KINtop Studies in Early Cinema – volume 5
series editors: Frank Kessler, Sabine Lenk, Martin Loiperdinger

Nordisk Films Kompagni 1906–1924

The Rise and Fall of the Polar Bear

KINtop. Studies in Early Cinema

KINtop Studies in Early Cinema expands the efforts to promote historical research and theoretical reflection on the emergence of moving pictures undertaken by the internationally acclaimed *KINtop* yearbook (published in German from 1992–2006). It brings a collection of anthologies and monographs in English by internationally renowned authors as well as young scholars. The scope of the series ranges from studies on the formative years of the emerging medium of animated photographs to research on the institutionalisation of cinema in the years up to the First World War. Books in this series will also explore the many facets of 19th and early 20th century visual culture as well as initiatives to preserve and present this cinematographic heritage. Early cinema has become one of the most dynamic fields of scholarly research in cinema studies worldwide, and this series aims to provide an international platform for new insights and fresh discoveries in this thriving area.

Series editors: Frank Kessler, Sabine Lenk, Martin Loiperdinger

Nordisk Films Kompagni 1906–1924

The Rise and Fall of the Polar Bear

Isak Thorsen

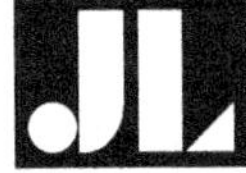

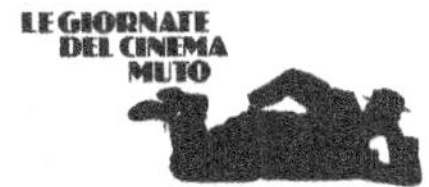

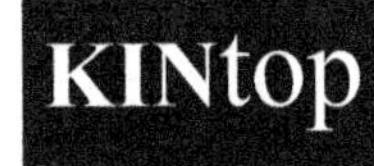

British Library Cataloguing in Publication Data

Nordisk Films Kompagni 1906–1924:
The Rise and Fall of the Polar Bear

Series: KINtop Studies in Early Cinema – volume 5

A catalogue entry for this book is available from the British Library

ISBN: 9780 86196 731 5 (Paperback)

ISBN: 9780 86196 930 2 (Ebook)

Published by
John Libbey Publishing Ltd, 205 Crescent Road, East Barnet, Herts EN4 8SB, United Kingdom
e-mail: john.libbey@orange.fr; web site: www.johnlibbey.com

Distributed worldwide by **Indiana University Press,**
Herman B Wells Library – 350, 1320 E. 10th St., Bloomington, IN 47405, USA.
www.iupress.indiana.edu

Printed and bound in the United States of America.

Contents

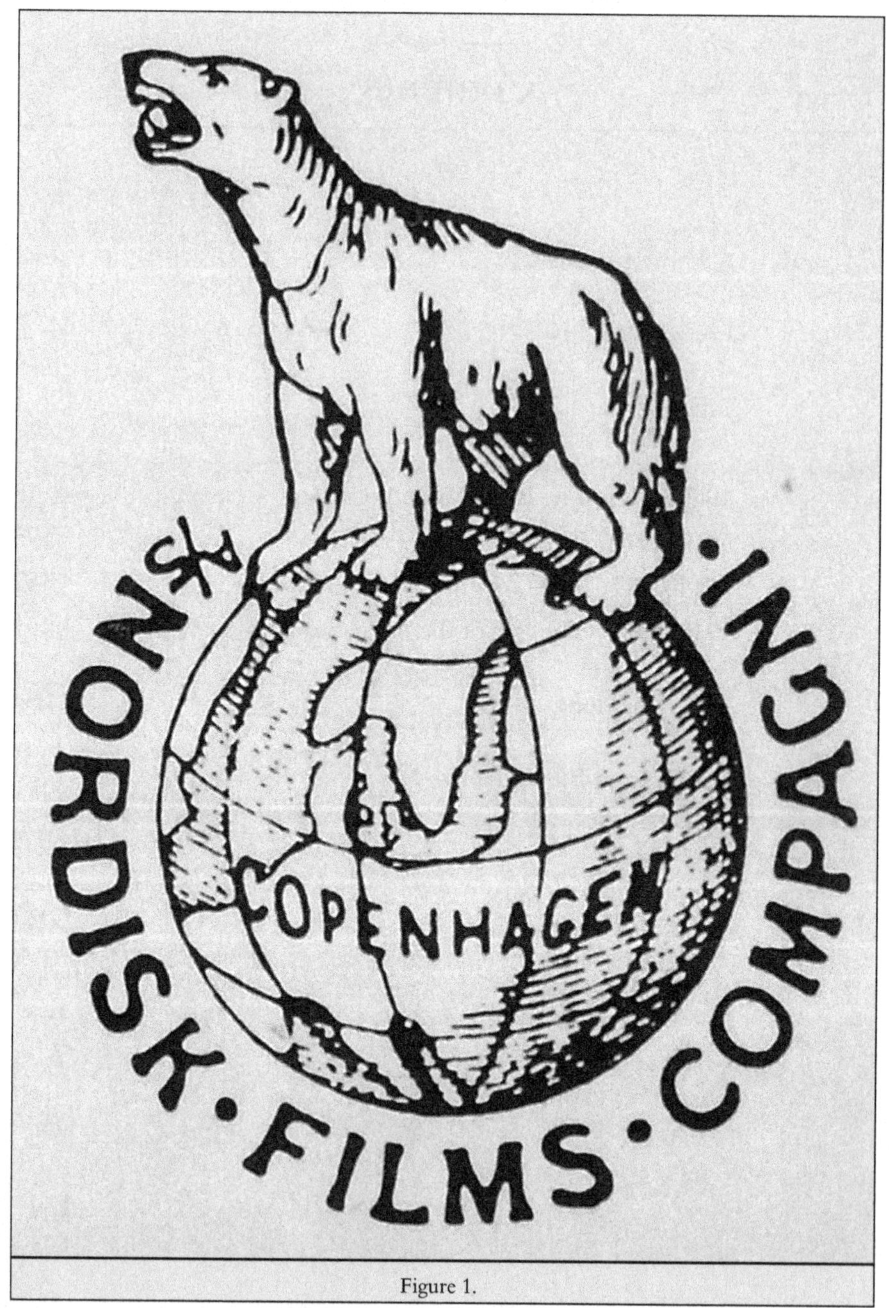

Figure 1.

Acknowledgements

This volume is a revised version of my Danish PhD Dissertation *Isbjørnens anatomi – Nordisk Films Kompagni som erhvervsvirksomhed i perioden 1906–1928* (The Anatomy of the Polar Bear – Nordisk Films Kompagni as a business enterprise 1906–1928) from 2009. As the attentive reader will notice, this volume ends in 1924, as the last part of the original dissertation is mainly of national Danish interest. The present publication has only been slightly revised and updated, and the revisions follow to a large extent the comments and suggestions of the original assessment committee members Per Boje, Peter Schepelern and Stephan Michael Schröder.

In the process of both writing the original dissertation and revising it into this publication I have many people and institutions to thank: first of all my supervisor Casper Tybjerg, who initially proposed the idea of examining Nordisk Films Kompagni as a business.

For their willingness to help and not least share their knowledge I would like to thank: Lauri Piispa and the late Rashit Yangirov, who generously dug up and translated Russian material; in Sweden: Anne Bachmann and Jon Wengström; in Germany: Annemone Ligensa; and in Denmark: Ib Bjarke Jensen, Karl Teglmand, Sven Philip Jørgensen, Lena Haugaard, Dennis Khadem, Henrik Zein, Kenn Tarbensen, Henrik Pedersen, Bente Ole Olsen, Hauge Marple, Jonas Hauvre, Kamel Bankaaba, Henning Bencard, Mogens Bencard and Palle Bøgelund Petterson. Kurt Jacobsen who followed the project on the side and his colleagues at the former Centre of Business History, Copenhagen Business School, especially Ole Lange, Steen Andersen and Mads Mordhorst. The ever supportive Lars Kaaber, who translated the whole lot into English, and Julie K. Allen and Claire Thomson who read and commented on the manuscript in the final stage.

I owe a great debt to the staff at the *Danish Film Institute*: Dan Nissen, Karen Jones, Lars Ølgaard, Lisbeth Richter Larsen, Madeleine Schlawitz, Thomas C. Christensen, Karina de Freitas Olesen, Birgit Granhøj, Karin Bonde Johansen, Werner Brakner, Mikael Braae, Henrik Fuglsang, Pernille Schütz, Juri Olsen, Christian Hansen and Tobias Lynge Herler; as well as to the *Danish Council for Independent Research* for granting me a scholarship and the *Department of Media, Cognition and Communication*, University of Copenhagen, for housing me.

Both my friend and archive-comrade Stephan Michael Schröder and David Bordwell followed the dissertation in the making, and they have persistently encouraged a translated version of the dissertation – thank you for your support. David Bordwell and Peter Schepelern for lending their names and goodwill in gaining support, because this volume would never have been possible without financial support: I am indebted to the *Danish Film Institute's almene støtte*, *Filmkopi*, *Lademanns Fond*, *Den Hielmstierne-Rosencroneske Stiftelse*, *Lillian og Dan Finks Fond*, *Letterstedtska Föreningen* and *Nordisk Film*.

Finally I am very grateful to the editors Frank Kessler, Sabine Lenk with the x-ray eyes, and Martin Loiperdinger for giving me the possibility to publish my work as a volume of *KINtop. Studies in Early Cinema*, and hereby reaching a wider audience as well as for their patience during the process, and for their detailed and constructive comments and suggestions.

Preface

This volume is based on extensive research into primarily one unique source: the Nordisk Film Collection. This collection constitutes the main source of this monograph and, from an international perspective, the collection is indeed unique: correspondence, accounts, contracts, minute books from general- and board meetings and much else is found here; quite an outstanding amount of written materials for a film company in the silent era. The collection provides a detailed impression of how Nordisk organized itself and developed as a business. A closer description of the collection and its associated data can be found in the list of sources and bibliography.

Therefore I have concentrated my principal research on this vast collection, and it is important to stress that the collection contains an enormous amount of material which can be approached from various angles and perspectives – this also creates some limitations. For instance, going through approximately 35,000 outgoing letters from 1906 to 1915 on topics as diverse as concerns about the formation of a monopoly in the American market and instructions to a carpenter, takes time. One might say that in comparison to many other researchers I have been privileged, because in many cases I had to exclude interesting details and perspectives due to the extent of material. In working with such an enormous amount of material, my intention has been to map out the general development of Nordisk as a business, but the collection can provide many other answers and new insights, depending on the questions asked. Nordisk's relation to the press and marketing is just one issue which could be investigated in greater detail.

Even though the Nordisk Film Collection is the main source, other sources have been consulted as well, including the Danish National Archives, Bundesarchiv, Nordisk Film's Archives in Valby, Ole Olsen's personal archives, a series of interviews done in the 1950s, 1960s and 1970s with persons active in film-making in the silent era, national and international film periodicals from the time, as well as correspondence with fellow researchers. A large amount of this material has either not previously been used in research, or only been used to a minor extent. This book is as detailed and factual as the sources permitted. Archival research is a laborious undertaking, and there are collections I did not have time to look into, such as those kept in Auswärtiges Amt in Berlin and the National Archives in Kew, England. Since completing my original main research nearly a decade ago, the archival situation has improved immensely:

for instance the access to national and international material online has grown rapidly, and in the revision of the text I have to some extent used the newly available resources.

To my best knowledge, the Nordisk Film Collection has not previously been scrutinized from the business angle proposed in the present study, and because of this, important sources such as the minutes from board meetings at Nordisk and the distribution protocols have not yet been included in research, either in Denmark or abroad. By empirically examining the sources available, this book contributes new knowledge about Nordisk's development, especially in the years from 1914 to 1924, which hitherto have been left somewhat in the dark. These new contributions include:

- A map out of Nordisk's distribution network and its development.
- The controversy concerning DEN HVIDE SLAVEHANDEL and the establishing of the limited company.
- Nordisk's control of the contents of its films through directives for script writers, Russian endings, and censorship memos.
- ATLANTIS' profitability.
- The organization of the film factory in Valby.
- Nordisk's expansion policy during World War I.
- The profitability and the sales of the company's films far into the war years.
- Nordisk's collaboration with UFA.
- The DAFCO investments.

Parts of this volume have either previously been published or incorporated in the following articles:

Isak Thorsen, "'We Had to Be Careful' – the Selfimposed Regulations, Alterations and Censorship-strategies of Nordisk Films Kompagni", *Scandinavian-Canadian Studies*, no. 19 (2010): 112–128. Reprinted in John Tucker (ed.), *Evaluating the Achievement of One Hundred Years of Scandinavian Cinema: Dreyer, Bergman, Von Trier, and others* (Lewiston: Edwin Mellen Press, 2012) and published online in a revised Danish version: Isak Thorsen, "'Vi maatte passe paa' – Selvcensur og selvregulering i Nordisk Films Kompagnis produktion", *Kosmorama*, no. 62 (2016) (www.kosmorama.org).

Isak Thorsen, "Nordisk Films Kompagni Will Now Become the Biggest in the World": *Film History: An International Journal*, vol. 22, no. 4 (2010): 463–478.

Isak Thorsen, "Ole Olsen's Sense of Film", *Journal of Scandinavian Cinema*, vol. 2, no. 1 (2012): 27–32.

Isak Thorsen, "Nordisk Film and Asta Nielsen", in Martin Loiperdinger and Uli Jung (ed.), *Importing Asta Nielsen* (New Barnet: John Libbey, 2014), 25–38.

Introduction

In the silent film era, Nordisk Films Kompagni ranged among the largest film companies in the world. Together with the two French companies Pathé Frères and Gaumont, Nordisk was at the core of the European film industry that dominated the global market before the outbreak of World War I. In 1924, German film producer Ludwig Gottschalk could write that "[...] for exactly fifteen years, Pathé, Gaumont and Nordisk were the kings of film production".[1]

Nordisk was founded in 1906 by Ole Olsen under whose auspices the company quickly grew to an international enterprise. On the strength of branches in Berlin, Vienna and London, a subsidiary company in New York, and a series of agents and distributors, the company's characteristic trademark – the polar bear on the globe – became known throughout most of the world, and the success of Nordisk remains unsurpassed by any other Danish film company.

Nordisk's heyday coincided with one of the most crucial stages in film history. "The years from 1910 to 1920 saw more radical changes than any other era in film history", asserts David Bordwell, adding that "Ole Olsen's company became a major player in a world market that was undergoing a critical phase of development".[2] In the course of a few years, film would transform and establish itself industrially, institutionally, artistically and stylistically. Due to its position as one of the leading international film companies, Nordisk played a significant role in this development.

No monograph has yet been published about the glory days of Nordisk. Our knowledge of the company is sporadic, often uncertain, and at times downright misleading. *Nordisk Films Kompagni 1906–1924* aims to describe and analyse the history of Nordisk from its foundation in 1906 and until 1924 when the original management stepped down. It focuses on the following questions:

How was Nordisk Films Kompagni able to rank among the leading film companies in the world, and why did the company eventually fail to maintain this position?

1 Ludwig Gottschalk, "15 Jahre Monopolfilm", *Lichtbild-Bühne*, no. 247 (1925), 14, quoted from Peter Lähn, "Afgrunden und die deutsche Filmindustrie. Zur Entstehung des Monopolfilms", in Behn, Manfred (ed.), *Schwarzer Traum und weiße Sklavin. Deutsche-dänische Filmbeziehungen 1910–1930* (München: edition text + kritik, 1994), 15.

2 David Bordwell, "Nordisk and the Tableau Aesthetic", in Dan Nissen and Lisbeth Richter Larsen (ed.), *100 Years of Nordisk Film* (Copenhagen: Det Danske Filminstitut, 2006), 81.

Previous research on Nordisk and Danish silent film offers no satisfactory answer to these questions. Attention has mostly focused on the artistic quality of the company's film productions as the major cause of the company's success and subsequent decline. However, one of the reasons that the development of the company has been attributed to the quality of the films is the fact that the company has never been investigated as a business enterprise. While the quality of the films was definitely a prerequisite for Nordisk's success, the company's organization of film production was equally important, in particular its advantageous network of distribution and its business organisation, which ensured the large-scale production and international distribution of the films. Empirically speaking, we actually have a better chance of analysing the business aspects of Nordisk than we have of analysing the films made there. Whereas only about 15 per cent of the 1,853 silent-film productions from 1906 to 1928 have been preserved,[3] large parts of the company's business archives still exist as mentioned in the Nordisk Film Collection at the Danish Film Institute.

Nordisk was created as a business enterprise, and its aim was profit. A general feature in the development of Nordisk was that the management continuously made radical changes to the company. These changes were based on the management's sense of, and reaction to, tendencies in the international film industry and an instinct for where a profit could be made. This book will argue that the ability and readiness of Nordisk to reorganize the company repeatedly was one of the main reasons that the company was able to maintain its position as one of the leading film companies. In his characterization of Olsen, Danish film historian Ebbe Neergaard emphasizes Nordisk's readiness to embrace change:

> He was [...] a brilliant organizer who constantly predicted the development of the industry over many years and was ready to meet it with a thoroughly prepared organization when stakes were raised.[4]

The reasons for the decline of Nordisk in the years following World War I must be found in a combination of the loss of business networks in Germany and Central Europe, failed investments, and the changes in finances and trade in which Nordisk had to manoeuvre after the war.

The significant role of Nordisk in Danish as well as international film history has caused the company to be mentioned and described in many places. In the following, I will give a chronological sketch of, respectively, the Danish and the international literature that have either contributed to creating the common perception of Nordisk, or dealt directly with the company as a business enterprise.

3 This number includes the 54 films which Nordisk produced, but to which the company assigned no negative number, as well as a few films produced by other Danish companies, and excludes the 33 American films which Nordisk distributed and gave a negative number.

4 Ebbe Neergaard, *Historien om dansk film* (Copenhagen: Gyldendal, 1960), 17.

In Danish research, Ole Olsen's memoirs *Filmens Eventyr og mit eget* (The Wonderful Tale of the Movies and Me, 1940), ghost-written by journalist Harald Mogensen, has been an important source for both Olsen's life and the history of Nordisk. Olsen was 77 when the book was published, and in her review of the book Danish film historian Marguerite Engberg warned: "All in all, we must view the autobiography as a delightful account of his life, but it cannot be trusted as a reliable source of dates and years."[5] In the only biography of Olsen, *Gøgler og generaldirektør: Ole Olsen, grundlæggeren af Nordisk Film* (Travelling Entertainer and Director General: Ole Olsen, Founder of Nordisk Film, 1997), Poul Malmkjær writes of the memoirs that "[...] they must be taken with a pound rather than a grain of salt".[6] I will not reject Olsen's memoirs as categorically as that, and I suppose Malmkjær does not either, since he bases large parts of his biography on *Filmens Eventyr og mit eget*. I do, however, share Engberg's and Malmkjær's view that Olsen's memoirs are not altogether reliable, but they still remain our only source for a series of reports on Nordisk's business dispositions, as well as Olsen's own reflections on the events. One may ask why Olsen felt a need to divulge this information. Some of the events described are important to the history of Nordisk and may be nuanced and verified by other source material, for which reason the memoirs will be referred to throughout this book. Malmkjær's biography draws heavily, and at times uncritically, on Olsen's memoirs, but Malmkjær does add information about Olsen's early youth which sheds further light on Olsen's entrepreneurial skills. Malmkjær's book has no notes and cites no sources, and Malmkjær emphasizes in his introduction that the book "[...] must not be considered an academic, historical work".[7]

Writer and journalist Arnold Hending describes the golden age of Danish film in a series of popular books, such as *Da isbjørnen var lille* (When the Polar Bear was a Cub) from 1945, in which Hending accounts for Nordisk's first years. Hending favours the good story above the truth, and the two major problems in Hending's books are his lack of source references and his metaphorical writing style which often leaves the reader in doubt as to what he actually means. Neither Olsen's memoirs nor Hending's book can be said to be of academic value, but since these are the first works on Nordisk, the books have greatly influenced the common view of the early years of the company.

The first book to contain academic essays on Nordisk is the anthology *50 Aar i dansk film* (Fifty Years in Danish Film, 1956), published to commemmorate the 50th anniversary of the company. The 23 essays in the anthology deal with various aspects of the history of Nordisk, from its foundation to 1956, and two of the essays directly concern the company as a business enterprise. In "Manden med Ideerne" (The Man with the Ideas), Svend Kragh-Jacobsen identifies

5 Marguerite Engberg, *Dansk stumfilm – de store år* (Copenhagen: Rhodos, 1977), 34.

6 Poul Malmkjær, *Gøgler og Generaldirektør* (Copenhagen: Gyldendal, 1997), 9.

7 Ibid., 11.

Olsen as: "The man who conceived of the company, caused it to be, unified it and controlled it."[8] However, Kragh-Jacobsen does not provide us with a clear impression of what exactly Olsen did. The other essay to treat Nordisk as a business is Erik Ulrichsen's "La belle époque". Ulrichsen discusses whether the root cause of the company's crisis is to be found in the outbreak of World War I or in the declining quality of Nordisk's productions. This article is significant for two reasons. First, Ulrichsen bases his research on archive material, such as the company's internal correspondence, and second, this is the first article to suggest that the company's crisis was primarily caused by the declining quality of its films.[9] Ulrichsen's assumption has influenced research on the subject since.

In *Historien om dansk film* (*The Story of Danish Film*, 1960), the usually level-headed Ebbe Neergaard shares Ulrichsen's belief that the quality of the productions was the main cause of the company crisis. Neergaard was the first to offer a thorough and balanced account of Nordisk's part in Danish film history. Neergaard touches upon the organization of Nordisk, the price of shares, the company's expansion in Germany during World War I, and the German company UFA's takeover of Nordisk's business network. While working on his book, Neergaard had access to the Nordisk archives, and *Historien om dansk film* contains the first statistical material on Nordisk's film production. On the whole, Neergaard gives a reliable and detailed account of the development of Nordisk and includes the industrial and financial aspects of the company.

The Danish film industry is also the subject matter of Knud Rønn Sørensen's thesis *Den danske filmindustri (prod., distr., konsumtion) indtil tonefilmens gennembrud* (The Danish Film Industry, Production, Distribution, Consumption, until the Advent of Sound Film, 1976). In his thesis, Sørensen offers a Marxist analysis of the Danish film industry, and the influence of Peter Bächlin's ideological critique in *Der Film als Ware* (Film as a Commodity, 1945) is evident. The Marxist rhetoric and conclusions appear outdated today, but Sørensen's analyses are basically sound; he positions Danish cinema in a new field of research by emphasizing the industrial and financial aspects of film history. Although the thesis rests entirely on books and articles available at the time and therefore reiterates the mistakes derived from these sources, Sørensen gives a solid presentation of Nordisk's development as a business. Regrettably, some of Sørensen's observations, such as Nordisk's crucial role in the transition period when longer films became standard in the industry, as well as the changed

8 Svend Kragh-Jacobsen, "Manden med Ideerne", in Svend Kragh-Jacobsen, Erik Balling and Ove Sevel (ed.), *50 Aar i dansk film* (Copenhagen: A/S Nordisk Films Kompagni, 1956), 14.

9 Ulrichsen was not the first researcher with access to Nordisk Film's archives. In 1938–1939, Ove Brusendorff was employed by Nordisk to sort out the archives while he was working on a three-volume publication entitled *Filmen: dens navne og historie* (Film: Its Names and History, published between 1939–1941). However, Brusendorff's work does not reveal any use of the archives (Poul Malmkjær, "I begyndelsen var billedet", *Film*, no. 40 (December 2004/January 2005): 26).

financial climate of the post-war period's influence on Nordisk, have been overlooked in later research.

The Nordisk Film Collection is the basis of Marguerite Engberg's pioneering *Dansk stumfilm – de store år* (Danish Silent Film – the Great Years) from 1977, which even today, 40 years after its publication, remains the primary reference work in the field of Danish silent film, together with Engberg's five-volume index to records *Registrant over danske film 1896–1930* (1977–1982). Engberg's work is monumental and she was the first to write at length about early Danish film history. In *Dansk stumfilm,* Engberg wanted to cover the entire Danish film history up to 1914. Among other things, the book describes the development of the early Danish film history, the most important film companies, directors, actors, and the changes in style and visual language. Of the 725 pages, Nordisk occupies the lion's share. Engberg meticulously accounts for the origins of the company and for parts of the production conditions in the company's studio at Valby. However, much of what Engberg includes is not placed in an explanatory context; the description of the development of Nordisk's distribution network leaves much to be desired, and Engberg omits to mention the importance of distribution to the success of the company. Engberg chooses to end her research in 1914, as she feels that the golden age of Danish film ended with the advent of World War I. I aim to show that the war in no way meant the end of Nordisk's golden age but actually offered an opportunity for expansion. In fact, the company became a multinational, vertically integrated enterprise during the war. Engberg shares Ulrichsen's and Neergaard's assumption that the stagnant quality of the films was the primary cause of Nordisk's crisis. Conversely, I intend to argue that this assumption leads to an insufficient explanation of the company's crisis.

Engberg uses the same sources as I do for this study, but our interpretations of the events differ greatly. It must be stated in all fairness that Engberg did not have access to the entire collection, parts of which were not submitted to the Danish Film Museum until after Engberg had finished *Dansk Stumfilm,* and moreover, I make use of material that was still in the company's possession at the time of her research.[10]

In two nearly identical articles, "Isbjørnens fald" (The Fall of the Polar Bear, 1997) and "Nordisk Films Kompagni and the First World War" (1999), Thomas C. Christensen, using Ulrichsen's, Neergaard's and Engberg's interpretations of the influence of World War I on Nordisk's development, has been one of the first to argue that previous research has been too biased. Christensen writes:

> In my opinion, most descriptions of the Danish film industry in the 1910s are, if not erroneous as such, then insufficient in their method and their balancing of cause and effect. I claim that it is causally problematic to explain financial matters

10 Most of this material is now held at the Danish Film Institute and has been integrated in the Nordisk Film Collection.

> by purely aesthetic observations, especially when such an explanation is based on material that is objectively inadequate.[11]

Christensen proceeds to argue that only few of Nordisk's war-time productions have survived; of the 496 productions from 1914 to 1916, only 22 actuality films and 29 dramatic films have been preserved, which amounts to about ten per cent of the production total. Consequently, the claim that Nordisk's crisis was caused by a decline in the artistic quality of the films rests on brittle ground, according to Christensen.[12] I agree with Christensen's objection and oppose the tendency of previous research to attribute Nordisk's decline to aesthetic shortcomings.

Among the most thorough researched academic works on Danish film history, however, are Casper Tybjerg's significant contributions to Danish film history. In his unpublished PhD-thesis, *An Art of Silence and Light* (1996), his chapters on Danish silent films in *100 års dansk film* (100 Years of Danish Film, 2001) and a series of articles, Tybjerg has researched early Danish film history, often from a cultural-historical perspective that includes recent research from international film studies. I have added to, and corrected, those of Tybjerg's interpretations that derive from a lack of information about Nordisk as a business and insufficient data concerning the company's development after 1914. Tybjerg himself has pointed to some of the deficiencies I have amended, such as the extent and the causes of Nordisk's financial losses after World War I.[13]

The anthology *100 Years of Nordisk Film* (2006), published in connection with Nordisk's centenary, contains contributions from a string of Danish and international scholars who present recent research in the history of the company. I wish to highlight David Bordwell's article "Nordisk and the Tableau Aesthetic" which analyses the alternative strategies used by Nordisk's film directors in the stylistic transition from theatrical tableaux to actual film editing, as well as mention my own contribution, "The Rise and Fall of the Polar Bear", which deals with Nordisk's development as a business enterprise from 1906 to 1928. The latter may be seen as a preliminary study for this present publication. The centenary featured one additional publication, Poul Arnedal's *Nordisk Film – en del af Danmark i 100 år* (Nordisk Film – a Part of Denmark for 100 Years, 2006), which is Nordisk's own account of the company's history. The chapters about Olsen and the early years at Nordisk are brief, and by and large only relate the story as told by Olsen himself and Hending sixty years earlier.

11 Thomas C. Christensen, "Isbjørnens fald. Nordisk Films Kompagni og første verdenskrig", in Helle Kannik Haastrup and Torben Kragh Grodal (ed.), *Sekvens 97. Filmæstetik og Billedhistorie. Filmvidenskabelig årbog 1997* (Copenhagen: Institut for Film og Medievidenskab, Københavns Universitet, 1997), 229.

12 See Christensen, "Isbjørnens fald", 229.

13 See Casper Tybjerg, *An Art of Silence and Light* (unpublished PhD-thesis, Copenhagen: Københavns Universitet, 1996), 241.

When we look at research into Danish business history in general, Nordisk is all but absent, and only in Per Boje's *Danmark og multinationale virksomheder før 1950* (Denmark and Multinational Companies Before 1950, 2000) do we find a cursory mention of Nordisk with an illustration and a caption.[14]

Yet Nordisk's business network spanned far and wide, and the company's activities have been recorded in international research. For many years, Ron Mottram's dissertation *Danish Cinema before Dreyer* (1988) has been the only extensive work in English on Danish silent films.[15] Mottram focuses on the films and their development and gives a detailed description of many of the films he has seen or found articles on. A valuable contribution of Mottram's book is his inclusion of reviews and articles in English on Nordisk's films. However, the interpretation of the reviews, especially Engberg's, could be more nuanced, and I will try to correct this deficiency while noting that in light of the research available in the 1980s, Mottram gives a fine impression of the development of Nordisk as a business enterprise. Moreover, using copies of letters sent from Nordisk in Copenhagen to its New York branch, Great Northern Film Company, Mottram describes the company's transatlantic activities in "The Great Northern Film Company: Nordisk Film in the American Motion Picture Market" (1988). Mottram's article is true to its sources and offers interesting and new insights into both the company's business methods and its role on the American market. However, the company's American office operated on conditions that were unlike those of Nordisk's other markets, partly because of the Motion Picture Patent Company's monopoly-like status in the US.

Due to Nordisk's influential role in the German market, several German articles which directly or indirectly describe Nordisk as a business enterprise have appeared over the last few decades. The anthology *Schwarzer Traum und weiße Sklavin: deutsche-dänische Filmbeziehungen 1910–1930* (Black Dreams and White Slave Girls: Dano-German Film Relations 1910–1930) from 1994 is a case in point; another is Manfred Behn's unpublished lecture "Reaktionen auf die Nordisk in Deutschland zwischen 1914 und 1917" (Reactions to Nordisk in Germany between 1914 and 1917, 1995), which, based on sources from the German film magazine *Lichtbild-Bühne,* describes Nordisk's role on the German market during the war. Behn's lecture has greatly influenced Danish film research. Tybjerg's presentation of Nordisk's expansion during World War I is largely based on it.

In 2011, Stephan Michael Schröder published his doctorate *Ideale Kommunikation, reale Filmproduktion. Zur Interaktion von Kino und dänischer Literatur in den Erfolgsjahren des dänischen Stummfilms 1909–1918*. Through extensive research in the Nordisk Collection and many other places, Schröder has contributed

14 See Per Boje, *Danmark og multinationale virksomheder før 1950* (Viborg: Odense universitetsforlag, 2000), 98.

15 It is worth mentioning that Ebbe Neergaard's *Historien om dansk film* was translated into English in 1963: *The Story of Danish Film*.

greatly to our knowledge, especially concerning Nordisk's script department, which was an important part of the organization of the company's film production. Some of Schröder's conclusions are available in his article "Screenwriting for Nordisk 1906–1918" from the anthology *100 Years of Nordisk Film.*

In *Vom Augusterlebnis zur UFA-Gründung* (From the Spirit of August 1914 to the Founding of UFA, 2004) Wolfgang Mühl-Benninghaus touches upon Nordisk's role in Germany from 1914 to 1917. Mühl-Benninghaus sheds light on Nordisk's part in the German film industry as well as the various attempts by the German military command to take over Nordisk's German and Central-European business. Both Behn's and Mühl-Benninghaus' view matter from a German angle. I will describe Nordisk's activities during the war from the viewpoint of the company itself and include Danish sources; I will also argue that the company's policy of expansion did not only apply to Germany.

The business-related aspects of Nordisk have been touched upon in Denmark and abroad, but many crucial questions about the company remain unanswered; our knowledge of the company from 1914 to 1924 is as yet insufficient, and we still need a full account of its early history.

Since the Brighton conference in 1978, the early history of cinema has been re-evaluated, and research in film history before the advent of sound is now constantly examined. The research results enable us to revise our perception of the period and to place Nordisk more accurately within international film history. In recent years, film historians have been influenced by two currents; one is research based on archival film material, while the other, rather than just concentrating on aesthetics, focuses on aspects like finances, production, distribution and exhibition. Of this latter trend, Thomas Elsaesser states:

> To do film history today, one has to become an economic historian, a legal expert, a sociologist, an architectural historian, know about censorship and fiscal policy, read trade papers and fan magazines, even study Lloyds Lists of ships sunk during World War One to calculate how much of the film footage exported to Europe actually reached its destination.[16]

I adhere to this tendency. However, the tradition of researching the sociological, industrial and financial aspects of film is not new; as early as in the 1910s, film was the subject of academic studies of the medium's social and financial role. Emilie Altenloh's *Zur Soziologie des Kino* (*A Sociology of the Cinema*, 1913) is a classic example, as is Peter Bächlin's later *Der Film als Ware.*[17]

Among Danish works on film history focusing on financial and business-related problems before the sound film, we find Gunnar Sandfeld's *Den stumme scene* (The Silent Scene, 1966) which gives a broad view of cinemas in Denmark, and Rønn Sørensen's aforementioned thesis. There is also Jens

16 Thomas Elsaesser, "The New Film History", *Sight & Sound*, vol. 55, no. 4 (Autumn 1986): 248.

17 William Uricchio has counted 200 theses about film in Germany between 1910 and 1945. See William Uricchio, "German University Dissertations with Motion Picture Related Topics: 1910–1945", *Historical Journal of Film, Radio and Television*, vol. 7, no. 2 (1987): 175.

Ulff-Møller's unpublished Master's thesis *Biografvæsenets udvikling, bevillings-sytemet og biografloven af 1922* (The Development of Cinemas, Licensing and the Cinema Law of 1922, 1988), and Jan Nielsen's extensive doctorate *A/S Film-fabriken Danmark SRH/Filmfabriken Danmarks historie og produktion* (A/S Film-fabriken Danmark: SRH/Filmfabriken Danmark's history and production, 2003), which includes a mixture of business history and a register.

In their introduction to cinema history, *Film History – Theory and Practice* (1985), Robert C. Allen and Douglas Gomery point to financial and technological film history as fields in which further research is still required. Even though it has mainly been American film research that has focused on the industrial aspects of film history, studies on European aspects of the subject have emerged. Independent studies that investigate the financial, industrial and organizational aspects which this present study draws upon include Kristin Thompson's *Exporting Entertainment* (1985), Klaus Kreimeier's *Die UFA-Story (The UFA Story*, 1992), Corinna Müller's *Frühe deutsche Kinematographie* (Early German Cinema, 1994), Ivo Blom's *Jean Desmet and the Early Dutch Film Trade* (2003), several contributions to the anthology *La firme Pathé Frères 1896–1909* (The company Pathé Frères, 2004) edited by Michel Marie, Laurent Le Forestier and Catherine Schapira, as well as Stéphanie Salmon's *Pathé. A la conquête du cinéma 1896–1929* (Pathé. Conquest of the Cinema, 2014).

The fact that the majority of studies have focused on the American film industry has made it difficult to find studies about the European film industry to compare with the development of Nordisk. In 1988 Ron Mottram called for investigations of the early European film industry, arguing: "It has become evident that the history of cinema can only be written from an international perspective",[18] and concluding: "Only as the industrial and artistic achievements of all the film-producing countries are studied and elucidated will a comprehensive and more objective history of the cinema be possible."[19] With the aid of the unique material in the Nordisk Film Collection, I will attempt to fulfil Mottram's request by contributing to mapping the early film history.

Nordisk's development from 1906 to 1924 spans many areas, and *Nordisk Films Kompagni 1906–1924* is an interdisciplinary investigation of film as culture, organization and business. Consequently, this present study cannot be confined to a single theory but has to include theories and concepts from primarily film studies as well as business studies. In the analysis of the development of Nordisk, the book makes use of Schumpeter's concept of entrepreneurship and Chandler's theory of *The Modern Industrial Enterprise*. My analysis of the development of Nordisk as a business enterprise fits in with David Bordwell's "mid-level research strategy". Bordwell calls for studies of the financial and production aspects of film history that are less confined by theory and

18 Ron Mottram "The Great Northern Film Company. Nordisk Film in the American Motion Picture Market", *Film History*, vol. 2, no. 1 (1988): 71.

19 Mottram, "The Great Northern Film Company", 84.

empirically limited.[20] In *The Theory of Economic Development* (1911),[21] in which Joseph Alois Schumpeter formulates his theory of the development of capitalist economy, the entrepreneur is a central figure. Schumpeter views the entrepreneur as someone who breaks former economic structures in order to create a more dynamic pattern. Schumpeter's starting point is the new type of entrepreneurs who, like Olsen, were successful businessmen in the Second Industrial Revolution. Nordisk emerged and had its heyday in this era which Ole Hyldtoft has described as "a swarm of innovations and the ensuing changes that revolutionized the world in the 1890s",[22] stretching from 1890 all the way to 1930. The Second Industrial Revolution can be characterized by a technological progress that created new markets and reorganized production; the railway, the steam ship and the telegraph paved the way for a global infrastructure in transportation and communication and made this infrastructure accessible to most people. Another important feature of the Second Industrial Revolution was mass production. Together with sound recordings, film became one of the first products in the entertainment industry to be mass produced like other industrial products.[23]

Several film historians identify the entrepreneur as a decisive driving force in the development of the early film industry. Through a relatively small investment with quick returns, the film industry was a "bonanza for entrepreneurs", as Lewis Jacobs puts it.[24] Economist Gerben Bakker also uses Schumpeter's terms when he writes about his own analysis of the underlying financial mechanisms of the industry:

> It investigates how motion pictures emerged from a world of traditional live entertainment, and how this emergence set in motion a continuous process of creative destruction, development and productivity growth that is still going on in the entertainment industry today.[25]

"Creative destruction" is the term which Schumpeter applies in one of his later works to the entrepreneur's replacement of old structures with new ones.[26] Schumpeter lists five different types of new combinations which an

20 See David Bordwell, "Contemporary Film Studies and the Vicissitudes of Grand Theory", in David Bordwell and Noël Carroll (ed.), *Post Theory: Reconstructing Film Studies* (Madison: University of Wisconsin Press, 1996), 26–30.

21 Schumpeter revised his book *Theorie der wirtschaftlichen Entwicklung* (1911) in 1934, and it is a reprint of this edition I quote here. When speaking of Schumpeter's entrepreneur theory, I mainly refer to his chapter 2. Schumpeter's subsequent economic theory that focuses on the entrepreneur has never gained much popularity in economic research. See Richard Swedberg (ed.), *Entrepreneurship* (Oxford: Oxford University Press, 2000), 15.

22 Ole Hyldtoft, "Den anden industrielle revolution – I forskningen og i Danmark", *Den jyske historiker*, no. 102–103 (December 2003): 18.

23 See John Sedgwick and Michael Pokorny (ed.), *An Economic History of Film* (London: Routledge, 2004), 7.

24 Lewis Jacobs, *The Rise of the American Film. A Critical History* (New York: Hartcourt, Brace & Company, 1939), 52.

25 Gerben Bakker, *Entertainment Industrialised* (Cambridge: Cambridge University Press, 2008), XX.

26 Joseph A. Schumpeter, *Capitalism, socialism and democracy* (London: George Allen & Unwin Ltd., 1976), 81–86, 131–134.

entrepreneur may use when exchanging old structures: (1) introducing a new commodity as yet unknown to the consumer or a new quality in a known commodity; (2) introducing a new production method; (3) finding new markets, which can be achieved either by launching an entirely new commodity or by relaunching a commodity in a new way; (4) finding new ways to get raw materials or partly produced commodities; (5) reorganizing, either by creating a monopoly or breaking one.[27] Schumpeter points to new combinations and innovations in the product, the process, the market, the supply or the organization. Bakker regards film as an innovation that contains all of Schumpeter's types of combinations.[28]

By Schumpeter's definition, the entrepreneur is not the one who creates the new ideas or inventions, but the one who either understands how to market these efficiently or discovers new ways to utilize already-existing factors of production. What matters to Schumpeter is the financial success of the entrepreneur's innovation and that the innovation adds to the social dynamics. Schumpeter deems it necessary for the entrepreneur to obtain a loan from banks or private investors in order to realize his innovations. Inherently, the entrepreneur can only be innovative in the initial phase of a new enterprise, as Schumpeter writes:

> [...] everyone is an entrepreneur only when he actually 'carries out new combinations', and loses that character as he builds up his business, when he settles down to running it as other people run their business.[29]

One objection to Schumpeter's concept could be his assumption that innovations always come from the entrepreneur. In his later research, Schumpeter went from seeing the entrepreneur as the sole source of innovation to finding innovative incentives in large companies as well. "In many cases, therefore, it is difficult or even impossible to 'name' an individual that acts as 'the entrepreneur' in a concern", Schumpeter wrote in 1949.[30] Nordisk is actually an example of an enterprise in which the innovations originally came from the entrepreneur and then continued to emerge in the established company. In spite of the fact that Schumpeter has no empirical support for his entrepreneur concept and assumes that the social structure in which the entrepreneur acts remains static, his definition, which is almost a century old, has spread from financial research to a series of other research disciplines.

In *Scale and Scope: The Dynamics of Industrial Capitalism* (1990), historian Alfred Dupont Chandler, Jr. shares Schumpeter's hypothesis that an established company may develop innovations like the ones conceived by the

27 See Joseph A. Schumpeter, *The Theory of Economical Development* (New Brunswick: Transaction Publishers, 2006), 66.

28 See Bakker, *Entertainment Industrialised*, 163.

29 Schumpeter, *The Theory of Economical Development*, 78.

30 Richard V. Clemence (ed.), *Essays on Entrepreneurs, Innovations, Business Cycles, and the Evolution of Capitalism. Joseph A. Schumpeter* (New Brunswick: Transaction Publishers, 1988), 261.

entrepreneur.[31] Chandler picks up where Schumpeter left off and analyses the historical development that follows the entrepreneur to the point when a successful company in the Second Industrial Revolution becomes a *Modern Industrial Enterprise* (MIE), a company able to produce a large quantity of commodities and distribute them widely. What is characteristic of an MIE is that the organization is made up of a series of units that each carries out its own function in the company's product development, production or distribution. In theory, any of these units in an MIE may act as an independent company.[32] Nordisk was organized in this way, with its studio in Valby, its printing laboratory in Frihavnen and offices in Berlin, London and New York, each with its own management and able to work like an independent company, even if top managers were needed to coordinate the product development, production and distribution carried out by first-line managers in the individual units. The emergence of top managers and directors is another characteristic of an MIE.

Chandler's theory lists some ideal characteristics required in a successful MIE, which he calls "organizational capabilities". These consist of the company's physical conditions of production, the skills of the employees – in particular the competence of the managers and middle managers – and the marketing of the product. Nordisk's organizational capabilities proved to be a decisive factor in the lasting success of the company. To carry out the strategies and new combinations planned by the company management, Nordisk brought to bear the structure and the organizational capabilities that enabled the company to reorganize – and in most cases, Nordisk succeeded.

Chandler's theory deals with companies characterized by mass production, a feature which at first glance seems fundamentally incompatible with film production, where every product, once shot and edited, is unique. But when the unique film is copied, sometimes in several hundreds of prints, the film becomes a mass-produced commodity. Another reservation when applying Chandler's concept to the film industry is the fact that Chandler bases his analysis on companies which require large investments in production facilities; this cannot be said of film production in the same way – basically, only a camera is needed – but it may in some respects be true of Nordisk's printing laboratory – the department which came closest to having actual production facilities. And by time the establishing of a studio with several stages also required large investments. All the same, Chandler's theory may encapsulate the essential features of Nordisk's organization of film production, distribution network and management structure.

Chandler bases his analysis on the 200 biggest industrial companies in the USA, Great Britain and Germany quoted on the stock exchange from the 1880s to

31 See Alfred D. Chandler, Jr., *Scale and Scope. The Dynamics of Industrial Capitalism* (Cambridge, Massachusetts: The Bellknap Press of Harvard University Press, 1990), 602.

32 See ibid., 14–15.

the 1940s. However by analysing only the biggest companies, Chandler fails to take into account both companies not quoted on the stock exchange, and smaller companies that actually do fulfil his idea of organizational capabilities, but failed to be successful, as well as other companies that succeeded although they scored poorly on organizational capabilities, are also excluded.

One can argue that the theories of both Schumpeter and Chandler are broad and general approaches, but they focus on the narrow time frame of the economic and industrial development coinciding with Nordisk's heyday. These theories have acquired the status of classics in research in business history and have proved valuable as company research tools. Chandler has previously been used in film-historic research, moderately so in Janet Staiger's analysis of the American film industry in *The Classical Hollywood Cinema* (1985)[33] and in Charles Musser's article "Pre-classical American Cinema: Its Changing Modes of Film Production". However, the interdisciplinary nature of this study and the specific questions it seeks to answer require the use of additional theories and concepts to supplement Schumpeter's and Chandler's; therefore Staiger's and Musser's discussion of the organisation and development of the film industry, and the research of economist Gerben Bakker will be currently included and discussed. Bakker's *Entertainment Industrialised* (2008), an analysis of the development of the film industry from 1890 to 1940, is based on economic as well as organizational theories. In recent years, Bakker's work has gained some footing in film research and may be nuanced when applied to Nordisk, especially because Bakker himself mainly analyses the British, French and American film industry and does not include Nordisk's largest markets: Germany, Russia and South America. Nordisk's strategy after World War I departs significantly from strategies in the countries which Bakker investigates.

On the whole, *Nordisk Films Kompagni 1906–1924* is structured chronologically, although I have found it thematically relevant to interject various events that deviate from this structure. Each of the four parts of this book investigate a specific period of change or reorganization in the development of Nordisk.

Part One deals with the period from 1906 to 1909. Nordisk's early years may be characterized as the pioneering years in which the company's organizational capabilities were founded with the printing laboratory in Frihavnen, the studio in Valby, the distribution network and the employment of managers. The company's early years will be compared to those of the international film industry, and I will examine how Nordisk could create a market, even though it was not the first company in its field.

Part Two analyses the extensive reorganization of Nordisk when the company became the first to concentrate on a production of multiple-reel films in

33 Whereas Bordwell, Thompson and Staiger only make sporadic use of Chandler, Bakker considers Chandler's ideas on the competitive advantage of "first movers"; production divided into departments and the vertically integrated company underly the analyses of the American film industry performed by Bordwell et al. See Bakker, "Entertainment Industrialised", 192, note 22.

1910–1911. The reorganization was Nordisk's response to the international crisis following the industry's overproduction of films. The transition meant that not only Nordisk, but the entire film industry had to change. When Nordisk reorganized itself into a corporation, with Olsen as the Director General and chairman of the board, the film production expanded and was divided into departments. A market for the films was ensured through distribution agreements favourable to the company, and Nordisk had a guarantee of sales of the films in years to come.

Nordisk's expansion policy will be examined in *Part Three*. The outbreak of World War I offered new opportunities and led to the next major change in the company. Since Denmark was neutral, Nordisk could maintain its exports to both sides. The company embarked on an expansion policy through which it bought foreign companies and cinemas, which turned Nordisk into a multinational enterprise and a vertically integrated company in Germany and Central Europe. In the first years of the war, Nordisk's expansion policy was lucrative but also politically dicey and would ultimately incur major losses for the company.

The period from 1918 to 1924 is described and analysed in *Part Four* which explores the widespread assumption that Nordisk's collapse was caused by the stagnating quality of the company's products. I will argue that this explanation is too one-sided in that it disregards the general lull in post-war international trade, and also ignores Nordisk's loss of investments during the war as well as the loss of favourable distribution deals that had been a prerequisite for the huge production in Valby. Moreover, the American film industry took over most of the world market and produced films at such huge costs with which the European industry could not compete. Additionally, the homemarket alone enabled the American companies to cover their expenses. Nordisk's reaction to these changes was to downgrade film production to fewer bigger films, inspired by American and Swedish productions. Instead of film production, Nordisk exploited its expertise and its close relations to German UFA and reorganized itself into a film-trading company. Nordisk invested massively in the distribution of American productions on the European market, but trade sanctions thwarted this venture and led to financial losses. Another strategy of Nordisk was the attempt to take over or control the UFA management, first through the purchase of shares and then through collaboration with American film producer Adolph Zukor and his company Famous Players. These plans foundered, and Nordisk was left with a huge debt that forced the company to write down its share capital, which in turn caused the management to lose control of the company, and in 1924, the entire management and Ole Olsen resigned.

1906–1909

The Birth of the Polar Bear

Ole Andersen Olsen (1863–1943) is the main character in the history of the Nordisk Films Kompagni. Initially as the sole proprietor, then as director general and chairman of the board, and finally as a rank-and-file member of the board, he was one of the decision-makers in the company until his retirement in 1924. More than anything, Olsen's decisions and abilities were the determining factors of the development of Nordisk.

Olsen was 43 years old when he founded Nordisk, and the company was the crowning achievement of his business experience in organization and leadership. Compared to other business managers in his day, Olsen was atypical. In spite of a slim empirical basis and some differences in the various industrial branches, Danish business historian Per Boje has managed to pin down some common factors of Danish managers and company owners in the period 1872–1972.[34] Danish top executives were rarely 'self-made men' and only a small percentage of them were sons of farmers or blue-collar workers. The majority had either a commercial or a technical education, which in most cases included spending time abroad; consequently, executives of this category often brought new technological know-how home to Denmark.

By contrast Olsen was a self-made man. He was born in Odsherred, a peninsula in the northwestern part of Zealand; his father was a carpenter and a smallholder and died in 1879, only 46 years old, but ill and broken down by alcoholism and hard physical labor.[35] Olsen said of his childhood: "It was so squalid, miserable and full of adversity and hardship that it deserves only to be forgotten."[36] Before his father died, Olsen was placed at the boys' reformatory Flakkebjerg near Slagelse after receiving a sentence for theft when he was ten. His academic skills were limited; Malmkjær reports that Olsen never learned to read or write.[37] However, Olsen's grandchild has stated in an interview that Olsen did learn to read but never to write and remained dependent on others to write for him.[38] It is difficult to determine whether some of the sparse

34 See Per Boje, *Ledere, ledelse og organisation 1870–1972. Dansk industri efter 1870*, vol. 5 (Odense: Odense Universitetsforlag, 1997), 125–150.

35 See Malmkjær, *Gøgler og generaldirektør*, 20.

36 Ole Olsen, *Filmens Eventyr og mit eget* (Copenhagen: Jespersen og Pios Forlag, 1940), 9.

37 See Malmkjær, *Gøgler og generaldirektør*, 40.

38 See Svend Aage Lorentz, *Eventyret om dansk film I – Filmen kommer til Danmark (1896–1909)* (Copenhagen: Det Danske Filminstitut, 1996).

material which Olsen left behind was written by himself;[39] in the case of some letters from the 1890s this is clearly not the case.[40] As the manager of Nordisk, Olsen had a secretary who took care of his correspondence, and his memoirs were taken down by the journalist Harald Mogensen, but neither of these facts serves as evidence that Olsen was altogether unable to write: it is certainly not out of the ordinary for an executive to have a secretary write his letters or for an unscholarly autobiographer to acquire the professional help of a journalist or a writer. It is temptingly romantic to think that the manager of one of the great multi-national companies was illiterate, but the truth is more likely that Olsen could read and that, to some degree, he was able to write as well. Moreover, Olsen travelled much in Northern Europe in his adult life and probably gained some proficiency in foreign languages. Joachim Nielsen, who was hired as a messenger in 1912 and did not leave Nordisk until 1957 when he was an office manager, is convinced that Olsen spoke German.[41] So although Olsen was certainly not an average top businessman for his time, he had travelled and worked abroad like other executives. According to Boje, Olsen's entrepreneurial skills and resourcefulness are characteristics he shared with other individuals who became the driving forces behind the industrial development in Denmark. As Boje writes, "[…] these individuals all knew how to interpret their surroundings and exploit the possibilities".[42]

Before Olsen established Nordisk, his enterprise had resulted in a series of other ventures, large and small. Among other things, he presented a peep-box with illustrations cut out from a magazine, and he embarked on various business ventures in Copenhagen before he really debuted in the entertainment industry in 1890. In the beginning, Olsen travelled around to fairs with his accordion, and before long his fairground attractions came to include a group of black people, lions and electric carousels. Olsen became a successful stallholder and made such a reputation for himself in Scandinavia that the city council of Malmoe in Sweden invited him to establish and manage a new amusement park in 1896, an equivalent of the Copenhagen Tivoli. Olsen successfully managed the amusement park until 1901, when the city council chose to close it down and Olsen, his wife and their five children returned to Copenhagen.

Olsen brought capital home from Sweden as result of this venture. A note in the newspaper *Dannebrog* from 1899 reports that Olsen "last summer had a net

39 Ole Olsen's private archives. Bente Ole Olsen.

40 The Olaf Fønss Collection. The Danish Film Institute (DFI).

41 Interview with Joachim Nielsen. DFI. The memoirs of Suzanne Pathé are another primary source that indicates Olsen's knowledge of German as she only spoke French and German, when she and Olsen traded films in 1906. Suzanne Pathé, *Souvenirs ensoleillés. D'une éducation à l'Américaine*. Unpublished manuscript kept at the Fondation Jérôme Seydoux-Pathé in Paris and by Suzanne Pathé's family. I am grateful to Frank Kessler and Sabine Lenk for the reference. See also NFS:II,1.DFI, 65. Letter from Ole Olsen to Suzanne Pathé, Paris (8 July 1907).

42 Boje, *Ledere, ledelse og organisation 1870–1972*, 242.

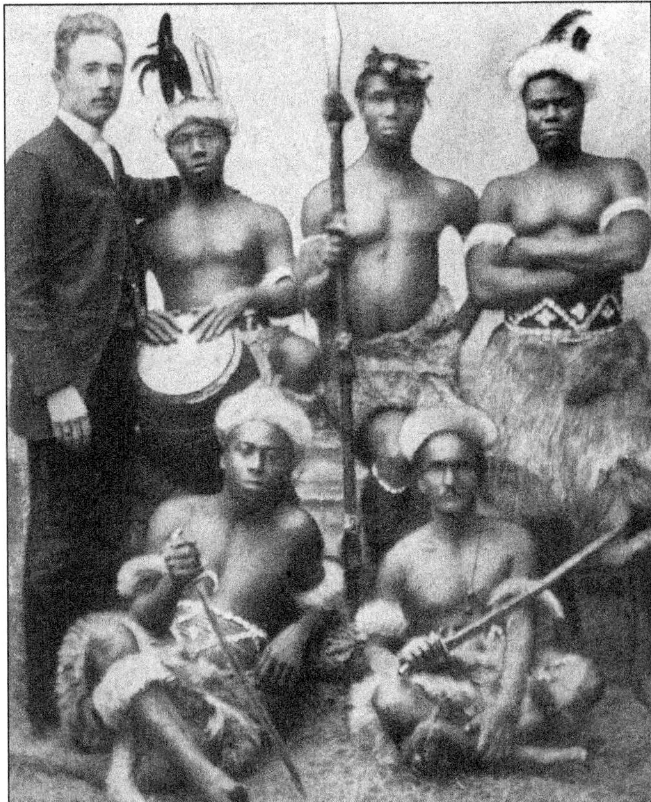

Figure 2. Ole Olsen together with his "Caravan", a group of Africans shown at fairs in Denmark. Source: Ole Olsen, *Filmens Eventyr og mit eget* (Copenhagen: Jespersen og Pios Forlag, 1940), 24.

income of about 60,000 kroner" from the amusement park.[43] (In order to get an impression of the relative value of Danish kroner, see Appendix 1.) However, what Olsen did after his return and until 1905, when he opened the cinema Biograf-Theatret, is not clear. Possibly, he opened a shop with "Benicia diamonds" in Østergade.[44]

Olsen's career as a film producer benefited from the experience acquired in his years as a travelling performer, a stallholder and an amusement-park manager. There are several similarities between fairground attractions and film; both are about processing an idea into an entertainment commodity and both involve a public demand for constant renewal. An idea may be said to be spent once it

43 Nordisk Film Samlingen (NFS):XIV,29.DFI, 1. Scrapbook, undated and untitled notice in *Dannebrog*, 1899.

44 See Arnold Hending, *Da Isbjørnen var lille* (Copenhagen: Urania, 1945), 25; Arnold Richard Nielsen, "Min Protege Milionæren", *Skandinavisk Films-Revue*, no. 1 (1913): 5; Arnold Richard Nielsen, "Fra Filmens første Dage", *Politikens Magasin* (17 January 1926): 10–11 and 15. It is uncertain what exactly Benicia diamonds are. Geological Museum, University of Copenhagen, has not been able to shed light on the matter.

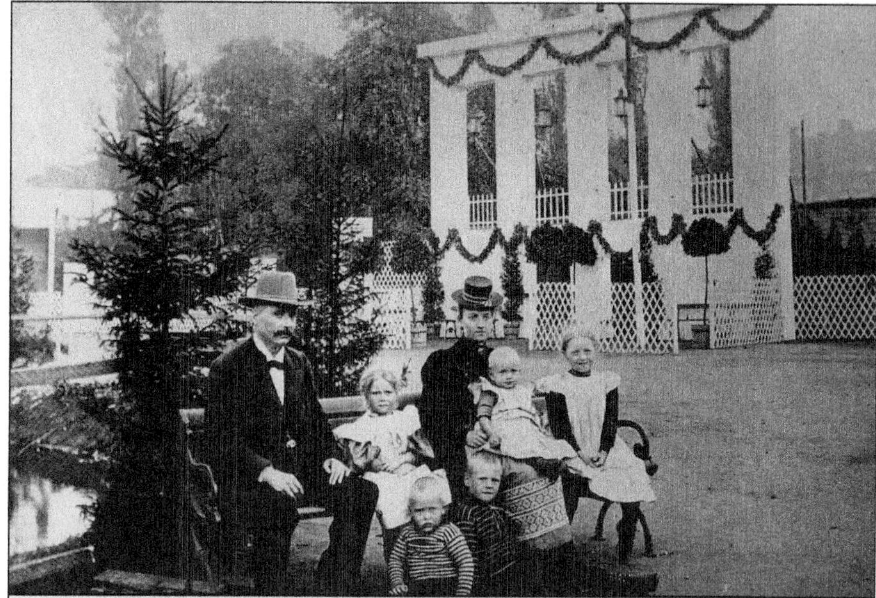

Figure 3. Ole Olsen with his wife and their five children in the Malmoe amusement park. Courtesy of Bente Ole Olsen.

has been turned into an act or a film, and new ideas or variations are needed. Moreover Olsen had formed an impression of what sort of entertainment people would pay for and knew that it would not do to disappoint them, if he wanted them to come back for more.[45] Furthermore, Olsen had acquired leadership skills and a knack for organization.

After working all over Scandinavia, moving on to an international market was an obvious progression for Olsen. The artistic environment and "the travelling folk" have always circulated internationally; circus, fun fairs and highly profiled opera performances all belonged to the small ensembles who offered live, transnational entertainment before the advent of film.[46]

"I've always been interested in being a pioneer when something new emerged", Olsen recalls in his memoirs,[47] and the technological novelties and advances of his day did not deter him. On the fairgrounds, Olsen had performed with an x-ray machine through which the customers could see their own bones; x-ray technology was a brand-new thing in 1895. That same year Olsen invested 4,000 kroner, at that time a small fortune, in making his carousels electrically powered.[48] He made an impression by being an amusement-park owner with a telephone installed in his caravan and by being one of the first

45 See Olsen, *Filmens Eventyr og mit eget*, 20.

46 See Bakker, *Entertainment Industrialised*, 165–166.

47 Olsen, Filmens *Eventyr og mit eget*, 41.

48 Letter from Ole Olsen to Gode Ven [Good Friend] (11 August 1895). Red Binder III, The Olaf Fønss Collection. DFI.

car owners in Malmoe. In 1898, Olsen was among the first in Sweden to show motion pictures. "The thing wasn't ripe yet, the public wasn't really interested",[49] Olsen later wrote about the motion picture shows. In the light of Olsen's enterprise and enthusiasm for new technologies, this new medium – film – was an obvious choice on which to embark.

Olsen recounted that he saw motion pictures at the first public viewing in Denmark at Pacht's Panorama in the Town Hall Square, Copenhagen, on 7 June 1896.[50] Initially, film was presented as a novelty at variety shows or as an attraction in travelling cinemas at fairs, and ten years would pass before film made its mark as an entertainment in its own right.

Gerben Bakker divides the history of the early film industry into three phases. In the first phase from 1890 to 1895, the basic and necessary technology was developed. The phase from 1895 to 1905 was when films were publicly shown in travelling cinemas, it was not until the third phase, 1905–1910, that films were shown in permanent cinema houses, a development that launched international growth in the film industry. Many companies were established and a film-distribution network was created in the industry in this third phase.[51]

Photographer Peter Elfelt, a Danish film pioneer, in both film-making and development of equipment, tried in vain to establish a cinema in Denmark, first with Hafnia Panorama in 1899, then with Kinografen in 1901, but no one succeeded with a cinema before Constantin Philipsen established Kosmorama in September 1904. Kosmorama in Østergade, Copenhagen, could seat about 150 people. Philipsen had also tried to open a cinema house in 1902, but the time was not yet ripe for this new medium, and he had to close it down after a short while due to the lack of audience demand. In the subsequent years, things had changed and new habits were formed that shaped public demand for entertainment.

On 5 April 1905, Olsen invited an audience into Copenhagen's second cinema, Biograf-Theatret at Vimmelskaftet 47. Olsen himself called Biograf-Theatret a "non-stop theatre";[52] there was no fixed schedule; people walked in and out of the cinema as they pleased. A show at Biograf-Theatret lasted somewhere between 30 and 45 minutes and featured four to five short films. A programme consisted of various genres or types of film, most often a newsreel or a documentary, a drama and a comedy.[53]

To the public, Olsen appeared as the manager of the cinema, but Biograf-Theatret was in fact a corporation, and Olsen's partner was Niels Evald

49 NFS:II,17.DFI, 870. Letter from Olsen to the Editorial office of *the Lichtbild-Bühne*, Berlin (9 December 1911).

50 "Ole Olsen fortæller om Film før og nu", *Kinobladet*, no. 7–8 (1920): 483–484.

51 See Bakker, *Entertainment Industrialised*, 170–171.

52 Olsen, *Filmens Eventyr og mit eget*, 48.

53 See Engberg, *Dansk stumfilm*, 41.

Jacobsen le Tort. Le Tort had worked as a magician and had toured with Olsen. He had also presented motion pictures in Stockholm for a brief period in 1901. It appears from the Copenhagen Trade Register that Biograf-Theatret was a private company with a capital of 24,000 kroner. The board of directors were Olsen and le Tort, both with the right to sign for the company.[54]

The demand for film entertainment was big since the films were only shown for a week at the time to make room for the next one.[55] Apart from Elfelt's sparse production, no one else produced films in Denmark, so films had to be imported from distributors abroad. Biograf-Theatret acquired films from Pathé Frères,[56] Gaumont[57] and Georges Méliès[58] in France; in Britain Olsen and le Tort obtained films from The Continental Warwick Trading Company,[59] Charles Urban Trading Company,[60] The Hepworth Manufacturing Co. Ltd.[61] and Robert William Paul;[62] in the USA from Edison Manufacturing Company Ltd.,[63] and in Italy from Cines[64] and Ambrosio.[65] Biograf-Theatret had an agreement with Gaumont and Urban for one copy of each of their new films,[66] and the supervisor of the cinema, Viggo Larsen, also went to London to get films.[67]

54 Copenhagen City Archives. The Trade Register, dpt. B, 1489. Engberg reports that there was a third partner, British Alfred James Gee. Nothing indicates that Gee was involved in Biograf-Theatret, but that he was a third partner remains a widespread assumption in Danish film research. See Malmkjær, *Gøgler og generaldirektør*, 104–106 and Jan Nielsen, *A/S Filmfabriken Danmark: SRH/Filmfabriken Danmarks historie og produktion* (Copenhagen: Multivers, 2003), 941. The assumption seems to derive from Engberg who interviewed Gee's daughter Mamie Gee in 1970. It is doubtful whether Mamie Gee could reliably testify to her father's partnership since she was not present 65 years earlier. Regrettably, the interview is not extant, but from the parts quoted by Engberg it appears that Gee left the company because Olsen wished to share the takings with as few people as possible and because Gee and le Tort were in constant disagreement (see Engberg, *Dansk stumfilm*, 43). Moreover, Engberg refers to a letter of October 1906, in which le Tort argues with Gee (see Engberg, *Dansk stumfilm*, 65). The actual letter does not mention Gee, but indicates that le Tort had a dispute with the manager of the Nordisk printing factory, Rasmus Bjerregaard (NFS: II,4.DFI, 456. Letter from Niels le Tort to Gode Ven [Good Friend] (Ole Olsen) (22 October 1906)). Gee is not mentioned as a partner in Biograf-Theatret in Hending's *Da Isbjørnen var lille* or in Sandfeld's reliable *Den stumme scene* (Copenhagen: Nyt Nordisk Forlag, 1966). Correspondence concerning Biograf-Theatret makes no mention of Gee as a partner, but solely as a customer and a distributor, e.g. in NFS:II,4.DFI, 59. Letter from Ole Olsen to A.J. Gee, Westend 15 (16 June 1906).

55 See Engberg, *Dansk stumfilm*, 46.

56 NFS:II,4.DFI, 35. Letter from Ole Olsen to Pathé Frères, Berlin (7 June 1906).

57 NFS:II,4.DFI, 136. Letter from Biograf-Theatret to Léon Gaumont and Co., Berlin (25 July 1906).

58 NFS:II,4.DFI, 162. Letter from Niels le Tort to Georges Méliès, Paris (4 August 1906).

59 NFS:II,4.DFI, 5. Letter from Ole Olsen to The Continental Warwick Trading Company (26 May 1906).

60 NFS:II,4.DFI, 601. Letter from Niels le Tort to Charles Urban Trading, London (26 November 1906).

61 NFS:II,4.DFI, 125. Letter from Niels le Tort to The Hepworth Manufacturing Co. Ltd., London (21 July 1906).

62 NFS:II,4.DFI, 611. Letter from Niels le Tort to Robert W. Paul, London (27 November 1906).

63 NFS:II,4.DFI, 84. Letter from Ole Olsen to Edison Manufacturing Company Ltd., London (2 July 1906).

64 NFS:II,4.DFI, 114. Letter from Niels le Tort to Cines, Rome (18 July 1906).

65 NFS:II,4.DFI, 44. Letter from Ole Olsen to Arturo Ambrosio, Torino (15 June 1906).

66 NFS:II,4.DFI, 600. Letter from Niels le Tort to Gaumont, London (26 November 1906).

67 Interview with Viggo Larsen. DFI.

Olsen and le Tort sold or rented their films on to Sweden, Norway and rural Denmark.[68] Olsen could sell the films to the network of contacts he had acquired in his years as a stallholder, and by distributing the films outside Copenhagen as well, Olsen prevented other cinemas in town from competing with Biograf-Theatret's films. Biograf-Theatret also sold equipment to people who wished to start their own cinema or motion picture show. It is not altogether clear whether this enterprise was Olsen's exclusively. In a letter, Olsen mentions this activity as going "through my main company via the firm Ole Olsen's Film Industry".[69]

Biograf-Theatret became popular with the Copenhageners. In 1906, the annual income of the cinema was 116,647 kroner and 60 øre,[70] and in the wake of the success of the first Copenhagen cinemas, more would follow. 1908 counted 16 cinemas in Copenhagen, the suburb of Frederiksberg included, and 17 or 18 in the rural areas.[71] The development history of cinemas in Copenhagen resembles that of other Western countries; in 1905, the first *Ladenkinos* opened in Berlin and Hamburg, and between 1907 and 1912, the number of Berlin cinemas varied between 300 and 400.[72] In the U.S. there was a "Nickelodeon boom" around 1905. In the spring of 1906 "[...] a dozen or more nickelodeons emerged in each of the metropolitan areas – New York, Philadelphia, Pittsburgh, Cleveland and Chicago. Within a year their numbers increased exponentially to include hundreds in New York and Chicago, and *Moving Picture World* estimated that there were between 2,500 and 3,000 throughout the country."[73]

Olsen and le Tort had picked the right moment to open their cinema, which gave them a competitive advantage. They had established contacts abroad so as to obtain a steady supply of films for their cinema, which enabled them to capitalize on the resale and rental of films, as well as the sale of equipment. However, Olsen and le Tort had the recurring problem of getting enough new titles for Biograf-Theatret.[74] This was the reason why Olsen eventually started his own film production.

In Olsen's memoirs Nordisk's first attempts at film production read like a fairy-tale: Olsen purchased a movie camera from France in early 1906, and his first long production was, by Olsen's own account, an immediate box-office hit at Biograf-Theatret, with audiences lining up to get in all the way down

68 E.g. NFS:II,4.DFI, 3. Letter from Ole Olsen to Gustav Molin, Kolding (26 May 1906), NFS:II,4.DFI, 11; Letter from Ole Olsen to Director Nielsen, Odense (29 May 1906), NFS:II,4.DFI, 158; Letter from Ole Olsen to Kvinssland, Kristiania (3 August 1906).

69 NFS:II,4.DFI, 65. Letter from Ole Olsen to Glazier I.A. Petersen, Næstved (29 June 1906).

70 See Jenss Ulff-Møller, *Biografvæsenets udvikling, bevillingssytemet og biografloven af 1922* (unpublished MA-thesis, Copenhagen: Københavns Universitet, 1988), app. 2.

71 NFS:II,8.DFI, 367. Letter from Ole Olsen to Consul Holbek (10 October 1906).

72 See Corinna Müller, *Frühe deutsche Kinematographie. Formale, wirtschaftliche und kulturelle Entwicklungen 1907–1912* (Stuttgart: J.B. Metzler, 1994), 29.

73 Richard Abel (ed.), *Encyclopedia of Early Cinema* (London: Routledge, 2005), 478.

74 Interview with Viggo Larsen. DFI.

Strøget, the most fashionable shopping street in Copenhagen.[75] In truth, however, things were not all that simple, as becomes evident from Viggo Larsen's recollection of this first shoot:

> We had a little cameraman by the name of Bjerregaard who didn't know the first thing about motion pictures, which the rest of us didn't, either. And they tried a couple of takes [...] and then they developed it and copied it, but it was no good. However, they believed that they had gained enough experience by now. And then we shot another film in the spring of 1906.[76]

The first shoot took place in H.C. Ørsted's Park in central Copenhagen and appears to have been the film DUER OG MAAGER (Pigeons and Seagulls, director unknown, 1906) which is the very first title registered in Nordisk's negative protocols, numbered 101.[77] The film was screened in two parts in Biograf-Theatret on 8 January 1906 under the title MAAGERNE FODRES I ØRSTEDSPARKEN (Seagulls are fed in H.C. Ørstedsparken, director unknown, 1906) and DUERNE VED KØBENHAVNS RAADHUS (Pigeons at the Town Hall, director unknown, 1906), with the label "[Nordisk's] own production".[78] However, the films which people lined up to see, according to Olsen's memoirs, were FREDERIK DEN 8'S PROKLAMATION (Frederik VIII's Proclamation, Ole Olsen, 1906) that premiered on 4 February, and CHRISTIAN DEN 9'S BISÆTTELSE (Christian IX's interment, Ole Olsen, 1906), shown on 19 February. The shooting of those films can be dated to 29 and 30 January, respectively, which postdates the screening of DUER OG MAAGER in Biograf-Theatret.[79] Throughout the spring and summer of 1906, the pace of film production increased steadily, and by 15 September 1906, Olsen had shot enough films to constitute a full programme of his own productions.[80] In the advertisement for the first programme made up of films from Nordisk it is worth noticing the highlightning of their national significance (see Illustration). "The first *Danish* programme", the headline states, while in the following text it is emphasized that the beautiful Danish nature is used, the actors are Danish and the subject should be to the liking of the Danish audiences. The three first films were actualities and the fourth was a comedy.[81] Actualities as a term covers factual films and can be divided into several sub-genres:

75 See Olsen, *Filmens Eventyr og mit eget*, 50.

76 Interview with Viggo Larsen. DFI.

77 Nordisk gave each film a negative number. The first film was numbered 101 in 1906 and JOKEREN (THE JOKER, Georg Jacoby, 1928) was no. 1880 in 1928. A series of American films and a few Danish productions purchased and distributed by Nordisk were given negative numbers as well and entered into the company's protocols along with Nordisk's own productions.

78 Engberg, *Dansk stumfilm*, 57–58.

79 Ibid.

80 See ibid., 46.

81 Martin Loiperdinger suggests that Nordisk may have started to produce films to satisfy a growing demand from Danish audiences for films related to their own local and cultural context. This idea is very interesting and worth considering, but I am not fully convinced by this suggestion because Nordisk was conceived as an international firm with export in mind. Judging from the few surviving films from Nordisk's first year, the national does not seem to be typical.

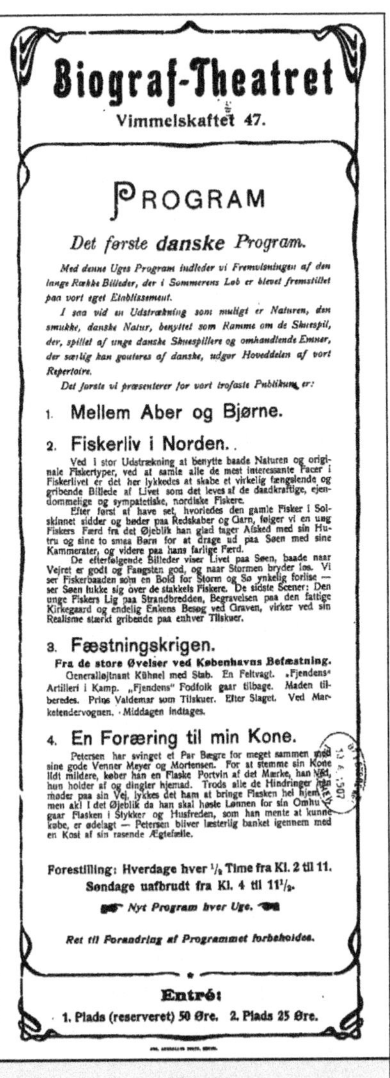

Biograf-Theatret

Vimmelskaftet 47.

PROGRAM

*Det første **danske** Program.*

Med denne Uges Program indleder vi Fremvisningen af den lange Række Billeder, der i Sommerens Løb er blevet fremstillet paa vort eget Etablissement.

I saa vid en Udstrækning som muligt er Naturen, den smukke, danske Natur, benyttet som Ramme om de Skuespil, der, spillet af unge danske Skuespillere og omhandlende Emner, der særlig kan gouteres af danske, udgør Hoveddelen af vort Repertoire.

Det første vi præsenterer for vort trofaste Publikum er:

1. **Mellem Aber og Bjørne.**

2. **Fiskerliv i Norden.**

Ved i stor Udstrækning at benytte baade Naturen og originale Fiskertyper, ved at samle alle de mest interessante Facer i Fiskerlivet er det her lykkedes at skabe et virkelig fængslende og gribende Billede af Livet som det leves af de daadkraftige, ejendommelige og sympatetiske, nordiske Fiskere.

Efter først at have set, hvorledes den gamle Fisker i Solskinnet sidder og bøder paa Redskaber og Garn, følger vi en ung Fiskers Færd fra det Øjeblik han glad tager Afsked med sin Hustru og sine to smaa Børn for at drage ud paa Søen med sine Kammerater, og videre paa hans farlige Færd.

De efterfølgende Billeder viser Livet paa Søen, baade naar Vejret er godt og Fangsten god, og naar Stormen bryder løs. Vi ser Fiskerbaaden som en Bold for Storm og Sø ynkelig forlise — ser Søen lukke sig over de stakkels Fiskere. De sidste Scener: Den unge Fiskers Lig paa Strandbredden, Begravelsen paa den fattige Kirkegaard og endelig Enkens Besøg ved Graven, virker ved sin Realisme stærkt gribende paa enhver Tilskuer.

3. **Fæstningskrigen.**

Fra de store Øvelser ved Københavns Befæstning.

Generalløjtnant Kühnel med Stab. En Feltvagt. „Fjendens" Artilleri i Kamp. „Fjendens" Fodfolk gaar tilbage. Maden tilberedes. Prins Valdemar som Tilskuer. Efter Slaget. Ved Marketendervognen. · Middagen indtages.

4. **En Foræring til min Kone.**

Petersen har svinget et Par Bægre for meget sammen med sine gode Venner Meyer og Mortensen. For at stemme sin Kone lidt mildere, køber han en Flaske Portvin af det Mærke, han ved, hun holder af og dingler hjemad. Trods alle de Hindringer han møder paa sin Vej, lykkes det ham at bringe Flasken hel hjem, men ak! I det Øjeblik da han skal høste Lønnen for sin Omhu gaar Flasken i Stykker og Husfreden, som han mente at kunne købe, er ødelagt — Petersen bliver læsterlig banket igennem med en Kost af sin rasende Ægtefælle.

Forestilling: Hverdage hver 1/2 Time fra Kl. 2 til 11.
Søndage uafbrudt fra Kl. 4 til 11 1/2.

Nyt Program hver Uge.

Ret til Forandring af Programmet forbeholdes.

Entré:
1. Plads (reserveret) 50 Øre. 2. Plads 25 Øre.

Figure 4. Biograf-Theatret's first programme made up entirely of own productions. Source: Marguerite Engberg, *Dansk stumfilm – de store år* (Copenhagen: Rhodos, 1977), 46.

travelogues, industrial films, scientific films, sports films etc. Actualities also included newsreels that captured events of a social nature, such as state visits, parades or acts of war. The attraction of these films was that they could show places and events which most people could otherwise only read about.

Film production was Olsen's responsibility, and the increase in production led to a break between Olsen and le Tort. On 11 December 1906, and for the sum of 10,000 kroner, Olsen took over "[...] Nordisk Films Kompagni with all its property, in Copenhagen and in Berlin, with all rights and responsibilities as the company owner".[82] As appears from the handover contract, Olsen had acquired several properties in less than a year. These included the printing laboratory of Nordisk in Frihavnen in Copenhagen and the studio in Valby, as well as the first foreign branch office of Nordisk in Berlin, established by Olsen on 18 November 1906.[83] After the break with le Tort, Nordisk got its first independent address in Frihavnen, and on 6 November 1906, Olsen managed to obtain a trade license in Copenhagen, an event that marks the official birth-date of the company.[84]

Le Tort took over the management of Biograf-Theatret and got the license of the cinema Kosmorama in the provincial town of Aarhus. Legally, Olsen was still the license owner of Biograf-Theatret, a fact which le Tort would come to regret a year later when Nordisk released LØVEJAGTEN (THE LION HUNT, Viggo Larsen, 1907). Olsen had bought two lions at Hagenbeck Zoo in Hamburg for the shoot. The film is about two big-game hunters and the film was shot on the small island of Elleore in Roskilde Fjord,

82 NFS:II,4.DFI, 710. Contract between Ole Olsen and Niels le Tort (11 December 1906).

83 Bundesarchiv-Filmarchiv R109-639. Universum Film Verleih G.m.b.H., Berlin.

84 Nordisk Films Kompagni and Biograf Theater Aktieselskab, Trade License from the Magistrate of Copenhagen (6 November 1906). Nordisk Films Foyer, Mosedalsvej, Valby, Copenhagen.

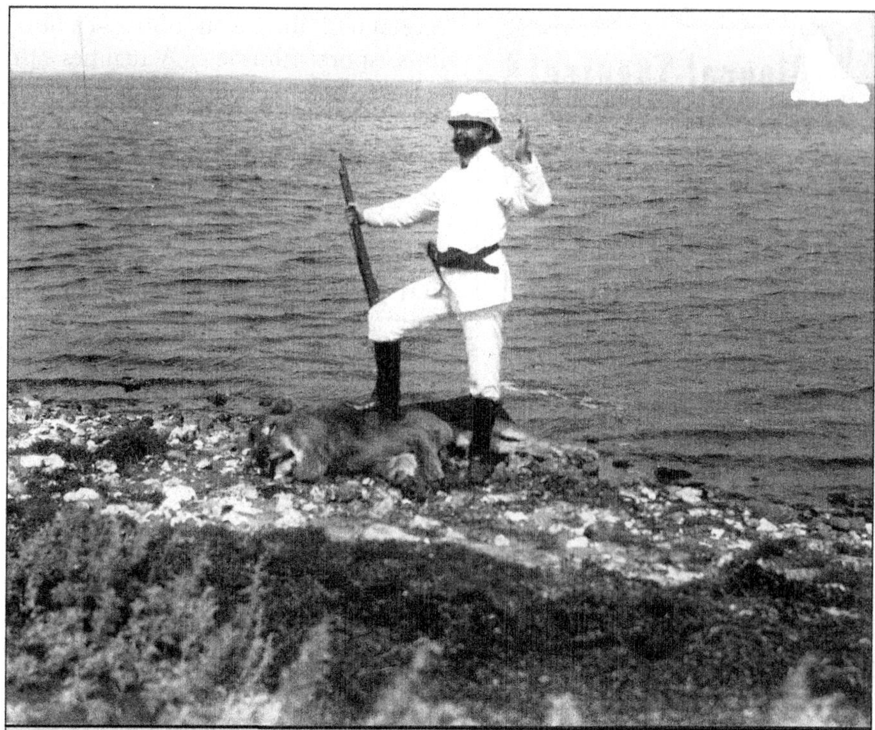

Figure 5. The big game hunter (Viggo Larsen) has finally killed the beast in LØVEJAGTEN. Courtesy of DFI/Stills & Posters Archive.

as were, indeed, the lions. Through an organization opposed to cruelty to animals, Minister of Justice Peter Adler Alberti was informed about the project, and he prohibited the shooting of the lions. Olsen, however, went ahead with the shoot and the shooting of the animals regardless, and afterwards the footage was sent to Sweden and distributed worldwide from there. With 259 copies sold,[85] the film became one of the company's greatest box-office hits and is counted as Nordisk's breakthrough on the international market.[86] It did not premiere in Danish cinemas until the following year.[87]

Alberti was so outraged at what Olsen had done that he withdrew the trade license of Biograf-Theatret and gave it to Otto Hennings and Mrs Køhlert, the widow of the Councillor of State whose husband had been a close friend of Alberti's. Le Tort and his new partner Alex Larsen, who ran the Biograf-Theatret, bore the brunt of Olsen's loss of license. Sandfeld writes that not

85 NFS:XI:1.DFI, 7. Protocol of Negatives.

86 See Lähn, "Afgrunden" (1994), 15; Georges Sadoul *Histoire générale du cinéma II: Les pionniers du cinéma 1897–1909* (Paris: Éditions Denoël, 1948), 416; Kristin Thompson and David Bordwell, *Film History. An Introduction* (New York: McGraw-Hill, 2004): 29.

87 Tybjerg, "Teltholdernes verdensteater", in Peter Schepelern (ed.), *100 års dansk film* (Copenhagen: Rosinante, 2001), 22.

only did Olsen lose his license, but the police commissioner in Copenhagen wished to investigate Peter Elfelt as well. Elfelt held the license of the cinema Kinografen, but the day-to-day management had been in the hands of Alexander Christian since the cinema opened. In Elfelt's case, however, LØVEJAGTEN would have no legal consequences.[88]

LØVEJAGTEN's case occasioned a change in the regulations concerning cinema licenses in Denmark. Before 1907, anybody could open a cinema. As with all other forms of entertainment, a permit from the police was needed, but these were summarily granted in all but a few cases until 1907, when the conditions to obtain a permit were tightened. For one thing, the applicant could not have a criminal record. Jens Ulff-Møller reports that the events around LØVEJAGTEN were the direct cause for this regulation; Alberti knew that Olsen did not have a clean record and that this would prevent him from obtaining a new cinema license.[89] Olsen had been convicted twice; he had committed fraud in 1882 by pawning a coat that did not belong to him, and he was sentenced in 1886 for having established a placement office which did not refer people to jobs, but simply cashed in the fees for registering with the office.[90]

Another consequence of the tightening of the license laws was that the license now became personal. It had previously been possible for a company to be licensed, as long as the signing licensee still ran the cinema and owned at least half of the shares in the company.[91] From now on, the licenses were issued individually from the Ministry of Justice directly to profitable Copenhagen cinemas. The apparent effect of this incursion of free trade was that Copenhagen cinemas were competitively protected, since not everyone could open a cinema in the Danish capital.

It was common in the international film industry for producers to run one or more cinemas. The change in the license laws limited Nordisk's opportunity to run cinemas in Denmark, since an individual person or company could no longer run a chain of cinemas after 1907.

Nordisk was the first film production company in Denmark, and according to Chandler, being a "first mover" on a market is the strongest competitive advantage for a company.[92] Engberg also emphasizes that Nordisk had the competitive advantage of being the first Danish company to produce films on a large scale.[93] However, Nordisk was not originally conceived as a national

88 See Gunnar Sandfeld, *Den stumme scene,* 24. The events concerning LØVEJAGTEN and Olsen's license became subjects of several government disputes, primarily between the social democrat Frederik Borgbjerg and the radical Carl Theodor Zahle on one side, and Alberti on the other. See Sandfeld, *Den stumme scene*, 36–38; Malmkjær, *Gøgler og generaldirektør*, 152–155.

89 See Ulff-Møller, *Biografvæsenets udvikling*, 52.

90 See Malmkjær, *Gøgler og generaldirektør*, 58–60.

91 See Niels-Jørgen Dinnesen and Edvin Kau, *Filmen i Danmark* (Copenhagen: Akademisk Forlag, 1983), 28–29; Ulff-Møller, *Biografvæsenets udvikling*, 52.

92 Chandler, *Scale and Scope*, 34.

93 See Engberg, *Dansk stumfilm*, 8.

firm, on the contrary; the company's production was aimed at export to the international market on which Nordisk was in no way a first mover.

The international film industry was dominated by companies established before the turn of the century. In her analysis of the early American film industry, Cadance Jones characterizes these as *technology entrepreneurs.*[94] Technology entrepreneurs were originally inventors, photographers, opticians etc., whose main interest was solving the technological challenges of the new medium, such as developing film stock from which the emulsion did not peel off; solving the problem of images that bounced about during projection; finding a common standard for equipment and raw stock; and finding a solution to the fire hazard of the highly inflammable material.[95] By patenting various technological solutions, technology entrepreneurs gained control over key resources and thereby a competitive advantage in the film industry.[96] Thomas Alva Edison, William Kennedy Laurie Dickson and Sigmund Lubin are Jones's examples of American technology entrepreneurs. To these may be added the French Léon Gaumont and the Pathé brothers, German Oskar Messter and British Robert William Paul as examples of European technology entrepreneurs.

Pathé Frères, which was the biggest film company in the international market and had been founded by the brothers Charles and Émile Pathé in 1896. Originally, the company produced phonographs and kinetoscopes for travelling amusement parks.[97] Around 1896, Charles Pathé started experimenting with cameras and projectors, and some years later with the production of raw stock, which gave Pathé a huge advantage when the company began its own mass production of film. In 1903, Pathé had representatives in Moscow and Berlin; 1904 they opened their own offices in Moscow, New York, Brussels; in 1905 in Berlin, Vienna, Chicago and St. Petersburg; in 1906 in Amsterdam, Barcelona, Milan, London and Odessa.[98] As Richard Abel reports: "Within another year, Pathé offices were monopolizing Central Europe as well as opening up the colonized areas of India, Southeast Asia, Central and South America and Africa."[99] According to Abel, in 1906, Pathé produced somewhere between a third and half of all the films seen in USA, and the company's film production division counted 1,200 employees. By the end of that year, Pathé produced 40,000 metres of positive film a day, which rose to 100,000 metres

94 Cadance Jones, "Co-evolution of Entrepreneurial Careers, Institutional Rules and Competitive Dynamics in American film, 1895–1920", *Organization Studies*, vol. 22, no. 6 (2001): 921–929.

95 See Jones, "Co-evolution of Entrepreneurial Careers", 922.

96 See ibid., 921.

97 The phonograph was a forerunner of the record player, and the kinetoscope was a viewing device consisting of a box with a peephole through which the viewer could see a series of illuminated images that would give the impression of movement.

98 Stéphanie Salmon, *Pathé. A la conquête du cinéma 1896–1929* (Paris: Tallandier, 2014), 97, 118–124, 130–131, 134–135.

99 Richard Abel, *The Cine Goes to Town. French Cinema 1896–1914* (Berkeley etc.: University of California Press,1994), 23.

in the years before the outbreak of World War I.[100] By comparison, Nordisk produced around 550 metres of positive film per day in 1906, and 11,300 metres in 1914.[101] Pathé was undoubtedly the biggest film company of its kind in the world. Over the years, Pathé based its film production on a large number of subcompanies, at home and abroad, affiliated to Pathé. Charles Pathé's motto was: "I did not invent cinema, but I industrialized it."[102]

Denmark was among the few countries in which Pathé did not gain a footing, and where distributors and cinema owners jointly pressed the French company out of the market in 1909. Letters from Olsen and Nordisk indicate that they were instrumental in forming this united front against Pathé.[103]

One third the size of Pathé, Gaumont was the other major French film company. The company was founded by Léon Gaumont, an optician. In 1895, he bought out the optical and cinematographic equipment business he had previously managed. He started selling actualities, the business grew rapidly, and in 1908, Gaumont had 14 international offices, and in 1914, Gaumont was a vertically integrated company with a share capital of four million francs.[104] With Pathé as leader, the French film industry had secured a leading position through a vertical integration of domestic film production, distribution, and exhibition, and internationally with a horizontal structure under which Pathé owned several production companies across the globe.

With the rise of cinema houses and new production companies around 1906 an international distribution network emerged. However, as Ivo Blom states in his work on the Dutch distributor Jean Desmet, up to now there has been little research in this area, and he identifies our lack of knowledge about distribution in the early European film industry as "the missing link" in research.[105] In his study, Blom distinguishes between two different types of film markets: open and closed markets. He characterizes the open market according to Kristin Thompson's description of film sales in Britain.[106]

100 See Abel (ed.), *Encyclopedia of Early Cinema*, 506.

101 See note to Table 1.

102 Charles Pathé, quoted in Bakker, *Entertainment Industrialised*, 331.

103 See Jens Ulff-Møller, "Edouard Partsch: Pathé's Danish affiliation 1909–1924", in Michel Marie, Laurent Le Forestier and Catherine Schapira, *La firme Pathé Frères 1896–1909* (Paris: Association française de recherche sur l'histoire du cinéma, 2004) and e.g. NFS:II,11.DFI, 807–808. Letter from Wilhelm Stæhr to A/S Th.S. Hermansen, Aarhus (16 December 1909).

104 See Abel (ed.), *Encyclopedia of Early Cinema*, 266.

105 Ivo Blom, *Jean Desmet and the Early Dutch Film Trade* (Amsterdam: Amsterdam University Press, 2003), 25. Since the publication of Blom's book, research into early film distribution has received some attention, and his idea of distribution as the "the missing link" in research has been investigated and discussed, for instance in the anthology *Networks of Entertainment* (2007). In my opinion, the overall development of film distribution has been mapped out by Kristin Thompson, *Exporting Entertainment. America in the World Film Market 1907–1934* (London: British Film Institute, 1985), by Müller, *Frühe deutsche Kinematographie*, and by Blom himself, but, in order to gain a full picture, we still need a series of detailed regional studies to shed more light on the importance of distribution in the early film history.

106 See Blom, *Jean Desmet*, 29.

In Great Britain, film producers sold their films to distributors who then sold or rented out the films to as many cinemas as possible. Cinema programmes changed frequently and there was competition for the popular films. If a cinema owner was unable to get the title he wanted from one distributor, he could get it from another. A film could be rented out to various cinema owners in the same area. It would have been more profitable for the distributors to have a smaller number of copies which they could rent out at a fixed price; in this way, the distributors would have exploited each title better and reduced the expenses of purchase. The result of the open market was that there were twice as many copies on the market than were actually needed, since many distributors were poised to supply the cinemas with the same title.[107]

The problem that Thompson points out – the oversupply of titles on the open market in Britain – did not become acute until 1908/1909. In 1906, when Nordisk started its own production, the opposite was the case. As Blom asserts, the open-market structure prevailed in Britain, Germany, the Netherlands and Italy.[108] As mentioned above, research into the distribution of films in the early period is scarce, but I venture to contend that the open-market structure was used everywhere save those two markets which Blom characterizes as closed markets, the French and the American.

In 1907, Pathé succeeded in dividing France into five regions, in each of which one single company purchased the rights to show Pathé films.[109] Pathé rented out films in a ready-made programme at a fixed price, and one-reel films became standard.[110] In 1909, Pathé repurchased all film rights from the regional distributors and established its own national distribution company.[111] Gaumont followed suit and started buying up shops and converting them into cinemas all over France, then established its own distribution network. The independent distributors who had no arrangements with Pathé or Gaumont were consigned to dealing with companies that only sold films or, alternatively, to deals with companies abroad. Pathé retained its monopoly-like status in France until 1910 when the advent of long feature films made it impossible for them to keep up.[112]

The other closed market was the United States, where trade was limited by a series of patent legislations that I will treat more thoroughly in connection with the establisment in 1908 of the *Motion Picture Patents Company*.

Nordisk entered a market dominated by a few companies that had embarked on film production at an early stage, but the generally unstructured interna-

107 See Thompson, *Exporting Entertainment*, 29–30.

108 See Blom, *Jean Desmet*, 30.

109 Abel (ed.), *Encyclopedia of Early Cinema*, 253–254.

110 Blom, *Jean Desmet*, 28–29.

111 Abel (ed.), *Encyclopedia of Early Cinema,* 254.

112 See Blom, *Jean Desmet*, 27–29; Abel (ed.), *Encyclopedia of Early Cinema*, 253–254.

tional film trade offered an opportunity for newly started companies to gain a footing.

Nordisk was not among the early established companies internationally, but Olsen chose to launch his film production and distribution at a time when films were very much in demand. Timing was of the essence, and Olsen also chose to make a series of crucial investments that became the foundation of Nordisk's "organizational capabilities". As described above, Nordisk was a latecomer on the international market where first movers like Pathé and Gaumont, as well as American, British and Italian film companies had established themselves early. To make its mark on the market, it is important for a latecomer company to invest in production facilities that match those of the existing companies, and this was precisely what Nordisk did.[113]

Contrary to Schumpeter's expectations that successful entrepreneurs are financed by bank loans,[114] Olsen had the capital to establish Nordisk. "[...] as I had no credit with the bank but invested my own money, I had to tread carefully", Olsen writes.[115] He had amassed his capital partly through the Malmoe amusement park, partly through Biograf-Theatret, and nothing in the records from Nordisk's first years indicates that Olsen obtained further loans to fund the company. As Nordisk grew, and until it became a limited company, Olsen personally supplied the capital necessary to invest and reinvest.

In one of the few investigations of the influence of banks on the early American film industry, Janet Wasko concludes that film entrepreneurs did not usually take out bank loans. The first film entrepreneurs in the USA either had their own capital in the launch phase, or they obtained private loans. Banks tended to disregard the film industry as "a novelty or a fad that eventually would fade into obscurity".[116] In fact Chandler documents that in the U.S. and Great Britain, the first entrepreneurs of the Second Industrial Revolution were rarely backed financially by banks, whereas in Germany banks financed new enterprises to a higher degree.[117]

We have no accounts from Nordisk before it became a limited company in 1911, but according to two of Olsen's own statements (which should not be unconditionally trusted), we get the impression that it required vast investments to establish the company. In August 1906, Olsen reported that he had raw stock worth more than 100,000 kroner lying in Frihavnen, since competing on the international market demanded such amounts.[118] And in a 1907 interview Olsen said of his investments:

113 See Chandler, *Scale and Scope*, 34.

114 See Schumpeter, *The Theory of Economical Development*, 94–127.

115 Olsen, *Filmens Eventyr og mit eget*, 75.

116 Janet Marie Wasko, *Relationships Between The American Motion Picture Industry and Banking Institutions* (unpublished PhD-thesis, Urbana, Illinois: University of Illinois at Urbana-Champaig, 1980), 23.

117 See Chandler, *Scale and Scope*, 597.

118 Olsen quoted in St. Martin, "Levende Billeder. Ny dansk Industri", *Klokken 12* (25 August 1906).

> [...] in the beginning, when the factory was founded, I spent a lot of money. Now, with the progress, I sell films abroad for one million kroner a year. 400,000 kroner of this amount goes out of the country, of course, to raw stock and the like, but the rest stays here in Denmark. This year, I calculate with sales of about 1.2 million kroner, which means that I sell 5,000 to 6,000 metres of film a day. But I could sell twice as much if the factory was bigger – that's how big the demand is.[119]

In both of Olsen's statements, the international perspective is evident. As early as March 1906 Olsen said: "The pictures are meant to be exported although they will be shown here in town as well, of course."[120] Nordisk was conceived as an international company from the very beginning. In 1906, a majority of Nordisk's films went to the export market; only 6.9 per cent of the films stayed in the domestic market, a percentage which dropped to 4.5 per cent in the following year (Table 1).

Table 1: Positive Metres Sold by Nordisk,1906–1909

Year	1906	1907	1908	1909
Positive metres in total	193,315	664,326	733,405	1,130,896
Positive metres sold in Denmark	13,375	29,219		
Percentage of positive metres sold in Denmark	6.9%	4.5%		

Note: No account exists of the sales to individual countries in 1908 and 1909, only accounts of the sales of individual titles, for which reason it is impossible to calculate the Danish share of the total sales.
In contrast to other big film-companies in the silent era, I have found no evidence that Nordisk produced catalogues of their production. This has been made up for by going through the quite detailed distribution protocols of which most have survived. The majority of quantitative data presented here is founded on a database developed by me in connection with the writing of this study. Facts about the titles and length of the films, when and in how many copies each film was distributed to various countries, are based on the distribution protocols NFS:XI,7.DFI. a+b and XXII,33–39.DFI. From around 1908 to the spring of 1912, no distribution protocols exist in the Nordisk Film Collection, which renders information about the number of copies and the countries in which they were distributed inaccessible. Data from this period are collected from NFS:XI,1.DFI, including information about negative numbers from 101 until 889 and the length and number of copies sold of a few other films. The information in NFS:XI,1.DFI differs slightly from that of the distribution protocols, and in some cases information concerning the number of copies sold is missing altogether, as in the case of DEN HVIDE SLAVEHANDELS SIDSTE OFFER, which according to correspondence from Nordisk sold more than 235 copies (NFS:II,15.DFI, 98. Letter from Wilhelm Stæhr to Ingvald C. Oes, New York dated 20 February 1911). I have not included this number or other scattered information in the database, but kept to information found in the protocols. The protocols often differentiate between the distribution countries; for example, it can be noted under "Cuba" that two copies have been sent to Mexico. This further specification has been transferred to the database. The length of the films have been subjected to random tests in NFS:XI,1.DFI and NFS:XI,3.DFI, as have the release dates of the films in NFS:XI,12.DFI. The production years differ from Engberg's register. Engberg refers to NFS:XI,1.DFI, while my dating relies on NFS:XI, 3.DFI and NFS:XI,5.DFI which are in accord with other dates in the Nordisk Film Collection, such as NFS:XXI.40.DFI. The information in the database has been subjected to random checks against in NFS:XII.22 and 23.DFI which have only been at odds with the protocols in rare instances.

119 "Næsten levende Billede!", *Dannebrog* (8 July 1907).

120 "Levende Billeder. Et Friluftsteater paa Amager. Humoresken under aaben Himmel", *Politiken* (2 March 1906).

Between 1906 and 1909 Nordisk film sales rose from 193,315 positive metres in 1906 to 1,130,896 positive metres in 1909. The films were not sold according to genre, title or artistic content, but by the metre, and the price of one metre was approximately one krone, which gives us a loose estimate of Nordisk's gross income in the first years, roughly corresponding to the sale of positive metres.[121] In 1906, the takings were less than 200,000 kroner, and three years later they had risen to roughly 1.3 million, which is at variance with Olsen's statements about an expected turnover of 1.2 million in 1907. We may not get a closer estimate of Nordisk's income in the first years, but to Olsen, the company was certainly a profitable business. In 1908, he could afford to invest 70,000 kr. in building bonds,[122] and that same year Olsen reported to the Inland Revenue Department that he calculated his net profit at about 70,000 kroner, as opposed to the previous year when his net profit as the licensee of Biograf-Theatret was 40,000 kroner.[123]

Chandler points out that the entrepreneur who wishes to obtain a maximum profit from his production must: 1. invest in production facilities large enough to exploit the potentials of technology; 2. invest in national and international marketing and distribution in order for the sales to keep up with production, and 3. invest in management, employ and train managers, not just to manage the business, but also to plan and develop.[124] This interplay of investments in production, distribution and management creates the successful MIE's organizational capabilities. Chandler asserts:

> The critical entrepreneurial act was not the invention – or even the initial commercialisation – of a new or improved product or process. Instead it was the construction of a plant of the optimal size required to exploit fully the economics of scale or those of scope, or both.[125]

When building up the organization of Nordisk, Olsen did indeed invest in the three items on Chandler's list. From Nordisk's birth in 1906 until around 1909, the foundation was laid for production facilities, management and distribution.

The printing laboratory and the studio in Valby, the cornerstone of Nordisk's film production, were the first parts to be established. Both facilities expanded as production grew, but always in such a way as to keep expenses low. When Nordisk was in its prime in the1910s, the company turned down an English journalist's request to publish an illustrated feature article about the film production at Nordisk:

121 The price of one metre of film from Nordisk was somewhat steady. In November 1906, one metre of film "of own manufacture" cost 1 kr. NFS:II,4.DFI, 557. Letter from Nordisk to Schive, Kristiania (19 November 1906). Engberg reports that the price of one metre rose from 1 kr. to 1, 25 kr. around 1911 (see Engberg, *Dansk stumfilm*, 99). There is some indication that the price was lower for the company's regular customers; De Giglio, for one, paid 88 øre per metre in 1913, NFS:XII,31:43.DFI. Unpagn. Agreement between A/S Nordisk Films Co. and A/S De Giglio (19 February 1913).

122 NFS:II,7.DFI, 422. Letter from Ole Olsen to Wholesale dealer Villadsen (28 May 1908).

123 NFS:II,7.DFI, 719. Letter from Ole Olsen to the Inland Revenue Department (11 July 1908).

124 See Chandler, *Scale and Scope*, 8.

125 Ibid., 26.

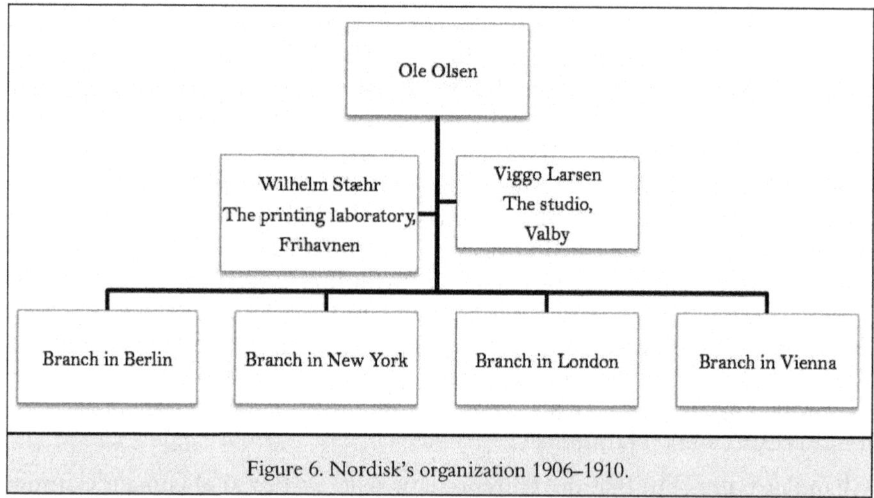

Figure 6. Nordisk's organization 1906–1910.

> Our facilities are hardly presentable since it has never been our intention to spend a fortune on unnecessary buildings and studios, quite the contrary: we have always endeavoured to minimize our expenses on buildings, and everyone who sees our establishments in Valby is amazed that a company of this size can thrive in such modest conditions.[126]

Olsen was keenly aware that the export of the films was essential to Nordisk's viability as an international company, and the first branch opened even before the company was officially started. Nordisk's offices in Berlin, London, Vienna and New York, as well as Nordisk's network of international agents were essential to the success of the company. The film industry was something new in Denmark and, with some efforts, Olsen gathered those co-workers who would be able to run and develop his company.

In the following, I will account for the development of Nordisk's organizational capabilities, a development previously unexplored in research. Nordisk has often been portrayed in history as an immediate success, but in reality, circumstances are likely to have been a bit more cumbersome. In the fledgling film industry, Olsen not only had to build up his organization, but also make allowances for the difficulties concerning the supply of raw film stock; he had to market the films and the company, protect the copyrights of the titles, and ensure the quality of the films, so that Nordisk could keep up with its competitors. Moreover, Olsen had to orientate himself in an international industry dominated by alliances and the creation of monopolies.

The printing laboratory was the first piece of Nordisk's organization to be established, and it remains a widespread myth that the development and copying of Nordisk's first films took place in Mrs Olsen's kitchen sink.[127] "The

126 NFS:II,30.DFI, 651. Letter from Harald Frost to Nordisk Films Co. Ltd., London (4 March 1914).

127 See Hending, *Da isbjørnen var lille*, 32; Engberg, *Dansk stumfilm*, 64–65; Malmkjær, *Gøgler og generaldirektør*, 119.

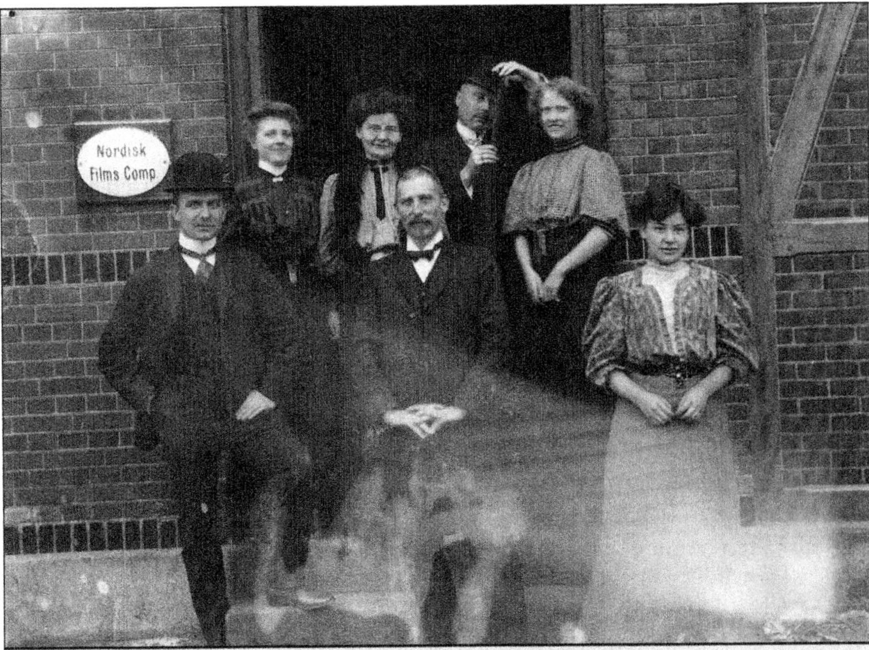

Figure 7. The first printing laboratory in Frihavnen. Wilhelm Stæhr standing in the middle and Ole Olsen behind him, looking at a filmstrip. Courtesy of DFI/Stills & Posters Archive.

humble beginnings took place in the privacy of Ole Olsen's villa",[128] Engberg reports, but "Mrs Olsen's kitchen soon became too small".[129] All evidence now points in the direction that Olsen commissioned the later cameraman and film director Alfred Lind, who had been trained as a carpenter, and photographer Rasmus Bjerregaard to build a developing system in a rented two-room apartment on H.C. Ørstedsvej.[130] "We had made a clever system with a hole drilled into the kitchen counter so the film could slip down into the 'darkroom' of pots and pans [...]",[131] as Leo Hansen, who sold souvenir programmes in Biograf-Theatret and later became a cameraman, has reported about the primitive contraption. The "kitchen-counter system" could not keep up with the rise in production, however and, moreover, the images developed there were "grainy".[132]

128 Engberg, *Dansk stumfilm*, 63.

129 Ibid., 64.

130 Interview with Alfred Lind. DFI. Lind mentions that the apartment was on the corner of H.C. Ørstedsvej and "Vinkelvej". The street names in Frederiksberg have changed several times since 1906, and "Vinkelvej" may have been either Stenvinkelsvej or Vinkelvej. On two separate occasions, the people at Frederiksberg City Archives have looked in vain for Olsen's apartment on the corner of H.C. Ørstedsvej. See Olsen, *Filmens Eventyr og mit eget*, 50; Palle Koch, "Hans egen verden – og Hollywoods ...", *Information* (15 August 1955).

131 Koch, "Hans egen verden – og Hollywoods...".

132 Interview with Alfred Lind. DFI.

In the summer of 1906, Nordisk established a printing laboratory on the fifth floor of Manufakturhuset (Manufacturing House) in Frihavnen, Copenhagen, and this was the official address of the company after Olsen's break with le Tort. Frihavnen was no random choice of location; it was a duty-free area, and until 1908, there was a ten per cent duty on raw stock.[133] This way Nordisk was spared tax on films and raw stock which the company imported as well as on the company's films shipped abroad. However, the rooms in Manufakturhuset were soon too small as well, and in January 1907, Nordisk built a new printing laboratory in the former rooms of Nordisk Kaffe Kompagni (Nordisk Coffee Company), also in Frihavnen. The following year, the printing laboratory was expanded,[134] and the number of employees in Frihavnen grew from eleven in September 1906[135] to 110 in the spring of 1908.[136]

Olsen hired photographer Rasmus Bjerregaard to manage the laboratory, but Bjerregaard lacked organizational skills. Axel Graatkjær has said of Bjerregaard's management in Frihavnen:

> Rasmus Bjerregaard was out there, and he was good at a lot of things, only not at running a printing laboratory. He couldn't delegate work, he did it all by himself. [...] Then we got Stæhr. He could put his foot down like some irate ram – he excelled at that. But he was good. He was the right man for the job.[137]

Wilhelm Carl Christian Stæhr (1861–1932) took over from Bjerregaard at the end of 1906, and Stæhr would prove important to the development of Nordisk. Originally, Stæhr was a photographer, so he had the technical skills to manage the printing laboratory. Besides his technical know-how, Stæhr turned out to be an "organizer of the first water".[138] In Stæhr's obituary notice, it says:

> Publicly, Ole Olsen was of course the great name in Danish film history back then when Danish films were world famous, but the weight of the entire daily work rested on Manager Stæhr's shoulders.[139]

In Stæhr, Olsen had found an efficient and a goal-oriented manager who could follow the company line and carry it into effect. Stæhr's manner and determination to fulfil the production targets of Nordisk often collided with the artistic staff, especially the directors and the actors:

> He became Olsen's right-hand man, and for some years he was in charge of the shoots in Valby where he tried to bully a greater sense of discipline into the artists; in these endeavours, he was not altogether successful.[140]

Stæhr was technically competent, loyal to Olsen, and his inexhaustible energy enabled him to multi-task. From 1913, Stæhr took care of both the production

133 See Engberg, *Dansk stumfilm*, 64, notes 5 and 6.

134 NFS:II,7.DFI, 359. Letter from Nordisk to Nordische Films Co., Berlin (18 May 1908).

135 See "Næste levende Billede!", *Dannebrog* (15 September 1906).

136 NFS:II,7.DFI, 17. Letter from Ole Olsen to the Editor of Industrial Report (16 March 1908).

137 Interview with Axel Graatkjær. DFI.

138 "En af dansk Films Pionerer død", *Berlingske Morgen* (10 April 1932).

139 Ibid.

140 "Direktør Stæhr død", *Politiken* (10 April 1932).

at the printing laboratory and the daily management in Valby. He was the only manager in Nordisk who stayed there from the early years and until Olsen retired.

In the printing laboratory, the recorded footage was rolled up on wooden frames, developed and dipped in huge tubs with fixer. The dried camera negative was copied to positive raw stock upon which the distribution print was edited together with titles and intertitles, and the finished film could then yield as many copies as were needed. The credits and intertitles were filmed at the printing laboratory, and, to meet the demands of the international market, Nordisk delivered it all in the various languages. The translations were not always impeccable, as Olsen lamented in a letter to the London office: "As for the English translation, a language can be translated in various ways, as you know, but in the future we shall endeavour to get it as correct as possible."[141] Joachim Nielsen has reported that Spanish audiences nearly died laughing at the poor translations of the intertitles, for which reason Nordisk from then on left the translations to the agents abroad. German translations had to be approved by the Berlin office,[142] and a letter from Nordisk to the Spanish agent reads:

> [...] we are willing to make Spanish titles for all ordered copies. We shall send all samples with English titles and exchange these with the Spanish ones according to your translation, at the time your orders are executed.[143]

It was common practice for European film companies to deliver the films with intertitles in the various main languages, but even Pathé Frères's films were released with the occasional grammatical slips and wrong idioms.[144]

The films were edited and collected at the printing laboratory. Carl Theodor Dreyer recalled how he used to sit all winter, editing the films with Stæhr. With neither script nor director, they were at complete liberty to make coherent stories out of the many thousands of metres of film that had been shot in the summer season.[145] Casper Tybjerg reports that Stæhr edited all of Nordisk's films up to 1915.[146] Although Stæhr was in charge of the editing of many of Nordisk's films in the first years, the directors were also involved; film director Viggo Larsen has stated that when he left Nordisk in the middle of the production of REVOLUTIONSBRYLLUP (A WEDDING DURING THE FRENCH REVOLUTION, Viggo Larsen, 1910) he quit so abruptly that he did not get to

141 NFS:II,6.DFI, 428. Letter from Ole Olsen to Nordisk Films Co., London (5 December 1907).

142 Interview with Mrs Elsas-Hansen and Joachim Nielsen. DFI.

143 NFS:II,10.DFI, 315. Letter from Wilhelm Stæhr to Marro y Tarre, S. en C., Barcelona (1 June 1909).

144 See Thomas Elsaesser, "The Presence of Pathé in Germany", in Michel Marie, Laurent Le Forestier and Catherine Schapira (ed.), *La firme Pathé Frères 1896–1909*, 127.

145 See Jean Drum and Dale D. Drum, *My Only Great Passion. The Life and Films of Carl Th. Dreyer* (Lanham Maryland: Scarecrow Press, 2000), 44–45.

146 See Tybjerg, "Spekulanter og Himmelstormere", in Peter Schepelern (ed.), *100 års dansk film*, 53.

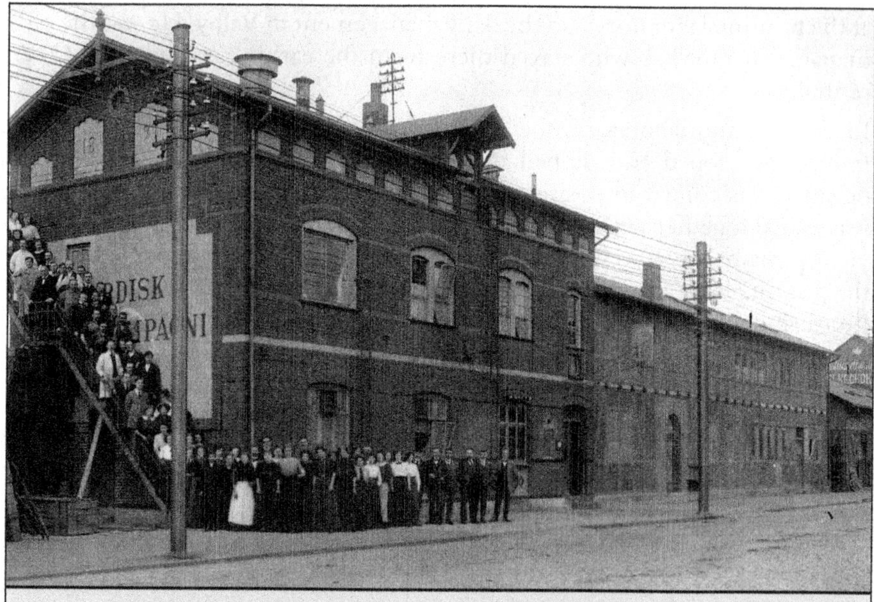

Figure 8. The new printing laboratory in Frihavnen around 1910. Manager Wilhelm Stæhr standing at the landing of the stairs. Courtesy of DFI/Stills & Posters Archive.

edit the film himself.[147] From the extant directors' contracts it appears that they were under obligation to edit if Nordisk so wished.[148]

Technical experience with film production was limited in Denmark in the 1910s, so Nordisk went abroad to hire expertise. In December 1906 Olsen wrote to a Mr. Bartram Tee from Brighton to ask him to come to Copenhagen at once and help out with "shooting, printing, developing etc. in fact everything appertaining to cinematography".[149] Whether Tee ever made it to Copenhagen or whether he may have been hired for a shorter or longer period is unkonwn. But the need for knowledge to solve both basic technological problems concerning film production and more specific problems were essential at Nordisk.

Technical problems played a major role in the first years of production at Nordisk, partly because quite basic impediments had to be overcome, partly because Nordisk aimed at an ambitiously high homogeneous quality in their films.

Nordisk not only had to go abroad to get cameras and machines for the printing laboratory – the indispensable raw stock had to be imported as well. Raw stock was sent to the factory, both negative film for the shoots and positive film onto which the finished film was copied. When the raw stock arrived in Frihavnen, it was first vacuum-cleaned, then perforated and packed in boxes before being

147 Interview with Viggo Larsen. DFI.

148 E.g. Nordisk Films Archives (NFA). Contract between Nordisk and A.W. Sandberg (24 February 1916).

149 NFS:II,2.DFI, 3. Letter from Ole Olsen to Mr. Tee, Brighton (12 December 1906).

delivered to the cameraman.[150] Perforation was among the first problems Olsen encountered in his film production. There was as yet no standard for perforation in the early days of the film industry, so the film was delivered without. The same machine was used to perforate both positive and negative film, but the positive film shrank in the chemical bath so it would no longer fit and the film would "shake" when it was run through the projector. In order to solve this problem, Olsen personally went to Paris to buy a perforation machine from Pathé Frères.[151] Later on, the perforation machines were purchased from the French company Debrie. Other machines, such as machines for copying film, were constructed by the company itself.[152]

Globally, only very few factories produced raw stock. The biggest producer was the American Eastman Kodak Company which was established in 1892 by photographer George Eastman. Eastman was the first raw stock producer who had systematized his production and his company more or less had the world monopoly.

In the beginning, Olsen bought his raw stock from various factories, such as Lumière,[153] but in May 1906 Nordisk struck a deal with Eastman who would remain the company's supplier until the 1910s.[154] Nordisk bought vast amounts of raw stock from Eastman; in the middle of 1907, Nordisk received between 500 and 1000 rolls of positive film a week.[155]

The production of raw stock was a complicated chemical process, and since no international standard of the format had yet been developed, either with regards to the thickness of the emulsion nor the perforation, the technological development of improving the raw stock was slow, and at the same time, the great demand for raw stock led to frequent shortages.

The quality of the raw stock was a continual problem for Nordisk, and Olsen complained to Eastman that the raw stock had 64 different emulsions, which presented Nordisk with the problem that they were, in effect, making 64 different films.[156] Another complication was that Eastman's negatives varied in thickness from 0.11 mm to 0.18 mm, which created problems during developing, and the films had spots on the emulsion.[157] Olsen wrote a letter complaining that Eastman's shipment of film did not meet the standards of the

150 Interview with H.F. Rimmen. DFI.

151 "Hvordan de skabte deres Livs Værk VII. Ved Leo Tandrup. Fhv. Generaldirektør Ole Olsen, skaberen af den første dramatiske film i verden siger: FORSTAA UNGDOMMEN!", *Berlingske Søndag* (10 February 1935).

152 NFS:II,11.DFI, 988. Letter from Wilhelm Stæhr to Messter Projektion, Berlin (8 January 1910).

153 NFS:II,4.DFI, 73. Letter from Ole Olsen to Lumière et son Fils [sic], Cours Gambetta, Lyon (28 June 1906).

154 NFS:II,4.DFI, 1. Letter from Ole Olsen to Kodak Ltd., London (25 May 1906).

155 NFS:II,1.DFI, 86. Letter from E. Hansen to Kodak Ltd., London (15 June 1907); NFS:II,1.DFI, 166. Letter from Nordisk to Kodak Ltd., London (4 July 1907).

156 NFS:II,1.DFI, 57. Letter from Nordisk to Kodak Ltd., London (6 June 1907).

157 NFS:II,11.DFI, 253. Letter from Wilhelm Stæhr to Kodak Ltd., London (13 October 1909).

sample Nordisk had initially received. The film was "[...] full of sparks and scratches between the celluloid and emulsion". The uneven quality of raw stock was a big problem; Nordisk received complaints from customers that the emulsion was peeling off and there were black spots on the films.[158]

The shortage of film was a further problem. At the beginning of 1907, the shortage was so severe that Nordisk repeatedly asked their Berlin branch to buy raw stock directly from Eastman's office in the German capital and have it shipped express to Frihavnen.[159] As an alternative to Eastman, Nordisk bought raw stock from Lumière in Lyon but had to admit that "the celluloid is too thick and quite impossible to work with".[160] Nordisk also tried to use film from Deutsche Rollfilm Aktiengesellschaft. Nordisk's appeal to the German factory testifies to the lack of standardization of raw stock: Nordisk preferred 35mm, they wrote, but 34.18 mm would do as well.[161] The raw stock from the German company was no success; Nordisk found the exposure of the film too slow.[162]

In August 1907, the shortage of film forced Nordisk to write to Eastman: "We have come into a bad fix through this. We have more than 20 plays ready and cannot get them out for want of negatives."[163] In September, Nordisk deemed the lack of negative film so critical that they shut down all production and decided to find another supplier if the situation did not change.[164] However, the situation did change in the autumn, and Nordisk informed Eastman that the quality now lived up to expectations.[165] The problems concerning quality and delivery improved but were not altogether solved in the company's early years.

Another problem was that the film came out unfocused in the middle of the frames after development. The solution, which Olsen according to his memoirs devised himself, was to place a small bit of velvet behind the glass plates during development to stop the film from bulging out in the middle.[166]

In some cases, Nordisk had to admit to its customers that the films were not always of the same high quality. Bad raw material was sometimes given as the cause, but at other times Nordisk actually confessed that the film was not

158 NFS:II,7.DFI, 370. Letter from Nordisk to Kodak Ltd., London (20 May 1908); NFS:II,6.DFI, 610. Letter from Ole Olsen to Hans Christensen, Vienna (7 January 1908).

159 NFS:II,3.DFI, 393. Letter from Nordisk to Nordisk Films Co., Berlin (4 April 1907); NFS:II,3.DFI, 427. Letter from Nordisk to Nordisk Films Co., Berlin (25 March 1907).

160 NFS:II,1.DFI, 180. Letter from E. Hansen to Lumière et son [sic] Fils, Lyon (8 July 1907).

161 NFS:II,1.DFI, 141. Letter from Ole Olsen to Deutsche Rollfilm Gesellschaft m.b.H., Frankfurt a/M (22 June 1907).

162 NFS:II,1.DFI, 185. Letter from Ole Olsen to Deutsche Rollfilm Gesellschaft m.b.H., Frankfurt a/M (9 July 1907).

163 NFS:II,1.DFI, 277. Letter from Nordisk to Kodak Ltd., London (3 August 1907).

164 NFS:II,1.DFI, 446. Letter from Nordisk to the Chief Manager of Kodak Ltd., London (10 September 1907).

165 NFS:II,6.DFI, 268. Letter from Nordisk to Kodak Ltd., London (6 November 1907).

166 See Olsen, *Filmens Eventyr og mit eget*, 82–84.

"beautiful" and gave a rebate of ten øre per metre, with the proviso that "[...] if this happened more often, it would render any trade with new films impossible".[167]

To ensure the quality of its films, Nordisk established a control system, so that any print could always be traced back to its processor in Frihavnen.[168] As a letter to the office in Vienna explained "[...] and we request that, in case of complaints, you always provide us with the two numbers scratched into the back end of the film so we can fire the employee responsible."[169] In connection with her work on restoring old films from Nordisk, Engberg has accounted for the intricate system of numbers and symbols which the company developed in Frihavnen to ensure that the films went through the many steps in production with the proper editing and colourization in the right places.[170]

About 80 per cent of all films from 1895 to 1930 were shown with some form of colourization.[171] The most frequently applied techniques were tinting and toning, monochrome colourizations in which the entire frame was given the same hue.[172] Nordisk's printing laboratory started producing tinted film in the autumn of 1906.[173]

Hand colourization was another method. With a magnifying glass and a very fine brush, colours were added to each frame of the copy. Among the earliest examples of hand-colouring in 1896 was Jacques Ducom's LA BICHE AU BOIS (The Deer in the Woods) and this practice had been used among others by French film-maker Georges Méliès around 1903, and Pathé and Gaumont had specialized in hand colourization and employed a large team of women were often employed to perform this laborious and time-consuming task. The demand for hand- and stencil-coloured films increased in the spring of 1907,[174] and the French companies' supply of coloured films was seen by Nordisk's Berlin branch as a threat Olsen reassured the staff in Berlin: "[...] as for Gaumont and their colourization of films, we will address that problem in time. But let us not lose our heads; it is no fun to be buried in a dunghill."[175]

167 NFS:II,3.DFI, 22. Letter from Nordisk to G. Knudsen, Kristiania (19 December 1906).

168 NFS:II,25.DFI, 614. Letter from Harald Frost to Ingvald C. Oes, New York (8 May 1913).

169 NFS:II,8.DFI, 930. Letter from Nordisk to Hans Christensen, Vienna (7 December 1908).

170 See Marguerite Engberg, "Er det nat eller dag? Om rekonstruktion af danske film", *Kosmorama*, no. 198 (Winter 1991): 40–43; Marguerite Engberg, "The Restoration of Silent Films Produced by Nordisk Films Kompagni", in Dan Nissen, Lisbeth Richter Larsen, Jesper Stub Johansen, and Thomas C. Christensen (ed.), *Preserve Then Show* (Copenhagen: Det Danske Filminstitut, 2002), 152–157.

171 See Daan Hertogs and Nico De Klerk, *Disorderly order. Colours in silent film: The 1995 Amsterdam Workshop* (Amsterdam: Stichting Nederlands Filmmuseum, 1996), 12.

172 *Tinting* is a process by which the developed film is dipped in dye that colours the light parts of the images while the black parts remain black. Conversely, *toning* applies a chemical solution to the positive film and colours the dark parts of the picture while the white parts remain more or less white.

173 NFS: II,4.DFI, 456. Letter from Niels le Tort to Gode Ven [Good Friend] (Ole Olsen) (22 October 1907).

174 E.g. NFS:II,3.DFI, 147. Letter from Christensen to Nilsson, Stockholm (26 January 1907); NFS:II,3.DFI, 384. Letter from Nordisk to Christofanini (22 March 1907).

175 NFS:II,3.DFI, 114. Letter from Ole Olsen to Partsch, Berlin (18 January 1907).

Engberg reports that Nordisk only hand-coloured nature films, and no more than four to six ladies were employed for this job in Frihavnen.[176] However, this was not how it began. In December 1907 Nordisk advertised for staff to colourize films at home after eight to ten days of free training;[177] they had no room for these people in Frihavnen.[178] On the day that the advertisement was printed, Nordisk told their London office that they were about to hire 75 women to colourize film, and that the product could only be expected after six weeks.[179] Nordisk had hired the Austrian colourizer Chocolus to train the women.[180] By mid-December, the colourization could commence, and a large order of high-gloss colours was placed with Günther Wagner in Vienna.[181] Half a year later, Chocolus had established the colourization department, and on 15 May 1908, his contract with Nordisk could be terminated.[182]

Coloured films were more expensive per metre since colourization by hand was considerably more time-consuming than tinting for which there was no extra charge.[183] In Germany, the price of hand-coloured films was ten pfennigs extra per metre.[184] Nordisk evaluated their hand-coloured films in this manner:

> [...] whatever was colourized in the last season was not of as high a quality as it ought to be, since it was carried out by beginners in this field, and you can lower the price upon customer request, and as much as you see fit. The colourized films you will get as of next season, however, will match the standards of any company.[185]

In time, Nordisk realized that the number of hand-coloured films being sold was too small for the company to compete with Pathé Frères and the French company's new machine-coloured films.[186] Technologically, Nordisk was lagging behind with regard to hand-colourization. With the films LA POULE AUX ŒUFS D'OR (THE HEN THAT LAID THE GOLDEN EGGS, Gaston Velle, Pathé Frères, F 1905) and ALADIN OU LA LAMPE MERVEILLEUSE (ALADDIN AND HIS WONDER LAMP, Albert Capellani, Pathé Frères, F 1906), Pathé launched films that were colourized on a stencil machine. A couple of other French companies such as Gaumont also started stencil-colourization, and Nordisk wanted to get

176 See Engberg, *Dansk stumfilm*, 75.

177 NFS:II,6.DFI, 400. Advert (2 December 1907).

178 NFS:II,6.DFI, 666. Letter from the Directorate to Ole Olsen (17 January 1908); NFS:II,7.DFI, 193. Letter to Nordisk from Mauritz Hansen (24 April 1908).

179 NFS:II,6.DFI, 405. Letter to the London branch (2 December 1907).

180 See Ivan Salto, *Nordisk Films 50 års jubilæum*, radio-montage aired 4 November 1956 (Copenhagen: Danmarks Radio, 1956).

181 NFS:II,6.DFI, 491. Letter from Wilhelm Stæhr to Günther Wagner, Vienna (14 December 1907).

182 NFS:II,7.DFI, 221. Letter from Wilhelm Stæhr to Chocolus (14 April 1908).

183 NFS:II,7.DFI, 348. Letter from Nordisk to Raleigh & Robert (14 May 1908).

184 NFS:II,7.DFI, 336. Letter from Nordisk to Christofanini (19 May 1908).

185 NFS:II,7.DFI, 932. Letter from Wilhelm Stæhr to Ingvald C. Oes, New York (11 August 1908).

186 NFS:II,12.DFI, 149–150. Letter from Wilhelm Stæhr to Nordisk Films Co., Berlin (28 January 1910).

a stencil machine, too,[187] but it was not easy to obtain, and Nordisk did not succeed in finding one at an auction until the end of 1910.[188] The machine rendered the women hired to colourize redundant, but a small department was maintained for hand-colourization. In 1911, six to eight women were still hand-colouring, and a manager of the department remained on the payroll, but mainly nature films were colourized this way.[189]

The problems concerning raw stock and the establishing of a department for the regrettably outdated colourization method exposed the advantage *technology entrepreneurs* had through their background as inventors in the early film industry.

Nordisk was continuously looking for technological novelties to test. Among these were the "Apparat Synchronisme", a mechanical system to synchronize image and sound,[190] an invention that could show images stereoscopically,[191] and a motorized projector which Nordisk sent to the Berlin branch for testing.[192] However, the company never established a department for technological development. As the industry acquired a common technological standard, the technical problems decreased and so did the competitive advantages of the *technology entrepreneurs*. One of Cadance Jones' points is that the early *technology entrepreneurs* dominated in the 1900s and lost ground around 1910 with the advent of longer films which brought the content of the films to the fore.[193]

The first films shot at Nordisk were actualities of a few minutes' duration – footage of topical events such as the company's film FREDERIK DEN 8'S PROKLAMATION or CYCLELØBENE I ORDRUP (The Bike Races in Ordrup, director unknown, 1906). The majority of films produced in 1906 were actualities,[194] and shooting these films did not require much organization. One person would film the events on his camera, and the footage could then be edited into the finished product. In the winter, Nordisk's permanently employed cameraman Graatkjær shot nature scenery,[195] but to get footage of big events abroad and of exotic places, Nordisk tried several options. The company F. Aubertin and E. Dinesen was hired for shoots in South America and Panama, but unfortunately, on their return to Copenhagen, their work turned out not to meet Nordisk's standards.[196] Another attempt was made by sending

187 NFS:II,11.DFI, 597. Letter from Wilhelm Stæhr to Nordische Films Co., Berlin (22 November 1909).

188 NFS:II,14.DFI, 613. Letter from Wilhelm Stæhr to Cadet frères, Paris (29 December 1910).

189 See Engberg, *Dansk stumfilm*, 75.

190 NFS:II,1.DFI, 111. Letter from E. Hansen to Georges Mendel, Paris (20 June 1907).

191 NFS:II,4.DFI, 334. Agreement between Ole Olsen and Olaf Verdelin (25 September 1906).

192 NFS:II,10.DFI, 8. Letter from Wilhelm Stæhr to Nordische Films Co., Berlin (15 April 1909).

193 See Jones, "Co-evolution of Entrepreneurial Careers", 919.

194 See Tom Gunning, "The Cinema of Attractions. Early Film, Its Spectator and the Avant-Garde", in Thomas Elsaesser (ed.), *Early Cinema. Space, Frame, Narrative* (London: BFI, 1990), 56.

195 See Salto, *Nordisk Films 50 års jubilæum*.

196 NFS:II,3.DFI, 107. Letter from Ole Olsen to F. Aubertin and E. Dinesen (18 January 1907); NFS:II,3.DFI, 612. Letter from Nordisk to F. Aubertin and E. Dinesen (4 May 1907).

photographer Alfred Lind on a Scandinavian tour to shoot footage of the Swedish landscapes, but these films were not usable either. In early 1907 Nordisk hired Edward Langhoff and Ludvig Lippert as full-time cameramen to film the company's actualities.[197] It appears from the company's correspondence that the two photographers constantly received instructions from Stæhr on how to record quality footage, by way of drawings and technical advice; after all, Stæhr had experience both as a photographer and as the manager of the printing laboratory.[198]

A permanent problem with the shooting of actualities was that reality sometimes proved quite unpredictable; in the summer of 1908, Langhoff was sent to Friedrichshafen to film a Zeppelin taking off. The launch, however, took quite a while, and Langhoff's footage was either over- or underexposed. Stæhr asked him to make the best of the wait and film something, giving him the following instructions:

> What really matters is to get something we couldn't have made at home, in Skovshoved for instance, but something out of the ordinary, something special to the country, some cultural activities or what have you; if you can find nothing like that, don't shoot anything, of course.[199]

Langhoff got some good takes of the Zeppelin launch,[200] and later that year he was sent to St. Petersburg.[201] This time, Stæhr's directions were: "[…] then we remind you that it would be an asset to every film if it contained some cultural activities, something from the poor quarters even if you have to pay to arrange it."[202] In the same letter, Stæhr expressed the idea that Langhoff should take the trans-Manchurian railroad to Port Arthur to film the American and British navies. Langhoff turned this offer down, and instead Lippert went to Constantinople and the Far East. Lippert managed to get some interesting footage, and Nordisk could proudly proclaim to its distributors that they were able to offer: "The first and the only motion pictures of the Sultan and his Harem."[203]

Those actualities, in which the news was the attraction, were troublesome to Nordisk because they required the photographer to be on the spot when the event took place, and even if a photographer was present, there was no

197 Information about Langhoff's and Lippert's travels and tasks is from Nordisk's books of correspondence copies; Langhoff worked for Nordisk until 1909; NFS:II,9.DFI, 746. Letter from Wilhelm Stæhr to Langhoff (11 March 1909). Lippert stopped in 1912; NFS:II,18. DFI, 607. Letter from Harald Frost to Lippert (1 February 1912)). Who shot Nordisk's actualities after 1912 is uncertain.

198 NFS:II,7.DFI, 448. Letter from Wilhelm Stæhr to Lippert, the Danish Consulate, Bangkok (6 November 1908); NFS:II,7.DFI, 520. Letter from Wilhelm Stæhr to Langhoff, Friedrichshafen, Bodensee (17 or 18 June 1908).

199 NFS:II,7.DFI, 521. Letter from Wilhelm Stæhr to Langhoff, Friedrichshafen, Bodensee (17 or 18 June 1908). Skovshoved is a small fishing village north of Copenhagen.

200 NFS:II,7.DFI, 576–577. Letter from Wilhelm Stæhr to Langhoff, Friedrichshafen, Bodensee (25 June 1908).

201 NFS:II,7.DFI, 740. Letter from Wilhelm Stæhr to Langhoff, poste restante, St. Petersburg (14 July 1908).

202 NFS:II,7.DFI, 752. Letter from Wilhelm Stæhr to Langhoff, poste restante, St. Petersburg (16 July 1908).

203 NFS:II,8.DFI, 437. Letter from Wilhelm Stæhr to Nordische Films Co., Berlin (17 October 1908).

guarantee that he would come home with usable footage or would have filmed the right things. In December 1907, Nordisk sent two photographers, one of whom was Langhoff, to Stockholm to film the interment of the Swedish King Oscar II. Nordisk informed their customers in advance that if they placed their order in good time, "the film will be delivered 24 hours after the event".[204] Olsen had written several letters directing what pictures to take and how, but he was not at all pleased with his two photographers. Even after other companies had sent out footage of the interment, Olsen had still received nothing in Frihavnen. Olsen wrote to the photographers in Stockholm:

> I don't understand what you were doing last Friday in Stockholm. The Nya Londoner Cinema has already shot the king lying in state so we are totally cut off from using that. Langhoff had express orders to film the king lying in state as soon as he arrived, but this he has not achieved, and now our competitors get the credit. I can't understand how this could happen, and you have let the others up there down terribly.[205]

The news value of actualities was paramount. Figures from the early 1920s show that the rental fee of actualities decreased by half only three days after the event; after nine days they cost 25 per cent of the original price, and the number of distributed copies was halved in the course of six days.[206] Nordisk kept constantly in touch with situations and events of newsreel value. In 1909, the Vienna office was instructed to send word to Copenhagen immediately if a war broke out between Austria and Serbia, and to get a cameraman to follow the troops.[207] Lippert, who was in Luzern in February 1909, was ordered to stand by and move at once if there were any signs of unrest in Greece.[208]

The competition to be first with actualities played a part in the planning of which events Nordisk would use its resources to shoot. In 1912, Nordisk gave up on getting footage of the war in North Africa since Pathé Frères, Gaumont and Itala had already distributed actualities from that event.[209] Pathé and Gaumont had special crews hired only to make actualities exclusively, and Nordisk's photographers could not compete with this. After a couple of years, Nordisk actually gave up on producing newsreels; the competition was too tough and the results too unprdeictable. However, Nordisk continued to produce one nature film or travelogue every week.

In 1917 and 1918, Nordisk started producing news-based actualities again. 31 newsreels were produced exclusively for the home market. However, they were expensive to make, and Nordisk eventually stopped producing these as

204 NFS:II,6.DFI, 442. Letter from Nordisk to Karlstadts Läskedricksfabrik og Biografteater, Karlstadt (9 December 1907).

205 NFS:II,6.DFI, 503. Letter from Ole Olsen to Fotograf Sørensen, Stockholm (16 December 1907).

206 See Bakker, *Entertainment Industrialised*, 214.

207 NFS:II,9.DFI, 607. Letter from Wilhelm Stæhr to Hans Christensen, Vienna (25 February 1909).

208 NFS:II,12.DFI, 299. Letter from Wilhelm Stæhr to Ludvig Lippert, Luzern (18 February 1910).

209 NFS:I,2:3.DFI, 2–3. Letter from Harald Frost to Ole Olsen (3 February 1912).

well.[210] Fiction films would turn out to be Nordisk's forte. The shoots were under control, the films sustained public interest for a longer time and consequently, fiction proved to be a better investment.

Nordisk's initial foray into making fiction film was hampered by the fact that no one in Denmark had any experience with doing fiction films. Prior to 1906, no one but Elfelt had ever made a fiction film, and he only made one, HENRETTELSEN (The Execution, Peter Elfelt, 1903). The film KONFIRMANDEN (The Candidate for Confirmation, Louis Halberstadt, 1906) was Nordisk's first attempt. Olsen hired the actor and impressionist Louis Halberstadt to direct the film. Halberstadt later said that Olsen did not want to see a script but just a pitch for the plot, and that what he wanted was "hullabaloo".[211] It turned out during the shoot, however, that Halberstadt was not up to the task of directing. Viggo Larsen, a former sergeant and the inspector of Biograf-Theatret, has given a report of the shoot:

> The impressionist Louis Halberstadt was to direct. He approached the job very solemnly and held a 'reading' in the cinema on Vimmelskaftet with the supernumeraries he had gathered. But when we started shooting in Søndermarken, he lost control. So I took command. It went well. From my days in the army I knew how to get respect and how to get people to obey; my experience helped me now, and Ole Olsen thought that I should be a director.[212]

Larsen took over the direction and, with a few exceptions, he directed all of Nordisk's films from 1906 to 1909.[213] The first employees at Nordisk had widely different backgrounds, and Larsen's impression of the staff was not encouraging: "Of course, we were all bloody amateurs as well as technically illiterate."[214] Arnold Richard Nielsen, a former sports reporter, worked as an ideas man and scriptwriter for Nordisk from 1906 to 1908 and has described the motley crew involved in the first fiction films:

> The new staff counted, among others, the ventriloquist *Gustav Lund*; the actor and tobacconist *Nylén;* the ballet dancer *Borgen*, the cartoonist *Ulk Jensen*; the editor at the Directory *Rasmussen*; actor *Valdemar Petersen* who was the theatre's first machinist; and actress *Gerda Jensen* from the Dagmar Theatre.[215]

Nielsen is certainly not the most reliable source – he has repeatedly claimed to be the true founder of Nordisk[216] – but his description of the widely different employees may still give us an idea of the degree to which the early Danish film industry had to learn everything from scratch.

Another employee of Biograf-Theatret, the former souvenir programme

210 Interview with Joachim Nielsen. DFI.

211 Interview with Louis Halberstadt. DFI.

212 Hr. Bert, "Dansk Film kan fejre sit 50 aars jubilæum", *Politiken* (24 April 1955).

213 It has not yet been possible to identify the directors of all of Nordisk's early films. We know that Ole Olsen directed a film in 1906 and that Gustav Lund directed one in 1907. This may indicate that Larsen directed all other fiction films.

214 Interview with Viggo Larsen. DFI.

215 Arnold Richard Nielsen, "Af Filmens Historie", *Folkets Avis* (29 September 1914).

216 E.g. Arnold Richard Nielsen, "Fra Filmens første Dage", *Politikens Magasin* (17 January 1926).

vendor Axel Graatkjær, was promoted to cameraman. In those days, cameras were cranked by hand and this had to be done in an even tempo to prevent movements on the screen appearing uneven. Ole Olsen was no good at filming; he would get nervous and excited at loud sounds and stop cranking whereas Graatkjær had a steady hand.[217] Larsen and Graatkjær were the nucleus of the film team of five to six people who shot all the company's fiction films in the years from 1906 to1909.[218]

In the first years, the crew members each had multiple functions during production. The cartoonist Robert Storm Petersen painted the sets and acted, while Larsen often played the lead in the films he directed. Larsen has said about his part in the productions:

> The best thing about the job was that in my quadruple capacity of scriptwriter, dramaturg, director and actor I was sovereign. My instructions were: make it fast, make it cheap, and never more than 165 metres.[219]

And it certainly did go quicly. "A couple of days. Some [films] were made in one [day]", Larsen recalled.[220] The very tight production schedule meant that Nordisk, in spite of having just one production crew, made an average of 60 fiction films a year from 1906 to 1909 (Table 2).

Table 2: Nordisk's production of fiction films and actualities, 1906–1909

	1906	1907	1908	1909
Fiction films	34	67	59	82
Actualities	55	47	74	59

Source: See note for Table 1 (on page 30).

The first fiction films were shot in public parks and in the streets, but as early as in 1906, Olsen announced that he intended to build a studio in Amager close to the old city moat: "The place is ideal because all the sets are there; water and trees and fields and roads, and there is space enough for crowd scenes as well as for little comic or idyllic scenes."[221] However, the final choice of location for the studio was not Amager but Valby. It is not known exactly when Olsen bought the plot there, but it must have been sometime in the summer of 1906.

Two wardrobe sheds were built on the Valby lot, one for the gentlemen and one for the ladies, along with a larger shed for decorations and a wooden platform that served as the studio, with everything screened off by a fence.[222] The platform functioned as a stage where backdrops could be hung up with decorations representing various locations. The problem with the outdoor

217 See Salto, *Nordisk Films 50 års jubilæum*.

218 Interview with Axel Graatkjær. DFI.

219 See Arnold Hending, "Det københavnske Hollywood", *Historiske meddelelser om København*, 4th series, vol. 4 (Copenhagen: C.E.C. Gad, 1954–1957), 644.

220 Hr. Bert, "Dansk Film kan fejre sit 50 aars jubilæum", *Politiken* (24 April 1955).

221 "Levende Billeder. Et Friluftsteater paa Amager. Humoresken under aaben Himmel", *Politiken* (2 March 1906).

222 Interview with Viggo Larsen. DFI.

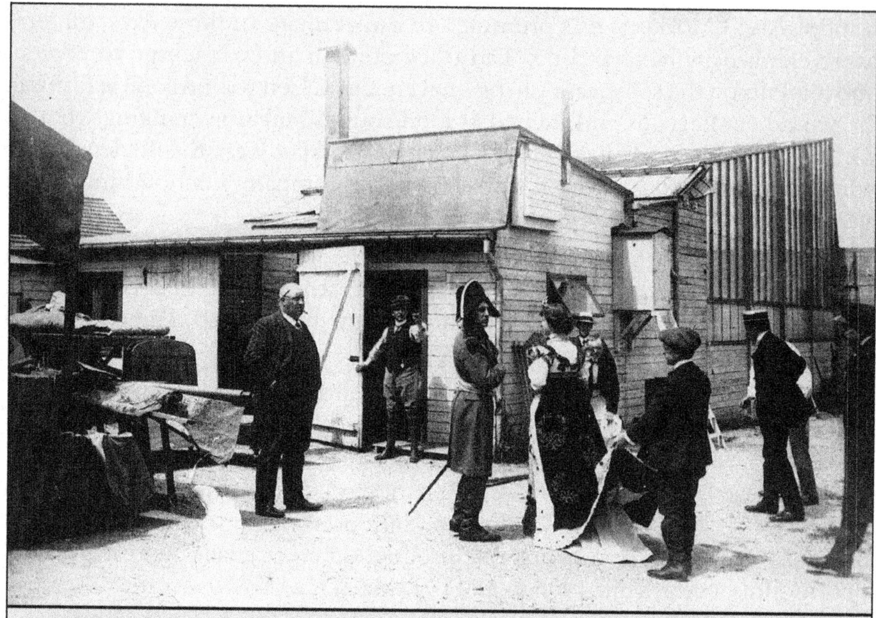

Figure 9. Actors on their way to shooting in Nordisk's first film studio built in 1907, stage 1, apparently for the shooting of the film MADAME SANS GÊNE (Viggo Larsen, 1909). Courtesy of DFI/Stills & Posters Archive.

stage was that the decorations would flutter at the slightest breeze during the shooting.[223] The makeshift wooden stage did not suit the studio's needs for very long, and in late May of 1907, Nordisk started building Denmark's first film studio in iron and glass, and also a smaller, wooden annex. It cost 4,700 kroner and was finished in five weeks.[224] Stage 1 would be Nordisk's only studio until 1910 when more production crews were employed.

The films were shot without artificial light, so sunlight was of vital importance. Consequently, the shooting season was limited to May through August.[225] In 1908/1909, after electric lighting had become more common, the season was extended to April through October.[226] Viggo Larsen was appointed inspector and artistic manager in Valby where the studio had 50 employees in 1908.[227] The printing laboratory in Frihavnen and the studios in Valby were the cornerstones of Nordisk's film production throughout the silent movie era.

Engberg identifies quality as the reason for the immediate success of Nordisk's films: "When things went so well for Olsen's company, it was first and foremost because the films soon acquired a reputation of being technically and

223 Interview with Axel Graatkjær. DFI.

224 NFS:II,3.DFI, 736. Letter from Nordisk to Carpenter Hansen (28 May 1907).

225 NFS:II,9.DFI, 34. Letter from Nordisk to Arnold Jørgensen, Odense (17 December 1908).

226 NFS:II,8.DFI, 700. Letter from Wilhelm Stæhr to Ole Olsen (10 November 1908).

227 NFS:II,7.DFI, 17. Letter from Ole Olsen to the Editors of the Industrial Report (16 March 1908).

artistically top notch."[228] Nordisk did indeed spend time and resources to make their films as technically perfect as could be, but it is difficult to form an opinion of the artistic quality since only few of the early films are extant. We cannot really know if Nordisk was perceived as superior in artistic style or plot when compared to other films on the market before 1910. In support of her argument that the films from Nordisk were considered more artistic, Engberg refers to Ron Mottram's study of film reviews in *Moving Picture World* from 1908 to 1913. Mottram reports that no other European film company received the kind of praise as Nordisk did in, for instance, a *Moving Picture World* review of EN KVINDE AF FOLKET (A WOMAN OF THE PEOPLE, Viggo Larsen, 1909):

> Great Northern films, which are going from success to success, have a polish and finish about them, which gives them that distinction of quality that lifts the moving picture onto the plane of the pictorial.[229]

Mottram points out some common features in the reviews of Nordisk's films: the magazine tends to commend their clarity of plot, their high technical quality and their realism.[230] However, since *Moving Picture World*'s reviews are among the few sources that give us an idea of how Nordisk was perceived by its contemporaries, and the theory about the artistic success of Nordisk shaping cinema history is based solely on *Moving Picture World*'s praise, this view cannot conclusively be considered representative. Mottram also quotes a less positive mention from another American magazine, *The New York Dramatic Mirror*, which states that REVOLUTIONSBRYLLUP (1910) fails "utterly in putting any life or feeling into the action",[231] so one may question whether Nordisk was the only company habitually praised by *Moving Picture World*. Richard Abel asserts that the magazine always praised the French company Éclair as well: "[...] winning consistent praise from *Moving Picture World,* the company was singled out for praise almost immediately."[232] Stæhr's own laconic view of Nordisk films in 1910 was: "Well, it cannot possibly all be golden, but that's the way with other companies' production as well; some of it is very good, some is good, and some is less so."[233]

In 1940, Danish critic Harald Engberg characterized Nordisk's early films in unflattering tones. He saw them as being just as childish and barbaric as the taste of the audience to which they catered:

> With a healthy appetite, which also devoured all good taste, they leapt at anything. Horrible murder stories, Biblical stories and classic drama, opera, ballet, fairy tales

228 Engberg, *Dansk stumfilm*, 72–73.

229 *Moving Picture World* (9 June 1908): 871, quoted from Ron Mottram, *The Danish Cinema before Dreyer* (Metuchen N. J.: Scarecrow Press, 1988), 51. In the U.S. Nordisk was known as the Great Northern Film Company.

230 See Mottram, *The Danish Cinema before Dreyer*, 52–53.

231 *The New York Dramatic Mirror* (18 March 1910): 18, quoted from Mottram, *The Danish Cinema before Dreyer*, 45.

232 Abel, *The Cine Goes to Town*, 52 and 483, note 297.

233 NFS:II,12.DFI, 179–180. Letter from Wilhelm Stæhr to Ingvald C. Oes, New York (1 February 1910).

and farces went into this sausage factory and were churned out as little film dramas at an impressive rate.[234]

Harald Engberg's view of the films as mass products devouring all good taste differs greatly from Marguerite Engberg's evaluation of their artistic merits, but other film historians have emphasized the popularity of Nordisk's films, such as Bardèche and Brasillach in their cinema history from 1935: "[...] one can only judge the early Danish film by hearsay today, but they were very popular before the war."[235] Bardèche and Brasillach establish that Danish films did not appear to be very different from the average productions of the time. Nevertheless, the films from Nordisk were highly esteemed and admired in France because of their dramatic intensity and their artistic quality.[236] The Russian film historian Semyon Ginzburg claims that Danish films from before World War I were the most popular among foreign films shown in Russia.[237] Neither Bardèche and Brasillach nor Ginzburg mention exactly when these films were considered so popular. It is tempting to surmise that they refer to Nordisk's multiple-reel films which were not produced until after 1910, at least in Russia it was around this time Nordisk's export of films took off to this country.

Olsen takes the credit for Nordisk being the first company to produce dramatic films. Olsen reports in his memoirs that he asked Charles Pathé if he would consider doing dramas, but Pathé replied that he had no intention of trying to improve on his own success and wished Olsen the best of luck.[238] This anecdote was never given a date, but in all likelihood it must have taken place before Olsen started his film production in 1906. In film-historic research, several researchers point to a turning-point in films around 1906 when Nordisk began producing its films and went from actualities to narratives.[239] Olsen may be right in stating that Nordisk was among the first companies to make drama films, but this also coincided with a general change in the film industry.

When comparing the relatively few films still in existence from Nordisk's production between 1906 and 1909 with films from other companies in this period, we find no remarkable differences. In general, the films are kept in long shots without inserts or close-ups, which gives them a stagy look. The sets are painted backdrops and very few props are used. A farce like ANARKISTENS SVIGERMODER (THE ANARCHIST'S MOTHER-IN-LAW, Viggo Larsen, 1906),

234 Harald Engberg, "Filmen", in Svend Dahl (ed.), *Danmarks Kultur ved Aar 1940*, vol. 8 (Copenhagen: Det Danske Forlag, 1943), 155.

235 Maurice Bardèche and Robert Brasillach, *The History of Motion Pictures* (New York: Norton, 1938), 56.

236 See ibid.

237 See Seymon Ginzburg, *Kinematograf dorevoliutsionnoi Rossii* (Moscow: Agraf, 1963), 163–65. I am grateful to Lauri Piispa for this reference.

238 See Olsen, *Filmens Eventyr og mit eget*, 74–75.

239 Abel, *The Cine Goes to Town*, 23; Noël Burch,"A Primitive Mode of Representation?", in Thomas Elsaesser (ed.), *Early Cinema. Space, Frame, Narrative*, 220; Gunning, "Cinema of Attractions", 56.

which to a great extent works because of its chase scenes, is not so very different from, for instance, LE CHEVAL EMBALLÉ (THE RUNAWAY HORSE, Louis J. Gasnier, Pathé Frères, F 1907). The Orientalist element in FLUGTEN FRA SERAILLET (THE FLIGHT FROM THE SERAGLIO, Viggo Larsen, 1907) is to be found in several of Pathé's films, such as ALADIN OU LA LAMPE MERVEILLEUSE. The cinematographic tricks of stop motion and reverse play used in the farce HEKSEN OG CYKLISTEN (THE CYCLE RIDER AND THE WITCH, Viggo Larsen, 1909) were, as Engberg writes, nothing new; in the British THE '?' MOTORIST (Walter Robert Booth, Robert William Paul, GB 1909) we find a similar melange of the same bag of tricks.[240] If we compare a Nordisk production like BARNET SOM VELGØRER (THE CHILD AS BENEFACTOR, Viggo Larsen, 1909) with the American THE COUNTRY DOCTOR (David Wark Griffith, Biograph Company, USA 1909) from the same year, the Danish production appears positively primitive.

The question is whether the artistic quality mattered at all in Nordisk's first years; Bakker emphasizes that the standardization of contents in films from the early years of the industry actually increased their trade value.[241] Therefore it is perhaps misleading to explain the success of Nordisk by the films' artistic quality since entertainment value was more significant at the time. However, the market Nordisk entered had a voracious demand for films, and what made a difference was whether the film company was organized in such a way that it could meet this demand with products of a visible quality. Artistic quality *per se* did not become a competitive advantage in the film industry until 1910 and the advent of longer films.

In a competitive market the new company needed a trademark and Viggo Larsen recalls that it was invented at a meeting where he, Olsen and the secretary Miss Gundestrup were present. They agreed that a globe was to feature in the trademark, and it was Miss Gundestrup who thought of putting a polar bear on top of it.[242] Nordisk's trademark appeared in ANARKISTENS SVIGERMODER which premiered on 25 October 1906, but Lisbeth Richter Larsen points out that it may have appeared earlier in a lost film. Richter Larsen surmises that the company stationery with Nordisk's letterhead most likely was ordered from the printer in January 1907.[243]

By choosing a triumphant polar bear roaring from the top of the world, Nordisk emulated Pathé Frères's trademark of a Gallic rooster. The most important function of the trademark was in marketing Nordisk; it differentiated and positioned the company's products from those of other companies and served as a quality mark. From his years at the amusement parks, Olsen understood the importance of branding one's product, and even if we have no

240 See Engberg, *Dansk stumfilm*, 192.

241 See Bakker, *Entertainment Industrialised*, 183.

242 See Salto, *Nordisk Films 50 års jubilæum*.

243 See Lisbeth Richter Larsen, "Isbjørnejagten", *Film*, no. 8 (April 2000): 12–13.

statements documenting it, Nordisk's marketing strategy seems thoroughly contemplated.

In the early years, Nordisk sold its films directly to distributors, cinemas and agents. The company had no share in the box office profits, and consequently, advertising was primarily targeted at distributors and cinema owners in the countries where Nordisk was represented. In Germany, Nordisk advertised in *Der Anker*[244] and *Der Komet*.[245] The London office advertised in *The Era*[246] and *The Stage*,[247] the Vienna branch in *Kinematographische Rundschau*,[248] and the American affiliate in *Moving Picture World*.[249] On all other markets, Nordisk's agents were left to do all the marketing themselves.

Nordisk's main office in Copenhagen stopped advertising in trade journals in 1911.[250] The company was offered ads but rejected them, for instance in *Lichtbild-Bühne*[251] and *Kinematographische Rundschau*.[252] As Stæhr explained to the Berlin office, "[...] you know, we place no value in magazine ads, even of the kind that the Rus-Scand. Commercial House uses".[253] What Stæhr is saying here is that another production company, Skandinavisk-Russiske Handelshus (Scandinavian-Russian Trading Company) was wasting its money. Nordisk would change its tune on this matter around 1912.

From early on, Nordisk produced commercial material to go with the films, primarily posters. The regular supplier of posters was the printing house Friedländer in Hamburg, and Nordisk gave very specific instructions as to how they wished the posters to look. For the poster of the film BJØRNEJAGT I RUSLAND (BEAR HUNTING IN RUSSIA, Viggo Larsen, 1909) the instructions were the following: "The five bears must lie dead (left upper corner); the horses must be seen in full gallop. The trees are pine and birch, no leaves. No snow."[254] In order for the posters to match the content of the films and ensure Nordisk's influence, a sketch[255] or a still photo from the film was enclosed, and Nordisk expected this material to be scrutinized and followed when the poster was designed.[256] Nordisk chose to have their posters printed abroad

244 NFS:II,3.DFI, 67. Letter from Ole Olsen to the Editor of *Der Anker*, Hamburg (4 January 1907).

245 NFS:II,4.DFI, 327. Letter from Ole Olsen to *Der Komet*, Pirmasens (24 September 1906).

246 NFS:II,6.DFI, 266. Letter from Wilhelm Stæhr to Partsch, London (5 November 1907).

247 NFS:II,6.DFI, 428. Letter from Ole Olsen to Nordisk Films Co., London (5 December 1907).

248 NFS:II,1.DFI, 174. Letter from Nordisk to Hans Christensen, Vienna (6 July 1907).

249 NFS:II,20.DFI, 805. Letter from A.W. Mammen and Harald Frost to Ingvald C. Oes, New York (27 June 1912).

250 NFS:II,13.DFI, 704. Letter from Wilhelm Stæhr to Nordische Films Co., Berlin (21 September 1910); NFS:II,16.DFI, 218. Letter from Wilhelm Stæhr to C. Nielsen, Berlin (24 June 1911).

251 NFS:II,9.DFI, 439. Letter from Wilhelm Stæhr to *Lichtbild-Bühne*, Berlin (8 February 1909).

252 NFS:II,9.DFI, 451. Letter from Wilhelm Stæhr to *Kinematographische Rundschau* (9 February 1909).

253 NFS:II,16.DFI, 140. Letter from Wilhelm Stæhr to C. Nielsen, Berlin (14 June 1911).

254 NFS:II,7.DFI, 369. Letter from Nordisk to Friedländer, Hamburg (19 May 1908).

255 NFS:II,3.DFI, 186. Letter from Nordisk to Friedländer, Hamburg (4 February 1907).

256 NFS:II,17.DFI, 748. Letter from A. Jensen to Stafford & Co. Ltd., London (1 December 1911).

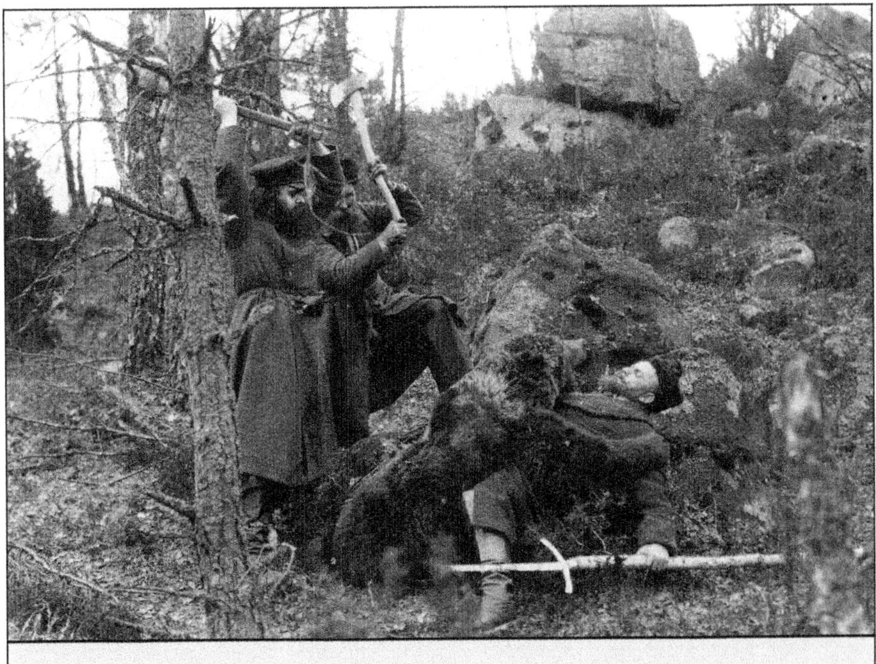

Figure 10. BJØRNEJAGT I RUSLAND. Courtesy of DFI/Stills & Posters Archive.

because it was cheaper, and they regularly changed printers[257] until finally settling on Stafford & Co. in Sheffield by December 1910.[258] Nordisk's offices and agents ordered whatever amount of posters was needed by telegraphing directly to Stafford who would then send the required amount of posters back to them.[259] Nordisk sent stills from the printing laboratory in Frihavnen together with the films, to be put on display with the posters and souvenir programmes as commercial material in the cinemas.

In the German trade journal *Der Kinematograph* we find a series of ads for Nordisk in 1908.[260] These ads coincide with the *Erste Internationale Kinematographen-Industrie-Ausstellung* (The First International Cinematograph Industry Exhibition) in Hamburg, June 1908. At the exhibition, the young film industry could show the state of the art and the newest technology. Nordisk's big hit at the exhibition was the film BJØRNEJAGT I RUSLAND, a follow-up to LØVEJAGTEN. Five brown bears had been purchased, and were then hunted down and shot in Sweden to make sure that Nordisk did not run into the same

257 NFS:II,1.DFI, 229 and NFS:II,1.DFI, 274. Letter from Nordisk to Seneca Andersen, Copenhagen (22 July and 3 August 1907); NFS:II,9.DFI, 354. Letter from Nordisk to Imprimerie Artistique, Louis Galice, Paris (28 January 1909).

258 NFS:II,14.DFI, 601. Letter from Wilhelm Stæhr to Stafford & Co., Sheffield (27 December 1910).

259 Interview with Joachim Nielsen II. DFI

260 E.g. *Der Kinematograph*, no. 74 (27 May 1908), and no. 79 (1 July 1908).

problems as with LØVEJAGTEN. In Hamburg, the tanned hides of the bears were supposed to be part of the exhibition at Nordisk's stall.[261] Unfortunately, the skins were completely ruined when they arrived at the tanner; they had been wrapped up while still wet rather than being dried before they were shipped from Sweden.[262] To make up for the missing bear hides, the Nordisk stall was decorated like an ice pavilion. "The ice pavilion with the company trademark, the polar bear on the globe, is indubitably one of the great attractions at the exhibition",[263] *Der Kinematograph* reported. What other professionals noticed was that Nordisk made a splash by presenting no less than "ten different colourizations",[264] and Nordisk won an honorary award and a gold medal for the excellent quality of the films. However, the attribution of the awards ended in protests and crises; several of the other exhibitors wanted a written statement concerning the jury's criteria and objected that the jury had not visited all the stalls at the exhibition.[265] The German trade press took exception to the awards, while Nordisk wrote to the editors of the trade journal *Der Komet* asking the magazine to publish the company's awards: "As far as our company is concerned, we understand from what we heard from several participants at the exhibition that according to our competitors, our awards were very much deserved."[266] In spite of the fact that the integrity of the awards had been called into question, Olsen still wrote proudly to the New York branch:

> [...] we have been praised to such an extent that we are the undisputed number one down there, and this although all the great companies in the world had exhibitions, too. I can report that producers of projectors for sale down there only wanted our films to run through as test material, since they were the only films that ran safe and sound through any machine.[267]

The prizes were used in the marketing of the company. In the period following the exhibition, Nordisk stamped all outgoing letters: "Hamburg 1908 Grand Prix and Gold Medal",[268] and for years, the two prizes were included on the company's letterhead.

Although the primary purpose of the trademark was to brand the company's films, it was at the same time a way to protect the products. Cinema owners

261 NFS:II,7.DFI, 376. Letter from Nordisk to Furrier Trolle, Østergade (20 May 1908).

262 NFS:II,7.DFI, 384. Letter from Ole Olsen to Hans Anderson, Immeln (21 May 1908).

263 Emil Perlmann, "I. Internationale Kinematographen-Industrie-Ausstellung Hamburg 1908", *Der Kinematograph*, no. 77 (17 June 1908).

264 "I. Internationale Kinematographen-Industrie-Ausstellung Hamburg 1908. II", *Der Kinematograph*, no. 78 (24 June 1908).

265 Ibid.

266 NFS:II,7.DFI, 755. Letter from Nordisk to the Editors of *Der Komet*, Pirmasens (16 July 1908).

267 NFS:II,7.DFI, 536. Letter from Ole Olsen to Ingvald C. Oes, New York (19 June 1908).

268 E.g. NFS:II,7.DFI, 740. Letter from Wilhelm Stæhr to Langhoff, poste restante, St. Petersburg (14 July 1908); NFS:II,7.DFI, 809. Letter from Ole Olsen to Khanjonkoff & Cie., Moscow (24 July 1908). For a detailed account (in Danish) of the events surrounding the exhibition in Hamburg in 1908 see Stephan Michael Schröder, "Den danske isbjørns sejr på den 1. Internationale Kinematograf- Industri-Udstilling i Hamborg 1908", in Stephan Michael Schröder and Martin Zerlang (ed.), *1908: Et snapshot af de kulturelle relationer mellem Tyskland og Danmark* (Hellerup: Spring, 2011): 124–156.

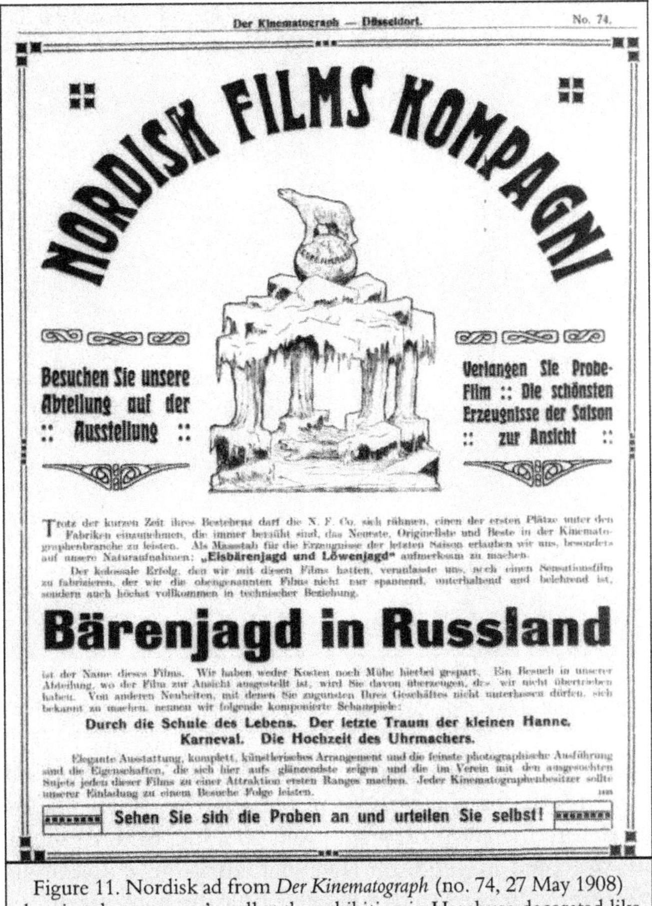

Figure 11. Nordisk ad from *Der Kinematograph* (no. 74, 27 May 1908) showing the company's stall at the exhibition in Hamburg decorated like an ice pavilion with the ice bear on top.

were not above re-editing the films before they showed them in their cinemas.[269] One way to prevent that the films were cut to pieces or that parts of them were re-used in films from other companies was to place the trademark in the film itself. In that way it was easy to prove theft of material. As mentioned, Nordisk's trademark appears in the film ANARKISTENS SVIGERMODER, and in this film, a cardboard or wooden slab sporting Nordisk's trademark is seen leaning against the sets in several scenes. Only a few of the early Nordisk films survive, so we cannot say for certain whether this demonstrative way of advertising was used in general, but it does not appear to be the case. Apparently only in one other surviving film, EKSPEDITRICEN (IN THE PRIME OF LIFE, August Blom, 1911), does the trademark appear more or less clearly in the sets.

269 See Sandfeld, *Den stumme scene*, 148; Gunning, "Cinema of Attractions", 58.

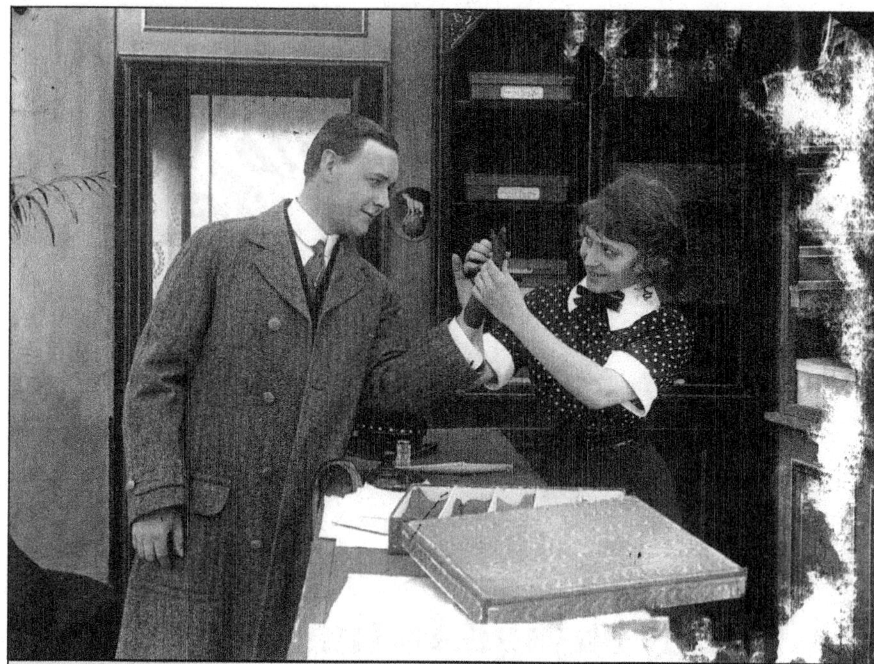

Figure 12. Carlo and Clara Wieth in EKSPEDITRICEN. The company trademark appears in the setting on the back wall between the two actors. Courtesy of DFI/Stills & Posters Archive.

This trademarking was necessary because of widespread plagiarism. André Gaudreault writes that in the early film industry they knew "neither law nor religion".[270] Before the Berlin Convention, an addendum to the Berne Convention, was accepted in 1908, no laws or regulations concerning the copyrights of motion pictures existed, and even after the convention it would take some years before the laws were implemented in the various countries; Denmark did not accede to the law until 1912.[271] Gaudreault thinks that "film piracy" was extremely widespread from 1900 to 1906. The pirates worked in two ways; either by copying another company's film and marketing it as their own product, or by plagiarizing an already made film in a remake.[272]

American producers protected their films by copying every single frame on paper. Before a premiere, the paper print was deposited at the U.S. Copyright Office in the Library of Congress. In case of a law suit, it would prove copyrights. This arrangement lasted until around 1912.[273]

270 André Gaudreault, "The Infringement of Copyright Laws and its Effects (1900–1906)", in Thomas Elsaesser (ed.), *Early Cinema: Space, Frame, Narrative*, 114.

271 Stephan Michael Schröder, *Ideale Kommunikation, reale Filmproduktion. Zur Interaktion von Kino und dänischer Literatur 1909–1918* (Berlin: Berliner Beiträge zur Skandinavistik, 2011), 429.

272 See Gaudreault, "The Infringement of Copyright Laws", 114.

273 Bebe Bergsten, *Ole Olsen. The Great Dane and the Great Northern Film Company* (Los Angeles: Locare Research Group, 1973), 27.

Another way to protect a given company's rights was to make an agreement with the competitors which mutually excluded plagiarizing. Nordisk and Pathé Frères had made such an agreement, but Pathé broke it. In a letter from 1907, Olsen directly asks Pathé if they had presented Nordisk's STORBRAND (The Great Fire, 1907) as a Pathé film. If this was true, Olsen intended to let it be publicized in all the European trade journals.[274] Nordisk had been obliged to pay 10,000 German marks to Ernst Durckel from Pathé's Berlin office as surety that Nordisk and Pathé would not copy one another's films. Olsen now regarded the agreement as null and void, and, as he later expressed in a letter to Pathé: "I consider it a question of honour, mine as well as yours, that we do not directly copy each other's film."[275] Pathé apologized and paid back the 10,000 marks to Nordisk.[276]

Nordisk had to be vigilant even with its own regular agents. In the British trade journal *The Era*, Olsen had read with amazement that the film TANTES FØDSELSDAG (Auntie's Birthday, Viggo Larsen, 1907) had been shown in London. Since the film had not been released in Britain, it had to be the company's agent in France, Raleigh & Robert, who had released it on his own recognizance, or else the film had been copied. Olsen had to tell the French agent in no uncertain terms: "[...] no one copies my films".[277] In April 1907, Nordisk contacted the Italian film company Ambrosio because Nordisk had been made to understand that Ambrosio sold films from Nordisk. Nordisk demanded to know if they had bought the films or copied them. Ambrosio was advised to answer honestly so that these pirates could be stopped.[278] Nordisk informed their Italian agent Christofanini that steps must be taken to teach these pirates a lesson and that Christofanini would no longer be troubled with these "calamities".[279]

Questions of copying and plagiarizing, as well as the need to protect its copyrights, would come to play a crucial role in Nordisk's later development. From around 1912, the Berne Convention would limit abuse of copyrights to some extent, but there were still cases of infringement, such as in the case of scenes from Nordisk's ATLANTIS (August Blom, 1913) which were cut out and edited into an American film that was shown in the Copenhagen cinema Kinografen.[280]

"O's role model is the mighty French company 'Pathé Frères' in Paris", the newspaper *Middagsposten* wrote about Olsen in January 1907.[281] Olsen

274 NFS:II,1.DFI, 43. Letter from Ole Olsen to Pathé Frères, Paris (3 June 1907).

275 NFS:II,1.DFI, 93. Letter from Ole Olsen to Pathé Frères, Paris (14 June 1907).

276 NFS:II,1.DFI, 142. Letter from Ole Olsen to Pathé Frères, Paris (28 June 1907).

277 NFS:II,3.DFI, 317. Letter from Ole Olsen to Raleigh & Robert, Paris (8 March 1907).

278 NFS:II,3.DFI, 567. Letter from Nordisk to Arturo Ambrosio & Co., Turin (29 April 1907).

279 NFS:II,3.DFI, 572. Letter from E. Hansen to A.M. Christofanini (29 April 1907).

280 Interview with Joachim Nielsen. DFI.

281 "Levende Billeder", *Middagsposten* (28 January 1907).

measured himself against Pathé. He explained in a letter from January 1907 to Eduard Partsch, the manager of Nordisk's Berlin office, how he "worked like a beast" to make Nordisk a success and that his ambition for Nordisk was "[...] for it to become next year's number one after Pathé Frères".[282]

In another letter to Partsch there seems to be no shortage of confidence on Olsen's part. As rumours in Berlin would have it, the two French companies wanted to lower their prices to 80 pfennigs per metre. Olsen warned, "Please make sure that Pathé and Gaumont hear this: if they reduce their prices, I will personally ruin the business for the lot of them."[283] In case of a price reduction, Nordisk's Berlin branch was to lower the price to 65 pfennigs per metre, he wrote. Olsen considered that the two French companies had vast administration expenses and would lose by reducing their prices, whereas Nordisk, according to Olsen, had very small expenses.[284] It would seem that Olsen was right. Thomas Elsaesser has pointed out that the profit for Pathé's shareholders was not very large in 1907–1909: only around 7.2 per cent against the expected 10–12 per cent.[285] Due to its sheer size, Pathé could undersell the industry's mutually negotiated prices in Britain in 1906.[286] Olsen knew Pathé's market strength and added the following concerning the price of films in a contract: "[...] our prices in England must at any time match those of Pathé and Gaumont."[287]

More examples of Nordisk's direct competition with Pathé and Gaumont exist. Nordisk used travelling salesmen for its foreign branches in Germany and Scandinavia. While travelling in Sweden, a salesman from Nordisk was told to hurry back to those customers who had not yet agreed to buy Nordisk films – in order to get there before a salesman from Gaumont who might bring twenty good films.[288] In a similar letter, Nordisk asked three Swedish cinema owners if they could advance the date of a premiere a couple of days; Pathé was releasing an almost identical film, and Nordisk wished to beat them to it.[289]

Apart from a short period in the French market and in the U.S. after 1908 onward, the companies in the early film industry cannot be called a collective monopoly. The competitive situation arose from the fact that the companies by and large produced similar kind of films, and even though they competed on prices, these were to some extent steady. The most important competition

282 NFS:II,3.DFI, 98. Letter from Ole Olsen to Partsch, Berlin (15 January 1907).

283 NFS:II,3.DFI, 114. Letter from Ole Olsen to Partsch, Berlin (18 January 1907).

284 NFS:II,3.DFI, 114. Letter from Ole Olsen to Partsch, Berlin (18 January 1907).

285 See Elsaesser, "The Presence of Pathé in Germany", 403.

286 See Jon Burrows, "When Britain Tried to Join Europe: The Significance of the 1909 Paris Congress for the British Film Industry", *Early Popular Visual Culture*, vol. 4, no. 1 (April 2006): 6.

287 NFS:II,1.DFI, 197. Agreement between Ole Olsen and Niels le Tort (12 July 1907).

288 NFS:II,10.DFI, 846. Letter from Wilhelm Stæhr to C.S. Dam, Helsingborg (25 August 1909).

289 NFS:II,12.DFI, 383. Letter from Wilhelm Stæhr to C.A. Friberg, Karlskrona (1 March 1910); NFS:II,12.DFI, 384. Letter from Wilhelm Stæhr to Svensk Film Co., Jønköping (1 March 1910); NFS:II,12.DFI, 385. Letter from Wilhelm Stæhr to Frantz Lundberg, Malmoe (1 March 1910).

for Nordisk during their first years concerned market shares on the international scene. The struggle for market shares is what sharpens a company's functional and strategic abilities that are part of an MIE's organizational capabilities:

> They [MIEs] did so *functionally* by improving their products, their processes of production, their marketing, their purchasing, and their labor relations, and *strategically* by moving into growing markets more rapidly, and out of declining ones more quickly and effectively than their other competitors.[290]

The conditions of Nordisk's distribution network have been insufficiently described in the existing literature and there is some confusion about the number of offices established by the company abroad, and also about its number of agents and distributors. In *100 års dansk film* (100 Years of Danish Film), Casper Tybjerg writes of Olsen's enterprise in 1906: "By the end of the year, he had established branches abroad in Sweden, Norway, Germany and Italy."[291] According to Neergaard, however, Nordisk established offices in Berlin, London, Vienna, Budapest, New York, Prague, Zurich, Amsterdam and St. Petersburg,[292] but in 2006, Marguerite Engberg asserted: "Already before the end of 1906, [Olsen] succeeded in establishing six branches and agencies abroad."[293] One cause of this confusion is that Nordisk referred to its agents and distributors as "branches". In 1907, letters from Nordisk referred to "our Paris branch",[294] but at this point, the company was represented in France by Raleigh & Robert and never actually opened an office in Paris. Prior to World War I, Nordisk established formal branches in Berlin in 1906, in London and in Vienna in 1907, as well as a subsidiary company, Great Northern, in New York in 1908. The one in Vienna, however, was short-lived. The rest of Nordisk's distribution network consisted of individuals or companies who obtained the exclusive rights to Nordisk's films on one or more markets.

Berlin was the obvious choice of location for the company's first foreign branch since it was one of the two major European film centres, alongside London. In October 1906, Olsen sent the Dane Eduard Partsch to the German capital with the mission of exploring the opportunities for a representation there. In Norway, Sweden and Finland, Nordisk sold its films through travelling representatives, a role that Partsch had filled in Sweden. Olsen gave him meticulous instructions as to what the office was to look like. It should be in the vicinity of those of the competing companies and have space enough for a business room, a storeroom and a projection room. If Partsch should find himself in doubt about how to furnish the office, he should pay a visit to Pathé

290 Chandler, *Scale and Scope*, 8.

291 Tybjerg, "Teltholdernes verdensteater", 21.

292 Neergaard, *Historien om dansk film*, 32.

293 Marguerite Engberg, "Plagiarism, and the Birth of the Danish Multi-Reel Film", in Dan Nissen and Lisbeth Richter Larsen (ed.), *100 Years of Nordisk Film*, 73.

294 NFS:II,1.DFI, 426. Letter from Christensen to Svensk Kinematograf Aktiebolag, Gothenburg (5 September 1907).

Frères's premises, but, as Olsen stipulated: "Under no circumstances should you mention who sent you; just pretend you're interested in the latest films."[295] On 18 November, Nordisk's first foreign branch opened at Friedrichstraße 23,[296] the street with all the film companies, among them Gaumont residing at number 20; Urban Trading Corporation at 43; Pathé Frères at 49a; Deutsche Mutoscope at 187, and Cines at 238.[297] Besides Partsch, a secretary was hired, and later a salesman, whose task was to look up potential customers, joined the other two.[298]

Before a film was officially circulated, the branches and the agents received a test copy which was only shown to the customers in the projection room on the premises. The customers then ordered whatever number of copies they desired. They then sent the orders back to Frihavnen where the required number of copies was produced. In this way, Nordisk avoided making more copies than they actually needed, and also avoided having to store old films in Frihavnen and at their offices abroad.

The Berlin branch did not only sell films in Germany but also in Russia,[299] Hungary,[300] Switzerland[301] and China.[302] As Nordisk acquired agents in the rest of Europe, Berlin stopped selling to those countries where Nordisk was represented; there were, for instance, no further direct sales to Austria-Hungary after Nordisk opened an office in Vienna, and in this way the company avoided competing against itself on the same market. On the other hand, Nordisk permitted the branches to sell to any market that did not have a permanent agent.[303]

Olsen demanded a daily report from Partsch on the office's progession, especially the sales, but also on general trends on the film market. Nordisk went to great lengths to keep up-to-date and now subscribed to all the leading film trade journals in the world.[304] At some point, Nordisk even subscribed to news from Ritzau's News Agency; Ritzau had to phone in news to Nordisk's office several times a day.[305] It appears from Nordisk's correspondence that the management sometimes knew from the international trade journals what the

295 NFS:II,4.DFI, 403. Letter from Ole Olsen to Partsch, Berlin (11 October 1907).

296 Bundesarchiv-Filmarchiv R109-639. Universum Film Verleih G.m.b.H., Berlin.

297 Michael Hanisch, *Auf den Spuren der Filmgeschichte. Berliner Schauplätze* (Berlin: Henschel Verlag, 1991), 168.

298 NFS:II,3.DFI, 373. Letter from Nordisk to Nordische Films Co., Berlin (20 March 1907).

299 NFS:II,3.DFI, 220. Letter from E. Hansen to Partsch, Berlin (12 February 1907).

300 NFS:II,3.DFI, 373. Letter from Nordisk to Nordische Films Co., Berlin (20 March 1907).

301 NFS:II,14.DFI, 984. Letter from Wilhelm Stæhr to Nordische Films Co., Berlin (9 February 1911).

302 NFS:II,14.DFI, 71. Letter from Wilhelm Stæhr to Hugo C.A. Fromm (4 November 1910).

303 NFS:II,12. DFI, 149–150. Letter from Wilhelm Stæhr to Nordisk Films Co., Berlin (28 January 1910); NFS:II,12. DFI, 240. Letter from Wilhelm Stæhr to Nordisk Films Co., London (10 February 1910).

304 Interview with Joachim Nielsen. DFI; NFS:II,7.DFI, 729. Letter from Ole Olsen to Great Northern Film Co., New York (13 July 1908).

305 NFS:II,6.DFI, 940. Letter from Ole Olsen to Ritzau's News Agency (2 March 1908).

branches were doing and what was happening on the individual markets even before the offices abroad reported back to Copenhagen. In other cases, Nordisk did not know what their own representatives were doing before they read about it in one of the journals.[306]

Olsen was often in Berlin to check up on his branch there, and when he was not able to be there, he sent instructions through Partsch. Olsen wrote to Berlin about a film he did not particularly like: "Don't strain yourself too much to sell DIE BEIDEN WEISEN [sic], since I am not too pleased with that play. See if you can fob it off on some idiot who can't tell the difference anyway [...]."[307] Olsen also gave Partsch permission to re-edit and shorten the film if this would improve sales.[308] If the technical quality of a film was not good enough, Olsen advised Partsch:

> When you find faults in the pictures, split them up and put something good in each so we avoid loss; I know for a fact that the other producers do this. Of course, do so only in cases when the fault is not too bad.[309]

The films were sold by the metre and the bills often occasioned discussions with customers who doubted that the prints had the length they paid for. The customers were actually right; Nordisk regularly cheated on the length. Partsch was instructed:

> In the future, seven per cent will be added to the actual length of all films, which is what Pathé does. You see, today we measured a Pathé film of which they gave the length of 95 metres, but it was in fact only 87 metres. If anyone complains and returns the films [...], then give them a rebate and explain away the length by stating that it is a mistake on the part of the photographer, but make sure to tell them that they should also measure Pathé's films. Do measure all the films you have now very meticulously, correct the measurements and add seven per cent. Make the adjustments in ink on the catalogues and please forward a note concerning the changed length, so we can enter it into the ads and our accounts.[310]

Nordisk continued to add metres to the films, a principle that applied to the other offices in the company. In 1911, Harald Frost wrote to the London branch where the new manager, Ludwig Landemann, appears not to have received the message about the added metres:

> As you know, this is an international arrangement and should be followed also in England. [...] If we do not make such an addition we shall be obliged to increase our prices as the profit will otherwise be too small.[311]

306 E.g. NFS:II,12.DFI, 934. Letter from Ole Olsen to Ingvald C. Oes, New York (2 June 1910).

307 NFS:II,3.DFI, 74. Letter from Ole Olsen to Partsch, Berlin (7 January 1907). Many of the films from Nordisk existed under several different Danish as well as international titles. I have not succeeded in finding the corresponding Danish title of DIE BEIDEN WEISEN [sic]. Herbert Birett, *Das Filmangebot in Deutschland 1895–1911* (München: Filmbuchverlag Winterberg, 1991), 764, mentions the Nordisk title ZWEI WAISEN (film number 16942). This film is 190 metres and could therefore be TO BØRN PAA LANDEVEJEN (Two Orphans, Viggo Larsen, 1906) which is also 190 metres.

308 NFS:II,3.DFI, 74. Letter from Ole Olsen to Partsch, Berlin (7 January 1907).

309 NFS:II,3.DFI, 24. Letter from Ole Olsen to Partsch, Berlin (19 December 1906).

310 NFS:II,3.DFI, 28. Letter from Ole Olsen to Partsch, Berlin (20 December 1906).

311 NFS:II,18.DFI, 366. Letter from Harald Frost to L. Landemann, Badenweiler (17 January 1911).

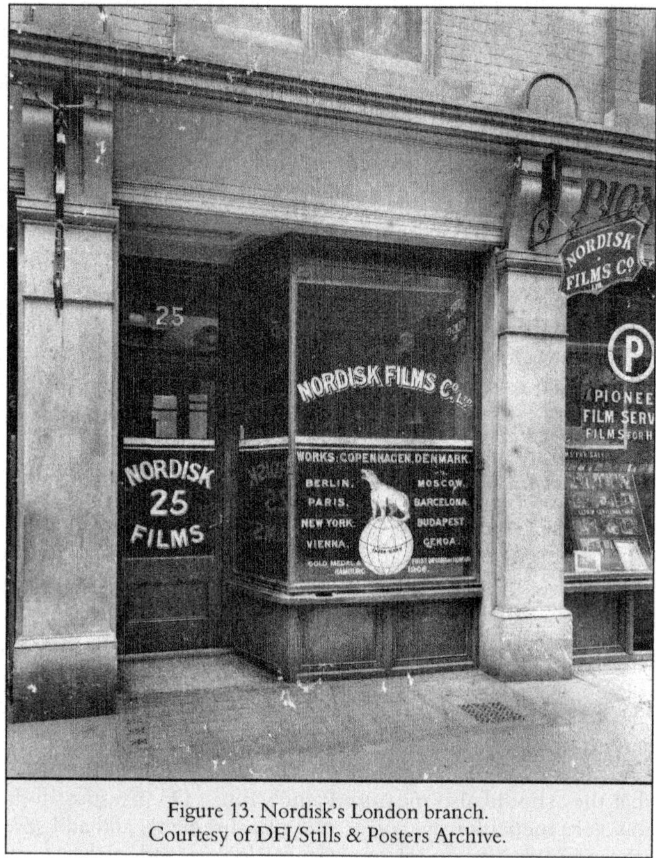

Figure 13. Nordisk's London branch.
Courtesy of DFI/Stills & Posters Archive.

In the case of Swedish A/B Svensk Kinematograf in Gothenburg, the added metres caused the company to discontinue their business with Nordisk. Nordisk responded that they followed the international regulations and continued:

> [...] we will, however, ask you to examine the length of your film very carefully, as we are inclined to believe that your measurement is wrong, since we time and again arrive at the very length for which we charge you.[312]

The producers' practice of adding metres must have been widespread. From the very comprehensive Dutch Jean Desmet archives it appears that distributor Desmet measured all the films he received and claimed a refund if he found that he had been charged for more than he got.[313] The New York subsidiary was also instructed to add some metres, although no more than three per cent of the proper length.[314] In 1907, Nordisk sold 664,326 positive metres film

312 NFS:II,3.DFI, 603. Letter from E. Hansen to A/B Svensk Kinematograf, Gothenburg (3 May 1907).

313 See Rixt Jonkman, "Any ID? Building a database out of the Jean Desmet archive", in Frank Kessler and Nanna Verhoeff (ed.), *Networks of Entertainment* (Eastleigh: John Libbey Publishing, 2007), 313.

314 NFS:II,7.DFI, 105. Letter from Wilhelm Stæhr to Ingvald C. Oes, New York (1 April 1908).

globally;[315] seven per cent of this amount is 46,502.82 metres and three per cent is 19,929.78 metres. At a price of about one krone per metre, the fraudulently added metres made the company a pretty penny indeed.

The second branch Nordisk established was in London, Europe's second-largest film trade centre. Via London, films travelled to and from the U.S. and Europe. The London office also sold films to Australia,[316] Singapore,[317] Africa[318] and Brazil.[319] In June 1907, Olsen offered le Tort, his old partner from Biograf-Theatret, the management of the agency, [320] but as it turned out, it was Partsch who went from Berlin to London instead.[321] The branch was supposed to be exactly like the one in Berlin, but Olsen was not pleased and wrote to Partsch that "[...] there must be a daily report of the sales etc. just like the one we get from Berlin".[322] A few days later, Olsen complained again:

> You were under express orders to hire a man from another film company, someone who is thoroughly experienced in the business, and I trusted that you would carry out this order since this would immediately give us the addresses of all customers in England. I deplore your negligence very much and it goes without saying that you need an Englishman more than a German. It is my wish that you hire a lady for the book-keeping presently. I want everything to follow the sure routine of the Berlin office. Be careful about giving credit. I don't want you to give credit to anyone that may give you the slightest cause for doubt.[323]

Olsen requested a native agent in order to create the best basis for the office, and a couple of weeks later, Olsen continued in the same tone of voice about the problems of hiring a female book-keeper: "I trust you can see that we must have a uniform system in our different offices that are all managed from the main office."[324] Olsen's instructions about the offices and how they should be run show how he insisted that all the branches looked the same, from rooms to personnel to book-keeping. A uniform pattern facilitated the central management from Copenhagen.

Austria-Hungary was another important European market in which Nordisk was interested, of course. In January 1907, Partsch was asked to go on a tour of the country where, hopefully, he would find a suitable agent. He was also offered the Austrian-Hungarian market for five per cent of the takings,[325] but in May 1907, Olsen started negotiations with Hans Christensen about a

315 See note for Table 1.

316 NFS:II,6.DFI, 401. Letter from Ole Olsen to Partsch, Berlin (2 December 1907).

317 NFS:II,7.DFI, 392. Letter from Ole Olsen to Nordisk Films Co., London (22 May 1908).

318 NFS:II,13.DFI, 547. Letter from Wilhelm Stæhr to K.M. Therkildsen, Copenhagen (2 September 1910).

319 NFS:II,16.DFI, 95. Letter from Wilhelm Stæhr to Nordisk Films Co., London (6 June 1911).

320 NFS:II,1.DFI, 197. Agreement between Ole Olsen and Niels le Tort (12 June 1907).

321 NFS:II,6.DFI, 183. Letter from Ole Olsen to Khanjonkoff & Cie., Moscow (19 October 1907).

322 NFS:II,6.DFI, 340. Letter from Ole Olsen to Partsch, London (23 November 1907).

323 NFS:II,6.DFI, 350. Letter from Ole Olsen to Partsch, London (25 November 1907).

324 NFS:II,6.DFI, 401. Letter from Ole Olsen to Partsch, London (2 December 1907).

325 NFS:II,3.DFI, 105. Letter from Ole Olsen to Partsch, Berlin (17 January 1907).

Nordisk's agency in Austria-Hungary. Christensen was to run the agency for three years if he could provide security and cover office and administration expenses; Nordisk would deliver films at one krone per metre. Olsen estimated that the annual turnover would be 150,000 metres.[326] The conditions of the agreement were similar to those presented to the company's Italian agent Christofanini; the agent would pay Nordisk per metre film, in Christensen's case 85 Austrian pfennigs, and add his own commission. Olsen admonished Christensen that "payments must be in cash".[327] The address and telegraphic address of the foreign offices would feature in Nordisk's ads in *Der Komet* and *Der Anker*. Moreover, Christensen was to advertise in the local Austrian-Hungarian *Kinematographische Rundschau*, yet keep the ad costs below 54 Austrian Kronen a month.[328]

Olsen gave Christensen precise instructions on how to establish and run an office, identical to the directions he gave when the offices in Berlin and London were established; there had to be a shop that would serve as an office and a projection room of at least seven metres in length for the screenings; the premises had to be close to Nordisk's competitors. The staff would consist of one female bookkeeper and a male projectionist.[329] Olsen recommended hiring a former employee of Pathé since such a person might give "[…] a quick insight into the clientele and the names of customers who can pay".[330]

Christensen opened the Vienna branch in July, but in the autumn, the collaboration between Christensen and Nordisk ran into trouble. Nordisk complained that they did not receive the weekly reports and money transfers.[331] Christensen ordered too many films that he could not sell, and when he made a sale, it was at 75 Austrian pfennigs per metre, which, according to Olsen, was an outrageously low price:

> If I wanted to sell my films at 75 Pf. per mtr. I could sell everything in the factory in less than 48 hours, but I would naturally lose money. I hope that you now understand that no films must be sold for less than the fixed price unless they are outdated and otherwise unsaleable.[332]

Furthermore, Olsen complained that Christensen had not yet prepared a projection room in which to show customers the films from Nordisk.[333] Olsen's dissatisfaction with Christensen's handling of the business in Vienna grew, and in July 1908 Olsen was able to cancel the contract with no further moral obligations since Nordisk learned that Christensen was about to sell the

326 NFS:II,1.DFI, 36. Letter from Ole Olsen to Hans Christensen, Vienna (1 June 1907).

327 NFS:II,1.DFI, 143. Letter from Ole Olsen to Hans Christensen, Vienna (28 June 1907).

328 NFS:II,1.DFI, 174. Letter from Ole Olsen to Hans Christensen, Vienna (6 July 1907).

329 NFS:II,3.DFI, 681. Letter from Ole Olsen to Hans Christensen, Vienna (5 May 1907).

330 NFS:II,3.DFI, 720. Letter from Ole Olsen to Hans Christensen, Vienna (23 May 1907).

331 NFS:II,6.DFI, 185. Letter from Ole Olsen to Hans Christensen, Vienna (21 October 1907).

332 NFS:II,6.DFI, 512. Letter from Ole Olsen to Hans Christensen, Vienna (17 December 1907).

333 NFS:II,6.DFI, 512. Letter from Ole Olsen to Hans Christensen, Vienna (17 December 1907).

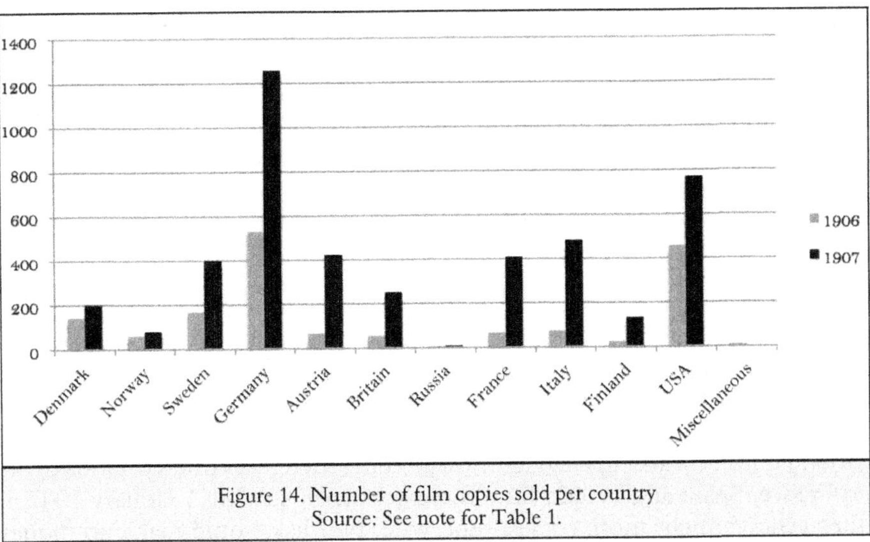

Figure 14. Number of film copies sold per country
Source: See note for Table 1.

agency to another party without informing Nordisk.[334] By mid-July the collaboration was definitely terminated,[335] and Olsen offered the Austria-Hungary agency to the company Neumann & Ungerleider.[336] However, collaboration with Christensen was resumed at the end of July; Christensen had accepted Nordisk's new conditions that Christensen had someone who would put up security for him.[337] In his eagerness to make money, Christensen started to offer the films at a price so low that Nordisk's regular customers, who usually bought their films from the Berlin office, were now able to buy the company's films at half the price in Vienna, to Nordisk's chagrin.[338] Nordisk wrote to Christensen: "[...] it now clearly appears from our business with you that you cannot be our representative in Austria-Hungary."[339] Nordisk contacted the Austrian distributor Projectograph that had a branch in Vienna and Budapest,[340] returned Christensen's bond of surety and terminated the arrangement.[341] The Vienna agency only existed for a few years.

Besides the foreign offices, Nordisk distributed its films through agents who represented the company in their respective countries or regions. Nordisk contracted Christofanini in Italy at an early stage, the company Raleigh & Robert handled Nordisk's films in France and Britain, and distribution in the U.S. was in the hands of Miles Brothers.

334 NFS:II,7.DFI, 664. Letter from Ole Olsen to Hans Christensen, Vienna (7 July 1908).

335 NFS:II,7.DFI, 750. Letter from Ole Olsen to Hans Christensen, Vienna (14 July 1908).

336 NFS:II,7.DFI, 751. Letter from Ole Olsen to Neumann & Ungerleider, Vienna (15 July 1907).

337 NFS:II,7.DFI, 797. Letter from Nordisk to Hans Christensen, Vienna (24 July 1908).

338 NFS:II,7.DFI, 920. Letter from Nordisk to Hans Christensen, Vienna (10 August 1908).

339 NFS:II,10.DFI, 7. Letter from Nordisk to Hans Christensen, Vienna (15 April 1909).

340 NFS:II,10.DFI, 717. Letter from Wilhelm Stæhr to Projectograph, Budapest (4 August 1909).

341 NFS:II,10.DFI, 722. Letter from Nordisk to Hans Christensen, Vienna (4 August 1909).

An account of Nordisk's regular customers shows that sales increased considerably in the first year (see Figure 14), but also that the company had regular agents in three markets: France, Italy and North America. In Denmark and Scandinavia, Nordisk sold its films through travelling representatives, and the three branches traded locally in Germany, Britain, and the U.S. – and sometimes they sold to territories in which Nordisk did not have an agent. Moreover, sales were sometimes made directly from the main office, for instance to Bangkok.[342]

Towards the end of the decade Nordisk was on the look-out for regular agents in more countries. The company approached consulates in France, Switzerland, Belgium, Greece, the Netherlands and Argentina to obtain recommendations for potential agents.[343] Nordisk also tried to make their regular agents sell films to more markets. Raleigh & Robert, operating for them in France and Britain until Nordisk opened their own offices there, was offered a monopoly in France, Spain and Britain for a three-year term starting 1 January 1907, if the agency bought more copies; otherwise, Nordisk would make no money on the deal. Moreover, Raleigh & Robert was offered the Netherlands, Belgium and North Africa, all of which were markets that Nordisk wished to enter.[344]

From the early years of the company until the outbreak of World War I, Nordisk received many offers from individuals and firms wishing to represent the Danish company.[345] Nordisk was careful in its selection of agents and rejected most applicants, even an agent in a country in which Nordisk had no contacts yet. One example of the difficulties in getting an agent in a foreign country was Russia, and this although Russia was one of the biggest export markets for the Danish industry before World War I and would later become Nordisk's biggest customer.[346] Sales to Russia started as early as 1906. Both via the Berlin and Vienna offices[347] and through deals made with distributors,[348]

342 NFS:II,10.DFI, 32. Letter from Wilhelm Stæhr to Hong Kong and Shanghai Banking Corporation, Bangkok (19 April 1909).

343 NFS:II,11.DFI, 588–594. Letter from Wilhelm Stæhr to Consul General Edvard Henrik Lund, Buenos Aires (22 November 1909); NFS:II,11.DFI, 590. Letter from Wilhelm Stæhr to Consul Jacob Boot, Amsterdam (22 November 1909); NFS:II,11.DFI, 591. Letter from Wilhelm Stæhr to Consul General Emil Hoskie, Paris (22 November 1909); NFS:II,11.DFI, 592. Letter from Wilhelm Stæhr to Consul Diethelm, Zurich (22 November 1909); NFS:II,11.DFI, 593. Letter from Wilhelm Stæhr to Consul General Leonidas Hadjdimitriou, Athens (22 November 1909); NFS:II,11.DFI, 594. Letter from Wilhelm Stæhr to Consul General Frederik G. Schack de Brockdorff, Antwerp (22 November 1909).

344 NFS:II,3.DFI, 342. Letter from Nordisk to Raleigh & Robert, Paris (14 March 1907).

345 E.g. Russia: NFS:II,1.DFI, 82. Letter from E. Hansen to B. Neuland (11 June 1907); NFS:II,1.DFI, 228. Letter from Nordisk to L.S. Finkelstein, Vladivostok (10 July 1907); Sweden: NFS:II,1.DFI, 340. Letter from E. Hansen to Jønköping Biografteatern, Jønköping (17 August 1907); Java: NFS:II,7.DFI, 238. Letter from Nordisk to M.S. Michael, Ned. Ind. Electr. Bioscoop, Satiga (Java) (30 April 1908); China: NFS:II,34.DFI, 881. Letter from Harald Frost to Viggo Meier, Russian Post Office, Shanghai, China (22 January 1915).

346 See Boje, *Danmark og multinationale virksomheder før 1950*, 100.

347 NFS:II,6.DFI, 189. Letter from Nordisk to Hans Christensen, Vienna (22 October 1907).

348 E.g. NFS:II,6.DFI, 70. Letter from Nordisk to Ph. Schwarzenberg, Kiev (28 September 1907).

a few of the company's films were exported to Russia, but an actual agreement with the potentially large and lucrative market never materialized. One of the reasons was that the French film companies sat firmly on the Russian market; the financial, political and cultural ties between France and Russia were strong around the turn of the century. Pathé Frères's first foreign office was established in Moscow in 1904, and Jay Leyda has argued that it was Pathé who cultivated and created a market for film in Russia, first through sales of projectors and films, later by having travelling projectionists touring towns and cities, which in time would lead to permanent cinemas.[349] After the American market, Russia was the source of the biggest foreign-market income for Pathé.[350]

Olsen hoped that he too would have an office in Moscow by the summer of 1907.[351] He opted to collaborate with one of the biggest production and distribution companies in Russia, Khanzhonkov & Co. in Moscow; but this partnership did not last.[352] In order to boost sales to the Russian company, Nordisk had claimed at an early stage that France and Italy bought at least 20 copies of each new title,[353] a number which was grossly exaggerated; Nordisk sold, on the average, 6.8 copies of its films in France and 7.7 in Italy.[354]

In July 1908, Henry Koch was given exclusive rights to negotiate Nordisk's films in Russia.[355] Koch was even given a list of those Russian customers who had hitherto bought films through Berlin.[356] However, Nordisk was not sure that Koch was the right man for the job and asked Frantsen, who represented the Danish shipyard Burmeister & Wain's Moscow branch, as well as the Danish vice consul Edström, for information on Koch.[357] Every time Nordisk started collaborating with agents abroad, they checked up on them, either through the Danish consulate[358] or at a credit institution in Copenhagen that also collected debts for Nordisk.[359] In the course of a few months it turned out that Koch was a slow payer.[360] Nordisk must have sensed that the outcome of a collaboration with Koch was doubtful, for they had conducted parallel

349 See Jay Leyda, *Kino. A History of the Russian and Sovjet Film* (New York: Collier Books, 1973), 24.

350 See Richard Abel, *The Red Rooster Scare. Making Cinema American, 1900–1910* (Berkeley, California: University of California Press, 1999), 242.

351 "Levende Billeder", *Middagsposten* (28 January 1907).

352 NFS:II,6.DFI, 101. Letter from Nordisk to Khanjonkoff & Cie., Moscow (5 October 1907).

353 NFS:II,6.DFI, 184. Letter from Ole Olsen to Khanjonkoff & Cie., Moscow (19 October 1907).

354 See note for Table 1.

355 NFS:II,7.DFI, 840. Letter from Nordisk to Henry Koch, Moscow (30 July 1908).

356 NFS:II,7.DFI, 848. Letter from Nordisk to Nordische Films Co., Berlin (30 July 1908).

357 NFS:II,8.DFI, 68. Letter from Nordisk to Frantsen, Burmeister & Wain branch, Moscow (2 September 1908).

358 NFS:II,3.DFI, 116. Letter from Ole Olsen to the Danish Consulate, Paris (19 January 1907); NFS:II,3.DFI, 629. Letter from Ole Olsen to the Danish Consulate, Vienna (7 May 1907).

359 NFS:II,3.DFI, 17. Letter from Gundestrup to Kreditreformforeningen, Copenhagen (18 December 1906).

360 NFS:II,8.DFI, 405. Letter from Wilhelm Stæhr to Henry Koch, Moscow (14 October 1908).

negotiations on the side with Aleksandr Drankov, St. Petersburg, who took over the Russian agency in 1908.[361] Drankov quickly amassed a great debt to Nordisk;[362] in May 1909, Nordisk reported Drankov's debt of 11,000 francs to their debt collector[363] and pursued legal action against him until October 1912.[364] Nordisk spent much energy on poor payers and seldom quit if money was due to them; they acquired a reputation of a company that was nobody's fool.

In the autumn of 1908 and the summer of 1909, Nordisk once again made an attempt at a Russian office, but the company was ready to give up if a suitable agent could not be found.[365] In August 1909, they finally succeeded in making contact with the newly formed production and distribution company Thiemann & Reinhardt, which secured Nordisk a place on the Russian market.[366] Denise J. Youngblood writes: "As distributors Thiemann & Reinhardt helped break the French hold on the infant Russian movie industry by introducing the distinctive artistic styles of American, Italian, and Danish film-makers to the Russian audience."[367]

Another important market was the American market. In the summer of 1907, the Danish newspaper *Dannebrog* interviewed Olsen about his sales:

> *Which country is your best customer?*
>
> – The North-American states! Every month I send films at the value of 45,000 kroner over there. The people on the boat to America are puzzled when we arrive with our small boxes that are insured for 30,000 kroner. I have made 48,000 kroner on THE POLAR BEAR HUNT alone; we shot that film last winter on the southern tip of Amager which had to serve as Spitzbergen, and most of the sales were in America.[368]

The biggest single market outside Europe was indeed the U.S. one, and it was dominated by European film companies. At times, 60 per cent of the films shown in the US were European.[369]

Nordisk's American distributor was the company Miles Brothers. An agreement was made when one of the Miles brothers personally came to Copenhagen in 1907, and in April of that year, Nordisk could sent 113 films to New York.[370] Nordisk's distribution records show that Miles Brothers did not

361 NFS:II,8.DFI, 209. Letter from Wilhelm Stæhr to Aleksandr Drankov (19 September 1908).

362 NFS:II,10.DFI, 198. Letter from Wilhelm Stæhr to Aleksandr Drankov (11 May 1909).

363 NFS:II,10.DFI, 200. Letter from Wilhelm Stæhr to Lawyer R.S. Lemoniks, St. Petersburg (11 May 1909).

364 NFS:II,22.DFI, 220. Letter from Wilhelm Stæhr to Lawyer R.S. Lemoniks, St. Petersburg (19 October 1912).

365 NFS:II,6.DFI, 486. Letter from Ole Olsen to Nordisk Films Co., London (13 December 1907); NFS:II,10.DFI, 663. Letter from Nordisk to M.A. Towbin, Warsaw (26 July 1909).

366 NFS:II,10.DFI, 713–714. Letter from Wilhelm Stæhr to P. Thiemann & F. Reinhardt (4 August 1909).

367 Denise J. Youngblood, *The Magic Mirror: Moviemaking in Russia* (Madison: University of Wisconsin Press, 1999), 22.

368 "Næsten levende Billede!", *Dannebrog* (8 July 1907).

369 See Thompson, *Exporting Entertainment*, 213.

370 NFS:II,3.DFI, 459. Letter from Nordisk to Miles Bros., New York (10 April 1907).

purchase a wide variety of titles but a great number of copies, between 25 and 50, of each title.

Unlike the European market, the American market was limited by various patent laws – it was the second closed market in Ivo Blom's analysis. Thomas Alva Edison, inventor and later producer, had tried to blow his competitors out of the water already in 1897 by claiming that he owned the patents for film cameras, projectors and raw stock. Some early American film companies paid a fee to Edison in order to be able to produce films. In 1904, a court order favoured Edison's claim, and more firms started paying royalties to Edison. The American Mutoscope & Biograph Company (AM&B) maintained however that their cameras had a different patented construction, and when Edison sued the company in 1907, the court ruled that AM&B's cameras were indeed different from Edison's. The upshot of this court case was that film producers and importers had to pay royalties to one of the two companies. Most American producers paid up to Edison, while AM&B made money on foreign producers and distributors, among them Nordisk.[371] The situation concerning royalties was untenable; Robert Anderson has argued that the battle between Edison and AM&B drained the industry of the energy it needed to establish a profitable business, and in 1908 the American film industry was at a crossroads between collapse and reformation.[372] In early 1908, Edison, AM&B and a string of other companies started negotiations which led to the establisment of the cartel known as the *Motion Picture Patents Company* (MPPC) in December.

The founding of the MPPC coincided with Nordisk's plans for an American branch. In the autumn of 1907, Nordisk had sent Christian Rabes to New York, partly to shoot two travelogues, one about sailing across the Atlantic and one about New York, and partly to develop business connections on the American market.[373] Olsen also asked Partsch to establish an office in the US, but Partsch declined the offer.[374] The position as manager of the New York office was offered to Clausen Kaas as well, if he could raise 40,000 kroner.[375] The branch had to materialize in a hurry. Miles Brothers had not paid their bills, and Olsen had films at the value of 30,000 kroner worth of films in New York. Olsen stated that he wanted "[...] this bill settled so the films can get on the market, or I shall suffer a substantial loss".[376] Norwegian Ingvald Carlo Aas was the final choice for manager of the American branch, and he subsequently anglicized his name into Oes. On 11 January 1908, Oes signed the contract

371 NFS:II,8.DFI, 120. Letter from Wilhelm Stæhr to Kodak Ltd., London (29 December 1908).

372 See Robert Anderson, "The Motion Picture Patents Company. A Reevaluation", in Tino Balio (ed.), *The American Film Industry* (Madison: The University of Wisconsin Press, 1985), 137.

373 NFS:II,1.DFI, 479. Letter from Ole Olsen to Christian Rabes, New York (15 September 1907).

374 NFS:II,6.DFI, 440. Letter from Ole Olsen to Nordisk Films Co., London (7 December 1907).

375 NFS:II,6.DFI, 514. Letter from Ole Olsen to Clausen Kaas (17 December 1907).

376 NFS:II,6.DFI, 486. Letter from Ole Olsen to Nordisk Films Co., London (13 December 1907).

with Nordisk to the effect that he was to establish and manage Nordisk's new office in New York, the subsidiary company Great Northern.[377]

Rumours at the time would have it that Edison and AM&B planned to form an alliance and that other big companies such as Pathé Frères would join. Olsen's 1908 correspondence shows how Nordisk, fearing that they would not be a part of this alliance, kept in close touch with the developments. Hearsay and fears abounded as to who would be part of the cartel and what would happen to those who were not. Olsen did what he could to strengthen Nordisk's chance of joining. In a letter to Eastman, he refers to a meeting he had with Charles Pathé:

> I just now returned from Berlin, and beg to tell you, that I had a conversation with Charles Pathe [sic]. Our discourse was pretty lengthy, but Pathe was rather supercilious, and no result could be obtained as to an agreement. He did not consider the matter quite impossible, but first some houses would have to be destroyed. Judging from his expression he seemed to mean Gaumont and Cines [sic].[378]

The letter to Eastman indicates that Pathé actually had the clout to get Nordisk into the MPPC, but also that Pathé intended to exclude its two European competitors. The meeting in Berlin must have resulted in some kind of rapprochement between Olsen and Charles Pathé; in a private letter to Christensen in Vienna, Stæhr writes that Pathé had offered to take over the Vienna branch in return for ten copies of each film released by Nordisk,[379] which would have been an excellent deal for the Danish company, but Olsen declined Pathé's offer since Nordisk was contracted to Christensen.[380] The letter may be read as a warning to Christensen to pull himself together and sell some films. Olsen remained in contact with Charles Pathé. In a letter to Eastman, Olsen writes: "I have to-day received a letter from Mr. Pathé from which I can only infer that his intentions are to ruin everybody else, in order to keep the market all to himself."[381] On that same day, Olsen warned Charles Pathé about a conspiracy of several big companies forming behind Pathé's back.[382]

Olsen pulled in all the favours he could, but as the year progressed, it became abundantly clear to him that his fears had come true; Nordisk was not to be part of the alliance.[383] In December 1908, the founding of the MPPC was made public. Anderson writes that the announcement was a formality and that the cartel had in fact been established behind closed doors already in May.[384]

377 NFS:IV,80.DFI. Agreement between Nordisk and Ingvald C. Oes (11 January1908).

378 NFS:II,8.DFI, 455. Letter from Ole Olsen to Kodak Ltd., London (19 October 1908).

379 NFS:II,8.DFI, 708. Letter from Wilhelm Stæhr to Hans Christensen, Vienna (11 November 1908).

380 NFS:II,8.DFI, 837. Letter from Ole Olsen to Pathé Frères, Usine de Vincennes, Paris (25 November 1908).

381 NFS:II,8.DFI, 820. Letter from Ole Olsen to Smith Esq., Kodak Ltd., London (23 November 1908).

382 NFS:II,8.DFI, 818. Letter from Ole Olsen to Charles Pathé, Paris (23 November 1908).

383 NFS:II,7.DFI, 534. Letter from Ole Olsen with addition from (W.S.) (Wilhelm Stæhr) to Great Northern Co., New York (19 June 1908).

384 See Anderson, "The Motion Picture Patents Company", 138.

The members of the MPPC comprised the American producers Edison, AM&B, Vitagraph, Essanay, Selig, Lubin and Kalem. Moreover, the distributor George Kleine and the two French companies Méliès and Pathé Frères were included. The cartel was created in the hope of monopolizing the American market with Edison's and AM&B's patents on cameras, film and projectors. Only members of the MPPC had the right to use Edison's patents which the nine cartel members had accepted as standard in the industry. Royalty fees now had to be paid to the MPPC by anyone who wished to produce, rent out, distribute or show films in the U.S. Furthermore, the MPPC signed a contract with Eastman to the effect that only MPPC members could obtain raw stock from Kodak.

As Anderson points out, the MPPC did not emerge from a vacuum but was inspired by other American monopolies based on patents. Bell Telephone, Standard Oil, International Harvester and General Electric are among Anderson's examples.[385] The Sherman Antitrust Act from 1890 banned monopolizing in the U.S., and in 1911, the American government took steps to break the trusts. Given this context, it is remarkable that no measures were taken against the MPPC. The MPPC did not lose its influence until 1915, and then only after the independent film producer William Fox had filed a lawsuit in 1913, after which proceedings dragged on for a long time. In the case of the MPPC, the authorities may have turned a blind eye, since the trust predominantly protected the American home market against European films, but at the same time also excluded some American companies.

Naturally, Nordisk was deeply disappointed when they were not allowed to join the MPPC. Stæhr called the exclusion of Nordisk dishonest and dirty and encouraged Oes to harass the trust with price reductions.[386] Nordisk was especially disappointed in AM&B, "under whose protection we have been working in America".[387] In desperation, Olsen suggested that Oes should sell Nordisk's films at half price to a distributor who was under the MPPC's protection. Oes was to sign a receipt for the full amount but actually only take half. As Olsen informed Oes: "[...] in business as well as in politics, we must interpret the law in subtle ways so as to circumvent but not break it. To my mind there exists no law that cannot be bent."[388]

Nordisk hoped that the film companies, distributors and cinemas who were outside the MPPC would collaborate and break the trust, even if this battle would be very uneven, "[...] like a tiny little mosquito against a big, big elephant".[389] Nordisk tried various constellations of collaboration with the European film companies Éclair, Itala and Messter, but nothing really came of

385 See ibid., 140–141.

386 NFS:II,9.DFI, 183. Letter from Wilhelm Stæhr to Ingvald C. Oes, New York (6 January 1909).

387 NFS:II,8.DFI, 120. Letter from Wilhelm Stæhr to Kodak Ltd., London (29 December 1908).

388 NFS:II,7.DFI, 839. Letter from Ole Olsen to Ingvald C. Oes, New York (29 July 1908).

389 NFS:II,9.DFI, 337. Letter from Wilhelm Stæhr to Ingvald C. Oes, New York (6 January 1909).

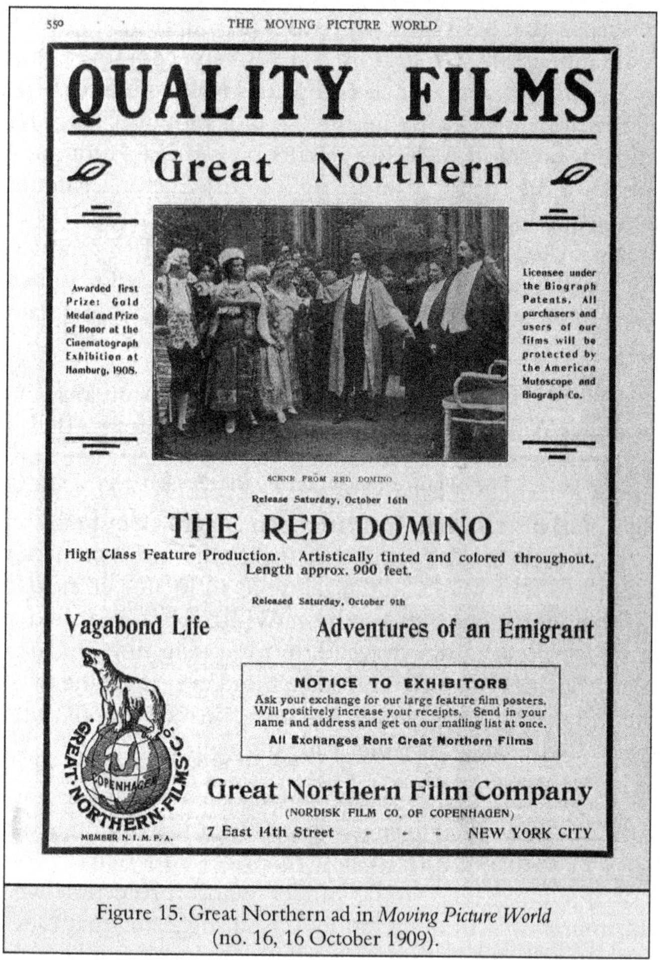

Figure 15. Great Northern ad in *Moving Picture World* (no. 16, 16 October 1909).

it. Nordisk persisted in the hope of being admitted into the MPPC as late as 1913.[390]

However, alternative ways of entering the American market presented themselves. Much to Oes' surprise, the independent Chicago Film Exchange purchased films from Nordisk in Europe and distributed them in the US; Stæhr had to caution the Berlin and London offices to stop this trade.[391]

In January 1909, without telling Nordisk, Oes contributed in establishing *The Independent Film Protective Association*, later changed into *National Independent Moving Picture Alliance*, of which Oes was a member of the executive committee. One of the goals of this independent alliance was to convince cinema owners

390 NFS:II,25.DFI, 333. Letter from Harald Frost to Ingvald C. Oes, New York (19 April 1913).

391 NFS:II,9.DFI, 430. Letter from Wilhelm Stæhr to Nordische Films Co., Berlin. NFS:II,9.DFI, 431. Letter from Wilhelm Stæhr to Nordisk Films Co., London (16 February 1909).

not to make deals with the MPPC.[392] This alliance was the first of various associations of film producers, distributors and cinema owners generally known as *"the independents"*, because they were outside the MPPC.[393] From 1909 onward, a fierce conflict raged in the American film industry between the MPPC and the independents, and the MPPC never succeeded in getting full control over the American market. They did however achieve the introduction of a standard technology. After 1909, the 35mm filmstrip with Edison's perforations and an aspect ratio of 1.33:1 carried the day. The MPPC also reformed and structured the American film industry. One day each week was designated for the release of new films. The price of new films went up, and was reduced when a film had been shown for a given length of time. One-reel films were made standard, and all films cost the same whatever their nature or contents, "since producers viewed films as standard products, like sausages".[394]

The MPPC was a hard blow to the European film industry. In 1907, the British companies had sold more films in the US than at home,[395] and Nordisk's American sales that year made up 17 per cent of the total.[396] While the plans of establishing the MPPC were in progress in 1908, the European film industry tried to form an alliance of its own. On 9 March 1908, the leading European producers met in Paris. Health problems prevented Olsen from participating, but he sent Raleigh & Robert to represent Nordisk.[397] According to film historian Jon Burrows, nothing came of the meeting save intentions of future collaboration.[398] Only when the MPPC was a fact did 31 of the leading European companies convene at a congress in Paris from 2 through 4 February 1909, at the behest of Star Film director Georges Méliès. *Congrès International des Éditeurs de Films* (IEF) was the official title of the congress. *Congrès des dupes* – Congress of Fools – is what Georges Sadoul dubbed it.[399] The participants included the biggest and most influential companies in the European film world:

Great Britain: R.W. Paul, Hepworth, British Gaumont, Cricks & Martin, Urban, Clarendon, Warwick, Walturdaw, Wrench, Williamson.

France: Pathé Frères, Star Film, Raleigh & Robert, Gaumont, Éclair, Le Lion, Lux, Radios, Éclipse.

Italy: Cines, Ambrosio, SAFFI-Comerio, Itala, Aquila.

Germany: Messter, Duskes, Deutsche Bioscope, Internationale Kinematographen- und Licht-Effekt-Gesellschaft mbH.

392 See Mottram, "The Great Northern Film Company", 76.

393 See Thompson and Bordwell, *Film History*, 33–35.

394 See Thompson and Bordwell, *Film History*, 35.

395 See Burrows, "When Britain Tried to Join Europe", 7.

396 See note for Table 1.

397 NFS:II,6.DFI, 976. Letter from Ole Olsen to the Kinematograph Manufacturer's Association of Great Britain, High Holborn (10 March 1908).

398 See Burrows, "When Britain Tried to Join Europe", 7.

399 See Sadoul, *Histoire générale du cinéma II*, 509.

Denmark: Nordisk Film.
USA: Vitagraph.[400]

Apart from a couple of photos of the participants, no official records seem to survive from this congress. We know that a set of rules was agreed upon and that there was a consensus that the participants must adhere to these regulations in the future. Through sources such as trade journals and memoirs, Burrows has pieced together the upshot of the rules which were intended to apply to the leading film companies in Europe. The overriding problem was the industry's over-production of films which led to a decline in prices and limited sales.[401] The German overproduction alone was estimated at 10,000 metres a week,[402] and in Britain, sales had dropped to an average of only three sold copies of each title.[403] There was also a market of older, unsellable films; titles that were two to three years old had started to re-circulate. The producers made no profit on these films, quite the contrary: the old titles impeded the sales of the new films. Instead of just selling films, the Congress agreed to let the producers start renting them out and reclaiming them after four months. The distributors could only get films from producers who had participated in the congress, and Nordisk agreed to a fixed price per metre.[404]

The date of the congress had been moved to accommodate Eastman. Eastman's presence is conspicuous, for which interests did he represent? Well, Eastman had struck a deal with the MPPC for exclusive rights to supply raw stock to the American market, and he was interested in making a similar deal with the European producers. Burrows maintains, however, that Eastman's authorized diary indicates that he was there to protect the interests of the MPPC. Members of the MPPC were in doubt as to whether Edison's patents applied to films imported from Europe as well, and it would be easier to make a deal with a European association than to observe the patent trust in America for each individual company.[405] Eastman agreed to give the members of the congress the European rights to his raw stock supplies from him in return for his refusal to supply producers who had not participated in the congress. It shortly turned out that such trade restrictions were a violation of French laws. The deal with Eastman was the first of the decisions made at the congress to fall apart. The next agreement was the fixed price on the films; this met with resistance among the distributors, and a new congress in April was scheduled.

400 See Burrows, "When Britain Tried to Join Europe", 8.

401 See Abel (ed.), *Encyclopedia of Early Cinema*, 127.

402 See Peter Lähn, "Paul Davidson, the Frankfurt Film Scene, and AFGRUNDEN in Germany", in Thomas Elsaesser (ed.), *A Second Life. German Cinema's First Decade* (Amsterdam: Amsterdam University Press, 1996), 83.

403 See Burrows, "When Britain Tried to Join Europe", 7.

404 NFS:II,10.DFI, 375. Letter from Wilhelm Stæhr to Marro y Tarro, Barcelona (8 June 1909).

405 See Carl W. Ackermann., *George Eastman* (London: Cable and Company Ltd., 1930), 220–221; Burrows, "When Britain Tried to Join Europe", 9.

At the second congress, Pathé Frères chose to withdraw from the European association, and without the biggest film producer in the world, the idea of a European counterpart to the MPPC collapsed. Charles Pathé had reservations already when the European alliance was being planned, and he had remained sceptical about joining.[406] After leaving the association, Pathé dumped his prices below what was agreed at the congress, which Nordisk construed as an attempt from Pathé to press the prices so far down that the other companies were ruined. This may indeed have been Pathé's intention.[407] In 1909, Nordisk tried their luck with several alternative collaborators to ensure their international position. In March, Olsen negotiated with the German film company Messter about making a joint venture backed by French capital.[408] The plan floundered, but Olsen made the offer that Nordisk's New York subsidiary could try to sell Messter's films in the U.S.[409] Another attempt was made when Olsen suggested to Gaumont that the two companies could establish a common rental bureau in various countries,[410] but this plan did not come off the ground, either.

A fundamental problem in the European film industry had still not been solved – the enormous overproduction of films. It was in the solution to this problem that Nordisk would come to play a decisive role.

406 NFS:II,8.DFI, 751. Letter from Wilhelm Stæhr to Director Smith, Esq. of Kodak Ltd., London (17 November 1908).

407 NFS:II,11.DFI, 702. Letter from Wilhelm Stæhr to the Directors of Kodak Ltd., London (4 December 1909)

408 NFS:II,10.DFI, 37. Letter from Ole Olsen to Oskar Messter, Berlin (19 April 1909); NFS:II,10.DFI, 56. Letter from Ole Olsen to Oskar Messter, Berlin (21 April 1909); NFS:II,10.DFI, 138. Letter from Ole Olsen to Oskar Messter, Berlin (1 May 1909).

409 NFS:II,10.DFI, 832. Letter from Ole Olsen to Oskar Messter, Berlin (23 August 1909); NFS:II,10.DFI, 863. Letter from Ole Olsen to Oskar Messter, Berlin (27 August 1909).

410 NFS:II,10.DFI, 737. Letter from Ole Olsen to Léon Gaumont, Paris (9 August 1909).

1910–1914

The Rise of the Polar Bear

Nordisk went through its first extensive structural changes in 1910. It became the first film company to base major parts of its production on multiple-reel films. Industry-wide, the transition to longer films led to a sweeping revolution with regard to the production, distribution and exhibition of films in the international industry.

The changes were manifest in the entire organizational structure of Nordisk. In 1911, Nordisk was converted into a limited company, and where Olsen formerly reigned supreme, he now had to answer to a board of directors and had managers working for him.

In order to plan its film production, Nordisk established a script department which was to supply the company directors with screenplays following a fixed set of rules that took into consideration the content prferences and the censorship regulations of the individual markets. In the Valby studios, Nordisk started working with several simultaneous production crews, and a sophisticated modus operandi was developed that anticipated the one which would later prove successful in Hollywood. It was not without reason that the Valby studios were dubbed "the film factory" after Nordisk's reorganization.[411]

Longer films meant a change in exhibition practice in cinemas; Germany and Great Britain introduced a new so-called monopoly or exclusive distribution system of through which a distributor could purchase the exclusive rights to a film in a particular area for a given period of time. Together with the advent of longer films, this system created new conditions for competition, and in order to enhance the competitive capacity of each film, the companies started to promote their own film stars and to include their names in the marketing of the films. Another step taken to make the films attractive and legitimate as entertainment for the middle classes was the introduction of the so-called *Autorenfilms*, i.e. a film based on a literary work by a famous author.

The film, DEN HVIDE SLAVEHANDEL (THE WHITE SLAVE TRADE, August Blom, 1910), became an important reason for Nordisk's thorough reorganization.

Nordisk was not the only film company in Denmark. Among the other Danish companies was the Aarhus-based Fotorama that would come to play a decisive role in the development of Nordisk on several occasions. In 1906, photographer

411 E.g. Emma Gad, "Film – Eventyret", *Politiken* (6 March 1913). Sandfeld points out that the term "film factory" was common at the time. See Sandfeld, *Den stumme scene*, 10.

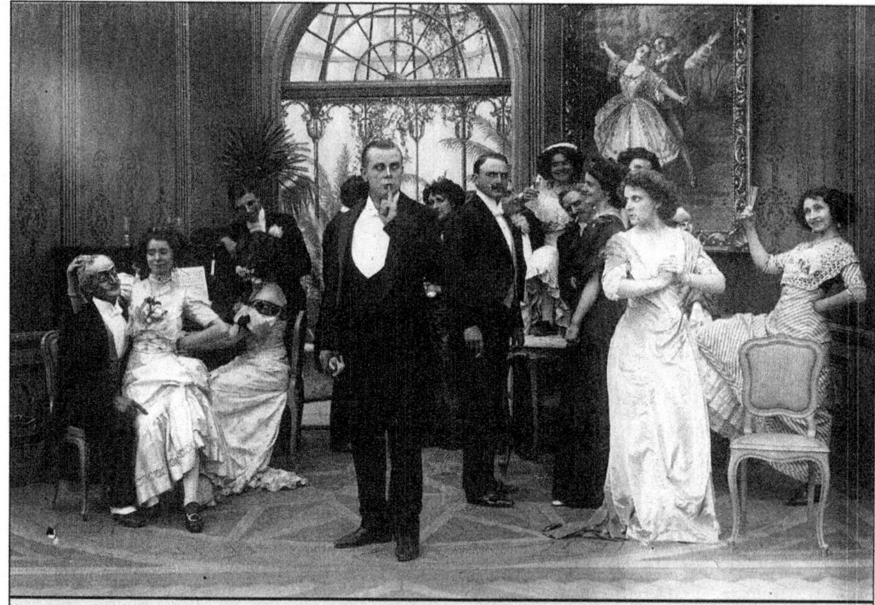

Figure 16. Anna (Ellen Diedrich) is about to be saved from the brothel by her childhood friend George (Lauritz Olsen) in DEN HVIDE SLAVEHANDEL. Courtesy of DFI/Stills & Posters Archive.

Thomas Sørensen Hermansen had obtained a license for the cinemas Fotorama and Biografteatret in Aarhus, and in 1908, with a capital of 125,000 kroner, he formed the limited company A/S Th. S. Hermansen for the purpose of renting out and selling films, and of running cinemas wherever possible. Frede Skaarup, a former grocer in Ringkøbing, was employed as a manager, and the following year Eduard Schnedler-Sørensen, who would become Skaarup's most trusted employee, was hired to help out.

In 1909, A/S Th.S. Hermansen started iss own film production. The company's first film, DEN LILLE HORNBLÆSER (The Little Hornblower, Fotorama, 1909), directed by Schnedler-Sørensen, was a success. In May 1910, when the company decided to expand into film manufacturing as well, it changed its name to Aktieselskabet Fotorama (Limited Company Fotorama). With Skaarup as manager, the business grew quickly in an occasionally aggressive way. Instead of charging a fixed rental fee, Skaarup demanded 20 to 25 per cent of the cinema owners' profits from the popular DEN LILLE HORNBLÆSER. Many cinema owners felt threatened by Skaarup, and as a reaction, Biograf Teater Foreningen for Provinsen (The Cinema Theatre Association of the Provinces) was founded in March 1910. But many cinema owners did not dare join the association for fear of not getting access to other films from A/S Th.S. Hermansen. In a very short time the company had gained control of large parts of the Danish cinema market.[412]

412 See Tybjerg, "Teltholdernes verdensteater", 27.

The connection between Nordisk and Hermansen goes back to the very beginnings of Nordisk. Hermansen purchased films from Nordisk, and the two companies appear to have been on friendly terms initially. Since Hermansen was such a good customer, Olsen gave him exclusive rights to Nordisk's films in Aarhus in 1907. Olsen and Hermansen may also have had a common interest, for as Olsen writes: "Mr. le Tort has wanted films from us, but we deemed it prudent to have only one buyer in that location."[413] Hermansen obtained the rights to Nordisk's films while Olsen kept his old partner le Tort at bay. Nordisk and Hermansen also stood together in 1909 when the Danish film industry succeeded in keeping Pathé out of the Danish market.[414]

Fotorama opened a branch in Copenhagen in early 1910 for buying and selling films, and also opened the cinema *Løvebiografen* (The Lion Cinema) on the ground floor of their Copenhagen office. On 11 April 1910, Fotorama's film DEN HVIDE SLAVEHANDEL (THE WHITE SLAVE TRADE, Alfred Cohn, Fotorama, 1910) premiered in Løvebiografen and was an instant success. The film tells the story of the young girl Anna (Ellen Diedrich) who accepts a position as a lady's companion in London far away from home, but soon discovers, to her great horror, that the position is in a brothel. Luckily her childhood friend George (Lauritz Olsen) discovers the deception, travels to London and manages with the aid of Scotland Yard to catch the villains and rescue Anna.

Audiences flocked to the film, and it was shown about 400 times in Løvebiografen.[415] What was extraordinary about the film was its length of 706 metres, approximately 35 minutes. Olsen's reaction was to send his director August Blom to the cinema to note down every scene from Fotorama's film.[416] Less than four months later, on 2 August, Nordisk released a nearly identical version of DEN HVIDE SLAVEHANDEL with the exact same title, 603 metres long. Only Nordisk's version is extant in its entire length. Engberg has compared the surviving fragments of the Fotorama version with the Nordisk version and convincingly argues that not only the plot but also camera angles and the composition of images are remarkably alike in the two versions.[417] Nordisk did not in any way attempt to conceal its plagiarism. The company wrote to a Swedish cinema owner:

> By request, we open with DEN HVIDE SLAVEHANDEL on August the first, executed in the exact same way as the one that ran here at the Løvebiografen but performed by better artists and with Miss Diedrich in the lead. It is a role she performs to perfection.[418]

413 NFS:II,6.DFI, 427. Letter from Wilhelm Stæhr to Hermansen, Aarhus (5 December 1907).

414 NFS:II,11.DFI, 203. Letter from Wilhelm Stæhr to A/S Th.S. Hermansen, Aarhus (8 October 1909); NFS:II,11.DFI, 807–808. Letter from Wilhelm Stæhr to A/S Th.S. Hermansen, Aarhus (16 December 1909).

415 "Hvor man morer sig", *Politiken* (10 May 1910), quoted from Engberg, *Dansk stumfilm*, 220–222.

416 Interview with Axel Graatkjær. DFI.

417 For a detailed comparison, see Engberg, "Plagiarism", 72–79.

418 NFS:II,13.DFI, 305. Letter from Nordisk to Frantz Lundberg, Malmoe (27 July 1910).

The film was even described to a Norwegian business acquaintance as "a picture whose content is exactly the same as the film of Scandinavian fame from Hermansen in Aarhus".[419] Just three days after the premiere of the Nordisk version, on 5 August, Fotorama reacted by placing adverts in the Copenhagen newspapers with the headline: "Warning to the Public."[420] Nordisk's version was called a bad copy which should not be compared with the Fotorama original, and the advert stated that "[...] this can only take place because the law as yet provides no protection against such things".

The circumstances surrounding DEN HVIDE SLAVEHANDEL scandal are some of the best-known incidents in early Danish film history, and Engberg's interpretation is the generally accepted one.[421] Engberg writes that Fotorama threatened to take Nordisk to court, and, to avoid any "unpleasantness", Olsen entered into an agreement with Fotorama under which Fotorama was granted, among other things, the rights to distribute films from Nordisk in Denmark, Norway, and later Sweden. Skaarup became a manager at Nordisk, and Schnedler-Sørensen was employed as a film director in Valby.[422] According to Engberg, the agreement was "fatal" to Nordisk in the long run.[423] In early 1911, when the agreement was finally signed, only a small percentage of Nordisk's sales went to the Scandinavian countries. But when World War I broke out, the borders closed and the export of film to nearly everywhere else than Scandinavia stopped, it was Fotorama that made the money on the films from Nordisk.[424] Nordisk and Fotorama did enter a distribution agreement on 3 December 1910,[425] which was finally confirmed on 6 February 1911,[426] and it is true that the text of this agreement reveals that Fotorama took over Nordisk's agencies in Denmark and Norway. Moreover, Nordisk made a commitment to produce twelve "art films", then the term for long feature films, and these were to premiere in Panoptikonteatret, a Copenhagen cinema in which Fotorama had a decisive financial interest.

All the same, Engberg's account needs some qualification; she confuses a series of events and, moreover, she interprets the sources available a bit liberally. The deal was hardly fatal for Nordisk. Denmark, Norway and later Sweden were small markets; the average sales to Denmark 1912–1914 made up only 2.6 per

419 NFS:II,13.DFI, 345. Letter from Wilhelm Stæhr to Norsk Films Co., Kristiania (1 August 1910).

420 *Politiken* (5 August 1910), quoted from Jan Nielsen, *A/S Filmfabriken Danmark: SRH/Filmfabriken Danmarks historie og produktion* (Copenhagen: Multivers, 2003), 66.

421 See for example Dinnesen and Kau, *Filmen i Danmark*, 29–20; Tybjerg, *An Art of Silence and Light*, 73–74; Christensen, "Isbjørnens fald", 235; Tybjerg, "Spekulanter og Himmelstormere", 31; Ulff-Møller "Edouard Partsch", 418.

422 See Engberg, *Dansk stumfilm*, 225.

423 See Engberg, "Plagiarism", 79.

424 See Engberg, *Dansk stumfilm*, 229.

425 NFS:II,14.DFI, 376–378. Letter from Wilhelm Stæhr to A/S Fotorama (3 December 1910).

426 NFS:I,1:12.DFI. Backside of page 4. Contract between Nordisk and A/S Fotorama (31 December 1910); NFS:I,1:8.DFI. Unpagn. Draft agreement between Aktieselskabet Nordisk Films Kompagni v/Ole Olsen and A/S Fotorama, undated.

cent of Nordisk's total sales, which was far from enough to maintain Nordisk's production.[427] Furthermore, Fotorama and Nordisk established the rental company Fotoramas Filmsbureau A/S in 1915, by which Nordisk acquired half the profits as well as the takings from other films that Fotorama sold or rented in Denmark, Norway and Sweden.[428] Nordisk got its share of the profits from its own films in Scandinavia during the war and in the years after it ended. It was in Nordisk's own best interest to hand over the distribution rights in Denmark, Norway and Sweden to Fotorama. Nordisk had actually tried to hand over the agencies for Sweden[429] and Norway[430] already in late 1910. The deal with Fotorama is very similar to the distribution deals Nordisk had closed for other territories, with an agent who bought a fixed number of films and thus guaranteed Nordisk a steady sale of films. Fotorama was the obvious choice for the Scandinavian countries. In March 1911, Martin Peter Drescher, chairman of Fotorama's board, reported at the company's general assembly that Fotorama now had 100 customers as compared to 60 the previous year.[431] The Aarhus-based company controlled a solid share of the Danish and Scandinavian market to which Nordisk now had access. From Fotorama's perspective, the deal was favourable, because, as Tybjerg writes: "[...] with the rights to the most attractive Danish films, [Fotorama] could impose their rental system by which the cinema owners had to pay a fixed share of the profit instead of a fixed price". [432]

The Aarhus company had given Nordisk access to a large part of the Danish and Scandinavian market. At the same time, Nordisk could save expenses on travelling salesmen in Scandinavia and on managing these markets. The deal secured Fotorama a steady supply of attractive and profitable films for the Danish market as well as for Norway which, at the time, had no film production of its own. Moreover, as Engberg writes, neither Skaarup nor Schnedler-Sørensen were attached to Nordisk when the two companies entered the agreement made in 1911; but Skaarup and Schnedler-Sørensen became attached when Nordisk was made into a limited company less than six months later.

Whether Fotorama would have been able to create any "unpleasantness" for Nordisk through a court trial, or even the threat of one is questionable. Stories about innocent girls abducted to work in brothels by nefarious characters were all the rage. As Tybjerg points out, such stories are to be found in countless

427 See note for Table 1.

428 In Sweden Fotorama's business started in January 1912. NFS:II,18.DFI, 329. Letter from Harald Frost to G.A. Hellström, Norrköping (15 January 1912).

429 NFS:II,13.DFI, 475. Letter from Wilhelm Stæhr to Numa Petersson, Stockholm (10 August 1910).

430 NFS:II,14.DFI, 324. Letter from Wilhelm Stæhr to Barrister Gundersen, Christiania (28 November 1910).

431 Danish National Business Archives: Generalforsamlingsprotokol f. Hotel Royal 1908–1923. Protocol of General Meeting of Hotel Royal 1908–1923 (2 March 1911).

432 Tybjerg, "Spekulanter og Himmelstormere", 31.

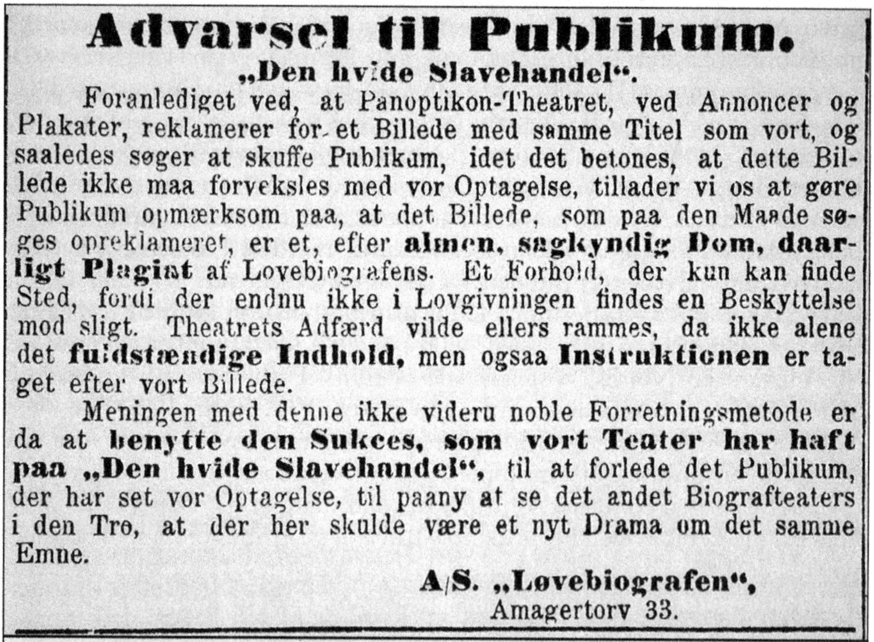

Advarsel til Publikum.

„Den hvide Slavehandel".

Foranlediget ved, at Panoptikon-Theatret, ved Annoncer og Plakater, reklamerer for et Billede med samme Titel som vort, og saaledes søger at skuffe Publikum, idet det betones, at dette Billede ikke maa forveksles med vor Optagelse, tillader vi os at gøre Publikum opmærksom paa, at det Billede, som paa den Maade søges opreklameret, er et, efter **almen, sagkyndig Dom, daarligt Plagiat** af Løvebiografens. Et Forhold, der kun kan finde Sted, fordi der endnu ikke i Lovgivningen findes en Beskyttelse mod sligt. Theatrets Adfærd vilde ellers rammes, da ikke alene det **fuldstændige Indhold,** men ogsaa **Instruktionen** er taget efter vort Billede.

Meningen med denne ikke videre noble Forretningsmetode er da at **benytte den Sukces, som vort Teater har haft paa „Den hvide Slavehandel",** til at forlede det Publikum, der har set vor Optagelse, til paany at se det andet Biografteaters i den Tro, at der her skulde være et nyt Drama om det samme Emne.

A/S. „Løvebiografen",
Amagertorv 33.

Figure 17. Fotorama's warning to the public. Printed in the newspaper *Politiken* (5 August 1910).

variations in the novels, dramas and films of the time.[433] In 1907, Nordisk had released DEN HVIDE SLAVINDE (THE WHITE SLAVE, Viggo Larsen, 1907), with a plot very similar to DEN HVIDE SLAVEHANDEL's. In the event of a lawsuit, Nordisk could have pleaded that Fotorama had actually plagiarized their film, and in fact, Fotorama's "warning advert" directly states that there were no copyright laws in Denmark, at least not for films. Had there been a copyright law in Denmark at the time, it would have been reckless of Nordisk to proclaim in its correspondence that its version of DEN HVIDE SLAVEHANDEL was identical with Fotorama's. Nordisk was well aware that intellectual rights were a potential future problem that had to be dealt with. As an example, Stæhr wrote to the Berlin office in the beginning of 1910 in order to be updated on the copyright problems.[434] Germany had signed the Berne Convention on 22 May 1910,[435] but Denmark did not agree to the revised convention until 1 July 1912.[436] There is no indications of legal action or even a threat of a lawsuit in Nordisk's correspondence or in the regional archives.[437] On the other hand, as Danish Film historian Jan Nielsen makes clear, the letters in the Nordisk

433 See Tybjerg, *An Art of Silence and Light*, 59–73.

434 NFS:II,12.DFI, 304–305. Letter from Wilhelm Stæhr to Nordische Films Co., Berlin (18 February 1910).

435 See Müller, *Frühe deutsche Kinematographie*, 126.

436 See Schröder, *Ideale Kommunikation*, 429.

437 The following collections were consulted in this search: Rigsarkivet; Landsarkivet for Sjælland: Landover, - samt Hof og Stadsretten: Fogedkontoret-kendelsesprotokoller 1910–1912; Navneregister 1892–1917; Forretningsregistre 1910–1912. (The Danish National Archives; High Court; the Bailiff's decree protocols 1910–1912; trade registers 1910–1912.)

Film Special Collection indicate that negotiations between Nordisk and Fotorama were carried out at meetings and over the telephone.[438]

Although there were no copyright laws protecting films, and apparently no official records of a court trial involving the two companies, the law actually did open one opportunity for Fotorama to cause trouble for Nordisk. *Lov om Forfatterret og Kunstnerret* (The Law on Copyright and Artistic Rights) from 1904 included a clause which protected authors from having their texts transferred to other media without the author's permission. It was actually used by the Danish author Johan Prægel against Fotorama in late 1910. Fotorama had to pay Prægel 500 kroner for adapting his stage play *Kapergasten* (The Privateer) into a film of the same title, not because of the adaptation from stage play to film, but because the stage play and the text of the film's souvenir cinema programme were too similar.[439]

In the case of DEN HVIDE SLAVEHANDEL, Nordisk copied the content of the Fotorama film, using the same settings and names, and in this context Louis Schmidt, who wrote the script for Fotorama's DEN HVIDE SLAVEHANDEL, could have taken Nordisk to court for transferring his script to the film's souvenir cinema programme. But in his memoirs Louis Schmidt reports: "In Aarhus, they tried to bring an injunction against the copy, but of no avail – living pictures were not yet copyrighted then."[440] One must assume that if Fotorama had been able to apply the 1904 law against Nordisk, Schmidt would surely have remembered using every means against such a spectacular case of plagiarism. It is also worth noting that the actual case involving Johan Prægel and Fotorama was not settled until 1912, which may indicate an uncertainty on the part of the courts about how to interpret the new copyright laws.[441]

While the plagiarism row concerning DEN HVIDE SLAVEHANDEL was still pending, Nordisk was involved in a similar case in Germany. The Danish author Karin Michaëlis' novel *Den farlige Alder* (The Dangerous Age) from 1910 had attracted a great deal of attention because it dealt with the sexuality of older women, a social taboo topic. Apparently, 60,000 copies of the book were sold in five weeks in Germany alone.[442] German film producer Oskar Messter chose to base his first long feature film, DAS GEFÄHRLICHE ALTER (The Dangerous Age, Adolf Gärtner, Messter Projection GmbH, GE 1911), on Michaëlis' novel. In his memoirs, Messter claims that neither he nor the film's scriptwriter knew the contents of the novel but just made something up.[443] Messter's film was scheduled for release in April 1911. At the same time, Nordisk had made

438 See Nielsen, *A/S Filmfabriken Danmark*, 66.

439 See Schröder, *Ideale Kommunikation*, 427.

440 Gandrup, Richardt, *Redaktør Louis Schmidt – en levnedsbeskrivelse* (Copenhagen: C.E.C. Gad, 1957), 38.

441 See Schröder, *Ideale Kommunikation*, 427.

442 See Annemone Ligensa, "'A Cinematograph of Feminine Thought': *The Dangerous Age*, Cinema and Modern Women", in Klaus Kreimeier and Annemone Ligensa (ed.), *Film 1900. Technology, Perception, Culture* (New Barnet: John Libbey, 2009), 225.

443 See Oskar Messter, *Mein Weg mit dem Film* (Berlin: Max Hesses Verlag, 1936), 102.

its own version of DEN FARLIGE ALDER (THE PRICE OF BEAUTY, 1911), directed by August Blom. Nordisk's version was to be sold unseen to the distributors, and was scheduled to premiere in Germany on 15 April.[444] Stæhr gave the following instructions for how the film should be presented to German cinema owners:

> [Nordisk] has spared no expense in producing the film DEN FARLIGE ALDER in a far better version [than Messter], yet with the same plot [...]. For a substantial fee, we have secured the consent of the author. We can assure you that this film, like all the films we have made recently, is performed by the best actors in Copenhagen, and the camera work is superb.[445]

The wording of this letter is reminiscent of Nordisk's presentation of their version of DEN HVIDE SLAVEHANDEL to cinema owners. Even though Nordisk had secured the rights to the novel, Messter reacted, and Nordisk asked its Berlin office to reply:

> We wrote in the German letter that you must deny any charges of copying Messter's film. We bought the rights to use the title and adapt its content for the cinema from Mrs Michaëlis. That two minds have thought alike is nobody's fault, and no one is to blame if our screenwriter has come up with scenes that are also in Messter's film. We deny the charges of simply having copied his film.[446]

The following day, Nordisk wrote to the company's attorney in Berlin, Arndt, and presented the case to him.[447] Arndt's reply is not extant, but three days later, Nordisk asked its bank, Den Danske Landmandsbank, to transfer 54,000 kroner to Messter in Berlin.[448] The same day, Nordisk could report to its Berlin branch that Messter had succeeded in postponing the release date of Nordisk's version of DEN FARLIGE ALDER: "We have paid Karin Michaëlis for the rights only to have to fight Monopolfilm; we have come so close to Messter's film that he now claims to have the rights."[449] Stæhr's explanation confirms Corinna Müller's thesis: "Nordisk lost the case on the charges that they had not adapted the novel but copied Messter's film."[450] This is likely to be the case; Nordisk had paid little or no attention to the literary material, but had once again sent August Blom to the movies to take notes of every single scene in Messter's film, and it was of no consequence that they had secured the rights to the novel. Nordisk paid its penalty, and in May, was able to release the delayed version of DEN FARLIGE ALDER in Germany.[451] A comparison of the two films confirms

444 NFS:II,15.DFI, 465. Letter from Wilhelm Stæhr to Nordische Films Co., Berlin (23 March 1911).

445 NFS:II,15.DFI, 513. Letter from Wilhelm Stæhr to C. Nielsen, Berlin (27 March 1911).

446 NFS:II,15.DFI, 658. Letter from Wilhelm Stæhr to C. Nielsen, Berlin (11 April 1911).

447 NFS:II,15.DFI, 664–665. Letter from Ole Olsen to Justizrat Arndt, Berlin (12 April 1911).

448 NFS:II,15.DFI, 666. Letter from Olga Christensen to Den Danske Landmandsbank (15 April 1911).

449 NFS:II,15.DFI, 677. Letter from Wilhelm Stæhr to Nordisk Films Co., Berlin (15 April 1911).

450 Müller, *Frühe deutsche Kinematographie*, 126.

451 Herbert Birett, *Das Filmangebot in Deutschland*, 226–227 reports the release date of neither Messter's nor Nordisk's version of the film. In a letter to the London branch, Stæhr writes that the original release date was 15 April 1911, but this date was postponed three to five weeks due to the Messter case. NFS: II,15.DFI, 744. Letter from Wilhelm Stæhr to Nordisk Films Co., London (21 April 1911).

that apart from somewhat different endings, Nordisk's version is barefaced plagiarism.[452]

Copyright violation continued to be a problematic issue to Nordisk, but not always as the offending party. In 1912, Nordisk became involved in a a case concerning the film DEN SORTE KANSLER (THE BLACK CHANCELLOR, August Blom, 1912). Shortly before its release in July, Nordisk discovered that the script which the company had bought from actor Christian Schröder was based on British author William Magnay's novel *The Red Chancellor* (1901). The Danish company Kinografen had also produced a film based on Magnay's novel, KANSLEREN KALDET "DEN SORTE PANTER" (The Chancellor known as "The Black Panther", director unknown, A/S Kinografen, 1912), but Nordisk exploited its international network, and had its London office secure the rights for Magnay's novel, then informed Kinografen that if they released their version, Nordisk would sue.[453]

On 8 May 1911, Nordisk went from being Olsen's private property to becoming a limited company. In his memoirs, actor Olaf Fønss writes that Fotorama, with Skaarup as its head, had made plans for a large, new, Copenhagen-based film company, and because of this, "[...] Ole Olsen became anxious and suggested a collaboration that resulted in the formation of the company 'Nordisk Film Co.' in 1911".[454] Arnold Hending likewise presents Fotorama as a threat to Nordisk that made "[...] Ole Olsen so nervous that he hastened to sign up their leading men with Nordisk".[455] Olsen's own version of the events is actually close to Fønss' and Hending's. In his autobiography, Olsen describes how more and more people became aware of the lucrative potential of the film industry: "Since the new men did not want too much of a hassle, they preferred to deviously lure my staff – whom I had trained in the business for years – away from me."[456] Olsen does not reveal who "the new men" were, but they can only have been people from Fotorama, since Olsen then recounts how he had to cut a deal with them, and so Nordisk was turned into a limited company. Olsen finishes his recollection with the following: "But I have never forgotten, and never will, their original plan to knock me to the ground if they could."[457]

452 I am grateful to Annemone Ligensa for having provided me with copies of both the Nordisk and the Messter version of DEN FARLIGE ALDER.

453 See Engberg, *Dansk stumfilm*, 454; Schröder, *Ideale Kommunikation*, 431; NFS:II,20.DFI, 819–821. Letter from Harald Frost to A.S. Paulsen, London (29 June 1912); NFS:II,20.DFI, 929. Letter from Harald Frost to A/S Kinografen, Frederiksberggade (10 July 1912). Nordisk's DØDSSPRING FRA CIRKUSKUPLEN TIL HEST (THE GREAT CIRCUS CATASTROPHE) premiered 26 August 1912. Almost simultaneously, Svenska Bio released DÖDSRITTEN UNDER CIRKUSPOLEN (THE LAST PERFORMANCE) which premiered 12 August. Nordisk's film is extant, whereas only fragments of Svenska Bio's film are preserved at George Eastman House in Rochester. A closer scrutiny of the films and an investigation of the conditions of their origin will reveal whether this, too, was a case of plagiarism.

454 Olaf Fønss, *Films-erindringer gennem 20 Aar* (Copenhagen: Nutidens Forlag, 1930), 66.

455 Hending, *Da isbjørnen var lille*, 82.

456 Olsen, *Filmens Eventyr og mit eget*, 91.

457 Ibid., 92.

However, it was actually Olsen who on 22 April 1911 presented the idea of establishing a limited company to a few select gentlemen. Except for the Nordisk managers Stæhr and Olsen, the gentlemen attending the meeting all came from, or were connected to, the management and/or the board of Fotorama: chairman of Fotorama's board, Martin Peter Drescher; Fotorama board members barrister Otto Gulmann, merchant Henrik Gielstrup and consul Eduard Bergmann; Alfred William Mammen, Drescher's partner in the shipping company Mammen & Drescher; and finally, there were Skaarup and Schnedler-Sørensen. At the meeting, Olsen outlined his plans for establishing a limited company. The board was to consist of four members: Olsen, Mammen and Johan Ramm (who was not present at the meeting, but was a shareholder in Fotorama), "[...] together with one of A/S Fotorama's board members. The choice of the latter is to be made by the shareholders of Nordisk Filmskompagni with the exception of O. Olsen."[458] This clause, however, never made it into the final instrument of foundation of the company.[459] The fact that the representatives from Fotorama were assured influence in the company, and the fact that Olsen had no say, in the first draft at least, in the fourth member of the board indicates that Olsen's position among the Fotorama crowd was somewhat precarious.

However, two days later, on 24 April, Drescher reported to the board of Fotorama that, Olsen had tried to sign up Skaarup to Nordisk with a generous offer, but Skaarup had refused because of his obligations to Fotorama. Drescher reported from the meeting with Olsen:

> Furthermore, Mr. Ole Olsen contemplated launching a film rental business that would have been troublesome and harmful to Fotorama, and one could expect that Mr. Ole Olsen, in the case an understanding could not be reached, could cause much harm to Fotorama Film Factory, partly by contracting the best actors, partly by making agreements with the two existing raw stock factories so as to make it difficult for Fotorama to acquire raw film.[460]

Under these circumstances, Drescher recommended a negotiation that would lead to a positive outcome for Fotorama, and after thorough debates, the board unanimously agreed to the outline of an agreement with Nordisk. In Drescher's minutes from the meeting of 22 April it appears that Olsen threatened to blow Fotorama out of the water by launching a distribution company as well as barring Fotorama from access to raw stock, and that the fear of such a move made Fotorama invest in the new company. In other words, Olsen had the means to force the Fotorama people into the founding of a limited company.

458 NFS:I,1:10.DFI. Unpagn. Minutes of the General Meeting (22 April 1911).

459 NFS:I,1:1.DFI. Unpagn. Laws for "A/S Nordisk Filmskompagni".

460 Danish National Business Archives: Generalforsamlingsprotokol f. Hotel Royal 1908–1923. (Protocol of General Meeting of Hotel Royal 1908–1923). Minutes of the Board of Directors are in the last part of the protocol (24 April 1911).

A couple of weeks later, on 8 May, the limited company was legally established at Barrister Oluf Bay's office in Niels Hemmingsensgade in Copenhagen. The limited company was to take over Olsen's film-factory business. From the minutes we can see how Nordisk was valued in the spring of 1911. Status per January 1911 plus assets later added on 24 April was:

Property in Valby	Kr. 25,699.10
Storeroom & building in Frihavnen	Kr. 18,145.33
Outstanding accounts	Kr. 172,043.07
Machines, equipment etc.	Kr. 49,228.06
Inventory	Kr. 220,401.49
Compensation for dismissal	Kr. 100,000.00
Debts	Kr. 71,011.13[461]

Olsen's company was valued at 514,702 kroner. The amount above 500,000 kroner was transferred to Olsen's private account. 200,000 kroner was issued as preference stock, i.e. shares that did not come with the right to vote and were to be paid before the returns from ordinary shares; 125,000 kroner was issued in ordinary shares; 250,000 kroner was paid in cash; and 50,000 kroner was converted into mortgage bonds.[462] In other words, Olsen was paid a lot more for his company than the 100,000 kroner mentioned by Engberg.[463] The statement leaves out an essential part of Nordisk's organization – the branches. They continued to be Olsen's private property for some years.[464] The first group of shareholders and the distribution of shares ended like this:

Eduard Bergmann	Kr. 5,000
Carl Henrik Wilhelm Gielstrup	Kr. 5,000
Johan Ramm	Kr. 26,000
Otto Gulmann	Kr. 24,000
Alfred William Mammen	Kr. 20,000
Eduard Schnedler-Sørensen	Kr. 20,000

461 NFS:I,23.DFI, 1–2. Minutes of the General Meeting (8 May 1911).

462 NFS:I,23.DFI, 1–2. Minutes of the General Meeting (8 May 1911).

463 See Engberg, *Dansk stumfilm*, 586.

464 Not until February 1913, and after much debate, was the London office converted into a private company in which Nordisk owned the majority of shares. NFS:II,24.DFI, 290. Letter from Harald Frost to Wilson & Son, London (18 February 1913). The Berlin branch became the property of Nordisk around 1913/1914. NFS:II,33.DFI, 846. Letter from Nordisk Films Kompagni to Steuerdeputation des Magistrats Abteilung II, Berlin (30 October 1914). The ownership of the New York business branch remains uncertain.

Frede Skaarup	Kr. 25,000
Ole Olsen	Kr. 125,000
–	Kr. 200,000 as preference stock.[465]

Seven out of the eight shareholders had connections to Fotorama, but Olsen still held half of the shares with voting rights and more than 72 per cent of the total share capital.

The board decided on the laws of the company and resolved to take over three contracts: one with Skandinavisk Kunstfilms Kompagni, one with A/S Panoptikonteatret, and finally the distribution agreement for Denmark and Norway between Nordisk and Fotorama. The contract with A/S Panoptikonteatret maintained the former agreement between Nordisk and Fotorama concerning the production of twelve art films that were to premiere in Panoptikonteatret.[466] Skandinavisk Kunstfilms Kompagni was founded by Gulmann, Mammen and Ramm who had made an agreement with film director Urban Gad that he should write and direct films for the company for a year.[467]

Stæhr and Skaarup signed their contracts and became managers.[468] Olsen was appointed chairman of the board but took no part in the day-to-day management.[469] Skaarup, who kept his position as the manager of Fotorama, was in charge of administration and the offices that now moved from Frihavnen to the Panoptikon Building at 3 Vesterbrogade in the heart of Copenhagen. Although now a manager, Stæhr continued to be in charge of the printing laboratory, the expansion of which was one of the first decisions made by the new board in order to enable the factory to reach 2.5 million metres a year.[470] Schnedler-Sørensen was hired as "overseer" which meant that he was to "supervise finances and accounts at the studio in Valby".[471] He later started to direct films again and completed sixty films between 1911 and his temporary departure from Nordisk in 1914.

Why was Nordisk converted into a limited company? Why was Olsen so eager to affiliate the Fotorama people with Nordisk? There are no clear answers to this. DEN HVIDE SLAVEHANDEL had shown that audiences were ready for longer films. A reorganization of production for the much more cumbersome and expensive long-film production with bigger investments and more distant

465 NFS:I,23.DFI, 3. Minutes of the General Meeting (8 May 1911).

466 NFS:I,I:7.DFI, 1–2. Agreement of collaboration of production between Nordisk and the Panoptikonteatret, undated.

467 NFA. Agreement between Urban Gad and Skandinavisk Kunstfilms Kompagni (11 April 1911). For the company, the signatories were O. Gulmann, A.W. Mammen and J. Ramm. Whether there were other interested parties and, if so, who they might be, is uncertain.

468 NFS:I,23.DFI, 3. Minutes of the General Meeting (8 May 1911).

469 NFS:II,16.DFI, 25. Letter from Wilhelm Stæhr to Ludwig Landemann (27 May 1911).

470 NFS:I,25.DFI. Unpagn. Minutes of the Board of Directors Meeting (8 June 1911).

471 NFS:II,33.DFI, 93. Letter from Harald Frost to Barrister Børge Jacobsen (24 August 1914).

profits called for risk/venture capital. The film industry was still relatively young, and perhaps Olsen had trouble finding investors. Olsen had contemplated making Nordisk a limited company for some time; in 1909, he had discussed plans with Oskar Messter, and throughout the spring of 1910, Olsen corresponded with Barrister Heinrich A. Müller concerning the establishment of such a company. Müller acted on behalf of an unnamed man, but it appears from the letters that Olsen supplied Müller with information about Nordisk's finances. However, these plans were dropped by Olsen when no concrete offer emerged from Müller or his client.[472] When neither of these plans materialized, Olsen may have found the investors he needed in the Fotorama group. Through their shipping agency, Drescher and Mammen had the requisite capital, and both had shown that they were willing to invest in film production. Or perhaps Olsen was actually pressurized by the Fotorama people into the founding of a limited company?

The film industry had been through its first crisis with the overproduction of films. In 1911 no one could be certain whether film was just a passing fad or whether it had taken root as an institution within entertainment. If the film industry ran into yet another crisis, Olsen would be at an advantage if he had someone with whom to share the losses.

There may also have been personal considerations on behalf of Olsen. By forming the new company, he liberated the capital he had accumulated for himself in the company. Olsen was 48, and with an average life expectancy of 56 in 1911, he would be wise to make provisions for himself and his family.[473] His wife, Anna Ludovika, had been hard hit by tuberculosis since she came home from Sweden. She grew weaker still and frequently visited health resorts for long periods of time until her death in 1916.

Olsen was also on the look-out for new managers. Viggo Larsen left his post as inspector and senior film director in Valby in November 1909. It appears that Olsen and Larsen had a falling-out, and Larsen left for Germany where he continued his work as a film director. Holger Rasmussen was hired as the new artistic manager in Valby from 1 January 1910.[474] However, Rasmussen proved "incompetent in all areas"[475] and was dismissed in October (effective 1 January 1911).[476] August Blom took over from Rasmussen. Already in December 1909, Blom had been among the candidates for the position of artistic manager.[477] In Skaarup and Schnedler-Sørensen, Olsen had two more managers who had already earned their spurs in the industry.

472 NFS:II,12.DFI, 172. Letter from Ole Olsen to Barrister Heinrich A. Müller (31 January 1910); NFS:II,12.DFI, 897. Letter from Ole Olsen to Barrister Heinrich A. Müller (28 May 1910).

473 According to Statistics Denmark, the average life expectancy in 1911–1915 was 56.2 years.

474 NFS:II,11.DFI, 712. Letter from Wilhelm Stæhr to Danske Dramatikeres Forbund (27 December 1909).

475 NFS:II,30.DFI, 968. Letter from Harald Frost to Barrister Børge Jacobsen (21 March 1914).

476 NFS:II,13.DFI, 813. Letter from Ole Olsen to Holger Rasmussen (5 October 1910).

477 NFS:II,11.DFI, 788. Letter from Wilhelm Stæhr to August Blom (15 December 1909).

All the same, Olsen lost influence through Nordisk's transition to a limited company. Stæhr reported to the Berlin branch: "In short, it goes like this: Mr. Frede Skaarup and I are the managing directors. Director Ole Olsen is the chairman of the board and does not take part in the daily decisions except when we ask his advice."[478] However, when Skaarup entered into a failed business venture with two German distributors, promising 60 copies of twelve upcoming feature films and 40 copies of the next Asta Nielsen film, a deal worth nearly one million kroner, he had exceeded his powers as a manager, and Olsen had to sort out the failed deal. The consequence of the case was a change in the procedures of decision-making in Nordisk's management. During a meeting of the board in August 1911, one of the new clauses specified:

> The board or at least the chairman is to be kept up to date concerning business, and neither the managing directors nor others may make decisions concerning anything outside the daily business without consulting the chairman or the executive committee. The managing directors and others have a duty to comply with the instructions of the chairman and the executive committee and to do their best to execute these.[479]

This clause makes it clear that Olsen had now regained his influence, except in the day-to-day business. By negotiating such a large contract without the board's or Olsen's approval, Skaarup had outmanoeuvred himself. His authority to make binding agreements on behalf of the company was withdrawn on 28 December 1911, less than six months after his engagement as manager.[480]

It is doubtful whether Olsen and Skaarup, both innovative and enterprising businessmen, could ever have worked together as managers in the same company; they were highly different personalities. Where Olsen was deliberate in his decisions, Skaarup seems to have been an impulsive and informal type. He rarely wore a jacket, and Sandfeld characterizes Skaarup as being chock-full of ideas and energy, with an unmistakeable talent for business.[481] In the years to come, however, Olsen and Skaarup collaborated closely on several large investment projects.

Yet another change in the company was to shift the power balance in the board at Nordisk. At a board meeting in June 1912, Olsen presented an approach from a syndicate who wanted to buy into Nordisk and raise the share capital to two million kroner. The syndicate had no links to the film industry but did have connections to two Copenhagen banks, Kjøbenhavns Laane- og Diskontobank and Revisionsbanken. The old shareholders would receive one million kroner in cash and shares in the value of one million kroner in the expanded company.[482] The board accepted the offer from the syndicate. The chairman

478 NFS:II,16.DFI, 25. Letter from Wilhelm Stæhr to Ludwig Landemann (27 May 1911).

479 NFS:I,25.DFI. Unpagn. Minutes of the Board of Directors Meeting (19 August 1911).

480 Copenhagen City Archives, the Trade Register, dpt. B. 2763. For a more detailed account of the events see Thorsen (2013), 25–38.

481 Interview with Joachim Nielsen. DFI. See also Sandfeld, *Den stumme scene*, 70.

482 NFS:I,25.DFI. Unpagn. Minutes of the Board of Directors Meeting (3 June 1912).

of the board of Revisionsbanken, stockbroker Aron Frederik Lamm, writes in his memoirs that one year prior to this, Olsen had asked the bank to participate in an expansion of Nordisk's share capital. It had been too risky then, but when Olsen was able to document "what an incredible amount of money he made", the bank was persuaded.[483] Lamm's memoirs confirm that Olsen had been looking for extra capital for some time, and was actually searching elsewhere than the Fotorama people around the time when Nordisk became a limited company.

On 12 June 1912, the new board was constituted, with eight members. Olsen continued as chairman, now with the title of director general. Barrister Børge Jacobsen became deputy chairman. He was a member of Diskontobanken's board with the authority to bind the bank. Bank manager Frederik Paulsen, a rank-and-file member of Nordisk's board, was also from Diskontobanken. A.F. Lamm and landed proprietor Carl de Neergaard represented Revisionsbanken. Of the old board only Gielstrup, Mammen and Ramm remained, all with connections to Fotorama.

In its new form, Nordisk took on the hierarchial management structure that charactarizes the Modern Industrial Enterprise. In his characterization of an MIE, Chandler operates with two types of managements; the "outside" and the "inside directors". These types of managers make decisions, each on their respective levels of the organization. Outside managers include the company board, shareholders, banks etc. who make the long-term, strategic goals. Inside managers are the hired managers and mid-level managers who performing the day-to-day duties. The two managements sectors of the company agree on decisions that secure the growth of the company.[484] In his capacity of director general at Nordisk, Olsen was head of the management, and as the owner of a large amount of shares and chairman of the board, he was both an outside and an inside manager.

Under Olsen were Stæhr, who continued as manager, and Harald Frost (1884–1942). With Stæhr and Frost as managers under Olsen, Olsen was the top-manager, answerable to the board. Under Olsen were the mid-level managers Frost and Stæhr, and through lower-level managers such as the supervisors in Valby, branch managers etc., they controlled the individual departments in Nordisk's organization.[485] Frost was office manager at Nordisk and was promoted to manager in 1912, the same year he married Olsen's daughter. Frost has been characterized as a reserved but extraordinarily upright and courteous man with outstanding pedagogical and administrative skills.[486] From his office at Vimmelskaftet, Frost took care of the company's international business and set long-term goals, such as the plans for the production

483 Alfred Lamm, *Erindringer og Tanker* (Copenhagen: Gyldendalske Boghandel, Nordisk Forlag, 1928), 189.

484 See Chandler, *Scale and Scope*, 33–34.

485 See ibid., 14–15 and 32.

486 Gtz., "Direktør Harald Frost død" ("Director Frost Passed Away"), *Politiken* (22 April 1942).

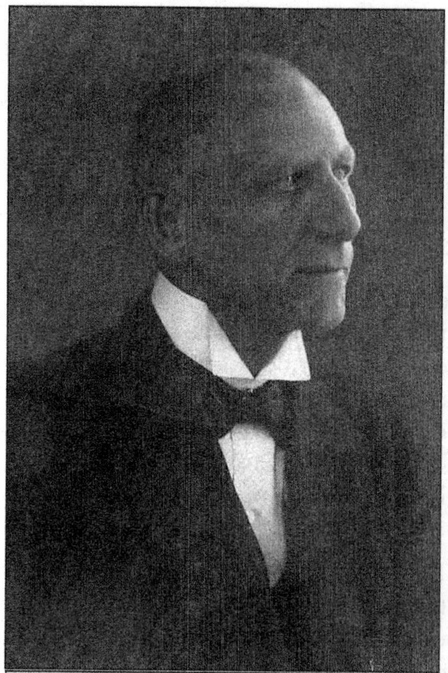

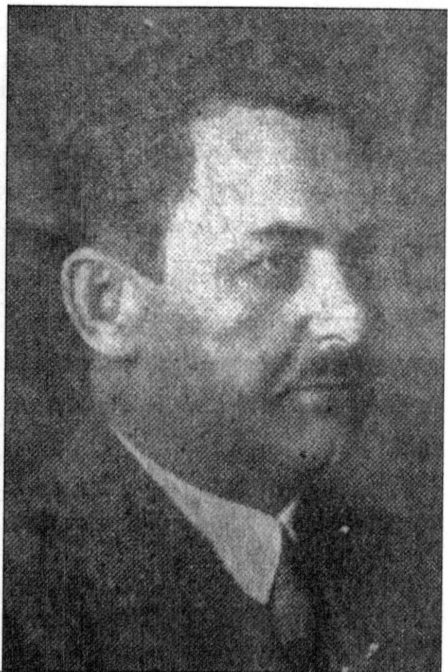

Figure 18. Olsen's trusted managers Wilhelm Stæhr (left) and Harald Frost (right). Courtesy of Museum of Slaughterhouses, Roskilde and *Politiken* (22 April 1942).

of films. Stæhr was the practical manager who distributed and supervised the work, first at Frihavnen and later also in Valby. Olsen, Frost, and Stæhr were the stable management team who controlled Nordisk all the way up to 1924. Letters and memos passing between them testify to a mutual trust and confidence, and the three of them socialized privately as well.[487] Like the management, the board remained the same until 1924, with very few exceptions.

Through its new board members, Nordisk acquired a foothold in both the upper political and financial echelons of Copenhagen society. Lamm was chairman of the social-democratic group in Copenhagen's city council and also an experienced stockbroker, well-connected at the Copenhagen stock exchange. Jens Hassing-Jørgensen, who had been in charge of negotiations with the syndicate concerning the expansion of Nordisk's share capital, was the founder and manager of Revisionsbanken. He left the bank in 1913 to become Minister of Traffic and Trade in the Danish Social Liberal Party government under Carl Theodor Zahle. When his term ended, he returned to the board of directors of the bank.

The new board composition created new business connections for Olsen and Nordisk. Per Boje emphasizes that a company manager's personal network as a prerequisite to the company's continued growth and states that it is difficult

487 E.g. NFS:II,54:20.DFI. Letter from Wilhelm Stæhr to Harald Frost (22 July 1917).

to draw a clear line between the professional and the social aspects of this network. Ties of loyalty may become a liability, partly because they imply blind trust, partly because they may bar the view to opportunities outside the network.[488] The national and international network Olsen created had immense importance for Nordisk's development, but to Olsen, business seems to have come before loyalty, and his personal network does not seem to have impeded with Nordisk's development in any way. Even when Skaarup had been ejected from Nordisk's management, Olsen continued to work with him. The German producer Oskar Messter, with whom Olsen was close in 1908 when they contemplated an amalgamation between their two companies, provides another example of business conflicting with personal connections. Olsen came on collision course with Messter, both in connection with DEN FARLIGE ALDER, and later about the services of actress Henny Porten. In both cases, Olsen favoured business over personal ties with Messter and Skaarup.

Through its close connections to two Copenhagen banks, Nordisk gained a financial safety net for the first time, which enabled the company to plan farther ahead. From 1916 to 1919, Olsen was a member of the board of Revisionsbanken,[489] and he had shares in both banks.[490] In her analysis of the American film industry, Janet Wasko emphasizes that it was only with the advent of long feature films that the industry started to gain a solid reputation and began to attract investors from the world of finance,[491] but, as Wasko adds: "Even though the industry had become more stable and offered quality products from around 1915–16, with only a few exceptions, it was still not considered eligible for substantial investment-bank support before 1919."[492] Comparisons between the American and the European film industries can only be made with several reservations, but there are some parallels. In 1897, Pathé had become a limited company with support from a group of industrials,[493] and Gaumont became a limited company with the aid of Banque Suisse et Française.[494] As Wasko explains, the transition to feature films and the industrial structure it entailed were important steps in securing the confidence of the banks in the first place, and in this, the European film industry was at least a few years ahead of the Americans. American banks were generally hesitant about investing in the new film industry because films were regarded a flash in the pan. This was also the prevailing view in Denmark. It appears from a newspaper coverage that the bank syndicate's involvement with Nordisk was viewed as an insecure investment. It was assumed that the old shareholders had received a substantial amount of goodwill for their shares. "These shares

488 See Boje, *Ledere, ledelse og organisation 1870–1972*, 147–148.

489 See Theodor Green, *Greens danske Fonds og Aktier* vol. 1916 (Copenhagen: Børsen), 181.

490 See Ole Olsen's private archives and Bergsten, *Ole Olsen*.

491 See Wasko, *Relationships*, 26.

492 Wasko, *Relationships*, 27.

493 Salmon, *Pathé*, 35–53.

494 See Abel, *The Cine Goes to Town*, 20.

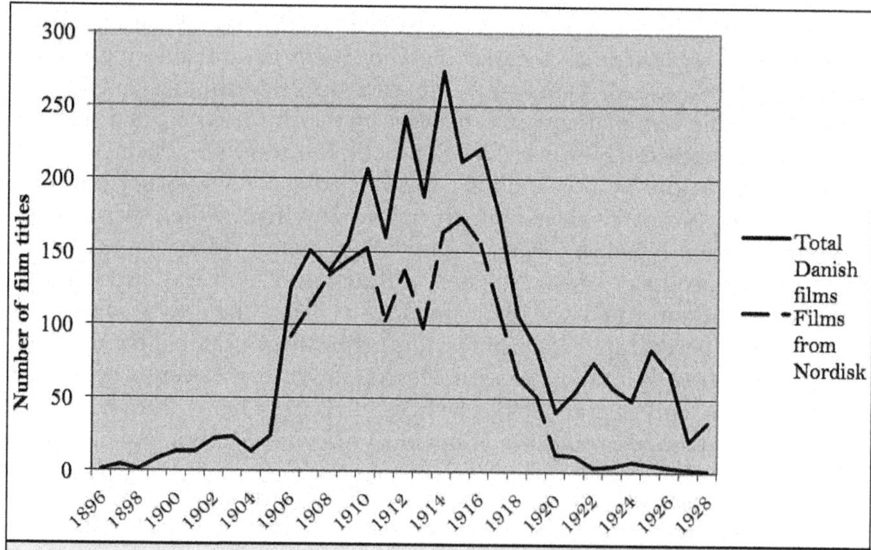

Figure 19. Total of Danish film production by title and Nordisk's share 1896–1928.

Note: The number of Danish films follows Engberg's *Registrant over danske film 1896–1930* I-V. In her work with the Danish Film Database, researcher Lisbeth Richter Larsen at DFI has found 32 films not on Engberg's list. 19 of these films have been dated and included in the above; those not dated have been excluded.
About the films made by Nordisk between 1908 and spring 1912, see note for Table 1 (on page 30).

were 'airy', i.e. there was a vast establishing account to write off", one newspaper reported.[495] In time, however, the syndicate's investment would prove highly profitable.

Olsen was not the only cinema owner who had started making films in Denmark. The owner of the cinema Biorama, Søren Nielsen, founded a film company by that name in 1909, the same year that Fotorama began producing films. Both companies started their production three years after Nordisk was established, during which time Nordisk had laid the foundation of its own production and the international network that enabled it to sell the films so widely. However, neither of the aforementioned competitors, and indeed no one since, came near the size of Nordisk, and they do not seem to have had any great influence on Nordisk's business. It was not until 1913 that a series of other Danish film companies arose in the wake of Nordisk's success. With regard to Nordisk's position in Denmark in the silent era, Ron Mottram assertes that "the history of Danish cinema is largely the history of this one company".[496] If we look at the collected production of films from 1906 to 1928 and Nordisk's share in these productions (Figure 19), it is evident that Nordisk dominated in Denmark from 1906 to 1920.

495 Undated anonymous article in *Børsen* probably from March 1913, in NFS.XIV:31.DFI, 1. Scrapbook.

496 Mottram, *The Danish Cinema before Dreyer*, 8.

However, Nordisk's sales of films had dropped at the end of 1909. In 1907, Nordisk had sold an average of 67 copies of each of their films; one year later, the average was down to 50, and in 1908 and 1909 this average fell to, respectively, 48 and 40 copies per film.[497] Engberg writes that this decline had two causes. Nordisk now had competition from other newly-started companies, and Viggo Larsen as a film director would no longer do.[498] Nothing indicates that Larsen's artistic skills were to blame for the decline in sales, although Engberg writes that "artistically, the Danish films were stagnating in a particular, primitive form",[499] but at the same time, she emphasizes that *Moving Picture World* incessantly mentioned Nordisk's high technical and artistic qualities, even in 1909.[500] Instead the decline was caused by the general crisis in the international film industry and the overproduction of films in the years before 1910. Nordisk was truly in doubt about how to get through the crisis, and doubts intensified when Larsen quit the company and a new manager had to be found; Nordisk also debated about the types of film they wished to produce.

> Since we have been doubtful as to which specific taste we should prefer in the upcoming season, we have not wanted to make a decision concerning your manuscript. We believe the adventurous genre has played itself out, and that public taste now favours grandiose, realistic stories, yet without crime or burlesque.[501]

In a letter from 1909, Stæhr mentions the possibility of making long feature films, but the company seems to have opted against it.[502] The international film industry was dominated by the conviction that films should not exceed one reel, i.e. 350 metres or fifteen minutes,[503] and Nordisk's production policy before 1910 was to refrain from making films longer than 300 metres.[504] With its 603 metres, DEN HVIDE SLAVEHANDEL became the first feature film produced by Nordisk, and these long films would eventually save the company. "Long and artistic films are our future motto", Stæhr announced in the spring of 1911.[505] From 1911 to 1917, Nordisk produced 944 actualities and fiction films of which 421 were long features.[506] Long films have been defined as films more than 500 metres long, and this was indeed the company's own definition.[507] The increase of the production of long films in the period 1910–1917

497 See note for Table 1.

498 See Engberg, *Dansk stumfilm*, 104.

499 Ibid.

500 See ibid., 74.

501 NFS:II,9.DFI, 156. Letter from Nordisk to Chr. Nielsen (4 January 1909).

502 NFS:II,11.DFI, 717. Letter from Wilhelm Stæhr to Nordische Films Co., Berlin (6 December 1909).

503 See Abel (ed.), *Encyclopedia of Early Cinema*, 452.

504 NFS:II,12.DFI, 746. Letter from Wilhelm Stæhr to O. Jensen, Helsingør (3 May 1910).

505 NFS:II,15.DFI, 464. Letter from Wilhelm Stæhr to Ingvald C. Oes, New York (23 March 1911).

506 See note for Table 1.

507 E.g. NFS:XII,31:43, DFI. Unpagn. Agreement between A/S Nordisk Films Co. and A/S De Giglio (19 February 1913).

is striking (Table 3). From having released a single long feature film in 1910, Nordisk went to releasing between 34 and 96 per year.

Table 3: The share of long feature films made by Nordisk by year, 1910–1917

	1910	1911	1912	1913	1914	1915	1916	1917
Films total	153	103	138	98	164	174	154	111
Long feature films	1	35	47	45	76	96	79	34
Percentage of long feature films	0.6	34	34	46	46	55	51	30

Source: see note for Table 1 (on page 30).

From 1911 to 1917, the rate of long feature films produced annually, if counted by the negative metres, amounted to 66 per cent of Nordisk's production total. In the course of 1911, their average length had reached 1,000 metres – about one hour of running time. In 1913, Nordisk released its first film with a running time of two hours: the prestigious ATLANTIS. The decline in the number of films in 1913 does not reflect a decline in production; quite the contrary: the company's production of negative metres rose steadily until 1915 (Figure 20).

Long films had been made before 1910, but they were rare. In 1903, the French company Pathé Frères had produced EPOPÉE NAPOLÉONIENNE (LIFE OF NAPOLEON, Lucien Nonguet) with a length of 430 metres, and LA VIE ET LA PASSION DE JÉSUS-CHRIST (THE LIFE AND PASSION OF CHRIST, Lucien Nonguet, Ferdinand Zecca) of 1,425 metres. The two films had been marketed as historical and religious specials and were shown over several evenings to accommodate the routine of the cinemas.

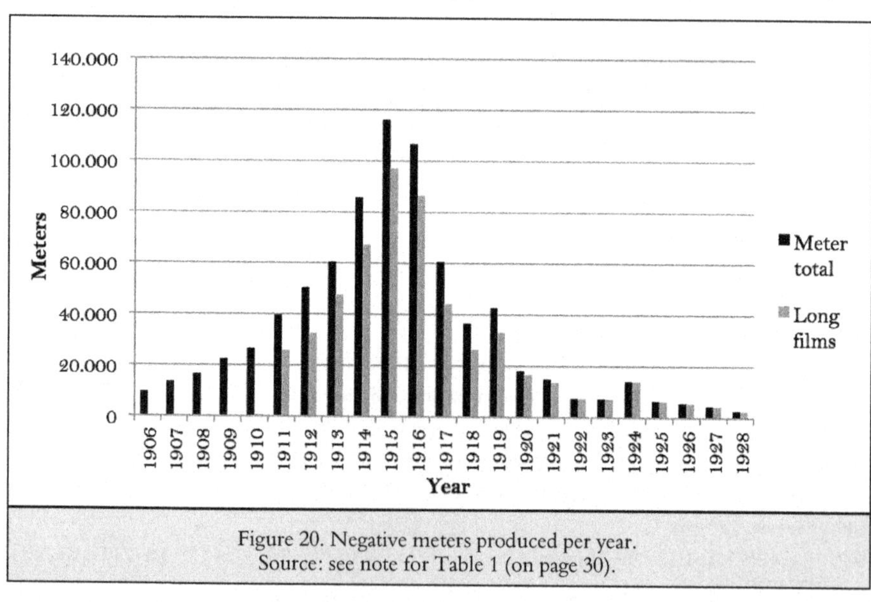

Figure 20. Negative meters produced per year.
Source: see note for Table 1 (on page 30).

However, many credited Nordisk with having introduced long feature films. In 1911 the British film magazine *The Kinematograph* wrote: "One company [Nordisk] seems to have started what is likely to be a new era in the trade [...]."[508] Another British film magazine, *The Kinematograph and Lantern Weekly*, wrote that the Italian Pasquali Company was the first to follow Nordisk's example and to launch the feature films in Italy.[509] It is doubtful whether Pasquali really was the first Italian company to produce a long film, but the influence from Nordisk and Denmark is also emphasized by film historian Aldo Bernardini who points to AFGRUNDEN (THE ABYSS, Urban Gad, Kosmorama, 1910), and the sequel to DEN HVIDE SLAVEHANDEL, DEN HVIDE SLAVEHANDELS SIDSTE OFFER (IN THE HANDS OF IMPOSTERS, August Blom, 1911) as the inspiration for the first long feature film in Italy, L'INFERNO (DANTE'S INFERNO, Francesco Bertolini, Adolfo Padovan, Giuseppe de Liguoro, Milano Film, IT 1911) which was 1,200 metres long and premiered in March 1911.[510] AFGRUNDEN was released in September 1910 and was 750 metres long.[511] It was produced by cinema owner Hjalmar Davidsen and directed by Urban Gad. Asta Nielsen played the female lead, and AFGRUNDEN made her one of the film industry's first and biggest stars.

In 1911, *Moving Picture World* wrote of Nordisk: "It was the first company to introduce 'features', starting in the early spring of 1911 with the three-reel picture TEMPTATIONS OF THE GREAT CITY (VED FÆNGSLETS PORT, August Blom, 1911) and has since been producing them regularly." The magazine continued:

> How auspicious the foresight of this aggressive company has been is best evidenced by the fact that since the inauguration of the above measures by Great Northern the same policy has been adopted by practically the entire film industry throughout the world.[512]

Nordisk's ground-breaking influence on the American market is also highlighted by Robert Grau, who writes in his 1914 book about the American film industry:

> It was the Great Northern Company that first introduced the multiple-reel subjects in this country, and from this beginning sprang the feature of to-day with its still-growing possibilities for the future.[513]

In his book about Dutch cinema owner Jean Desmet, Ivo Blom writes that also on the Dutch market, DEN HVIDE SLAVEHANDELS SIDSTE OFFER paved the way

508 *The Kinematograph* (22 June 1911), quoted from Mottram, *The Danish Cinema before Dreyer*, 95.

509 See Mottram, *The Danish Cinema before Dreyer*, 93.

510 See Aldo Bernardini and Vittorio Martinelli, *Il cinema muto italiano 1911, prima parte* (Roma: Centro Sperimentale di Cinematografia, 1995), 12–13 and 238.

511 The length is according to the Danish version of the film.

512 Bergsten, *Ole Olsen*, 19.

513 Robert Grau, *The Theatre of Science. A Volume of Progress and Achievements in the Motion Picture Art* (New York, London: Broadway Publishing Company, 1914), 76.

for feature films.[514] He states: "The share of Danish movies remained small, but in 1911 and 1912 almost half of Desmet's long features came from Denmark", and Blom adds that most of the Danish films came from Nordisk.[515]

Over the course of 1911 and the spring of 1912, the rest of the European film industry started to produce feature-length films on a regular basis.[516] In early 1911, SCAGL, one of Pathé's subsidiary companies, released the 750-metre-long LE COURRIER DE LYON (THE COURIER OF LYONS, Albert Capellani, F 1911), at the same time as the long Danish films reached the French market.[517] Gaumont followed suit with LA TARE (THE DEFECT, Louis Feuillade, F 1911) of 810 metres in the autumn of 1911. By then, Nordisk had already shot 36 long films.

The transition to long feature films was not entirely smooth. In September 1910, the German trade journal *Der Kinematograph* reported of the new Danish films that played to packed houses in Denmark: "All these Danish films share the fault of being too long, 700–1000 metres."[518]

Without mentioning Fotorama's film at all, Olsen writes in his memoirs how DEN HVIDE SLAVEHANDEL was shown at a closed viewing to a group of cinema owners in Germany. Not one of the Germans dared venture into longer films; they feared losing money because the audiences would stay away. However, Olsen found a cinema owner in Hamburg and made him a favourable offer: if he made no money on the film, he could have it for free. When the cinema owner still declined, Olsen threatened to stop supplying him with films from Nordisk unless he put DEN HVIDE SLAVEHANDEL on the programme. The cinema owner agreed to Olsen's "offer".[519] Olsen writes of the Hamburg premiere: "Word got out all over town. The next day the cinema was packed and on the third day it took twenty police officers to retain order since people were queueing around the block to get tickets."[520] Nordisk's version of DEN HVIDE SLAVEHANDEL was a success and sold 103 copies worldwide, in comparison to a 1910 average sale of 40 copies per film.[521] All the same, Olsen's version of the story should probably be taken with a grain of salt; Corinna Müller observes that the film's length was not stated anywhere in the German ads for DEN HVIDE SLAVEHANDEL. Rumours of the success of the film in Denmark had spread to Germany, and they eclipsed the length of the production.[522] Film

514 Blom, *Jean Desmet*, 192.

515 Ibid., 185.

516 See Abel, *The Cine Goes to Town*, 299.

517 See Abel (ed.), *Encyclopedia of Early Cinema*, 454.

518 "Die Kinematographen-Verhältnisse in Dänemark", *Der Kinematograph*, no. 196 (28 September 1910).

519 Olsen, *Filmens Eventyr og mit eget*, 85–88.

520 Ibid., 87.

521 NFS:XI,1.DFI, 19. Protocol of Negatives.

522 See Müller, *Frühe deutsche Kinematographie*, 114–115.

historians agree that DEN HVIDE SLAVEHANDEL, together with AFGRUNDEN and the boxing film JEFFRIES-JOHNSON WORLD'S CHAMPIONSHIP BOXING CONTEST, HELD AT RENO, NEVADA, JULY 4 (J & J Co., director unknown, USA 1910), paved the way for long feature films in Germany.[523]

Only two years after *Der Kinematograph*'s sceptical article about films becoming far too long", the magazine changed its tune and wrote:

> The Danish film art then brought the great atmospheric and lively drama like those we read in novels; the artistic films that win our hearts through calm pictures and tell a simple story which almost imperceptibly rises in suspense – things we had not thought films capable of. That is how AFGRUNDEN works in Germany, and this is where Danish films are best received and best understood.[524]

The risk of producing feature films cannot be underestimated, nor can the difficulties in persuading the cinema owners to screen them. Long films meant that the entire culture of going to the movies changed. For one thing, the cinemas had to introduce a fixed time schedule, unlike the early days of continuous looped screenings that allowed audiences to enter and leave the darkness of the cinema as they pleased.

Nordisk did not invent long feature films, but the fact that the company so ventured into longer films so early on set a standard which was quickly followed by the rest of the world. The venture gave Nordisk a competitive advantage and marked the beginning of what several authors have called the Golden Age of Danish film.[525]

With the advent of feature films, new distribution systems were introduced in Britain and Germany. Rachael Low writes that DEN HVIDE SLAVEHANDELS SIDSTE OFFER was the first film in Britain to be distributed through the new *exclusive system*.[526] The exclusive system, or *Monopolfilm*, as it was called in Germany, was a forerunner of the distribution system known today. A distributor or cinema owner had exclusive (or monopoly) rights to a film in a certain area and for a specified period of time. Bypassing rental bureaus, the distributor could control how many copies of a film were needed to cover a certain area. Instead of having the same film competing against itself by being shown in several cinemas in the same town, the distributor could guarantee a good profit from the film.

The system was not new; it also applied to those markets where a film company sold to an agent who had the sales and distribution rights of the company's films in one or more countries. What was new about this system was that the producers could sell a single film to a distributor at a much higher price than

523 See Abel (ed.), *Encyclopedia of Early Cinema*, 453; Lähn, "Paul Davidson", 85; Müller, *Frühe deutsche Kinematographie*, 112–119.

524 "Dänemark und Deutschland. In der Filmkunst", *Der Kinematograph*, no. 280 (8 May 1912).

525 See e.g. Engberg, *Dansk stumfilm*, 8; Neergaard, *Historien om dansk film*, 56; Christensen, "Isbjørnens fald", 238.

526 See Low, Rachael, *The History of British Film 1906–1914* (London: George Allen & Unwin Ltd., 1949), 46.

before. With exclusive rights it took fewer copies to cover an entire country. Müller writes that fifteen to twenty copies would have sufficed for all of Germany.[527]

To begin with, Nordisk was nervous about the distribution system in Germany; it claimed that DEN FARLIGE ALDER was made in protest against *Monopolfilm*.[528] Messter had sold his version as a *Monopolfilm*, and Nordisk hoped that cinema owners who had not secured the rights for Messter's film in a given area would buy Nordisk's free-trade version instead.[529] Nordisk sold its version as a "Terminfilm", i.e. a film in free trade but with a fixed release date that had been announced in advance in the trade press. In this way, attention was duly created, and the sales of copies rose. The *Terminfilm*, which according to Müller appeared on the German market near the end of 1908, was a step in the direction of the release procedure used from the early 1910s onward, when the big companies could issue a selection of various films each week and advertise the films months ahead.[530] Nordisk quickly started selling its films on the British and German markets as exclusive films and *Monopolfilms*. On all other markets, the company still distributed through an agent.

Plans for expanding the *Monopolfilm* system from a region to an entire country were still far away in 1912. But in Germany, film manufacturers and distributors formed a nationally controlled organization, Film-Industrie-Aktien-Gesellschaft (FIAG). Nordisk joined the organization[531] and committed itself to delivering 1.15 million metres of film annually to FIAG for three years. Nordisk's conditions for entering the league were that sixteen German distributors should sign up for a share, and that FIAG obtained exclusive rights for Germany from Pathé Frères, Gaumont, Itala, Vitagraph, Edison and "three good German companies and one American".[532] Moreover, Nordisk stipulated in the contract that Nordisk "obtained the same rights as the companies Pathé and Gaumont".[533] Nordisk's terms show that they counted themselves among the leading European film companies, and the contract also reflects German film's inferior status – no German company is even named in the agreement that would come to dominate the German film industry completely. The contract between Nordisk and FIAG was signed 17 February 1912, but the agreement foundered. Müller writes that FIAG was stillborn from the outset. The opposition against a monopolization of the film industry was too strong in Germany.[534] Nordisk's advantage of entering FIAG was the guarantee of

527 See Müller, *Frühe deutsche Kinematographie*, 102.

528 NFS:II,15.DFI, 677. Letter from Wilhelm Stæhr to Nordisk Films Co., Berlin (15 April 1911).

529 NFS:II,15.DFI, 465. Letter from Wilhelm Stæhr to Nordische Films Co., Berlin (23 March 1911).

530 See Müller, *Frühe deutsche Kinematographie*, 88–94.

531 NFS:I,25.DFI. Unpagn. Minutes of the Board of Directors Meeting (7 October 1912).

532 NFS:I,2:43.DFI. Unpagn. Contract between FIAG and Nordisk (17 February 1912).

533 NFS:I,2:43.DFI. Unpagn. Contract between FIAG and Nordisk (17 February 1912).

534 See Müller, *Frühe deutsche Kinematographie*, 157.

steady sales years ahead, and at that point, the FIAG contract resembled the agreements which Nordisk entered into in the early 1910s.

An good example of such a contract is the one between Nordisk and the company A/S De Giglio concerning the agencies for two smaller markets, Finland and Italy.[535] The contract was signed in February 1913 and ran from 1 May 1913 to 30 April 1916. De Giglio agreed to buy at least five copies of Nordisk's art films, which here mean films of a length of 500 metres or more. Moreover, De Giglio was to buy at least three copies of Nordisk's other films. The art films cost 0.88 kroner per metre and the price of the others was 0.75 kroner per metre. If De Giglio could not buy the amount agreed upon, he was to "pay Nordisk Films Co. 0.38 kroner per metre of art film for not meeting the terms of the contract, and 0.25 kroner for the other films".[536] Should one of the films be prohibited by Italian or Finnish censorship, De Giglio was bound by the contract to take at least a smaller number of copies of the censored film – even if it could not be shown to the public. In one case, Nordisk charged De Giglio for some metres which the Italian censorship had ordered to be removed from the film.[537]

That the buyer should pay for a film from Nordisk even if it was prohibited by the censor was a business principle to which the company had adhered for a long time. The film DEN HVIDE SLAVINDE had been outlawed by the censor in Norway, and Nordisk had told the Norwegian buyer that "[...] items bought and paid for and viewed here at our factory cannot possibly be returned".[538] A similar answer was given to Hermansen in Aarhus in connection with the film MORDET PAA FYN (Murder on Funen, 1907) which was prohibited in Denmark in 1907.[539]

The De Giglio contract is interesting for several reasons. De Giglio must have had confidence in the quality of Nordisk's films and bought them sight unseen. The agreement guaranteed Nordisk earnings on films three years ahead regardless of censor intervention; the long films, which were more expensive to make, cost more to buy than other films, and furthermore, the contract is an early example of what the American film industry would later call "block booking" and "blind selling". Block booking is a type of distribution agreement through which cinemas and distributors agree to buy a bulk of films – even the ones they are not interested in – in order to obtain the rights to attractive films – in this case, the more expensive long films. Blind selling means that the distributor bought films unseen, and in some cases even before they were made.

535 NFS:XII,31:43.DFI. Unpagn. Agreement between A/S Nordisk Films Co. and A/S De Giglio (19 February 1913).

536 NFS:XII,31:43.DFI. Unpagn. Agreement between A/S Nordisk Films Co. and A/S De Giglio (19 February 1913).

537 NFS:II,32.DFI, 324. Letter from Harald Frost to A/S De Giglio (23 June 1914).

538 NFS:II,3.DFI, 129. Letter from Nordisk to G. Knudsen, Kristiania (23 January 1907).

539 NFS:II,3.DFI, 508. Letter from E. Hansen to Hermansen, Aarhus (17 April 1907).

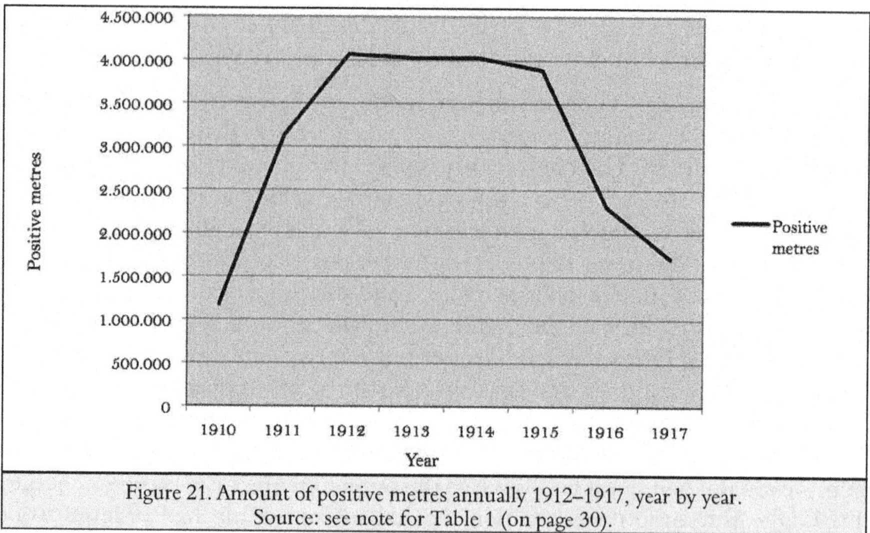

Figure 21. Amount of positive metres annually 1912–1917, year by year. Source: see note for Table 1 (on page 30).

The De Giglio contract is not unique; similar contracts exist, for instance the one for the Russian market between Nordisk and the company Thiemann & Reinhardt.[540] One of the big international distributors, the Frenchman Louis Aubert, who among other things had access to the South-American market, entered into similar contracts with Nordisk.[541] Aubert applied to Nordisk for the new long films, which no other company could deliver on a regular basis.[542] Aubert became one of Nordisk's biggest customers in the company's glory days. Nordisk's competitive advantage consisted of being the first company to reorganize its production to accommodate feature films, and this enabled Nordisk to obtain the advantageous distribution agreements.

In 1913, Nordisk started bypassing intermediate agents by selling directly through the exclusive rights system to cinemas in Germany. Frost claimed that Nordisk was the first company to rent directly to the cinemas.[543] In October 1913, Nordisk established its second branch in Frankfurt am Main, Germany, and yet another one in Düsseldorf in the spring of 1914.[544] In Britain, Nordisk launched direct rental in November 1914.[545]

Nordisk's production increased when it started making long feature films. From having produced 1,168,462 metres positive film in 1910, the number rose to about 4 million metres a year until 1915 (see Figure 21).

540 NFS:XII,31:21.DFI. Unpagn. Agreement between A/S Nordisk Films Co., Copenhagen, and the gentlemen P. Thiemann & F. Reinhardt (20 November 1912).

541 E.g. for Brazil. NFS:XII,31:5-19.DFI. Agreement between Nordisk Films Co. and L. Aubert, Paris (28 May 1912).

542 See Blom, *Jean Desmet*, 29.

543 NFS:II,30.DFI, 140. Letter from Harald Frost to Nordisk Films Co. Ltd., London (3 February 1914). Pathé Frères was probably the first as the company rented to its local firms in France and Germany.

544 *Der Kinematograph*, no. 355 (15 October 1913).

545 NFS:II,33.DFI, 760. Letter from Harald Frost to Nordisk Films Co. Ltd., London (24 October 1914).

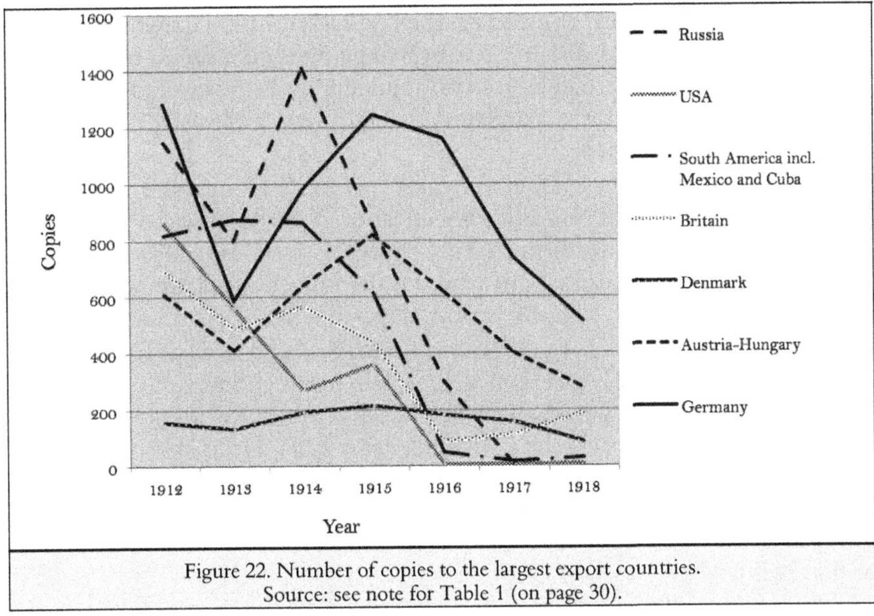

Figure 22. Number of copies to the largest export countries.
Source: see note for Table 1 (on page 30).

In the years just before World War I, the millions of metres of film were exported worldwide, largely speaking. In Europe, the biggest markets were Germany and Russia, and outside Europe, South America was the company's biggest customer (see Figure 22).

The films from Nordisk reached far and wide through a small but steady network of agents. In the early 1910s, the company's network consisted of nine agents and three main foreign offices (see Table 4).

Table 4: Nordisk's distribution-network in the early 1910s

Foreign Offices:	**Nordische Films Co., G.m.b.H. Berlin:** Germany, The Netherlands Offices in Frankfurt am Main and Düsseldorf **Nordisk Films Co. Ltd., London:** Great Britain, Australia, New Zealand, the British colonies, China, Japan **Great Northern, New York:** USA, Canada Office in Minneapolis
Agents:	**J.B. Turull Fournols, Barcelona:** Spain, Portugal, the Philippines, Chile **A/S De Giglio, Copenhagen:** Italy, Finland **Oestereicher & Szilagvi, Sofia:** Bulgaria, Rumania, Turkey, the Balkans **Louis Aubert, Paris:** France, Belgium, Switzerland, Brazil, Argentine, Chile, Paraguay, Uruguay, Bolivia, Peru **Fotorama, Copenhagen:** Denmark, Norway, Sweden **Santos y Artigas, Havana:** Cuba, Mexico **Projectograph, Budapest:** Hungary **Projectograph, Wien:** Austria, Northern Italy **Société Thiemann, Reinhardt, Osipov & Co., Moscow:** Russia

The favourable multiyear contracts and its well-established network of agents and branches placed Nordisk in a position to plan production more systematically than if its films were to be sold off individually as they were made, and it guaranteed sales, which was mandatory if such a large and costly film production was to be maintained.

The transition to the more demanding feature films and the rise in production led to a radical change in Nordisk's organization. Film production was divided into departments, and decision-making processes were moved from the production team to the management who did the long-term planning and coordinated production between the various departments.

Before 1910 it is somewhat unclear who actually decided what films were to be made at Nordisk. To a certain degree, the production team under Viggo Larsen decided on its own productions. Olsen contributed ideas for the films and had some say in the choice of subject. After 1907, Nordisk received script ideas, but again, it is uncertain who approved or rejected the ideas.[546] The minutes of a board meeting in August 1911, after Nordisk had become a limited company, shed some light on who made the decisions about what films to make at that point:

> From now on, Skaarup, Stæhr, Schnedler Sørensen and Blom bear the responsibility for the film texts that are accepted for production until an arrangement can be made concerning a weekly reading in the presence of the above mentioned gentlemen and Kjerulff [sic] together with a representative of the board.[547]

Responsibility for the selection of scripts was divided between the two managers Skaarup and Stæhr, who represented the business, whereas Schnedler-Sørensen and August Blom were in charge of the artistic aspects. Moreover, journalist Alfred Kjerulf was present at the meetings. In April 1911, he had been hired to "read, revise and prepare film ideas submitted to us for consideration and possible purchase".[548] The employment of Kjerulf should be seen in connection with the transition to the production of feature films which demanded more planning already at the script stage. It is doubtful whether the weekly meetings allowed time to read scripts aloud to each other; it was probably more a matter of pitching and discussing which ideas and scripts could pass muster.

When Kjerulf was hired, Nordisk established a script department that was to be expanded when they hired Laurids Skands in the winter of 1912 or spring of 1913. It was further expanded in April 1913 with Carl Theodor Dreyer, Arnold Vilhelm Olsen in 1914, Valdemar Andersen in April 1915 and finally with Carl Gandrup in January 1916,[549] each of whom had a special field in the

546 E.g. NFS:II,1.DFI, 243. Letter from E. Hansen to Particulier L. Bønnelykke (26 July 1907); NFS:II,3.DFI, 650. Letter from E. Hansen to E. Rasch, Kolding (10 May 1907).

547 NFS:I,25.DFI. Unpagn. Minutes of the Board of Directors Meeting (19 August 1911). Schnedler Sørensen changed his name to Schnedler-Sørensen with a hyphen around 1913.

548 NFA. Agreement between Alfred Kjerulf and Nordisk Films Kompagni (21 April 1911).

549 See Stephan Michael Schröder, "Screenwriting for Nordisk 1906–1918", in Dan Nissen and Lisbeth Richter Larsen (ed.), *100 Years of Nordisk Film*, 102–103.

department. Dreyer chiefly worked with scripts based on novels, and A.V. Olsen was hired to work with short comedies and farces. The department was first based in the company offices at Vimmelskaftet, but at the behest of film director Robert Dinesen, it moved to Valby in order to be closer to the sets, which was practical in the case of scenes that had to be changed. A small pavilion was erected for the writers, and in the winter, when there were no shoots, they convened in the actors' dressing rooms.[550]

In 1916, Kjerulf could report that Nordisk received around 2,000 manuscripts a year from all over the world, mostly from Germany.[551] A. V. Olsen's estimate was, however, that 95 per cent of the submissions were useless.[552] Among the preserved scripts, several have notes added by the management. In the script VAGABONDENS HÆVN (THE TRAMP'S REVENGE, director unknown, 1912), Stæhr has noted: "No – the last trick in the idea may be used – either more comical situations must be added, or we will pay 15 kroner for the idea and then write the script ourselves."[553] "Much too strong, but good, can be used as it stands", Ole Olsen noted in the script for DEN UNDVEGNE (CONVICTS NO. 10 AND NO. 13, August Blom 1911).[554] The notes on the scripts show that the management closely followed the suggestions and not least that they had influence on them.

The goal of the weekly meetings at which the selection of scripts took place changed over time. It appears from a set of rules carried on a director's meeting in November 1915 that Blom, the artistic manager of the company, together with the other directors, was given the mandate to decide which scripts they wanted to realize. The final word, however, remained with the management,[555] and the reason for this was probably to achieve certain standards in the transition to feature films. It was not only a matter of selecting the stories but also of developing a clear strategy for the content of the films. In his memoirs, Ole Olsen writes:

> We had to be careful and make the films in such a way that they could be understood everywhere. As an example I might mention that a film could not be sold in England if a man walked through a bedroom, even if no one else was in the room. At the peak of our production we had, in addition to actors and artists, seventeen hundred employees, all of whom needed a steady income, and because of this it was of no use at all having loads of clever people telling us what we should shoot. They couldn't pay the bills, when they came in, if we shot the wrong pictures.[556]

550 Interview with A.V. Olsen. DFI.

551 "Akademiet for 'Tilskæring' af Filmskomedier", *Folkets Avis* (22 April 1916).

552 Interview with A.V. Olsen. DFI.

553 Manuscript no. 914, NFS. DFI. Version A, backside of page 3.

554 Manuscript no. 786, NFS. DFI, 1.

555 NFS:VIII,22:19.DFI. Unpagn. Minutes of Directors Meeting (13 November 1915).

556 Olsen, *Filmens Eventyr og mit eget*, 105.

What is striking about Olsen's statement is that in his mind there is little difference between making a film "understood everywhere" and getting it past the often obscure and culturally contingent censorship regulations – in this case the British censors and their monitoring of sexual morality. Although Olsen doesn't explain the exact reason for the banning of the unnamed film, he was right: indeed, British censorship would not, in fact, accept a film in which a young man invited a young woman into a room that contained a bed, even if it was actually a divan.[557]

In-house censorship and self-regulation were integrated parts of Nordisk's film production. "Scholars usually distinguish broadly between two kinds of control over the movie content", writes Matthew Bernstein, and continues: "One is the external control of the film industry."[558] External control is the official censorship enforced by the state or local officials to prevent themes, subjects or plots that run counter to morality. "A second type of effort at controlling movie content is frequently characterized as 'self-regulation'", Bernstein notes.[559] Self-regulation is founded on the film company's assumptions about what the audience wants and what will make people buy tickets for the film.

To a significant degree, Nordisk's self-regulation rested on the censorship rules of the various countries, and the question remains whether Nordisk actually distinguished between external censorship and the company's own internal self-regulation. In its production policy, Nordisk tried to satisfy censors and audiences alike around the world. Janet Staiger writes of the film companies' self-regulation: "Self-censorship was also profitable in that it encouraged a product acceptable to all cultural groups."[560] Staiger's point corresponds with Olsen's notion of making films "understood everywhere". Olsen had an obligation to make money for the company, the employees – and himself. In his memoirs, Olsen is very specific about the type of films his company should produce:

> I certainly knew the taste of the people so well that I knew that they wanted to see something from lives far from their own, as life was lived in places they couldn't go. The young people wanted to see beautiful parties with elegant dresses [...]. They would also like to see how a count, a baron or a king lived, and how he ate his dinner.[561]

Judging by the success of Nordisk's films, Olsen may have been right. The audience wanted to see how life was lived in the upper strata. Conversely, Nordisk had found out which films not to make; Olsen reports that he quickly

557 See Schröder, *Ideale Kommunikation*, 357.

558 Matthew Bernstein, *Controlling Hollywood. Censorship and Regulation in the Studio Era* (New Brunswick, New Jersey: Rutgers University Press, 1999), 1.

559 Bernstein, *Controlling Hollywood*, 2.

560 David Bordwell, Janet Staiger and Kristin Thompson, *The Classical Hollywood Cinema. Film Style and Mode of Production to 1960* (London: Routledge, 1985), 104.

561 Olsen, *Filmens Eventyr og mit eget*, 77–78.

discovered that literary adaptations were unprofitable.[562] Olsen repeatedly stated that he focused on young audiences, and Viggo Larsen declared the following:

> He had a special talent for finding out what people wanted to see. He would point with his crooked finger and say: "Larsen, if you wish to know what people want to see, listen to what young people are talking about. What they talk about is what we're going to make."[563]

What Olsen chose not to make was erotic films. In the late 1908, Stæhr could report to the Vienna branch: "We definitely don't make risqué films, and we are surprised that you can use such when you or the police discard DRONNINGENS KÆRLIGHED (LA TOSCA, Viggo Larsen, 1908) due to the risqué double bed."[564] In 1907, Nordisk had caused a scandal with the film MORDET PAA FYN, based on a real murder case in April that same year in the town of Holse, where an imbecile farmhand had murdered the farmer's daughter. The film gave Nordisk a hint of how far they could go before offending public morals. The film was partly the reason that the first censorship rules were introduced in Denmark. Film censorship was managed in Copenhagen by the theatre censor, and in the provinces by local commissioners of police. SHERLOCK HOLMES II/RAFFLES' FLUGT FRA FÆNGSLET (RAFFLES' ESCAPE FROM PRISON, Viggo Larsen, 1908) exemplifies the censorship rules; it was forbidden in the town of Kolding. Olsen approached the local police chief who was also the mayor:

> I write to you partly because it is of the utmost urgency for my business to know which moral precautions to take, and partly because the film in question has been outlawed nowhere else in the world but by you, Mr. Mayor.[565]

Already in 1908, Olsen was interested in knowing which measures to take regarding avoiding censorship. Nordisk's correspondence shows how important it was to observe the censorship rules in the various markets if export levels were to be maintained. To a potential Russian agent, Olsen wrote in 1907 that Nordisk produced films that passed muster in all countries: "Our factory does not produce anything that is not in accord with Russian censorship."[566] Olsen advertised Nordisk's talent for adapting to censorship rules almost like a marketing tool. Censorship compliance was indeed part of the planning, as Nordisk explained to a Swedish customer:

> In the course of the season, we will release many finely written and well-acted plays made with those countries in mind that have new censorship rules, and we expect that you will be pleased with our new productions.[567]

562 Ibid., 76.

563 Interview with Viggo Larsen. DFI. "Hvordan de skabte deres Livs Værk VII. Ved Leo Tandrup. Fhv. Generaldirektør Ole Olsen, skaberen af den første dramatiske film i verden siger: FORSTAA UNGDOMMEN!", *Berlingske Søndag* (10 February1935).

564 NFS:II,8.DFI, 494. Letter from Wilhelm Stæhr to Hans Christensen, Vienna (23 October 1908).

565 NFS:II,8.DFI, 860. Letter from Ole Olsen to the Mayor in Kolding (28 November 1908).

566 NFS:II,6.DFI, 184. Letter from Ole Olsen to Khanjonkoff & Cie., Moscow (19 October 1907).

567 NFS:II,1.DFI, 257. Letter from E. Hansen to Particulier L. Bønnelykke (26 July 1907).

Despite such caution, some Nordisk films were still banned outright; as menitioned above, DEN HVIDE SLAVINDE was banned in Kristiania (today Oslo) in 1907.[568] It was not always easy for Nordisk to anticipate censorship regulations and public taste. The cultural differences between the countries played a part. The flaying of a bear in ISBJØRNEJAGT (Polar Bear Hunt, Viggo Larsen, 1907) caused offence in London and rendered the film unsellable;[569] nudity would not do in USA.[570]

The company's experiences with public taste was formalized around 1910. In a letter, Stæhr advised scriptwriter Holger Ibsen to adhere to four guidelines. The first two were concerned the formal requirements of a script, but the last two dealt with censorship and self-regulation:

> 3. Illegalities like murder, adultery, procuring and the like must not be included.
>
> 4. The plot must not cater specifically to the taste of a Danish audience but must be suited to an international audience as well.[571]

These directions reappear in Nordisk's official set of "Guidelines for Scriptwriters" which the company had formulated around January 1912, and which were translated into German later that year.[572] The instructions were often sent to scriptwriters whose works had been rejected by Nordisk, and they consisted of ten items to keep in mind if the scriptwriter wished to have a script accepted by Nordisk. Many of the guidelines concerned practical or pragmatic issues; for example that the script should be typewritten or at least written in a legible hand; how much one could expect to be paid for a script; that a film should include at least one amiable character; and so on. But some of the guidelines derived from the internal self-regulation of the company, and they are quite revealing. We find the following instructions about the content of the films:

> 5. Crimes like murder, theft, counterfeiting and the like, must absolutely not be shown but only suggested.
>
> 6. The action has to take place in the present day and play out among the upper classes. Dramas that take place among people of humble means and farmers will not be accepted. Stories about knights, historical and national dramas are equally unacceptable.
>
> 7. Nor is it allowed to write anything derogatory or unfavourable about royalty, persons of authority, priests or military officers. Nihilism, anarchism and suchlike may not be introduced.[573]

The instruction given under item number six that national matters must be played down is consistent with the letter in which Stæhr wrote that the films should cater to an "international audience", and in which he emphasizes

568 NFS:II,3.DFI, 117. Letter from Ole Olsen to G. Knudsen, Kristiania (19 January 1907).

569 NFS:II,3.DFI, 483. Letter from E. Hansen to Raleigh & Robert, Paris (13 April 1907).

570 NFS:II,8.DFI, 896. Letter from Wilhelm Stæhr to Ingvald C. Oes, New York (2 December 1908).

571 NFS:II,14.DFI, 92. Letter from Wilhelm Stæhr to Holger Ibsen (7 November 1910).

572 See Schröder, "Screenwriting for Nordisk 1906–1918", 100.

573 Erik Nørgaard, *Levende Billeder i Danmark* (Copenhagen: Lademann, 1971), 99. The official "Guidelines for Scriptwriters" have been lost, but the original document is reproduced in Nørgaard's book.

Nordisk's international profile. The obscuring of the films' Danish origin could be seen in various ways. Already during production, Nordisk would change or delete Danish identifiers and target the films at other countries. For a film that was to be exported to Portugal, Nordisk asked the translator of the intertitles to come up with the name of a Portuguese park that looked like the local Frederiksberg Gardens, and the characters Lilli Stine, and Jens were to be given Portuguese names.[574] Nordisk asked the various branches and agents to send samples of the telegram forms, magazines and newspapers of their respective countries so these could be inserted in the film to provide as much local authenticity as possible.[575]

Items 5 and 7 express the morals of the time and the efforts to accommodate the censorship regulations of the various countries. Political subjects were a minefield in the years prior to World War I, and item 7 attempts to prevent disputes. An example of the downplaying of political subjects is to be found in a 1913 letter from Alfred Kjerulf, head of the Story Department, to the scriptwriter Harriet Bloch. Kjerulf had intended to buy Bloch's script *Socialistens Hustru* (The Wife of the Socialist), but after conferring with Olsen he chose to reject the script for the following reason: "In Germany the censor is particularly watchful of a workers' revolt."[576] Two years earlier, in 1911, Nordisk had actually produced DØDSFLUGTEN (FLIGHT TO DEATH, Eduard Schnedler-Sørensen, 1911) about a group of nihilists whose awful plans are revealed by a young count. The film had a successful sale of 138 copies, against the average of 60 copies that a film could expect to sell in 1911.[577] This success suggests that there was a market for films about nihilists, anarchists and other revolutionary groups, but censorship rules must have changed enough after the release of DØDSFLUGTEN that films with revolutionary or subversive themes no longer got past the censor.

Olsen's assumption that most people wanted to get a keyhole view of life in the upper classes is evident in item 6 which states that Nordisk did not accept stories about people in the lower strata. Yet even though the guidelines clearly state that historical films would be rejected, Nordisk did indeed make historical films, such as REVOLUTIONSBRYLLUP (THE HEART OF LADY ALAINE, August Blom, 1915), but they are exceptions to the rule. The reason for not accepting scripts with knights or historical themes is likely to be found in the international film industry of the time. The Italian film companies had specialised in spectacular historical dramas with elaborate sets and hundreds of extras, and Nordisk could not compete. In her book *History of British Film* (1949), Rachael Low notes the tendency of national film industries to specialize in particular genres. Low writes that the Americans made romantic dramas, the Italians

574 NFS:II,16.DFI, 442. Letter from Frede Skaarup to Translator Roepstorff (21 July 1911).

575 NFS:II,17.DFI, 374. Letter from Harald Frost to L. Aubert (2 November 1911); NFS:II,17.DFI, 398. Letter from Harald Frost to Ingvald C. Oes (3 November 1911).

576 Schrøder, *Ideale Kommunkation*, 356, note 1131.

577 NFS:XI,1.DFI, 23. Protocol of Negatives.

favoured spectacular films, the British preferred the situation drama, whereas Nordisk focused on the social drama which Low defines as "the dramatic conflict of human emotions with social conventions".[578] The Danish film historian Ebbe Neergaard agrees with Low's assessment, but with the following caveat: "The term 'social' is not to be understood as the kind of attitude towards society or class issues, as the word presently denotes", Neergaard explains.[579] On the contrary, the social drama is about the contrast between the upper classes and the lower levels in society, "depicted not as a socially (changeable) phenomenon, but as a destiny which could be changeable only for the individual".[580] Neergaard emphasizes that the reason for the repetition of this theme was because it was interesting to audiences at the time.[581]

Perhaps the most characteristically Danish film genre at the time was the "erotic melodrama". "Star-crossed love affairs, the *ménage à trois*, and jealousy, justified or baseless, were subjects endlessly taken up and explored", writes Marguerite Engberg.[582] Already by 1910, AFGRUNDEN, starring Asta Nielsen, had established the erotic melodrama as a Danish speciality in the mind of the audiences:

> Danish films soon got a reputation for being daring, and, consequently, they were heavily cut by the censors in many places, if not totally banned. It was not only the choice of subject, but also the execution that caused Danish film to be considered both "lascifs" and "scabreux".[583]

American film historian Mark Sandberg emphasizes that the reputation of Danish film was due to by a combination of their multi-reel length and their sexual themes,[584] and Sandfeld quotes a request to the Minister of Justice in 1913 from the right-wing politician Oscar Ellinger, who protested that "morally subversive films do not come from Paris, but from Copenhagen".[585]

Like Low, Richard Abel points to special national characteristics in European films:

> "While producers such as Cines in Italy concentrated on lavish historical reconstructions and those in Denmark specialized in sometimes risqué, contemporary films, the French ranged across the spectrum of so-called serious drama."[586]

An awareness of the international competition probably lay behind the rule

578 Low, *The History of British Film*, 206.

579 Neergaard, *Historien om dansk film*, 39.

580 Ibid.

581 See ibid.

582 Engberg, *Dansk stumfilm*, 441.

583 Ibid. Engberg quoted "lascifs" and "scabreux" from Sadoul, *Histoire générale du cinéma II*, 183 and translated them as "lascivious" and "lewd".

584 See Mark Sandberg, "Pocket Movies. Souvenir Cinema Programmes and the Danish Silent Cinema", *Film History*, vol. 13, no. 1 (2001): 10.

585 Sandfeld, *Den stumme scene*, 278.

586 Abel, *The Cine Goes to Town*, 299.

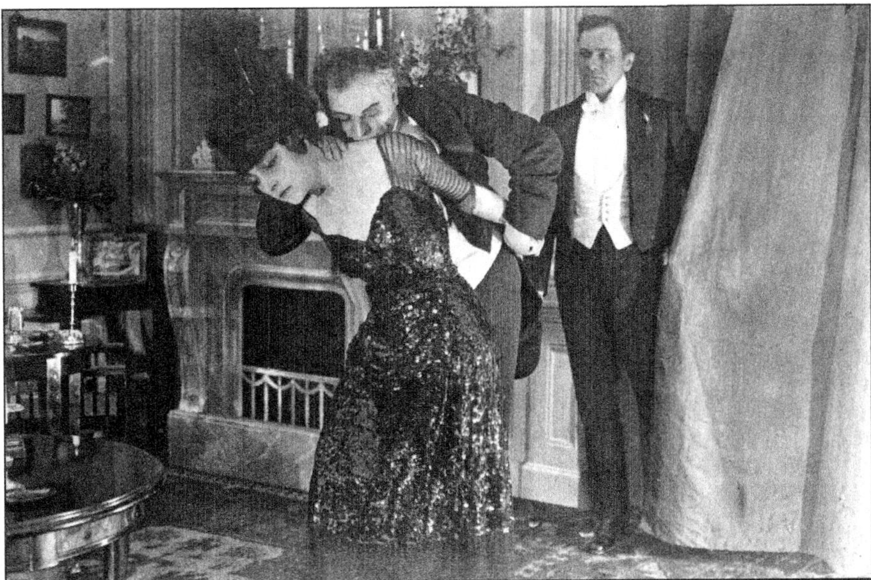

Figure 23. The erotic melodrama. Count Waldberg (Valdemar Psilander) surprises the jeweller Hirsch (Gunnar Helsengreen) and Stella (Asta Nielsen) in DEN SORTE DRØM. Courtesy of DFI/Stills & Posters Archive.

rejecting historical screenplays. Nordisk did not want to compete with film genres that other companies specialized in. At the same time, Nordisk sent a clear signal to its buyers about what kind of film to expect from Nordisk. A slightly altered version of the guidelines was made in 1917 and included a new provision:

> In view of the strict censorship codes, the author must be extremely careful in his choice of subjects and material. Everything that can be considered unaesthetic, titillating or brutalizing must be avoided.[587]

In contrast to the guidelines from 1912, the consideration of censorship is explicitly included in the new version. According to these guidelines, a script could be rejected by Nordisk either for being "[...] unoriginal, too ordinary in its content or contrary to censorship codes".[588]

The problem of censorship had become an important issue for the Danish film industry. As Schröder emphasizes, it is striking that the entire first chapter of the first Danish manual for scriptwriting, Jens Locher's *Hvorledes skriver man en film* (How to Write a Film) from 1916, concerns censorship restrictions.[589] Even before addressing the directions and principles of the art of scriptwriting, Locher warns: "Almost all countries have introduced a special film censor who has the power to prohibit films."[590] Later in the manual, the entire set of

587 NFS:VIII,1:4.DFI. Instruktioner for Filmsforfattere, Copenhagen (1 March 1917).

588 NFS:VIII,1:4.DFI. Instruktioner for Filmsforfattere, Copenhagen (1 March 1917).

589 See Schröder, *Ideale Kommunikation*, 353.

590 Jens Locher, *Hvorledes skriver man en Film?* (Copenhagen: V. Pios Boghandel – Povl Branner, 1916), 8.

Nordisk guidelines for scriptwriters is reproduced, and Locher's comment clearly indicates the importance of censorship and self-regulation in the Danish film industry; his inclusion of all of the Nordisk guidelines indicates how dominant a position the company held in Denmark. Locher, the editor of the trade magazine *Filmen*, had no great personal success as a scriptwriter; in 1915 and 1916, four of his scripts were rejected by Nordisk.[591] It was not until he became artistic director at Nordisk in the second half of the 1920s that his scripts were accepted and produced.

The novelty of the long feature films wore off in a few years, however, the London branch began to shorten the films, to the dismay of the management in Copenhagen. But, Nordisk allowed:

> [...] if it is your firm conviction that sales in England will improve (disregarding the number of copies) by reducing the length of the films, we will overcome the technical difficulties and allow you to reduce the length wherever you find it financially necessary, and where we find it artistically defensible.[592]

The upshot was that instead of letting the London branch edit the films, the printing laboratory shortened the films sent to Britain so they did not exceed 900–1,000 metres.[593] When this decision was made, the management sent the following memo to their directors: "Due to the change in sales, no production must exceed 1,000–1,200 Metres unless it has been discussed at the main office of the company."[594] This regulation exemplifies how sensitive Nordisk was to changes. The company was quick to respond to new conditions, in this case by adapting the films to the requirements of the British market.

On the whole, Nordisk kept a close eye on developments in various international markets; all through the silent era, the company subscribed to all the major international trade magazines. These sources allowed the company to follow the ways in which censorship rules changed around the world. In 1915, this attentiveness resulted in yet another initiative to adapt Nordisk's films to different markets. At a meeting in November 1915, a new set of rules for the directors was decided upon. One of the rules was: "If a film should contain scenes which might be banned by the censor in certain countries, the director must shoot two different scenes, one decorous and one more explicit."[595] Censorship considerations were no longer something that applied only to scriptwriting; it also had to be taken into account during the film shoots. In connection with the release in Britain of MIDNATSSOLEN (THE MIDNIGHT SUN, Robert Dinesen, 1916), Frost could inform the London branch that "[...]

591 NFA. Letter from Anne Christensen to Jens Locher (10 July 1915). Letter from Anne Christensen to Jens Locher (28 October 1915). Letter from Valdemar Andersen to Jens Locher (30 October 1915). Letter from Jens Locher to Nordisk Films Kompagni (26 August 1916).

592 NFS:II,28.DFI, 133. Letter from Harald Frost to Nordisk Films Co. Ltd., London (10 October 1913).

593 NFS:II,28.DFI, 415. Letter from Rotkjær to Nordisk Films Co. Ltd., London (30 October 1913).

594 E.g. NFS:II,28.DFI, 441. Letter from Wilhelm Stæhr to August Blom, Nordisk Films Co.'s Studio, Valby (31 October 1913).

595 NFS:VIII,22:19.DFI. Unpagn. Minutes of meeting of film directors (13 November 1915).

the scene with the Negro execution has been made in such a way that it may be edited out with no damage to the film."[596] In other words, the scene in question had been incorporated in the plot so gingerly that its removal would not render the story unintelligible.

Another point from the 1915 rules specifies that Nordisk's management would keep directors and scriptwriters informed about censorship regulations in various countries so that measures could be taken already in pre-production, and on 6 December 1915, Censorship memorandum no. 1 was distributed to directors and the Story Department at Nordisk. Issuing internal memoranda, which were often stamped "confidential", remained standard company procedure until no. 50, issued on 6 October 1920.[597] In these memos, excerpts from letters and information from Nordisk's branches and distributors were passed on to the directors and the Story Department of the company. The information they contain mainly deals with individual films and the reasons why they had been banned in a particular country, or what cuts and alterations had been necessary to get a film approved by a censorship board. The memoranda also contained general information about the management's decisions about future policies regarding the content of films. Many of the recurring reasons for cuts or bans correlate with the topics warned against in the guidelines for scriptwriters. The depiction of crime in whatever form was often the cause of prohibition and frequently earned the censors' verdict of "brutalizing".[598] Another theme that drew the censor's attention was eroticism. The New York branch reported that an intertitle saying "The following morning" had to be removed because it contained a hint of a sexual encounter.[599] Besides information about which films had been censored and why, the memoranda also informed about the company's production policy. Due to Denmark's neutrality in World War I, Nordisk could maintain its export to both the Entente- and the Central Powers[600], for which reason Nordisk advised its affiliates about the use of uniforms:

> Under certain circumstances, we repeat again, uniforms must be avoided if possible, and they should therefore only be used in cases of unavoidable necessity, when the person in question appears in uniform according to his official position. This precaution is dictated not only because of censorship concerns, but mainly because it is extraordinarily difficult at present to sell films with uniforms in them. As mentioned earlier, there have been occasions in which uniforms, even when they had been diligently designed to be as neutral as possible, still caused offence in Britain for being "German" and in Germany for being "English".[601]

596 NFS:II,30.DFI, 332. Letter from Harald Frost to A/S Fotorama (14 February 1914).

597 Only censorship memo no. 44 is lost; the remaining 49 are kept in the Nordisk Film Collection.

598 NFS:II,56:12.DFI, 1–2. Censur Cirkulære no. 12 (6 June 1916).

599 NFS:II,16.DFI, 128. Letter from A. Jensen to Nordisk Films Kompagni, Valby (14 June 1911).

600 The two overall belligerent powers during World War I were the Entente and the Central Powers. The Entente was an alliance between the French Republic, the British Empire and the Russian Empire. On the other side, the Central Powers consisted of Germany, Austria-Hungary, the Ottoman Empire and Bulgaria.

601 NFS:II,56:8.DFI, 2. Censur Cirkulære no. 7 (9 May 1916).

During World War I, subjects like war, espionage and military matters were avoided: "[...] films in which war scenes, battlefield scenes, camp hospital scenes and the like occur will in the first place not pass the censorship in any of the belligerent countries, and secondly will not be tolerated by audiences in these countries",[602] stated the Nordisk management in a memo. In this case, the company tried to please both censorship and audiences.

The memoranda also reported positive comments from the branches and agents. About the film HOTEL PARADIS (HOTEL "PARADISE", Robert Dinesen, 1917), the German branch writes: "The film is in every detail so cleverly thought out that the censorship board could hardly have any reason to object."[603] The German branch praised the way in which the well-executed film got away with including criminal actions and themes by only hinting at them, and thereby dodging the censors. Nordisk's management concludes that this "[...] confirms that nearly any subject can be treated in such a way that the finished film will observe the censorship rules".[604] In another memorandum, the Berlin branch informs the company that it is sceptical of the film HVO, SOM ELSKER SIN FADER (HE WHO LOVES HIS FATHER, Holger-Madsen, 1916) because the branch believes it is "avowedly a man's film".[605] This remark from the German branch caused Nordisk's management to stress later in the memorandum that such male-centred films are considered problematic:

> This is undoubtedly correct. In all countries the 'weaker' sex makes up the majority of the cinema audience, and it is mainly due to films that please the ladies that the theatres make a profit. This information is for you gentlemen directors to consider in your choice of subjects.[606]

When the management encouraged the directors and writers to make films that appeal to an important section of the ticket-buying audience, i.e. women, this proves Staiger's point that self-censorship also meant making a product acceptable to different cultural groups, and thereby ensuring the profits of the films.[607] The necessary consideration of the spectators arises again in the memorandum's discussion about the choice of actors. The Berlin branch warns of the danger of using one of the stock actors, Alf Blütecher, as a villain because filmgoers had grown accustomed to him playing the part of a young attractive lover.[608] The objection to actors playing both heroes and villains is repeated in a later memorandum.[609]

Often the censorship rules changed, as the London branch reported: "There have to be as many bathing ladies as possible in the comedies, and the bathing

602 NFS:II,56:11.DFI. Censur Cirkulære no. 11 (30 May 1916).

603 NFS:XII,86:5.DFI. Censur Cirkulære no. 21 (26 February 1917).

604 NFS:XII,86:5.DFI. Censur Cirkulære no. 21 (26 February 1917).

605 NFS:II,56:10.DFI. Censur Cirkulære no. 10 (30 May 1916).

606 NFS:II,56:10.DFI. Censur Cirkulære no. 10 (30 May 1916).

607 See Bordwell, Staiger and Thompson, *The Classical Hollywood Cinema*, 104.

608 NFS:II,56:14.DFI, 2. Censur Cirkulære no. 14 (10 July 1916).

609 NFS:II,56:40.DFI. Censur Cirkulære no. 46 (16 September 1916).

suits must be smart and tight-fitting."[610] This could suggest that the British censors were beginning to soften up on erotic subjects. Unsurprisingly, it was difficult to deal with the different individual tastes in so many countries. Or as the Berlin branch despairingly complained when the censor had cut a scene because it contained an accident: "If accidents are also prohibited, what then are we going to film?"[611]

Nordisk's censorship memos are early examples of organized marketing research in the film industry. Both Adolph Zukor and Carl Laemmle have reported that, as nickelodeon owners, they observed the reaction of their audiences. Apart from such unstructured surveys, market polls became popular in the inter-war period and thereby followed the development in other lines of business.[612] Nordisk's self-regulation and self-censorship, present from the beginnings of the company, were formalized with the advent of long feature films. The guidelines to scriptwriters as well as the rules for directors and censorship memos all exemplify the efforts of the company to control the contents of the films in order to meet the varying demands and expectations of audiences on the international markets.

In 1912 and 1913, Russia was Nordisk's second-largest export market, surpassed only by Germany, and in 1914 the Russian market became Nordisk's largest. An article from the Russian film magazine *Kinogazeta* from 1918 reads:

> All's well that ends well! This is the guiding principle of foreign cinema. But Russian cinema stubbornly refuses to accept this and goes its own way. Here it's "All's well that ends badly" – we need tragic endings.[613]

The Russian audiences preferred tragic or unhappy endings for the films, so film companies in Russia had made a standard of often producing two endings for their films, a happy ending for export, and a tragic one for the domestic market. Yuri Tsivian believes that this custom originated with the the Moscow-based branch of the French company Pathé which produced films for export. Tsivian mentions NEVESTNA OGNYA (THE BRIDE OF FIRE, André Maître, RUS [1911]) as the first film to be produced with two endings.[614]

Around the same time, Nordisk started producing alternative tragic endings for films made for the Russian market. The idea of alternative endings was not new at Nordisk; in 1908, Stæhr asked the Vienna branch, the company's Italian agent Christofanini and Drankov, Nordisk's the Russian agent at the time, whether an alternative ending would improve the sales potential of DRONNINGENS KÆRLIGHED:

610 NFS:II,56:40.DFI. Censur Cirkulære no. 46 (16 September 1916).

611 Schröder, *Ideale Kommunikation*, 357.

612 See Bakker, *Entertainment Industrialised*, 344–347.

613 *Kinogazeta* quoted in Yuri Tsivian, "Some Prepatory Remarks on Russian Cinema", in *Testimoni silenziosi: Film Russi 1908–1919*, research and co-ordination by Yuri Tsivian (Pordenone: Biblioteca dell'Immagine, London: British Film Institute, 1989), 24.

614 See Yuri Tsivian, "Some Prepatory Remarks on Russian Cinema", 26.

> Since there have been complaints from several places that the film DRONNINGENS KÆRLIGHED does not sell so well because there is a murder near the end, we hereby inform you that the film is available with and without this murder.[615]

It remains uncertain whether the murderless ending was merely an offer or whether it was actually made. With either BALLETDANSERINDEN (THE BALLET DANCER, August Blom, 1911) or JERNBANENS DATTER (THE LITTLE RAILROAD QUEEN, August Blom, 1911), the production of alternative endings became a part of Nordisk's production policy, which coincided with the closing of a distribution deal with the Moscow-based company Thiemann, Reinhardt, Osipov & Co.[616] Russia became an important market for Nordisk and was decisive in the company's decision to produce alternative endings. In a letter, Nordisk writes to Thiemann & Reinhardt in 1913: "Rest assured that we will always, if possible, make a special dramatic ending for Russia. We have already repeatedly given clear orders about this to our directors and literary employees."[617] The practice of making alternative endings spread, and Nordisk soon also provided happy endings for films which originally ended tragically. In a letter from 1916 from Nordisk's artistic manager, August Blom, to director Hjalmar Davidsen, we may read the following: "I beg to remind directors of the previously approved rule, that every film with a sad ending, even if it seems misleading, must always be supplied with an extra ending scene [...]."[618] This appears to be a standard letter issued to all of the directors at Nordisk in the 1916 season. The happy endings were meant for the British and American markets. On occasion, Nordisk would mistake the taste of the audiences in a certain country. Frost responded to a letter from the London branch:

> We have noted your comments about the endings that would be most suitable for Britain. By the way, if it's possible, we do in all cases always create different endings according to the tastes in the different countries. We always aim to hit the English taste, but it is pretty difficult to be consistently lucky in this.[619]

It was not only in Britain that Nordisk could misinterpret the taste of the audience; a similar mistake occurred in Italy: "[...] we note that in the future you [...] desire the same endings of your films for Italy as those we use for Russia."[620]

Whenever the company had released a film with an inpopular ending, another was readily available. For instance, Thiemann & Reinhardt wanted a dramatic ending for SKANDALEN PAA SØRUPGAARD (THE VICAR'S DAUGHTER, Hjalmar

615 NFS:II,8.DFI, 384. Letter from Wilhelm Stæhr to Hans Christensen, Vienna (12 October 1908); NFS:II,8.DFI, 385. Letter from Wilhelm Stæhr to Aleksandr Drankov (12 October 1908); NFS:II,8.DFI, 386. Letter from Wilhelm Stæhr to Christofanini (12 October 1908).

616 NFS:XII,31:20.DFI, 1–3. Copy of contract between Nordisk and P. Thiemann & F. Reinhardt (23 January 1911).

617 NFS:II,24.DFI, 468. Letter from Harald Frost to P. Thiemann & F. Reinhardt, Moscow (26 February 1913).

618 NFS:II,37.DFI, 551. Letter from August Blom to Hjalmar Davidsen (9 October 1916).

619 NFS:II,23.DFI, 630–631. Letter from Harald Frost to Nordisk Films Co., London (14 January 1913).

620 NFS:II,29.DFI, 39. Letter from Harald Frost to A/S de Giglio (6 December 1913).

Davidsen, 1913), in which they desired the main character to commit suicide. Nordisk had made no extra ending for this film, but it was made in the course of a week and was ready to be shipped to Moscow.[621] On one single occasion, Nordisk declined the wish for an alternative ending for the Russian version, since they found that the original ending of HAMMERSLAGET (IN THE HOUR OF TEMPTATION, Robert Dinesen, 1914) was the only logical solution.[622]

It is not easy to say exactly how widely these alternative endings were used. More than half of the scripts of the over 1,100 films Nordisk made between 1911 and 1928 have survived in the Nordisk Special Collection, and amid these we find various indications that at least some had alternative endings. The script for DRAMAET I DEN GAMLE MØLLE (THE DRAMA IN THE OLD MILL, Robert Dinesen, 1913) reads: "N.B. For Russia: it must end with all three dying in the mill, while Bjørner, powerless, looks on".[623] And in the script for MANDEN UDEN SMIL (FATHER SORROW, Holger-Madsen, 1917) we find the following typewritten note: "Note – for England an end scene has to be shot in which the father survives".[624] Mostly, the endings are typewritten, which indicates that they were planned during the development of the script, and only in very few cases does a hastily-written note in shorthand indicate that an alternative ending should be shot, for example for the film DEN DØDSDØMTE (CONDEMNED TO DEATH, Holger-Madsen, 1916).[625]

Aside from the endings we find in the scripts, the nearly 35,000 outgoing letters that have survived from Nordisk's headquarters provide a further resource for identifying films with alternative endings from the company. Six of the actual endings have survived: ET DRAMA PAA HAVET (FIRE AT SEA, Eduard Schnedler-Sørensen, 1912), ATLANTIS, EVANGELIEMANDENS LIV (THE CANDLE AND THE MOTH, Holger-Madsen, 1915), EN FARE FOR SAMFUNDET (LOVE THE CONQUEROR, Robert Dinesen, 1918), BLADE AF SATANS BOG (LEAVES FROM SATAN'S BOOK, Carl Theodor Dreyer, 1921) and PRÆSTEN I VEJLBY (THE HAND OF FATE, August Blom, 1922). For EVANGELIEMANDENS LIV we even have two alternative endings, a Russian and a Swedish one. The Swedish ending is interesting, because it was most likely conceived in order to get the film past the very strict Swedish censorship board, but it is actually the most dramatic version. Contrary to the normal custom of creating Russian and English endings which were employed simply to provide extra choices for Nordisk's

621 NFS:II,27.DFI, 693. Letter from Harald Frost to P. Thiemann & F. Reinhardt, Moscow (13 September 1913). According to Jay Leyda's notes, Russian filmmakers themselves made alternative endings for films with Psilander if such were not delivered from Nordisk. The actor Aleksandr Volkov was Psilander's Russian "double". Tamiment Library NYU, Jay Leyda Collection Box 2, notes on Russian and Soviet film, cuttings 1920–1940. I am grateful to the late Rashit Yangirov for this information. However, I doubt that extra endings with Volkov as Psilander have been common.

622 NFS:II,30.DFI, 344. Letter from Harald Frost to Thiemann, Reinhardt, Osipov & Co., Moscow (14 February 1914).

623 Manuscript no. 1035, NFS.DFI. Version B, last page.

624 Manuscript no. 1496, NFS.DFI. Version A, last page.

625 Manuscript no. 1342, NFS.DFI. Version B, last page.

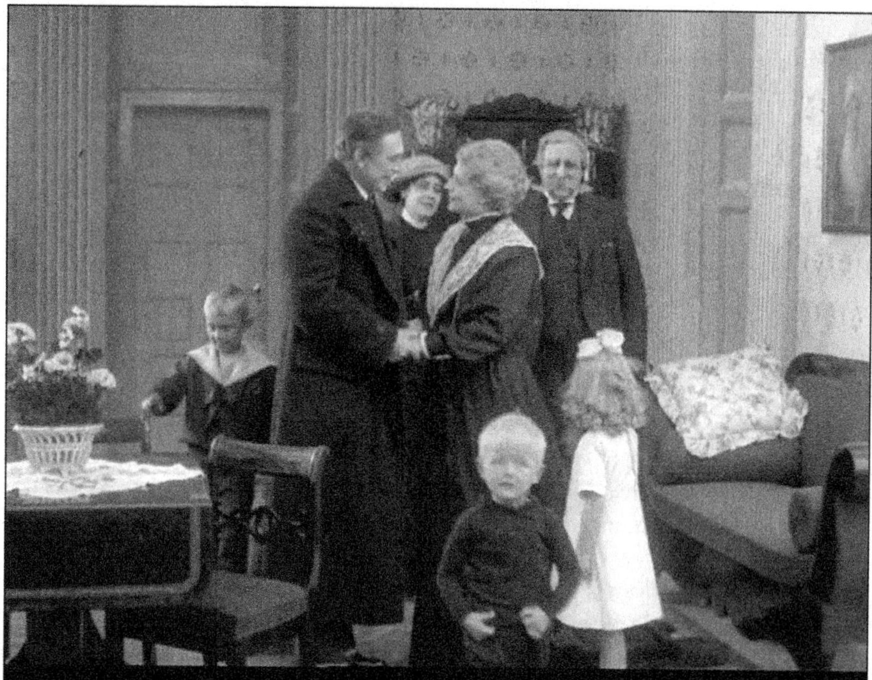

Figure 24. *Above*: in the happy ending of ATLANTIS, Kammacher returns to his children and family with his new wife. *Below*: the Russian ending in which Kammacher suddenly dies of a heart attack. Framegrab: ATLANTIS (August Blom, 1913), Danish Film Institute (DVD).

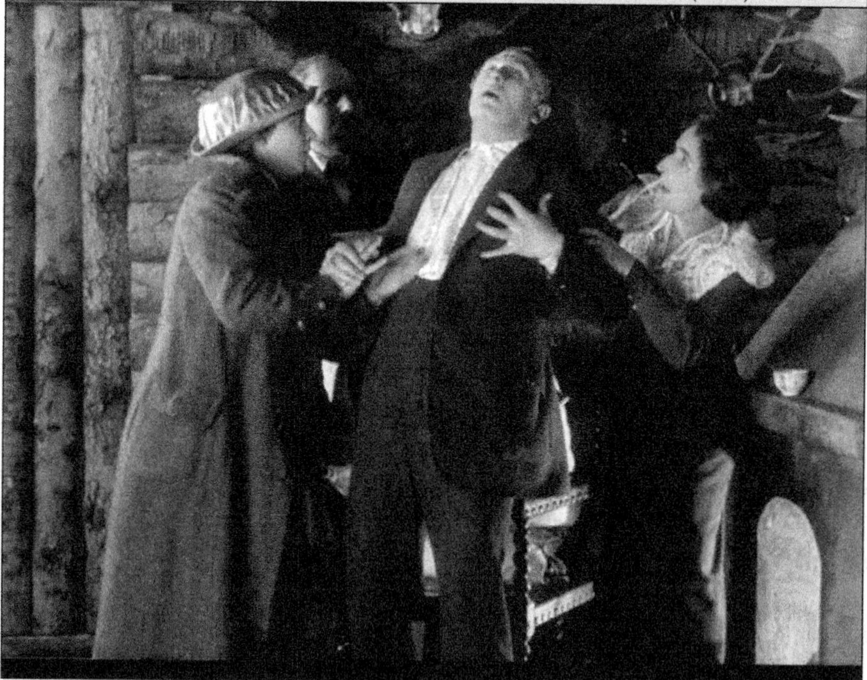

customers, the two endings in this case were a matter of necessity – to get the film approved by the censors. On the basis of surviving films, letters and scripts, we know that at least 55 alternative endings were made from 1911 to 1928 (see Appendix 2). In the scripts for the five films for which alternative endings have survived there are no hints that these endings were planned in advance.[626] This indicates that alternative endings may have been shot even if this was not noted in the script.

The archival material indicates that the habit of making alternative endings was an integral part of Nordisk's production and distribution policy from around 1911 to the late 1920s, and that it was introduced with the advent of long feature films. Apart from small Russian companies, no other company so consistently incorporated the practice of shooting alternative endings. Examples of these are to be found in the Swedish DÖDSRITTEN UNDER CIRKUSPOLEN (THE LAST PERFORMANCE, Georg af Klercker, S 1912) and in American films from the 1920s, such as SUDS (John Francis Dillon, USA 1920), FLESH AND THE DEVIL (Clarence Brown, USA 1926) and THE CROWD (King Vidor, USA 1928), but among the major companies, only Nordisk made it part of its production policy to make endings that would satisfy the varying tastes of the audiences on different markets.

In August 1911, Skaarup predicted: "This year, all the companies are making long films. There are weeks in which ten different films are released, and then you'd better have the best one."[627] Nordisk realized that the other companies would follow suit and start producing feature films as well. With the Exclusive/*Monopolfilm* System, competition between these expensive films had become tougher. The trick for the companies was to brand their films. One way in which Nordisk positioned and differentiated itself on the market was through the company's guidelines for scriptwriters and their censorship memoranda – initiatives that gave the buyers a clear indication that the films from Nordisk probably would not be banned by the censors. The national genre differentiation mentioned by Low and Abel was another way in which Nordisk stood out from its competitors.

Gerben Bakker emphasizes that in the 1910s, when films became more expensive to make, branding became essential to maintaining sales.[628] As an investment, film comes at a great risk. New films are released all the time, and given the relatively short commercial lifespan of a film, the producer has no guarantee of recovering his investment; hence, branding became a way of ensuring a film's success with the audience. Bakker mentions three ways in which the companies chose to brand a film:

626 Peter Schepelern (ed.), *100 års dansk film* (Copenhagen: Rosinante, 2001), 59 states that a Russian ending is outlined at the end of the script for ATLANTIS. The text informs: "In the original scripts these scenes are set apart with an added note, "to Russia" at the top of the page". Several copies of the ATLANTIS script still exist in the Nordisk Collection, but none of these matches the description.

627 NFS:II,16.DFI, 526. Letter from Frede Skaarup to Nordische Films Co., Berlin (1 August 1911).

628 See Bakker, *Entertainment Industrialised*, 277.

1. by extending the brand beyond one product into a series of successive products, using the trademark, the series, or the star.
2. by acquiring an existing brand about which the consumers already had reached a high level of awareness, such as famous plays, novels, or music.
3. by using the film itself as a brand to turn intrinsically unbranded products into premium branded products – for example, by using stars as spokespersons for products or by licensing of what we today call "merchandise-tie-ins".[629]

Bakker concludes that even though film star fees and purchase of literary rights were expensive, it was money well spent. Branding could not guarantee success, but created public attention for the films.[630] Nordisk branded its films through the trademark, film series, film stars and by connecting the films to literary works and famous authors. Nordisk also made use of the third possibility listed by Bakker, although to a lesser degree.

After the advent of long feature films, the company's use of its polar bear trademark intensified. In 1913, Nordisk encouraged the London branch to continue to use the trademark in ads.[631] As for the public, Nordisk stepped up its campaign by printing 10,000 posters with the trademark and the words in German, English or French: "Nordisk film shown today."[632] These posters were sent to branches and agents who would pass them on to the cinemas for display. Later, 100 polar bear posters for marketing in Germany were printed without text.[633] In another marketing initiative Nordisk sent between 2,000 and 5,000 personalized stamps to each of its branches and agents. The stamps could be added to packages, letters etc.[634] Nordisk repeated this marketing action in connection with the film ELSKOVSLEG (LOVE'S DEVOTEE, Holger-Madsen, August Blom, 1914), and for this release, Nordisk also manufactured stickers with stills from the film.[635] The stickers were on sale in the cinemas, and Nordisk regarded this initiative as an experiment.[636]

629 Ibid., 278.

630 See ibid., 312–313.

631 NFS:II,27.DFI, 543. Letter from Harald Frost to Nordisk Films Co. Ltd., London (5 September 1913).

632 NFS:II,27.DFI, 165. Letter from Harald Frost to Nordisk Films Co., London (15 August 1913); NFS:II,27.DFI, 654. Letter from Harald Frost to Andreasen & Lachmann, Copenhagen (11 September 1913).

633 NFS:II,34.DFI, 982. Letter from Harald Frost to Nordische Films Co., Berlin (27 January 1915).

634 NFS:II,27.DFI, 200. Letter from Harald Frost to Great Northern, New York (18 August 1913); NFS:II,27.DFI, 201. Letter from Harald Frost to De Giglio (18 August 1913); NFS:II,27.DFI, 202. Letter from Harald Frost to J.B. Turull Fournols (18 August 1913); NFS:II,27.DFI, 205. Letter from Harald Frost to Aubert (18 August 1913); NFS:II,27.DFI, 206. Letter from Harald Frost to Nordisk Films Co. Ltd., London (18 August 1913); NFS:II,27.DFI, 207. Letter from Harald Frost to Oesterreicher & Szilyagi (18 August 1913); NFS:II,27.DFI, 208. Letter from Harald Frost to P. Thiemann & F. Reinhardt (18 August 1913); NFS:II,27.DFI, 209. Letter from Harald Frost to Projectograph AG, Vienna (18 August 1913); NFS:II,27.DFI, 210. Letter from Harald Frost to Projectograph AG, Budapest (18 August 1913); NFS:II,27.DFI, 211. Letter from Harald Frost to Nordische Films Co., Berlin (18 August 1913); NFS:II,27.DFI, 212. Letter from Harald Frost to Fotorama (18 August 1913).

635 NFS:II,30.DFI, 699. Letter from Harald Frost to Projectograph AG, Budapest (7 March 1914); NFS:II,30.DFI, 700. Letter from Harald Frost to Projectograph AG, Vienna (7 March 1914); NFS:II,30.DFI, 701. Letter from Harald Frost to Thiemann, Reinhardt, Osipov & Co., Moscow (7 March 1914); NFS:II,30.DFI, 702. Letter from Harald Frost to Oesterreicher & Szilyagi, Sofia (7 March

That the audiences knew which companies made which films is evident; in Kharkov, Russia, the cinema Modern issued a questionnaire for its patrons, and when asked "From which country do you prefer your film dramas?" the majority answered France, with Denmark and USA next. In reply to the question of a favourite film company, 916 out of 1313 spectators answered "Nordisk", with Pathé and Vitagraph in second.[637]

Nordisk's films and Nordisk as a company had a good reputation, which others sought to exploit. Frost had heard the following story from an acquaintance in Italy and passed it on to Nordisk's local agent De Giglio:

> In Rome, where I've spent some time, there is a highly-frequented cinema in the main street which advertises "Nordisk Films Co's Pictures". These are usually more successful than the numerous films from Milano and Turin, and they are announced on posters and in souvenir programmes, but it has happened a couple of times that I went to see Danish actors performing (enticed by the announcement: Nordiks [sic]), only to watch films that had nothing whatsoever to do with your company. One time it was an Asta Nielsen Film with German (?) actors, another time I believe they were French.[638]

Frost's letter is not the only example indicating that people other than Nordisk's regular agent in Italy, De Giglio, claimed to have the rights to Nordisk's films. The Italian company Roatto advertised its "monopoly on the famous Nordisk" in Italy,[639] while in Cuba, Nordisk had to advise its Cuban agent Santos y Artigas that other companies' films could not be marketed under Nordisk's name.[640] There are also examples of Nordisk's trademark being registered and patented by other companies. Santos y Artigas patented it in Cuba, but with the aid of the Ministry of Foreign affairs, Nordisk tried to reclaim it,[641] convinced that Santos y Artigas wanted to blackmail Nordisk,[642] and it took a court case to protect the trademark.[643] In Argentina, someone registered Nordisk's trademark in his own name in order to blackmail the company; Nordisk's films were confiscated and would only be released in return for a large sum. Nordisk contacted the temporarily appointed Head of Mission in the Danish embassy in Argentina to solve the case. The

1914); NFS:II,30.DFI, 703. Letter from Harald Frost to A/S Fotorama (7 March 1914); NFS:II,30.DFI, 704. Letter from Harald Frost to Nordisk Films Co. Ltd., London (7 March 1914); NFS:II,30.DFI, 705. Letter from Harald Frost to Great Northern Film Co., New York (7 March 1914); NFS:II,30.DFI, 706. Letter from Harald Frost to Santos y Artigas, Cuba (7 March 1914); NFS:II,30.DFI, 707. Letter from Harald Frost to Turull Fournols, Barcelona (7 March 1914); NFS:II,30.DFI, 715. Letter from Harald Frost to A/S De Giglio (7 March 1914).

636 NFS:II,30.DFI, 859. Letter from Harald Frost to Nordische Films Co. Ltd., London (16 March 1914).

637 *Sine-fono*, no. 8 (1913): 31. I am indebted to Lauri Piispa for this reference.

638 NFS:II,27.DFI, 217. Letter from Harald Frost to A/S De Giglio (19 August 1913).

639 NFS:II,31.DFI, 697–698. Letter from Harald Frost to A/S De Giglio (11 May 1914).

640 NFS:II,30.DFI, 252. Letter from Harald Frost to Santos y Artigas, Havana (10 February 1914).

641 NFS:II,27.DFI, 95. Letter from Harald Frost to the Foreign Ministry's 2nd Department (9 August 1913).

642 NFS:II,34.DFI, 751. Letter from Harald Frost to Ingvald C. Oes, New York (13 January 1915).

643 NFS:I,61:139.DFI. Letter from International Patent Bureau A/S to A/S Nordisk Films Kompagni (22 September 1915).

correspondence does not reveal how the matter ended, but it must have been in Nordisk's favour since the company continued its export to Argentina.[644] The company trademark was effective, and in the early 1920s, Nordisk compared the "polar bear on the globe" with other well-known Danish trademarks such as that of Lurpak Butter and the three wavy lines on Royal Danish Porcelain.[645]

Nordisk had used series of films as a way of branding itself from the very beginning. ISBJØRNEJAGT was followed by other films about exotic big game hunting such as LØVEJAGTEN and BJØRNEJAGT I RUSLAND. DEN HVIDE SLAVEHANDEL led to a series of films about women who were abducted and ended up in brothels. Nordisk even produced films about male victims of slave trade: SHANGHAI'ET aka MÆND SOM OFRE FOR SLAVEHANDEL (SHANGHAIED aka IN THE HANDS OF SHARKERS, Eduard Schnedler-Sørensen, 1912) in which a drunken sailor is tricked into signing on to a ship. Nordisk's slave-trade films launched a wave of similar films. Müller writes about "die 'weiße-Sklavin'-Film-Welle" (the White Female Slave Wave) in Germany,[646] and as early as February 1911, Nordisk complained that the American company Yankee had released the film A SON OF OLD GLORY (director unknown, Yankee Studios, USA 1911) with a plot that was very like one of Nordisk's productions.[647] The following years saw a string of films on the theme of white slave trade, such as TRAFFIC IN SOULS (George Loane Tucker, Independent Moving Pictures Co. of America, USA 1913), THE INSIDE OF THE WHITE SLAVE TRAFFIC (Frank Beal, Moral Feature Film Co., USA 1913) and THE HOUSE OF BONDAGE (Pierce Kingsly, Raymond B. West, Photo Drama Company, USA 1914).

Nordisk chiefly produced series with regular main characters in the detective genre, including twelve Sherlock Holmes films in the years 1908 to 1911, to which was later added a series about the master criminal DR. GAR EL HAMA I-V (DR. GAR EL HAMA, THE ORIENTAL POISONER I-V, Eduard Schnedler-Sørensen [I+II], Robert Dinesen [III-V], 1911–1918) and MANDEN MED DE NI FINGRE (THE MAN WITH THE MISSING FINGER I-V, Anders Wilhelm Sandberg, 1915–1917). Remakes of earlier successes were also fairly common for instance REVOLUTIONSBRYLLUP, which was produced first in 1910 and again in 1915. Also KLOVNEN (THE CLOWN, both versions A.W. Sandberg) which exists in a version from 1917 and another from 1926; and MAHARADJAENS YNDLINGSHUSTRU (A PRINCE OF BHARATA, Robert Dinesen, 1917, August Blom, 1919), of which parts I and II, from 1917 and 1919 respectively, were remade in 1926. The Maharajah films were so popular that the German company PAGU released DIE LIEBLINGSFRAU DES MAHARADSCHA, 3. TEIL (ORIENTAL LOVE,

644 NFS:II,28.DFI, 237. Letter from Harald Frost to Otto Wadsted, acting Deputy Head of Mission, Buenos Aires (16 October 1913).

645 NFS:I,17:I.DFI, 5. Blade af Aktieselskabet Nordisk Films Kompagnis Historie (pages from the story of the limited company Nordisk Films Kompagni). No author, no date.

646 Müller, *Frühe deutsche Kinematographie*, 115.

647 NFS:II,15.DFI, 17. Letter from Wilhelm Stæhr to Ingvald C. Oes (22 February 1911).

Max Mack, Pagu, DE 1921).[648] These Maharajah films became so familiar to audiences that Nordisk could even make a spoof on them in 1919, with the comedy MAHARADJAENS YNDLINGSFLAMME (THE MAHARADJA'S FAVOURITE FLAME, Lau Lauritzen, 1919).

Based on MAHARADJAENS YNDLINGSHUSTRU, a novel was published, intended to be the first in a series of literary adaptations from Nordisk entitled *Eisbärbücher* (Polar Bear books). Marie Louise Droop, who was employed by the Berlin branch as translator and dramatic adviser, was the author of the novel which contained a combination of the plots in the first two Maharajah films. Books based on films exemplify the merchandise-tie-ins which Bakker mentions as a way of branding. However, the first book in the *Eisbärbücher* series would be the only novel which Nordisk published.[649]

Droop also participated in the marketing of Nordisk in Germany. From 1917 to 1919, she edited the German magazine *Der Eisbär* which was published every two weeks. It promoted Nordisk's films through lavish portraits of the stars and still photos. The Nordisk writers helped out with articles for the magazine.[650] From around 1916, a "hit list" was published for the branches in Budapest, Vienna and Prague which had been established during the war. The list announced which films would be released in the near future and also included stills from the films as well as small portraits of the stars at Nordisk. From 1917, it was published as a regular magazine, the *Wiener Eisbär.*

Around 1909, established actors started making films, but contracted film actors who did not just see film work as a way to fast money beside stage work did not emerge at Nordisk until 1911. Film acting was looked down upon and considered less genteel than stage performances. Edith Buemann, one of the first trained actresses to do films, bluntly stated: "You didn't tell anyone that you had been there."[651]

Furthermore, the Copenhagen theatres objected to actors doing film work while they were employed in stage productions. In July 1913 the Danish film companies had to strike a bargain with actors and theatre managers in Copenhagen to the effect that actors who acted in films while under contract with a theatre had to pay ten per cent of their film fees to the theatre of their employment. In order not to reveal the amount of money an actor made on films, it was agreed that the Danish Actors Guild should collect the money and then settle accounts with the theatres. The only theatre who did not impose

648 See Casper Tybjerg, "Orientalisme i dansk stumfilm", in Helle Kannik Haastrup and Torben Kragh Grodal (ed.), *Sekvens 97. Filmæstetik og Billedhistorie. Filmvidenskabelig årbog 1997*, 221–228.

649 Writer Niels Th. Thomsen rewrote his script for the film HVORLEDES JEG KOM TIL FILMEN (THE SILENT ACTOR, Robert Dinesen, 1916) entitled *Hendes Filmshelt. En Dollarprinsesses Kærlighedsroman* (Her Film Hero. A Dollar-Princess' Love Novel) in 1927, see Schröder, *Ideale Kommunikation,* 859. In 1921, Sophus Michaëlis's literary version of HIMMELSKIBET (A TRIP TO MARS, Holger-Madsen, 1918) was published. Nothing indicates that either of the two publications was used in the marketing of the films or of Nordisk.

650 Interview with A.V. Olsen. DFI.

651 Interview with Edith Buemann. DFI.

this tax on actors was the Scala Theatre, run by manager Frede Skaarup. Olsen found the dispute ridiculous and inconsequential to Nordisk since, as he said: "Our best actors are permanently employed by us."[652]

Prior to1911 Nordisk had an unwritten policy not to reveal the names of its actors. A letter from 1908 reads:

> We take the liberty of informing you that actors in our future films for the time being are under contract to theatres in town, and that their names must not be used in advertising or in connection with the individual films in which they perform. We therefore ask you to respect that no ads are to be published with the names of the actors in question; otherwise, we dare not release the film for your consideration.[653]

Even with their names withheld, the actors were still recognized since the films reached a wide audience. Viggo Larsen, who played Sherlock Holmes in five films from 1908 to 1909, has reported:

> Nordisk Films was known throughout the world, and I had been noticed – "There goes Sherlock Holmes" boys shouted at me in the streets of Berlin. They had seen me as the detective in a series of films shot in Valby, but they did not know my name. Our names never appeared, neither in the films nor in the souvenir programmes. Everyone, actors, directors, writers and cameramen, appeared in perfect anonymity.[654]

Nordisk's policy of keeping the actors anonymous was the rule until the era of feature films. Valdemar Psilander was to become the greatest star at Nordisk in the silent era; from 1911 to 1916, he appeared in more than 80 of Nordisk's films, most of which were long films. He was immensely popular with cinema audiences, especially in Germany, Russia, Central Europe and South America. On the question: "Which film actor or actress do you regard your number one?" 382 readers of a German film magazine named Psilander. Asta Nielsen came second with 271 votes, and only then followed the local German stars.[655] In Russia, Psilander was known and admired under the name of Garrison, and he was undoubtedly the most popular male star in Russia, with Asta Nielsen in the lead among actresses.[656] In Brazil, Psilander was the object of "[...] a veritable idolization among the fair sex".[657] On the strength of his popularity, Psilander was able to perform two and a half months in 1914 to packed houses in Budapest with a film made for the occasion, GREV DAHLBORGS HEMMELIGHED (Count Dahlborg's Secret, Eduard Schnedler-Sørensen, 1914), as part of his performance. Psilander had planned a similar tour to Russia that never came about because of the war.[658]

652 "Skuespillernes Filmtilladelse", *Politiken* (9 July 1913).

653 NFS:II,7.DFI, 174. Letter from Nordisk to unknown recipient (22 April 1908).

654 Hr. Bert, "Dansk Film kan fejre sit 50 aars jubilæum", *Politiken* (24 April 1955).

655 "Stumper og Strimler", *Filmen*, no. 8 (1914).

656 *Sine-fono*, no. 8 (1913): 31.

657 Irv., "Dansk Film i Brasilien", *Berlingske Tidende* (20 January 1925).

658 *Kine-Zhurnal*, no. 2 (25 January 1914): 23.

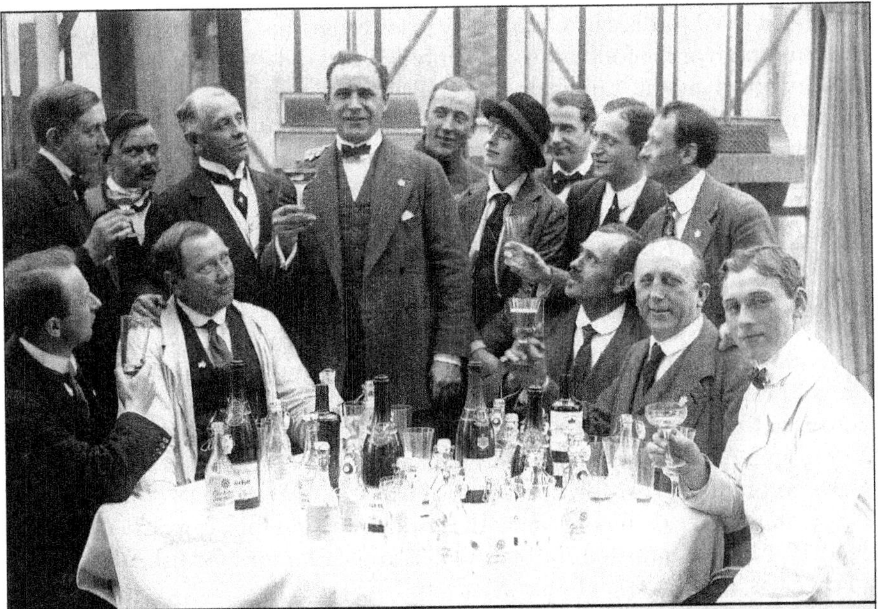

Figure 25. The greatest star at Nordisk: Valdemar Psilander in the middle celebrating his birthday in the studio (1916). Courtesy of DFI/Stills & Posters Archive.

Nordisk used Psilander mercilessly in its marketing; in Germany, he was dubbed "the darling of the audiences", and "a sure box-office success in difficult times".[659] Psilander postcards were sent from Copenhagen to Nordisk's branches and agents by the tens of thousands.[660] He was the highest-paid actor at Nordisk; in the 1916 season, Psilander was engaged to star in ten films, at a salary of 10,000 kroner per film. When he demanded 250,000 kroner to appear in eight films to be shot over six months in the 1916 season, Frost had to turn him down.[661] By comparison, Nordisk's second man, Olaf Fønss, got 14,000 kroner for the entire 1915 season,[662] and the popular comedian Oscar Stribolt's entire fee for eleven films in 1916 was 6,500.[663] Among the highest paid actresses was Else Frølich who received 8,500 kroner in 1915, and Rita Sacchetto who was paid 18,000 marks for that same season.[664]

659 *Der Kinematograph*, no. 381 (15 April 1913).

660 E.g. 7,000 postcards of Psilander were sent to Russia. NFS:II,23.DFI, 11. Letter from Harald Frost to Nordische Films Co., Berlin (4 December 1912). A couple of months later, another 10,000 were sent to Russia. NFS:II,24.DFI, 288. Letter from Harald Frost to P. Thiemann & F. Reinhardt, Moscow (18 February 1913). And yet another 10,000 went to Russia half a year later. NFS:II,27.DFI, 142. Letter from Harald Frost to Nordische Films Co., Berlin (13 August 1913).

661 NFS:IV,75.DFI. Letter from Valdemar Psilander to Harald Frost (25 September 1916); NFS:IV,75.DFI. Letter from Harald Frost to Valdemar Psilander (27 September 1916).

662 NFS:IV,60.DFI. Contract between Nordisk and Olaf Fønss (10 July 1914).

663 NFS:IV,71.DFI. Contract between Nordisk and Oscar Stribolt (31 January 1916).

664 NFS:IV,71.DFI. Contract between Nordisk and Rita Sacchetto (15 February1914).

Psilander left Nordisk in October 1916 to found his own company, and he died in March of the following year, only 32 years old. After his death, Nordisk was involved in the publishing of a Psilander memorial booklet, and the company had so many unreleased Psilander films in store that they could market these as "Psilander memorial films" as late as 1920.[665] In 1917, the Russian film company Drankov produced a fiction film about Psilander's career, THE LIFE OF GARRISON, but, due to the turbulent times in Russia that year, it may never have premiered.[666] Norwegian actor Gunnar Tolnæs took over from Psilander as the company's star, but his popularity never reached the heights of Psilander's.

The other major Danish film star was Asta Nielsen. Fotorama had contracted her and her future husband, the director Urban Gad,[667] and they were both connected to Nordisk through their contract with Skandinavisk Kunstfilms Kompagni. Asta Nielsen made DEN SORTE DRØM (THE BLACK DREAM, Urban Gad, Fotorama, 1911) for Fotorama, and BALLETDANSERINDEN for Nordisk before they broke their contract with Nordisk and left for a career in Germany. In 1918, Nielsen returned and starred in a single film for Nordisk, MOD LYSET (TOWARDS THE LIGHT, Holger-Madsen, 1918).

Nordisk also promoted other actors, of course, and they often became popular too. In the aforementioned Russian questionnaire, we find the names of Nordisk's actors Else Frölich, Kiri Maja (Lili Beck), Robert Dinesen and Ferdinand Bonn,[668] and Nordisk delivered postcards of Robert Dinesen, Ebba Thomsen, Poul Reumert, Zanny Petersen, Augusta Blad, Carl Alstrup, Frederik Buch and Oscar Stribolt to its foreign branches and agents.[669] When actor Carl Alstrup performed in a theatre in London, Nordisk immediately wrote to the London branch that Alstrup's performance should be used in the marketing of the films he had made at Nordisk.[670] Nordisk's films were often produced long before they were released, and the company continuously kept its foreign branches up to date concerning which actors to promote; the actors might no longer be employed by Nordisk when the film opened. Actor Aage Hertel was mentioned in ads from the New York branch although he was no longer with Nordisk, as Frost had to tell branch manager Oes.[671] Famous actors were hired from the Copenhagen theatre world – Karl Mantzius, who had been

665 E.g. anonymous article, *Aftenbladet* (26 August 1920).

666 *Kine-zhurnal*, no. 17–24 (1917): 62. Katalog filmov chastnogo proizvodstva (1917–1921). In *Sovetskie chudozestvennye fil'my: annotirovannyj katalog*, T.3: Prilozheniia. Iskusstvo, Moskva (1961), 263. I am grateful to Lauri Piispa for the reference. For a more detailed account on Valdemar Psilander as a star on the Russian market see Lauri Piispa, "Garrison, Star of the Russian Screen", *Kosmorama*, no. 267 (2017) (accessed on 1 May 2017, http://www.kosmorama.org/Artikler/Garrison-Star-of-the-Russian-Screen.aspx).

667 NFA. Contract between Asta Nielsen and Frede Skaarup (2 May 1911).

668 *Sine-fono*, no. 8 (1913): 31.

669 NFS:II,23.DFI, 896. Letter from Harald Frost to Nordisk Films Co., London (27 January 1913).

670 NFS:II,31.DFI, 586. Letter from Harald Frost to Nordisk Films Co. Ltd., London (4 May 1914).

671 NFS:II,25.DFI, 956. Letter from Harald Frost to Ingvald C. Oes, New York (2 June 1913).

the manager of the Royal Danish Theatre and was known as a character actor, and Betty Nansen, Copenhagen's uncrowned stage queen, who acted in ten films before her contract with Nordisk expired at the outbreak of World War I. Nordisk did not mind letting Nansen go, since her films did not turn out to be as successful as hoped. In 1915, Nansen went to the United States, where she made five films.

Besides its Danish actors, Nordisk also brought in a few actors from abroad, such as Ferdinand Bonn and Rita Sacchetto. In September 1912 Olsen succeeded in engaging Henny Porten, Germany's most celebrated actress, to appear in at least 20 films over a span of two years, which was a scoop for Olsen since Porten had been under contract with Messter for some time.[672] Together with Asta Nielsen, Porten was the greatest female star in Germany, and they were each other's antithesis: Nielsen was dark and seductive, Porten the fair-haired girl next door.

To Olsen's great consternation Porten announced that she had prolonged her contract with Messter in October and November 1912[673] and was therefore unable to fulfil her promise to Nordisk.[674] Due to the terms of the contract, Nordisk could not prevent Porten from continuing to make films with Messter. Of course, Porten had to pay Nordisk for breach of contract, but the amount was nowhere near the profits Nordisk might have made on Porten's films; they calculated their losses to the tune of at least 540,000 marks.[675] Porten's desertion was quite serious to Nordisk; several German clients felt cheated by Nordisk who had promised them films with her,[676] and the fight between Nordisk and Messter was covered by German trade magazines. In full-page ads, Messter, Nordisk and Porten reported decisions and letters from the court case.[677] Messter ultimately paid an indemnity of 35,000 mark to Nordisk.[678]

Getting stage actors to act in films was one way of branding Nordisk's productions and linking them to an already established and culturally accepted institution. In the early 1910s, bigger and more luxuriously furnished cinemas started to appear. The time span of a feature film resembled a stage play, and both cinemas and the demographics of their audiences changed in response. In Germany alone, 150 small cinemas had to close down in 1912; people wanted to see films in big cinemas.[679]

In Copenhagen, Constantin Philipsen rebuilt the former central station into

672 NFS:II,24.DFI, 615. Letter from Harald Frost to Lawyer Bruno May, Berlin (4 March 1913).

673 NFS:II,24.DFI, 318. Letter from Ole Olsen to Henny Porten, Berlin (19 February 1913).

674 NFS:II,24.DFI, 615. Letter from Harald Frost to Lawyer Bruno May, Berlin (4 March 1913).

675 NFS:II,24.DFI, 615. Letter from Harald Frost to Lawyer Bruno May, Berlin (4 March 1913).

676 NFS:II,25.DFI, 435. Letter from Harald Frost to Emil Schilling, Köln (24 April 1913); NFS:II,25.DFI, 522. Letter from Harald Frost to Schreiber & Klefish, Köln (29 April 1913).

677 E.g. *Der Kinematograph*, no. 325 (19 March 1913) and no. 336 (4 June 1913).

678 NFS:II,27.DFI, 799. Letter from Harald Frost to Lawyer Bruno May, Berlin (19 September 1913).

679 "Lille Film-Interview", *Politiken* (13 April 1913).

the cinema Paladsteatret. Nordisk had applied in vain to get a license for the old station building in April 1912,[680] but in the end Philipsen inaugurated Paladsteatret on the 18 October 1912 with pomp and circumstance. The cinema seated 2,500, and a thirty-man band played both before and after the show. Much had happened since the first Copenhagen cinemas opened. Sandfeld muses:

> What can better illustrate the enormous development in the six years that had passed since Constantin Philipsen had found the courage to open his little Kosmorama? Now you could go to the movies and still be genteel.[681]

Film had developed from a fairground attraction into a respectable form of entertainment that adopted the institutional conventions of the theatre – at least in the big cities. Film shows lasted as long as theatre performances, and the newly-erected cinema palaces resembled the theatres with lobbies, an orchestra, intermissions and souvenir programmes.[682]

Another step towards legitimizing film as culture and branding individual films was made by making a closer connection between writers and films based upon their literary works."It had taken years for literary works to build up their fame, but their accumulated 'brand awareness' could be instantly used by the film studios", writes Bakker.[683] On 6 November 1912, the day of the sixth anniversary of the founding of Nordisk, Nordisk's Berlin branch announced in a circular letter that the company had bought picturization rights from several prominent German writers: Gerhart Hauptmann, Arthur Schnitzler, Hugo von Hofmannsthal, Felix Salten, Max Halbe and Jakob Wassermann were among the writers whose works were to be dramatized.[684]

In Germany in the early 1910s, the so-called "cinema debate" took place, in which several celebrated artists decried film as a vulgar substitute for culture: "Zichorie statt Kaffee für das Volk" (substitute coffee for the people), wrote the German author Carl Hauptmann.[685] To deflect this criticism, the German film industry tried to associate film with men of letters and render their art form more house-trained, as it were.[686] Nordisk's circular letter was ahead of

680 National Archives: Københavns Politi. 1. politiinspektorat. Protokol over bevilligede og nægtede andragender om biografbevillinger 1905–1929 (Copenhagen Police, Protocol of granted and refused licenses for cinemas 1905–1929).

681 Sandfeld, *Den stumme scene*, 48.

682 Vito Adriaensens has argued that the Danish 'Kunstfilm' (art films) which emerged with the long feature films drew from the bourgeois realism found in paintings in the early twentieth century and hereby mirrored the values and daily life of the middle classes. See Vito Adriaensens, "'Kunst og Kino': The Art of Early Danish Drama", *Kosmorama*, no. 259 (2015) (accessed on 1 May 2017, http://www.kosmorama.org/Artikler/Kunst-og-Kino.aspx).

683 Bakker, *Entertainment Industrialised*, 281.

684 See Ludwig Greve, Margot Pehle and Heidi Westhoff (ed.), *Hätte ich das Kino! Die Schriftsteller und der Stummfilm* (Stuttgart: Ernst Klett, 1976), 118.

685 Hauptmann quoted in Deniz Göktürk, "Market Globalization and Import Regulation in Imperial Germany", in Karel Dibbets, Bert Hogenkamp (ed.), *Film and the First World War* (Amsterdam: Amsterdam University Press, 1995), 193.

686 See Helmut H. Diederichs, "The Origins of the Autorenfilm", in Paolo Cherchi Usai and Lorenzo Codelli (ed.), Prima di Caligari. Cinema tedesco, 1895–1920 (Pordenone: Biblioteca dell'Immagine, 1990), 384.

these plans. It was launched by German Karl Ludwig Schröder, the manager of the script department in Berlin in September 1912.

In Germany, Nordisk's new move led to a wave of films under the name "*Autorenfilm*" – films either based on the works of well-known authors or written in collaboration with respected men of letters. In 1908, the French company Film d'Art had built its reputation on film adaptations of famous novels and using famous and named actors in the lead roles, so the idea of basing film on literary works was not new. Before 1910, Nordisk had made film versions of works by Hans Christian Andersen and Alexandre Dumas the Younger, but according to Olsen, that was not the proper path to take,[687] partly due to the length of these films; in Nordisk's 1907 version of KAMELIADAMEN (THE LADY OF THE CAMELLIAS, Viggo Larsen, 1907), the entire plot was played out in ten minutes, and this could only be done with the aid of some very long, explanatory intertitles.

Another problem with filming literary works was the unclear copyright legislation that made it possible for other companies to dramatize the same novel or play. The introduction of new copyright laws in the early 1910s enabled the companies to protect their film versions.

Nordisk had experience with copyright disputes about DEN HVIDE SLAVEHANDEL and DEN FARLIGE ALDER, discussed above, and one of the tasks allotted to Schröder was to secure the rights to the works of famous authors and adapt them for the screen. Nordisk also used its network to get these rights. The company's Russian agents, Thiemann & Reinhardt, were asked to investigate whether the works of Leo Tolstoy, Fyodor Dostoyevsky and Ivan Turgenev could be obtained.[688] Nordisk was especially interested in Dostoyevsky's *The Gambler* and Tolstoy's *War and Peace*.[689] Nordisk's French agent, Louis Aubert, was asked about the rights for Émile Zola, Alphonse Daudet, Guy de Maupassant and George Sand.[690] The authors were offered a fee and 3 to 4 per cent of the takings.[691]

Autorenfilms became part of Nordisk's distribution at the level of art films, which were defined as films of more than 500 metres. In the weeks when Nordisk released an *Autorenfilm*, it replaced the weekly art film.[692] Nordisk was confident that *Autorenfilms* would be the new craze in the film industry: "We have always been the first among trailblazers, such as when we took the lead with the introduction of long films, and we believe that we have also struck gold this time."[693]

687 See Olsen, *Filmens Eventyr og mit eget*, 76.

688 NFS:II,25.DFI, 996. Letter from Harald Frost to P. Thiemann & F. Reinhardt, Moscow (5 June 1913).

689 NFS:II,26.DFI, 67. Letter from Harald Frost to P. Thiemann & F. Reinhardt, Moscow (10 June 1913).

690 NFS:II,25.DFI, 997. Letter from Harald Frost to Louis Aubert, Paris (5 June 1913).

691 NFS:II,28.DFI, 232. Letter from Harald Frost to Wm. Heinemann, London (16 October 1913).

692 NFS:II,25.DFI, 10. Letter from Harald Frost to Projectograph AG, Budapest (27 March 1913).

693 NFS:II,27.DFI, 203–204. Letter from Harald Frost to Nordisk Film Co. Ltd., London (18 August 1913).

ATLANTIS was Nordisk's first major *Autorenfilm* venture. The plot was based on Gerhart Hauptmann's novel of the same title from 1912. The book had generated much attention because this story about the wreck of a luxury liner was published at almost at the same time as the Titanic disaster. *Atlantis* was serialized simultaneously in the German *Berliner Tageblatt* and the French *Le Temps* from 16 January to 24 April 1912 and the Titanic went down on 14 April 1912.[694]

Even before the film was made, it was sold throughout Germany via Ludwig Gottschalk's Düsseldorf company Atlantis Film G.m.b.H., a company established for the occasion and holding the monopoly film rights. The marketing of the film was massive: Leonardo Quaresima reports that advertising started almost a year before the release,[695] via articles such as "Atlantis and the Women",[696] and excerpts from the novel were printed in German newspapers.[697] This was followed by a commercial campaign, and in *Der Kinematograph*, Atlantis Film had full-page and double-page ads a month before the premiere. The budget of the film and the fact that it was based on a novel were constantly mentioned in the marketing. After the premiere, the campaign continued with the good reviews,[698] and cinema owners reported the splendour of the film which they had seen in Copenhagen.[699] In Britain, the agents put in ads for ATLANTIS in *Kinematograph Weekly*.[700] Other companies followed suit in the marketing of their own films. The German branch could report that in Germany the company Vitagraph advertised the release of DER OZEANRIESE (THE NEXT GENERATION, L. Rogers Lytton, USA 1913) characterizing it as a "Grossartiges Schiffsdrama – Kessel Explosion – Panik an Bord – Schiffsuntergang" (Great drama at sea – Boiler explosion – Panic on board – Shipwreck) all elements familiar from ATLANTIS.[701]

The finished film was far too long and had to be drastically truncated to 2,280 metres "for commercial reasons". Nordisk had doubts whether Hauptmann would accept the film version at all,[702] and after the release of the film, Nordisk's agents and branches made further cuts. In France Aubert reduced the film to 1,500 metres, 100 metres were cut out in Vienna, and the London office reduced it by 2,000 feet (628 metres).[703] Suddenly Nordisk faced the

694 See Tybjerg, *An Art of Silence and Light*, 196.

695 See Leonardo Quaresima, "Dichter, heraus! The Autorenfilm and the German Cinema of the 1910's", *Griffithiana*, no. 38/39 (October 1990): 106.

696 "Atlantis und die Frauen", *Der Kinematograph*, no. 350 (10 September 1913).

697 *Der Kinematograph*, no. 351 (17 September 1913).

698 *Der Kinematograph*, no. 364 (17 December 1913).

699 *Der Kinematograph*, no. 361 (26 November 1913).

700 NFS:II,27.DFI, 60. Letter from Harald Frost to Nordisk Films Co. Ltd., London (8 August 1913).

701 NFS:II,29.DFI, 498. Letter from Rotkjær to Harald Frost p.t. Davos Platz, Switzerland (31 December 1913).

702 NFS:II,28.DFI, 438. Letter from Harald Frost to Karl Ludwig Schröder (30 October 1913).

703 NFS:II,29.DFI, 432. Letter from Rotkjær to Harald Frost p.t. Davos Platz (27 December 1913).

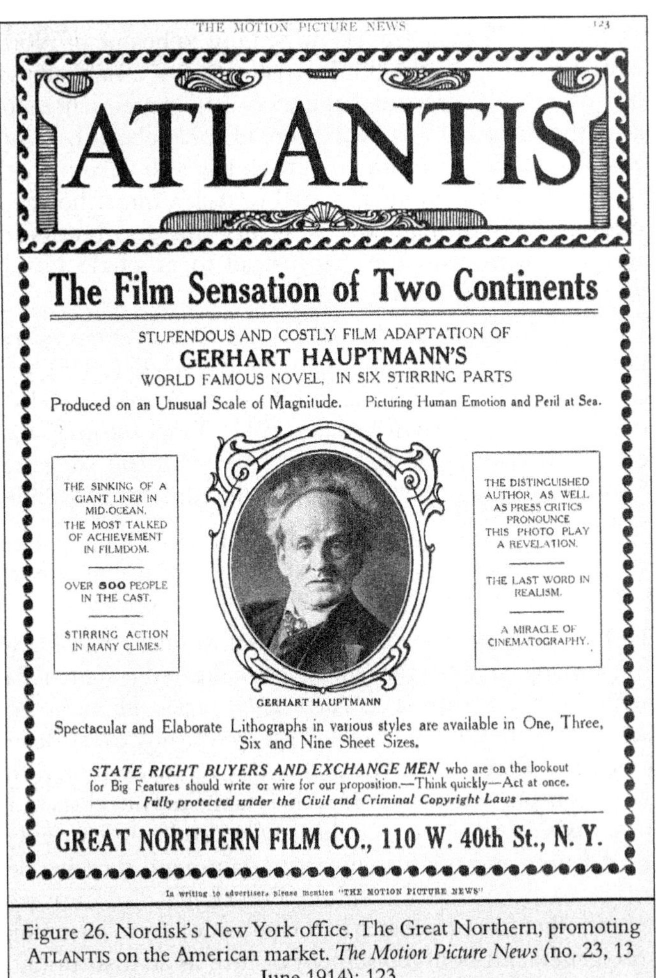
THE MOTION PICTURE NEWS

ATLANTIS

The Film Sensation of Two Continents

STUPENDOUS AND COSTLY FILM ADAPTATION OF
GERHART HAUPTMANN'S
WORLD FAMOUS NOVEL, IN SIX STIRRING PARTS

Produced on an Unusual Scale of Magnitude. Picturing Human Emotion and Peril at Sea.

THE SINKING OF A GIANT LINER IN MID-OCEAN. THE MOST TALKED OF ACHIEVEMENT IN FILMDOM.

OVER 500 PEOPLE IN THE CAST.

STIRRING ACTION IN MANY CLIMES.

THE DISTINGUISHED AUTHOR, AS WELL AS PRESS CRITICS PRONOUNCE THIS PHOTO PLAY A REVELATION.

THE LAST WORD IN REALISM.

A MIRACLE OF CINEMATOGRAPHY.

GERHART HAUPTMANN

Spectacular and Elaborate Lithographs in various styles are available in One, Three, Six and Nine Sheet Sizes.

STATE RIGHT BUYERS AND EXCHANGE MEN who are on the lookout for Big Features should write or wire for our proposition.—Think quickly—Act at once.

Fully protected under the Civil and Criminal Copyright Laws

GREAT NORTHERN FILM CO., 110 W. 40th St., N. Y.

In writing to advertisers please mention "THE MOTION PICTURE NEWS"

Figure 26. Nordisk's New York office, The Great Northern, promoting ATLANTIS on the American market. *The Motion Picture News* (no. 23, 13 June 1914): 123.

problem that ATLANTIS was being circulated in many more or less reduced and different versions. The situation was so critical that Stæhr suggested releasing ATLANTIS with a different title and removing Hauptmann's name in the countries where the film had been most mangled.[704]

The results of this endeavour were mixed. Göktürk calls ATLANTIS a "loss-making transaction",[705] and both Neergaard and Engberg conclude that ATLANTIS was an artistic and economical failure.[706] This, however, is not altogether correct, for ATLANTIS was in fact a financial success. It had cost 73,296.86 to produce, grossed a total of 504,888.88 kroner, and made a profit

704 NFS:II,29.DFI, 454. Letter from Rotkjær to Harald Frost p.t. Davos Platz (29 December 1913).

705 Deniz Göktürk, "Atlantis oder: vom Sinken der Kultur. Die Nobilitierung des frühen Kinos im Autorenfilm", in Manfred Behn (ed.), *Schwarzer Traum und weiße Sklavin. Deutsch-dänische Filmbeziehungen 1910–1930* (München: edition text + kritik, 1994), 81.

706 See Engberg, *Dansk stumfilm*, 499; Neergaard, *Historien om dansk film*, 76.

of 348,276.62 kroner,[707] so ATLANTIS turned out to be one of Nordisk's most profitable enterprises. As for the film's artistic qualities, Engberg writes: "The Atlantis flop – as it must be agreed that it was – had consequences for Nordisk. Confidence in the company was rattled abroad, and nobody bought Nordisk's films unseen any more."[708] Nothing substantiates the claim that ATLANTIS created any doubts about the quality of Nordisk's films, however, and the advantageous contracts through which agents and distributors in the early 1910s committed themselves for years ahead to purchase Nordisk's films unseen continued after the release of ATLANTIS.

After ATLANTIS, Nordisk produced several more *Autorenfilms* such as ELSKOVSLEG (1914), based on Arthur Schnitzler's *Liebelei* (1895), and SKYLDIG? – IKKE SKYLDIG? (THE FATAL THREE, Karl Ludwig Schröder, 1914) after Max Halbe's novel *Die Tat des Dietrich Stobäus* (1911). Frost summed up Nordisk's experience with *Autorenfilms* in a letter to Oes, who had suggested that the names of famous authors were connected to the films, in November 1914:

> We notice your comment about advertising the name of a famous author in connection with the film. As you may know, we tried that in Europe some time ago. It didn't last long, half a year at the most.[709]

Helmut H. Diederichs arrives at the same conclusion: *Autorenfilms* were a flash in the pan that disappeared because the investments rarely matched the profits. Why Nordisk did not continue its *Autorenfilm* series when ATLANTIS was a financial success is unclear. As a cinematic wave, however, *Autorenfilms* are important because they helped heighten the reputation of film with the authorities and censors who respected well-established novelists more than the anonymous scriptwriters. Moreover, *Autorenfilms* broke the barrier between the classy men of letters and popular film entertainment, thereby elevating the prestige of film art.[710] One might add the French *film d'art* films from around 1907–1908 as another important step in the transition from low to high culture, but the more general embourgeoisement of film as an institution came with the transition to feature film and the emergence of cinemas, which coincides with the wave of *Autorenfilms*.

This transition entailed a completely new production mode in the film studios in Valby. The script department made sure that there were scripts in different genres and lengths to choose from, so that the management could plan ahead long before the shooting season started. Harald Frost planned the shoots and sent out lists to foreign branches and agents well before the films premiered,

707 NFS:IX,21.DFI, 65–66, 91. Film-account; NFS:XII,41.DFI, 1–3. Film Account Protocol. For a more detailed account of the calculation of the profit of ATLANTIS, which includes Hauptmann's fee and percentage, percentage to Nordisk's literary staff in Berlin, returns and rebates see Schröder, *Ideale Kommunikation*, 419.

708 Engberg, *Dansk stumfilm*, 499.

709 NFS:II,34.DFI, 159. Letter from Harald Frost to Ingvald C. Oes (24 November 1914).

710 See Diederichs, "The Origins of the Autorenfilm", 394–396.

which was on the same day all over the world.[711] This was a way of preventing the buyers from purchasing copies from Nordisk's branches and releasing them before the regular Nordisk agents did, and also ensuring that competing companies did not copy the film and distribute it before Nordisk agents and offices did so. As mentioned, it was important to keep the schedule; still photos had to be shipped to Stafford in England to get the posters ready in time, and for the USA a paper copy of the film was needed to protect the copyrights. Finally, the release date had to be observed in order to fulfil the various distribution contracts made by Nordisk. Nordisk had to deliver a feature film every week, together with a short film and an actuality which could be a travelogue, scenery shots or a documentary of news value.

The company's administrative department grew. In January of 1913, Nordisk moved from the Panoptikon Building to 45 Vimmelskaftet[712] where the company rented a few offices to begin with and in time occupied the entire second floor. In the heyday of Nordisk, 20 to 22 people were employed under Frost and Olsen.[713] In Valby, August Blom was the manager and, as production increased in September 1913, Stæhr was moved to Valby, to take charge:

> Based on the experiences from the summer season concerning the amount of negative film shot at the theatre, it will be impossible for the company to meet the demands under the current procedures at the theatre, and the management has ordered Manager W. Stæhr to assist at the theatre as of today; he will be considered your superior.[714]

Blom continued as the artistic manager, but Stæhr controlled and organized production, and from a letter from an administrative employee it appears that Stæhr's presence in Valby was much needed:

> If he [Stæhr] can enforce [...] that the directors meet on time, which is to say at eight in the morning, and especially that also Blom arrives at this hour, he would indeed make a great progress. [...] Usually, the mornings are wasted.[715]

From the board of directors and the management at Vimmelskaftet, Blom and Stæhr received directives about how the "theatre" in Valby should be run, how scripts should be distributed among the directors, how to make the best use of Psilander's contract,[716] and which tasks were assigned to Blom's and Stæhr's respective jobs.[717] The recurrent guiding theme of the directives was to "make the most of time".[718]

711 NFS:II,18.DFI, 158. Letter from Harald Frost to Nordisk Films Co., London (4 January 1912).

712 NFS:II,23.DFI, 688. Letter from Harald Frost to Købmagergades Postkontor (16 January 1913).

713 Interview with Joachim Nielsen II. DFI.

714 NFS:IV,80.DFI. Letter from Nordisk to Lauritz Maaløe (12 September 1913).

715 NFS:II,40.DFI, 7. Letter from Lauritz Maaløe to the Management of Nordisk (16 September 1913).

716 NFS:II,34.DFI, 252–254. Letter from Harald Frost to August Blom (1 December 1914); NFS:II,34.DFI, 255–257. Letter from Harald Frost to Wilhelm Stæhr (1 December 1914).

717 NFS:II,34.DFI, 503–504. Letter from Harald Frost to Wilhelm Stæhr (22 December 1914); NFS:II,34.DFI, 548–549. Letter from Harald Frost to August Blom (24 December 1914).

718 NFS:II,34.DFI, 503–504 Letter from Harald Frost to Wilhelm Stæhr (22 December 1914); NFS:II,34.DFI, 548–549. Letter from Harald Frost to August Blom (24 December 1914).

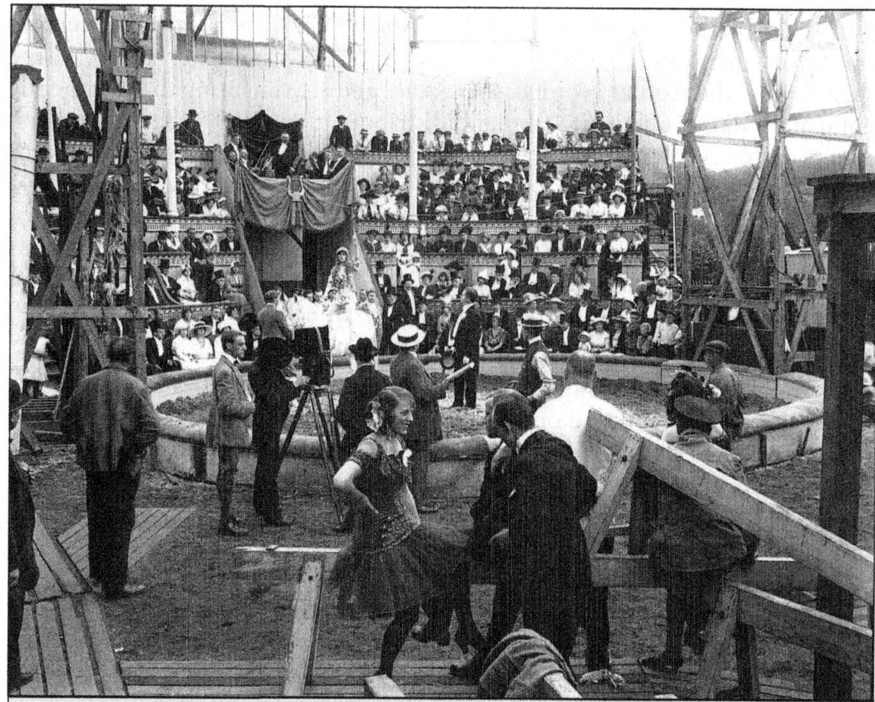

Figure 27. Stories about circus were popular, and Nordisk built a permanent circus ring on the lot. From the shooting of DEN HVIDE RYTTERSKE (THE WHITE RIDER, Alfred Cohn, 1915). Courtesy of DFI/Stills & Posters Archive.

In order to keep up with the rigorous production schedule, Nordisk built several new studios. In 1907, the temporary outdoor stage from the summer of 1906 was replaced by a real studio, Stage 1. Then followed Stage 2 in 1910, Stage 3 in 1912, Stage 4 one year later and, finally, the biggest studio, Stage 5, was built in 1915. Furthermore, a permanent circus ring was built, and locations outside Valby were often used. After Stage 2 had been built, there was an opportunity to shoot with two crews simultaneously. Cameraman Axel Graatkjær reported about the conditions: "When we started having two directors, they were Blom and Dinesen. I had to go back and forth between the studios. While they built sets on one, I went down to the other, shot and rehearsed."[719] Graatkjær was Nordisk's only cameraman for fiction films, and with the rise in production, it was no longer enough to have only one man in each field of work. It did not take long before a second cameraman was hired. The number of employees in the various fields rose significantly between 1910 and 1911 (see Table 5). In 1910 there were two cameramen, and this number went up to ten by 1913. The same increase applied to directors: two in 1910, four in 1911 and ten different directors in 1913. Many of the directors had a theatrical background, either as actors or directors. The number of actors

719 Interview with Axel Graatkjær. DFI.

employed by the company also increased after the feature films arrived, from 82 in 1910 to 133 in 1911.

Table 5: The development in selected workfields 1906–1914

	1906	1907	1908	1909	1910	1911	1912	1913	1914
Directors	1	1	1	1	4	4	6	10	10
Cameramen	1	1	1	1	1	2	3	6	8
Actors	11	16	30	45	82	133	93	102	126

Source: For directors see Danish Film Database. For cameramen and actors see Engberg (1977), 288 and 332–340. As mentioned, Ludvig Halberstadt and Ole Olsen directed films in the pioneer phase of the company, but are not counted here for1906.

The number of people employed during the shooting season, which now lasted from March to October, varied. In a status report to the main office dated May 1914, cashier and bookkeeper at the studios Lauritz Maaløe wrote that there were 65 regular actors, about 50 extras each day, seven directors and eight cameramen besides the seven administrative workers and 63 workmen, messengers, cleaning women, wardrobe personnel, stagehands etc. On a given spring day in 1914, around 200 people would be employed in Valby.[720]

The increase in staff led to a greater degree of specialization in several ways. Whereas Viggo Larsen used to direct all genres, many of the directors at Nordisk found specific genres to work with after 1911. Lau Lauritzen preferred comedy and directed 196 of these between 1914 and 1919. Comedies were only about fifteen minutes, which explains Lauritzen's impressive track record. Other directors such as Schnedler-Sørensen specialized in crime stories.

The directors were hired on standard contracts with few variations. Holger-Madsen,[721] Robert Dinesen and Hjalmar Davidsen were employed to direct as many films as possible per season, though not more than twenty. The directors were paid per film and by the length of the films. Dinesen received 1,000 kroner per film, usually between 500 and 1,250 metres, and 400 kroner per film of less than 600 metres.[722] For a film of less than 325 metres, Lau Lauritzen was paid 200 kroner, 300 kroner for a film of up to 600 metres, and 400 kroner for a film between 600 and 800 metres.[723]

720 NFS:II,40.DFI, 267. Letter from Lauritz Maaløe to A/S Nordisk Films Kompagni (20 May 1914).

721 Holger-Madsen was born Holger Madsen, and he changed his name to Holger-Madsen (with a hyphen) in 1911. In much English-language literature he is mistakenly given the first name Forest or Forrest. This originates in a misreading of an illustration caption in Arnold Hending's book *Stjerner i Glashuse* (Valby: Winkelmanns Forlag, 1936), 28, which reads, "Forrest Holger-Madsen". In Danish *forrest* means "in the front" or "in the foreground", and is not Holger-Madsen's first name.

722 NFA. Contract between Nordisk and Robert Dinesen (26 November 1915).

723 NFA. Letter from Nordisk to Lauritz Lauritzen (10 December 1914).

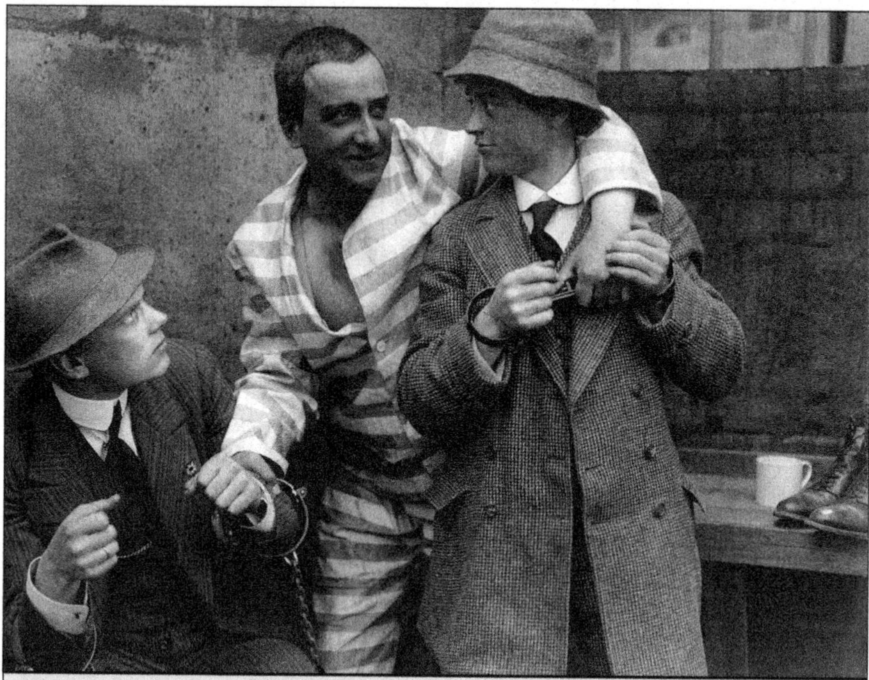

Figure 28. Director Eduard Schnedler-Sørensen, actor Aage Hertel and cameraman Axel Graatkjær having fun during the shooting of the DR. GAR EL HAMA (1911).
Courtesy of DFI/Stills & Posters Archive.

Directors were obliged to prepare their scripts themselves, and the scripts were to be approved by the management eight days before the shoot started; if the management requested it, the directors had to edit their films, too. The finished film was to be screened in Frihavnen in the presence of three members of the management, and the director had to re-shoot unsatisfactory scenes for no extra fee, if the management so desired.[724] The directors were not only hired for the shooting season; the management expected them to work through the winter season as well. In December 1914, Stæhr wrote to director Anders Wilhelm Sandberg that he was expected to fully prepare "eight to ten plays before mid-February".[725]

A list of the directors employed and the number of films they made for Nordisk show that a handful of the 26 directors hired between 1911 and 1917 supervised most of the production (see Table 6).

724 NFA. Contract between Nordisk and A.W. Sandberg (24 February 1916).

725 NFS:II,36.DFI, 345. Letter from Wilhelm Stæhr to A.W. Sandberg (14 December 1914).

Table 6: Directors and number of films they directed for Nordisk 1911–1917

Director	1911	1912	1913	1914	1915	1916	1917	Total
August Blom	31	18	10	14	11	2		86
William Augustinus	21							21
Eduard Schnedler-Sørensen	16	32	6	6			5	65
Urban Gad	1	1						2
Robert Dinesen		8	9	14	17	10	3	61
Leo Tscherning		6						6
Christian Schrøder		7	5					12
Holger-Madsen			10	18	21	16	3	68
Lauritz Olsen			1					1
Axel Breidahl			5					5
Hjalmar Davidsen			7	13	12	11	2	45
Sofus Wolder			19	6				25
Karl Ludwig Schröder			1					1
A.W. Sandberg				12	11	11	2	36
Lau Lauritzen				28	43	44	29	144
Alfred Cohn				9	2			11
Karl Mantzius				3				3
George Schnéevoigt					3	2		5
Alexander Christian					10	10	2	22
Martinus Nielsen					4	7		11
Robert Schyberg					1		2	3
Oscar Stribolt							3	3
Alfred Kjerulf							3	3
Emanuel Gregers							1	1
Gunnar Sommerfeldt							1	1
August Blom/Thorleif Lund							1	1

Source: See note for Table 1 (on page 30). Though Urban Gad left Nordisk in 1911, he is credited for the 1912 film DET BERYGTEDE HUS (IN THE HANDS OF THE IMPOSTERS).

August Blom, Eduard Schnedler-Sørensen, Robert Dinesen, Holger-Madsen, Hjalmar Davidsen and Lau Lauritzen directed 469 out of the 642 films produced at Nordisk between 1911 and 1917, which amounts to 73 per cent of the production total. Such an extensive annual output ensured that the directors' noses were kept to the grindstone and that they continuously improved at what they were doing. The permanently employed directors often used each their own regular cameraman[726] and a regular team of actors.[727] Production was made more efficient by forming small, close-knit production teams in which everyone knew each other, and this also helped to ensure a certain standard of the results.

Director Robert Dinesen has reported that one of the rules that applied to the job was that Stæhr only handed out 100 metres of film at a time. If the director

726 Interview with H.F. Rimmen. DFI; see also Engberg, *Dansk stumfilm*, 283–287.

727 Interview with Zanny Petersen. DFI.

did not turn in anything useful on those 100 metres, he had to account for his failure before he was given the next hundred metres.[728] David Bordwell refers to a similar arrangement with Gaumont's top director Louis Feuillade: "[…] Gaumont pegged part of Feuillade's salary to the amount of finished footage turned out, and he got a bonus if a film proved popular. So he enforced ruthless efficiency."[729]

Like the scriptwriters, Nordisk's directors had directives to follow as well. In a letter to Blom, Olsen refers to the company's regulations of 31 October 1913, which have not survived, but they appear to state that:

> Before the shooting starts and already when he plans the production, the director must make a note of how many metres will be recorded to ensure that the film will be made on the estimated amount of film. Moreover, at the rehearsal before the shoot, the director must confer with his cameraman to make sure that they agree how many metres are required for the shoot. If they do not agree, adjustments must be made so the film can be kept within the estimated length.[730]

A similar demand from Olsen appears in a memo from 1917. Olsen complains that the finished films time and again have to be cut down by several hundred metres. As a consequence, the director must henceforth make a note in his script as to how many metres any given scene will require. This will state the length of the finished film even at the script stage.[731]

In his analysis of the films from Nordisk in the 1910s, Bordwell emphasizes the tableau-like style that dominated European films at the time. It seems a qualified guess that Nordisk's rules of only giving the directors 100 metres at a time and tying the directors down to a pre-planned estimate were industrial constraints that encouraged the directors to stick to and develop the tableau style. With the longer films, the scripts became more detailed and were to a greater extent used as a tool in the planning of the shoots. Following the success of VED FÆNGSLETS PORT and DEN HVIDE SLAVEHANDELS SIDSTE OFFER, Nordisk's first long feature films, the company began breaking down the scripts and ceased to shoot them chronologically,[732] and it was the actors themselves who had to keep track of the continuity.[733] Robert Dinesen saw the years as a director at Nordisk as excellent training which came to good use in his later career,[734] and the education which the directors received at Nordisk made them attractive to other companies. "Abroad, you're considered highly qualified if you've been working with Olsen", stated director Leo Tscherning when he was relieved of his contract to go to Germany to work for Messter

728 Interview with Robert Dinesen. DFI.

729 David Bordwell, *Figures Traced in Light* (Berkeley: University of California Press, 2005), 44.

730 NFS:II,32.DFI, 549. Letter from Ole Olsen to August Blom, The studios, Valby (6 July 1914).

731 NFA. Letter from Ole Olsen to Holger-Madsen (5 March 1917).

732 NFS:XIV,35.DFI, 57. Scrapbook. Handwritten note by Wilhelm Stæhr. Interview with Alma Hinding. DFI.

733 Interview with Alma Hinding. DFI.

734 Interview with Robert Dinesen. DFI.

Film.[735] Graatkjær, who had been with Nordisk since its beginnings, went to Germany in 1913 to become one of the highest paid cameramen in the world.

Specialization and rules did not just apply to the directors, but also to the staff of the studio in Valby. In 1914, the distribution of the technical personnel in various groups was as follows: ten painters, three carpenters, two joiners, three saddle makers, eight cameramen, three electricians, fourteen machinists, and two unskilled labourers.[736] The theatre painter Carlo Jacobsen, who was employed by Nordisk in 1914, reported that the painters were divided according to their individual fields of speciality.[737] Specialization raised the speed of production. Scriptwriter Arnold Vilhelm Olsen stated that a new decoration for the studio could be ready in an hour.[738] From the lists of employees it appears that there was no costume department in Valby. The reason was that the actors were required to bring their own costumes. Since most of the films were set in the present day, the actors could wear their own clothes. For historic films, such as those featuring medieval knights, Nordisk rented costumes in Germany,[739] and eventually, Nordisk collected a wardrobe of costumes made and purchased abroad.[740] Some costumes, however, were tailor-made for the event. The "neutral uniforms" used in war films during the World War, or the leather suits which the explorers wear on their expedition to Mars in HIMMELSKIBET (A TRIP TO MARS, Holger-Madsen, 1918) were made for these films only. Nordisk rented props, furniture, carpets, curtains etc. in antique shops and from art dealers.[741] Military costumes were borrowed from the Danish Army.[742]

The many rules and directives flooding Nordisk's organization led to a rise in bureaucratization in Valby. In an interview, Carlo Jacobsen related how even painters had to report to the management about what they had been doing,[743] just like the directors who had to report if they had not turned out something useful. Moreover, the offices in Valby filed reports to the main office at Vimmelskaftet about the various film projects, and detailed accounts were given of how many scenes and negative metres were shot every month.[744]

735 '-o-', "De filmede Skuespillere", *Centrum* (4 March 1913).

736 NFS:II,33.DFI, 330. Letter from Rotkjær to The studio, Valby (17 September 1914).

737 Interview with Carlo Jacobsen. DFI.

738 Interview with A.V. Olsen. DFI.

739 NFS:II,1.DFI, 157. Letter from E. Hansen to Customs (2 July 1907); NFS:II,3.DFI, 426. Letter from E. Hansen to Atelier Verck & Flotow (4 April 1907); NFS:II,36.DFI, 237. Letter from Maaløe to F. & A. Diringer, München (6 April 1914).

740 NFS:II,12.DFI, 427. Letter from Wilhelm Stæhr to the General Directorate, Copenhagen (4 March 1910).

741 NFS:II,33.DFI, 171. Letter from Harald Frost to Barrister Teilmann-Jørgensen (31 August 1914).

742 NFS:II,12.DFI, 604. Letter from Wilhelm Stæhr to Upholsterer [Edvard Hann] (5 April 1910); NFS:II,36.DFI, 224. Letter from Maaløe to the Army Technical Corps (26 January 1914).

743 Interview with Carlo Jacobsen. DFI.

744 E.g. NFS:II,40.DFI, 36. Monthly status of production, September 1913; NFS:II,40.DFI, 59. Monthly status of production, October 1913.

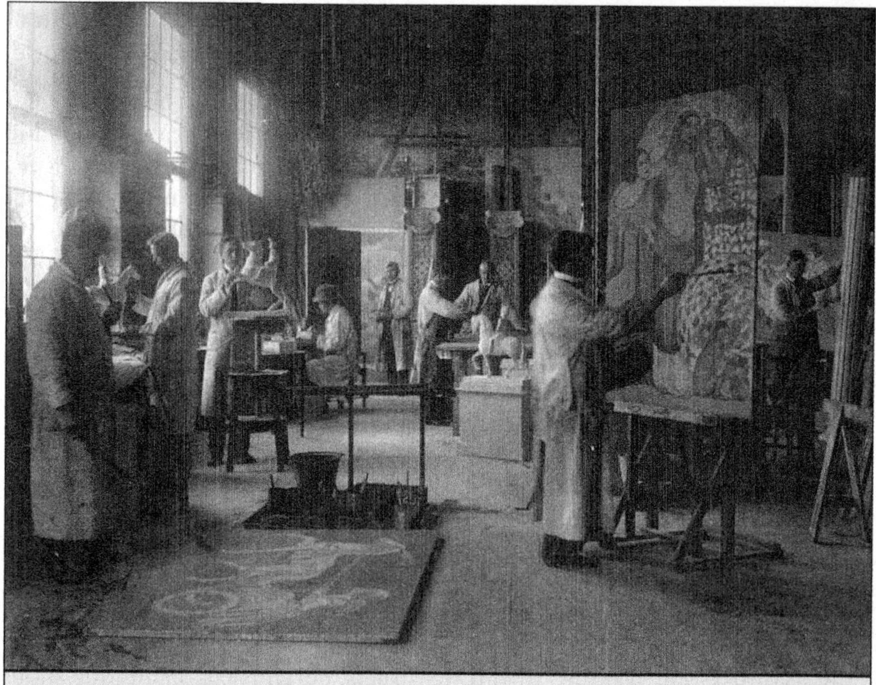

Figure 29. The painter's workshop in Valby ca. 1915. Courtesy of DFI/Stills & Posters Archive.

A ringtone system was introduced in order to control the many films shot simultaneously in Valby; each director had his own signal. Blom had a long ring, and each stage had a corresponding ring signal. Stage 1 had one short ring, and a manual for this system explains,"one long ring and three short means that Director Blom is called to Stage 3".[745]

Regulations for Valby in 1915 are extant, according to which the following applied to actors' costumes: "Forgetting your costume, private clothes, or props which the performer has to provide will be fined with 1 to 5 kroner."[746] Penalties were quite extensive; it cost half of a krone to arrive fifteen minutes late and two kroner for up to half an hour's delay. For being late for more than thirty minutes, the fine would be set according to the damage incurred on the company,[747] and in the case of repeated delays, the management had to be notified. Actor Olaf Fønss, who was employed in 1913 and acted in 30 films for Nordisk, wrote about the working conditions in Valby:

745 NFS:I,87:4.DFI. Notice of the ringtone system in Valby.

746 *Nordisk Films Kompagni, NF 1906–1981* (Copenhagen, 1981). The publication was made for the press in connection with the company's 75th anniversary. It was held at the Danish Film Institute's library, but is apparently now lost. The documents referred to in the publication was scanned, and are in my possession.

747 Ibid.

> Dissatisfaction with Stæhr's tyranny in Valby grew. Thunder and electricity were always looming, and each day there was an altercation between some actor or director and Manager Stæhr who tried to bully his subordinates. The working speed increased, and the demands on us grew still more unreasonable until both actors and directors lost that joy of working without which all artistic efforts must fail. Fines were dished out for everything, and the previously cordial and friendly atmosphere, under Stæhr's rule, had turned into cursing and scolding.[748]

The actors protested against the working conditions in Valby. In July 1915 they joined in protest against the management. What ignited the conflict was Stæhr's decision that actors now had to travel third class on trips to locations outside the studios, instead of first and second class as before. A letter of protest was written, signed by 39 actors and directors, and sent to the management at Nordisk.[749] Olsen responded that the signatories had to comply with the decisions of the management and the board of directors, and if anyone was unsatisfied with the working conditions, he or she could be released from his or her contract within three days.[750] The reaction to Olsen's letter was yet another letter of complaint against the new travelling arrangement and Olsen's threat.[751] This time, the number of signatories had dropped to 18.

Olsen's threat had worked and nothing came of the actors' protest. On her own behalf, actress Ebba Lund, one of the original signatories, penned a mollifying and explanatory letter to Olsen,[752] and the newspaper *Ekstra Bladet* reported that Robert Dinesen and A.W. Sandberg had revoked their signatures from the first letter of protest in a private letter to Olsen. When Dinesen and Psilander, co-signatories of both letters, met in Valby, Psilander caught Dinesen by the neck and shouted: "Look at this, Comrades, this is the biggest a – h – at 'Nordisk Film.'"[753] The only actors who maintained their protest were Carl Alstrup and Olaf Fønss, who discontinued their contracts with Nordisk.[754] The press reported that both Psilander and Holger-Madsen had handed in their resignations, but that Nordisk's management had refused them.[755] In the case of Psilander, however, nothing indicates that he really wished to be released from his contract.[756] One thing did come of the protest,

748 Fønss, *Filmserindringer*, 146–148.

749 NFS:IV,20:1.DFI, 1–2. Letter of protest to the management of A/S Nordisk Films Kompagni (2 July 1915), signed by 39 actors and directors.

750 NFS:IV,20:2.DFI, 1. Letter from Ole Olsen (6 July 1915).

751 NFS:IV,20:3.DFI, 1. Letter from actors and directors to the Management of A/S Nordisk Films Kompagni (9 July 1915), signed by 18 actors and directors.

752 NFS:IV,20:4.DFI, 1–3. Letter from Ebba Lund to Ole Olsen (9 July 1915).

753 P., "Et Sammenstød paa 'Nordisk Film'", *Ekstra Bladet* (12 July 1915).

754 NFS:IV,60.DFI. Letter from Olaf Fønss to the Management of A/S Nordisk Films Kompagni (9 July 1915); NFS:IV,55.DFI. Letter from Carl Alstrup to the Management of Nordisk Films Kompagni (12 July 1915).

755 "Røret Indenfor Nordisk Filmskompagniet", *Politiken* (23 July 1915).

756 NFS:IV,75.DFI. Letter from Valdemar Psilander to the Management of Nordisk Films Kompagni (9 July 1915).

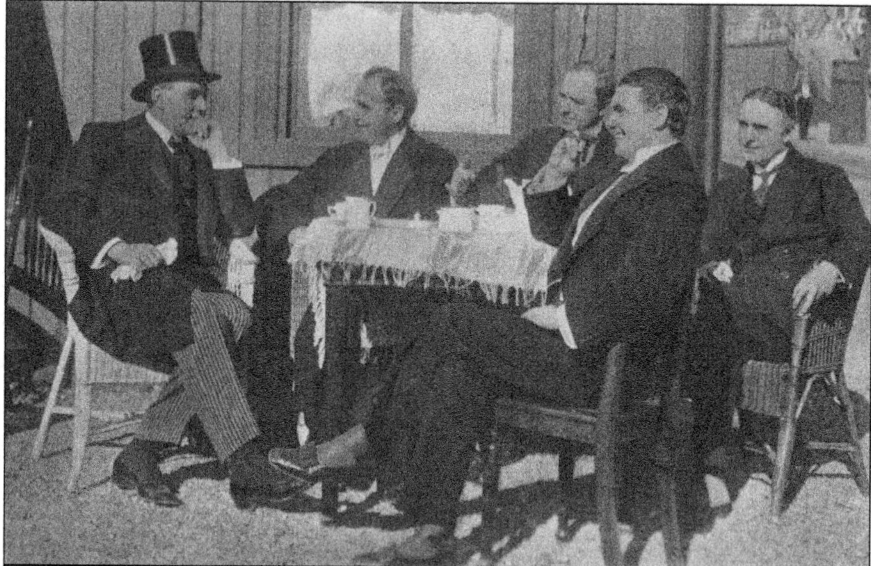

Figure 30. Actors Carl Alstrup, Valdemar Psilander, Thorleif Lund, Gunnar Sommerfeldt and Olaf Fønss relaxing between takes. Source: Arnold Hending, *Stjerner i Glashuse* (Valby: Winkelmanns Forlag, 1936), 66.

however: a subdivision of the Danish Actors Guild, the Screen Actors Guild, was formed and existed until April 1925.[757]

The reason that no one followed the example of Alstrup and Fønss, and that the protests were not more tenaciously upheld, was the power Nordisk had in the Danish film and theatre industry. By now, film work had become a normal and important source of income for actors. In 1913, when several small film companies had to close down, the Danish Actors Guild supplied legal assistance to the actors who were caught in the disaster.[758] In the 1920s, when Nordisk scaled down its production, the Danish Actors Guild viewed this as the direct cause of unemployment for 258 out of its total of 611 members.[759]

The reason that the directors, among whom A.W. Sandberg and Dinesen, were the first to withdraw from the protest and continued working for Nordisk was partly that the salary was good, partly that it was next to impossible to find other work in Europe during the war. Furthermore, both actors and directors had agreed, when signing their contracts, not to work for another film company.

757 Minutes of the Danish Actors' Association's board meeting (21 April 1925). Held at The Danish Actors' Association. An undated document with the signatures of the guild members exists in the Olaf Fønss Collection at the DFI.

758 Membership Magazine of the Danish Actors' Association (31 October 1913). Held at The Danish Actors' Association.

759 Membership Magazine of the Danish Actors' Association (1 October 1922). Held at The Danish Actors' Association.

The penalty for breach of contract for the directors was 50,000 kroner.[760] That is what Fønss would have been fined, if he broke his contract stating that he could not make films for other companies before the end of 1916.[761] In spite of walkouts and organized labour, conditions did not change significantly until 1918 when Nordisk reorganized its film production.

"Hollywood in Copenhagen" is what Hending calls Nordisk,[762] and the comparison between Nordisk and Hollywood is obvious. Nordisk's organization of its film production was controlled by the management down to the smallest detail. From scriptwriting to forgotten costumes, the company reigned supreme through a deluge of rules, regulations and directives and aimed for rationality and effectivity. But can Nordisk's production mode really be compared to Hollywood's? And how and in which ways did it resemble or differ from the production modes of other companies of the time?

In her investigation of the American film industry from 1896 to 1930, Janet Staiger divides this development into periods characterized by each their own production mode.[763] In this connection, "production mode" is to be understood as a series of conventions which together form the organization of the film production: where do the material and financial resources come from, who makes the decisions, and how is the work distributed during production? Staiger operates with the following four modes which she also defines according to periods:

1. *The cameraman* system (1896–1907)
2. *The director* system (1907–1909)
3. *The director-unit* system (1909–1914)
4. *Central producer* system (1914–1930)

In the *cameraman system* there is no actual distribution of work. One person executes everything according to an idea, he finds out how this idea can be realized technically, he directs, shoots, develops and edits. At this stage, the cameraman was quite often his own employer, and he financed the production himself. The *cameraman system* was mainly used for actualities.

With the transition to fiction, the *director system* evolved; the director was in charge and influenced the entire production from idea to editing. The cameraman was then reduced to a mere technician. Synopses or drafts for the films were usually not written by the director, but he still had final say in the matter.

The *director-unit system* resembled the *director system*, but deviated in that the film production was divided among several production units which could produce simultaneously, and also shoot footage for films that other units were working on. The individual *director-unit* worked in relative autonomy and was still part

760 E.g. NFA. Contract between Nordisk and Holger-Madsen (12 April 1915).

761 NFS:IV,60.DFI. Contract between Nordisk and Olaf Fønss (10 July 1914).

762 Hending, "Det københavnske Hollywood", 641.

763 See Bordwell, Staiger and Thompson, *The Classical Hollywood Cinema*, 87–141.

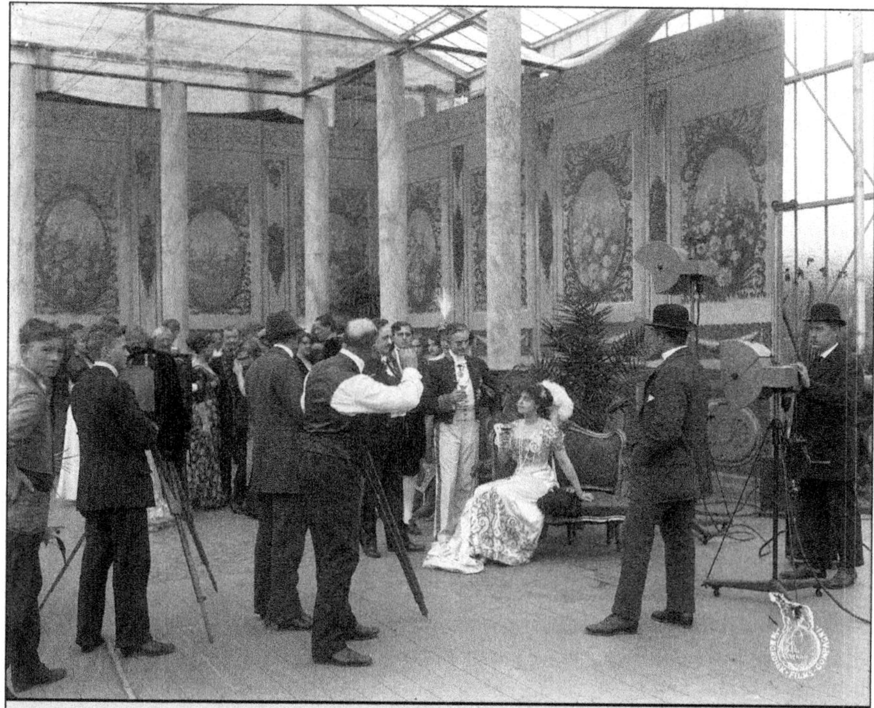

Figure 31. August Blom in shirtsleeves directing Robert Dinesen and Ebba Thomsen on stage 2 in DEN TREDIE MAGT (THE STOLEN TREATY, August Blom, 1913). Courtesy of DFI/Stills & Posters Archive.

of a greater organisation which could contribute to the production with a regular group of actors, sets, costumes etc.

As the films grew longer, this system was replaced by the *central producer system*. "'The central producer', the modern manager of a well-organized mass production system was now necessary to produce the quality multiple-reel film", writes Staiger.[764] The organization of film production at this stage was divided among various departments, each with their own task in the production, and the producer managed and distributed the undertaking. The *central producer system* was the production mode that characterized Hollywood.

Charles Musser sees Staiger's model as largely representative of the development of American film production, but he also raises a few objections. The transition from one stage to the next did not happen simultaneously across the entire industry. While some companies quickly developed a *central producer* mode, others lingered in the *cameraman system* or the *director system*. Musser's main objection is that according to Staiger's typology, the great divide in the early American film industry was the transition from the *director-unit system* to

764 Ibid., 134.

the *central producer system*. Musser believes that this transition did not occur in 1914 but much earlier:

> [...] the 1907–1909 period was a fulcrum, the breakpoint between (1) the film-making process built around traditional forms of organization, of partnership, that was consonant with structures of small-scale capitalism; and (2) production based on modern corporate structures and industrial capitalism.[765]

According to Musser, the real turning point occurred in the transition to an MIE structure.

Nordisk's organization of its film production exemplifies Musser's objection to Staiger's categorization. When Nordisk was founded in 1906, the company worked with several laterally operating stages: cameramen Langhoff, Lippert and Graatkjær worked according to the *cameraman system*, and Viggo Larsen managed the production team in Valby according to something akin to the *director system*. Olsen and Stæhr coordinated and managed the various production teams. In other words, Nordisk had a centrally controlled management even though the production mode cannot be likened to the *central producer system* before the early 1910s. Nordisk's organization of film production went through a massive change with the transition to feature films. The departmentally divided and specialized film production that Nordisk launched in the beginning of the 1910s is very like Staiger's definition of the *central producer system* that is characteristic of Hollywood.

Nordisk's organization resembles Hollywood's in several other ways, too. An important element ignored by Staiger's definition or categorization in periods is distribution and exhibition. The foundation of Hollywood's glory days from 1915 to 1960 was the vertical integration of the film companies. Blind selling and block booking are concepts that derive from this period in which each of the big studios had their own network of cinemas. Nordisk was not a vertically integrated organization before World War I, but still had distribution contracts containing both blind selling and block booking-like clauses that guaranteed future sales of the films. In this, too, Nordisk strikingly resembles the conditions of Hollywood's most successful period.

The studio system in which actors and directors were compelled by contracts to remain loyal to a single film company also resembles what Nordisk had established with its artistic staff. It makes good sense to compare Nordisk to Hollywood, and even to argue that Nordisk organized its film production according to a *central producer system* before Hollywood did.

Staiger's definition of the *central producer system* bears a strong resemblance to Chandler's definition of an MIE, and Musser points to this likeness in his critique of Staiger's typology.[766] Olsen referred to Nordisk's films as the

765 Charles Musser, "Pre-classical American cinema: its changing modes of film production", in Richard Abel (ed.), *Silent Film* (New Brunswick, N.J.: Rutgers University Press, 1996), 97.

766 See Musser, "Pre-Classical American Cinema", 91.

"company's film-fabricata, or consumer film-goods",[767] and Staiger's definition of the *central producer system* contains the assumption that the films are mass-produced consumer products. Musser questions the widespread assumption that "Hollywood is a form of mass production and employs the factory system".[768] By comparing film production with the assembly line in a motorcar factory, Musser argues that film production is in fact incomparable to this. It is only very late in the genesis of a film that the assembly line plays a part. In pre-production, shooting and editing, a film may be compared to the manufacturing of a prototype of a car. Only when the edited negative film lies ready can the actual copying of the film begin, and only in this phase can one speak of a mass production of identical products; only then the assembly-line workers of the film industry take over. I agree with Musser: every film is a unique product, and a direct comparison between film and a mass product is invalid. The effective and rational modus operandi which Nordisk developed may be the closest we get to mass-produced films, or films produced according to *economy of scale*, which is Chandler's term for the competitive advantage which a company gains by producing so many units that the cost of production per unit drops.[769] With its central management and division in departments, the organization of film production at Nordisk, when seen in the view of Staiger's *central producer* mode, looks like an MIE.

Staiger's categorization focuses on the American film industry and does not take European film production into consideration, especially during the transition to the production of feature films when the companies organized themselves differently. If we compare Nordisk's production mode with the world's largest company at the time, Pathé Frères, there are some decisive differences. Whereas Nordisk by and large only produced its films in Valby and in Danish or Scandinavian locations, Pathé fanned out to a series of smaller, independent production companies around the world.

Richard Abel writes that from around 1911, Pathé Frères' influence on the world market started to dwindle. In the US, the company's share of the annually released negative films plummeted to below ten per cent, and in France, the number of American films shown in the last three months of 1913 surpassed the home market: 308 American films against 268 French.[770] Charles Pathé started to dissolve the vertically integrated organization he had built. The connection to the parent company, and the influence it had on the many production companies, fell apart, and Pathé focused on distribution and exhibition. The decentralization of Pathé in the years from 1911 to 1914 brought the French film industry to what Abel has characterized as a "cottage-industry" structure – precisely the opposite of the specialisation which the

767 NFS:I,25.DFI. Unpagn. Minutes of the Board of Directors Meeting (13 October 1916).

768 Musser, "Pre-Classical American Cinema", 98.

769 See Chandler, *Scale and Scope*, 17.

770 See Abel, *The Cine Goes to Town*, 46.

American film production went through in those same years.[771] "Cottage industry" denotes the production mode from before the industrial revolution – industries which can be managed from home by a family with the available tools.

Musser argues that the *director-unit system* was in fact never widespread in the USA, but was the dominant production system in France. Abel partly agrees with Musser, but emphasizes the differences: the French directors for a large part wrote their own scripts, and the *director-units* could plan their economy and production to a large extent. The degree of division of labour in the production units was not high. Abel writes that there was no move toward the *central producer system*, quite the contrary:

> [...] the French companies continued to rely on camaraderie of their production teams (especially at Gaumont) or on a "merit system" of responsibility and compensation rather than on "scientific management" – apparently there were no "clock watchers" at Pathé-Frères.[772]

Research into the organization of the early film industry is still insufficient, but it appears that Nordisk's organization of its production was unique in Europe. Whereas the organization of film production in the big French companies developed toward decentralization, Nordisk was based on a centrally controlled, departmental division of labour that looked like, and indeed anticipated, the organization of the American film industry.

In view of the position Nordisk had achieved, one may wonder why the company did not follow Pathé's example and start a film production outside Valby. Olsen must have reached the conclusion that his way of organizing the film factory was the cheapest and most controllable way of producing. Only few of the company's accounts survive, but a series of statements from the golden years gives us an impression of how much the company made on the individual films. The efficient mode of production shortened the shooting period. From a statement covering 108 films shot in 1913 and 1914, it appears that an average of four days were spent on shooting a film under 500 metres which cost 1,639.97 kroner to produce, and it took thirteen days to shoot a long feature film of which the average price was 5,190.73 kroner. We also have figures for what Nordisk earned on eleven of these films: they cost 10,814.24 kroner on average and made 73,732.86 kroner, which amounts to an average profit of 62,918.62 kroner per film.[773] The account is not detailed and the

771 See ibid., 47.

772 Ibid., 48.

773 Only the dates when the shoot started and ended are noted in the protocol, for which reason the actual shoot may have been shorter if not all the days in between were used. When counting the shooting days, the calendars for 1913 and 1914 have been checked, and Sundays have been excluded. This concerns 108 films from 1913–1914. NFS:IX,21.DFI, and NFS:IX,22.DFI. Production costs; NFS:IX,21.DFI, and NFS:IX,22.DFI; Profits; NFS:XII,41.DFI, 1–3. As for ATLANTIS, the production costs differ greatly from those of the few films we have figures on. Since ATLANTIS tips the general image of the average film, it has been left out of the equation.

average cost of the films can probably be compared to below-the-line figures, in which the salaries of directors, actors etc. are not included.

Joel Finler writes that the American films, Universal's TRAFFIC IN SOULS and William Fox's first feature film, LIFE'S SHOP WINDOW (J. Gordon Edwards, Box Office Attractions Company, 1914), were produced at "a rock-bottom cost" of 6000 dollars (22,380 kroner), and the average price of an American feature film in 1914 was 20,000 dollars (74,600 kroner).[774] Bakker informs us that in Britain, a film would cost an average of 100 pounds (approx. 550 kroner) in the years 1905 and 1907, and the more expensive productions would cost 600–700 pounds (approx. 3,500 kroner). In the 1920s, the price had risen to 10,000–12,000 dollars (approx. 60,000 kroner). A Pathé Frères film cost between 16,000 and 17,000 francs (ca. 22,742 kroner) to produce in 1905.[775] Figures are scarce and it is difficult to make an exact comparison, but the picture nevertheless emerges that Nordisk produced at very low costs. With average production costs of approx. 11,000 kroner and average earnings of approx. 70,000 kroner per film, the film production was very good business indeed.

Financially, Nordisk was doing fine. At the company's first general meeting on 25 January 1912, Olsen received his 200,000 kroner worth of preference shares, after which the preference shares were put out of circulation, and a unanimous board decided to pay a further bonus of 1,000 kroner for each ordinary share, which amounts to a dividend of 100 per cent per share.[776] One year later, a dividend of 60 per cent per share was paid, and in 1914, a dividend of 33 per cent per share. Put together, dividends of 193 per cent were paid for each Nordisk share after the first three general meetings. To this must be added commissions of profits for the board, management and trusted employees, who were paid before the shareholders. All in all, a total of 2,803,811.10 kroner was paid from 1912 to 1914, which would equal around 166 million kroner in 2015.[777] Nordisk's board of directors could actually have chosen to pay more than 33 per cent dividends in 1914, but opted instead to consolidate by writing off and depositing 700,000 kroner on a company account. The consolidation indicates that the board of directors believed in the future film industry. The scepticism which the press expressed when the bank syndicate purchased Nordisk's shares at overprice in June 1912, at a quotation of 130, turned out to be unjustified.

Olsen claimed in 1913 that Nordisk was the world's second-largest film company, only surpassed by Pathé Frères, and with Gaumont coming in third.

774 See Joel W. Finler, *The Hollywood Story* (London: Wallflower Press, 2003), 41.

775 See Gerben Bakker, "Stars and stories. How films became branded products", in John Sedgwick and Michael Pokorny (ed.), *An Economic History of Film*, 48. According to *Salmonsen's Encyclopedia*, second edition 1915–1930, the rate of exchange for a 100 kroner was in American dollars 3,73; British pounds 18,16; French francs 72; Engberg gives the following rates of exchange for 1914: dollars 3,74; British pounds 18,22 and French francs 72,45. See Engberg, *Dansk stumfilm*, 658.

776 NFS:I,25.DFI. Unpagn. Minutes of the Board of Directors Meeting (25 January 1912).

777 Calculated according to Denmark's Statistical Consumer Index.

According to Olsen, Nordisk was a more profitable enterprise which yielded a greater dividend than all other film companies. Olsen asserted that an unnamed company had had a turnover of 17 million francs, but posted a profit of a mere 750,000 Francs and a dividend of eight per cent.[778] In 1913, Pathé had a net profit of over seven million francs, and the company could pay a dividend of 13 per cent. It had been 17,5 per cent in the previous year.[779] Engberg agrees with Olsen's claim that Nordisk was the second-largest film company in the world, based on a comparison of the negative production at Nordisk, Pathé and Gaumont from various years between 1902 and 1908.[780] Bordwell also counts Nordisk as one of the big European companies: "Nordisk took its place alongside Pathé and Gaumont as a major producer and distributor."[781] Schröder also discusses Nordisk's size, but questions which parameter to use:

> [...] according to the company's financial clout? The dividends? The number of productions of feature films or negative metres? According to the amount of positive metres purchased? Or number of employees?[782]

Olsen refers to the profits, and Engberg to the production of negative metres, but whatever the parameter, comparative data from other companies are hard to find. Although it is difficult to give a precise statement concerning Nordisk's size and position on the global market, it is my estimate that with the reorganization due to the production of feature films, the company had moved from being an established national enterprise to carving out a niche among the top contenders.

The Nordisk share were not quoted on the stock market until July 1916, so information concerning the development of the shares had to be obtained from the newspapers. The astounding development of the share is described in an article from the spring of 1913. In September 1912, the Nordisk shares had risen to 165, in November further to 175, and then to 185 in February 1913. In the course of March, the shares went up "day to day" and "hour to hour" until they reached 280. "Small wonder that this precipitate, unprecedented boom creates attention", the article stated.[783] In March 1913, Nordisk shares reached a rate of 340.[784] *Social-Demokraten* said of the extraordinary event: "It is no secret for those in the know that most film-production companies (with the exception of Nordisk) have not been lucrative."[785]

A string of small Danish companies followed in the wake of Nordisk's success, hoping to share in the financial fairy-tale. Knud Rønn Sørensen has counted

778 Anker, "Men hvad siger Ole Olsen?", *Politiken* (10 April 1913).

779 "Films- og Biograf-Industrien", *Berlingske Morgen* (24 July 1913).

780 See Engberg, *Dansk stumfilm*, 72.

781 Bordwell, "Nordisk and the Tableau Aesthetic", 81.

782 Schröder, *Ideale Kommunikation*, 44.

783 Undated anonymous article, *Børsen* (1913) probably from March. XIV:31.DFI, 1. Scrapbook.

784 J.P.B., "I Filmens Himmeltegn", *Social-Demokraten* (22 March 1913).

785 "Dansen om Films-Guldkalven", *Social-Demokraten* (2 March 1913).

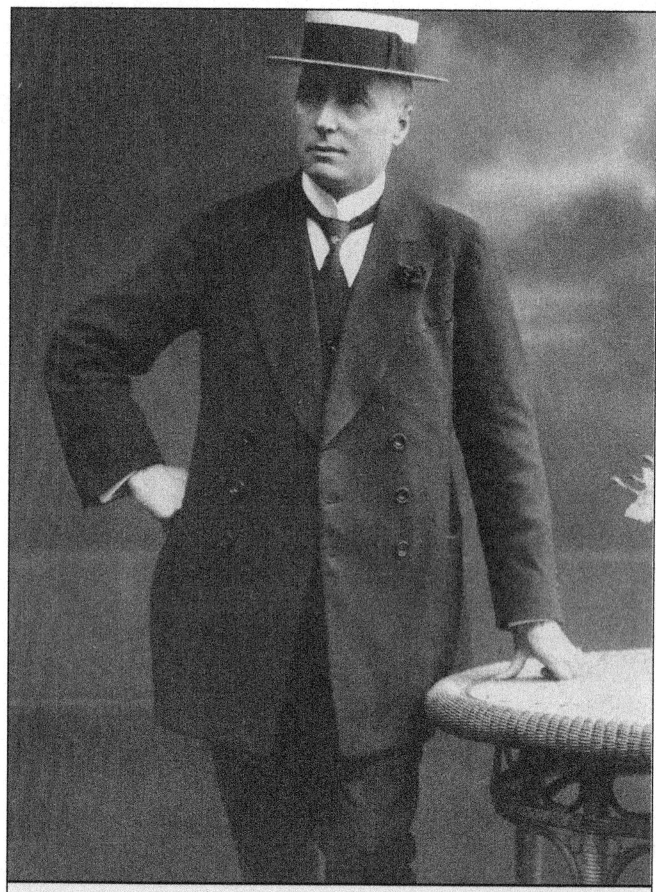

Figure 32. Ole Olsen: "But in order to find a market for their films, I think they'll have to settle the South Pole." Courtesy of DFI/Stills & Posters Archive.

the emergence of 22 new Danish film companies in the years from 1911 to 1914.[786] In a newspaper interview from 1913, Olsen replied to the question of whether these new companies had a chance of succeeding: "[…] if they can groom good managers, and if they can find a loophole in the world market, yes. But in order to find a market for their films, I think they'll have to settle the South Pole."[787] Olsen's point is simple: without a market, there is no basis for a turnover and hence no reason to produce films. Through its own distribution network and its contracts, Nordisk had secured a market for its films. The majority of the newly started film companies had to close quickly, partly for the reason that the markets were already taken.

786 See Knud Rønn Sørensen, *Den danske filmindustri (prod., distr., konsumtion) indtil tonefilmens gennembrud* (Copenhagen: Københavns Universitet / Institut for Filmvidenskab, 1976), 74.

787 Anker, "Men hvad siger Ole Olsen?", *Politiken* (10 April 1913).

During the spring and summer of 1914, Nordisk received a lot of press coverage. The company was used to publicity since film usually made the news, but this time, the press focused on aspects of the company's and Olsen's business transactions. One week after the general meeting in May 1914, Nordisk's shares came under pressure. In June, under the headline: "Will the Nordisk Film Company be Crushed?" the *Social-Demokraten* published a sensational article written by the reporter Jarlbak. The article claimed that Pathé Frères and Gaumont had attempted to crush Nordisk because Nordisk had succeeded in keeping Pathé Frères out of the Danish market in 1909. The way for Pathé Frères to destroy Nordisk was to drop the prices on their own films to such an extent that Nordisk could not keep up. The article further reported that even if Nordisk had made more money in 1913 than in the previous years, the profits had dropped, partly because of the huge salaries paid to their stars. The French film companies were reportedly behind this, and several companies abroad had discontinued their contracts with Nordisk. "The golden days are over", the article claimed.[788] The price of Nordisk shares, which had hit an unprecedented 357, was now at 162. "The panic has spread to the stockbrokers who do their level best to be rid of the film shares". The article claimed that even Olsen had sold off most of his shares, and also insisted that Olsen was on his way "abroad to find a new market for his films" but deemed it unlikely that he would succeed.[789] The allegations of the article were reprinted throughout most of the Danish press, and on the following day, Nordisk's board of directors issued the following statement which was printed verbatim in most of the papers:

> Regarding the article in *Social-Demokraten* printed Thursday, bearing the headline "Will Nordisk be Crushed?" the board of directors at Nordisk is compelled to state that nothing untoward has happened to justify such a doubt in the future as expressed in the article, and the company has experienced no aggressive move on the part of competing companies.[790]

Nordisk shares were put up for sale in ads and box numbers,[791] and the price of shares teetered. *Politiken* wrote about the crisis that "[…] on the whole, we get the impression that a stock-market manoeuvre is at the bottom of this".[792] The rumour spread that Nordisk's shares had been dropped from the stock market because of the financial turbulence surrounding them.[793] Nordisk had in fact tried in vain to get their shares listed at the stock exchange in May 1914.[794] Some weeks after the first article in *Social-Demokraten,* Jarlbak aimed

788 Jarlbak, "Vil Nordisk Filmskompagni blive knust", *Social-Demokraten* (4 June 1914).

789 Jarlbak, "Vil Nordisk Filmskompagni blive knust", *Social-Demokraten* (4 June 1914).

790 "Nordisk Films-Kompagni", *Berlingske Tidende* (5 June 1914). The notice was also published in *København*, *Ekstra Bladet*, *Børsen* and *Social-Demokraten*.

791 "Nordisk Filmsfabrik", *Berlingske Tidende* (12 June 1914); "Nordisk Films", *Politiken* (19 June 1914); "Nordisk Films Aktier", *Politiken* (1 July 1914).

792 "Børserne", *Politiken* (12 June 1914).

793 "Ugens Fondsbørs og Pengemarked", *Politiken* (14 June 1914).

794 NFS:II,31.DFI, 938. Letter from Børge Jacobsen to the Stock Rate Committee at the Copenhagen Stock Exchange (27 May 1914).

another blow at Nordisk. *Berlingske Tidende* found the new attack "tendentious",[795] and *Børsreferenten* wrote: "It is an unparalleled web of lies that has been printed." The newspaper accused Jarlbak of being an errand boy for stockjobbers[796] who tried to bring down the rate of shares for their own gain. In late July 1914, *Politiken* wrote:

> [...] and the shares went up to 350. We have it on good authority that even the Director General could not resist temptation at this enormous rate but sold his shares – at one million – to a local bank which immediately sold the shares on to some stockbrokers who on the following day scattered them far and wide. These private shareholders now suffered an immense loss when the shares went down from 350 to 115 – the minimum reached yesterday. Such a fall in the exchange rate is unprecedented in Denmark, and possibly even abroad.[797]

The rumour that Olsen had sold his shares in the spring was in fact true. In his memoirs, Olsen writes: "I cannot give you a reason why I sold my shares in Nordisk already before the war."[798] Olsen states that he started by selling one set of shares at the value of one million kroner in 1913, and reports that Diskontobanken bought shares for further 400,000 kroner at the rate of 365. "Even in the worst war-time speculation, they never reached such a rate", Olsen recalls. According to the magazine *Filmen*, Diskontobanken helped to inflate the rate of the Nordisk shares: "The banks that supported these shares, not least Diskontobanken, helped to raise expectations that these shares would reach 500 per cent, and at 300–320, most of the old shareholders sold out."[799] When Olsen and the other board members started selling out, a large percentage of Nordisk's shares was put up for sale on the open market. Still, a large number of the shares stayed within the reach of the board, probably with Revisionsbanken or Diskontobanken who maintained the board's control of the company. After Olsen sold his shares, he was no longer the owner but an employed managing director. The separation between ownership and management is one of the characteristics of an MIE.[800] Olsen kept his influence, however, and as before, Nordisk's course rested on his decisions.

Not until May 1914, after Olsen and most likely other board members had sold off the majority of their shares in the company, did the board decide to consolidate the company with 700,000 kroner. It seems an obvious conclusion that since that the board had now secured themselves personaly, they wished to consolidate the company with capital from the new shareholders.

However, at this time, Nordisk embarked on a period of long-term strategies which called for larger investments, first in film production, and then in expansion. Chandler concludes that there is a tendency to pay large dividends

795 "Nordisk Films-Kompagni. Tendentiøse Angreb", *Berlingske Tidende* (24 June 1914).

796 NFS:XIV,32.DFI. Scrapbook, 73. Anonymous article, *Børsreferenten* (1 July 1914).

797 "Omkring Filmen. Er det mon saa galt?", *Politiken* (19 July 1914).

798 Olsen, *Filmens Eventyr og mit eget*, 148.

799 E.H., "Gaar Filmindustrien en vanskelig tid imøde?", *Filmen*, no. 19 (1914).

800 See Chandler, *Scale and Scope*, 2.

in companies owned by the manager, whereas a company with an employed management is more apt to invest in the maintenance of the company's organizational capabilities.[801] The consolidation of Nordisk and the drop in the payment of dividends coincided with Olsen's changed position in the company from owner to employee. With the larger investments, the dividends never again reached 100, 60 or 33 per cent but stayed around ten per cent.

It is difficult to say who started the rumours about Nordisk, but it may have been people close to Olsen or to the board. In his memoirs, Olsen emphasizes in two different places that he never stockjobbed or speculated in shares.[802] Nevertheless, Olsen has been connected to the stockjobber "Carousel Charles", who was called Olsen's "buddy" and agent,[803] and also to the stockjobber "Jeweller Smith".[804] Stockbroker Lamm, a member of the board at Nordisk's, influenced the rate of Nordisk's shares on several occasions.[805] When Olsen in 1918 passed on crucial information concerning Nordisk's financial situation to the public, a board meeting was called at which in particular Børge Jacobsen from Diskontobanken and Lamm expressed that this information should not have reached the press without the consent of the board.[806] Both Jacobsen and Lamm probably wanted to take precautions before the news went public and influenced the rate of shares.

Nordisk shares became an object of speculation. The newspaper *Politiken* characterized the shares as papers bought and sold more passionately than any other shares,[807] and in 1921, *Social-Demokraten* wrote the following: "Film belongs among the most famous war-time securities. For a long time, film was the regular refrain of stockjobbers."[808] In some cases, the rumours surrounding Nordisk were pure fiction; in other cases, they sprang from actual events that were subsequently blown out of proportion.

An example of the latter is Nordisk's price reduction on the Germany market in the summer of 1914. Nordisk dropped its prices by 50 per cent in Germany in June; Olsen attributed the reduction to overproduction of film, and said that Pathé Frères, Nordisk's competitor, had a competitive advantage in producing its own raw stock.[809] Rumour had it that Pathé would lower its prices in Germany, and Nordisk wished to pre-empt this move.[810] *Social-Demokraten* predicted:

801 See ibid., 594–596.

802 See Olsen, *Filmens Eventyr og mit eget*, 147 and 149.

803 "Sukker og Film", *Social-Demokraten* (23 June 1921).

804 NFS:I,25.DFI. Unpagn. Minutes of the Board of Directors Meeting (13 March 1924).

805 "Børsen. Storkamp i Film", *Social-Demokraten* (14 August 1920); Merkur, "Fra Børsen", *Ekstra Bladet* (28 June 1921).

806 NFS:I,25.DFI. Unpagn. Minutes of the Board of Directors Meeting (2 June 1918).

807 Pis, "Nordisk Film", *Politiken* (23 January 1915).

808 "Sukker og Film", *Social-Demokraten* (23 June 1921).

809 "En Omvæltning i Filmsindustrien", *Berlingske Tidende* (Evening edition) (17 July 1914).

810 "En Omvæltning i Filmsindustrien", *Berlingske Tidende* (18 July 1914).

> The enormous capital which the French companies have will enable them to counter Nordisk Films Co's reductions – and the question is who will come out of the fight victorious. For a fight will surely ensue – a fight to the death.[811]

The price reduction came as a surprise to most of the Nordisk board members, who had been told at the general meeting two months before that the situation looked promising.[812] Olsen's Swedish competitor Charles Magnusson, the managing director of Svenska Biografteatern, expressed his opinion of the consequences of a price reduction in a newspaper interview. Magnusson asserted that both Nordisk and Pathé rented out their films rather than selling them. The price of the films varied according to their quality. "In that respect, a 50 per cent price reduction is rather a vague concept", Magnusson stated.[813] Partsch, Pathé Frères' Danish representative, also played down the consequences of a price reduction; summer was the low season of the cinemas, and a reduction of prices was ordinary at this time of year. Partsch continued that "[...] the reductions are temporary and only advertised in the trade magazines as 'up to 50 per cent'".[814] Still, the Germans reacted. The management of the German company Projektions-Aktiengesellschaft Union (PAGU) feared "a fierce price fight",[815] and the German film industry held protest meetings against Nordisk.[816]

In yet another interview, Magnusson stated that "[...] you can hardly rid yourself of the suspicion that private speculation lies behind the reduction, arranged by an interested party who wishes to appropriate a large amount of shares".[817] The price reduction influenced the shares which fell to the rate of 115.[818] On the day that the Magnusson interview was printed, Nordisk made the headlines again. Rumour had it that an international trust consisting of Nordisk, Pathé Frères and Gaumont was in the offing, with the intention of crushing all the small film companies. This would indeed have been possible since the three companies together would command a share capital of about 35 million kroner.[819] The rumour was backed by the fact that Olsen had been abroad and had not yet returned home. Frost and Partsch dismissed the rumours as "fanciful".[820] Together with the news that Nordisk's accounts looked good, the rumour of an international trust made the prices of the shares

811 "Katastrofe paa Filmsmarkedet", *Social-Demokraten* (18 July 1914).

812 "Films-Krachet. Ole Olsen kom de franske Fabriker i Forkøbet", *Social-Demokraten* (19 July 1914).

813 "Nord. Films Co.s Prisreduktion", *Ekstra Bladet* (22 July 1914).

814 "En Films-Sammenslutning? Er det mere end Varmerygter?", *Nationaltidende* (22 July 1914).

815 "Preiskämpfe im Filmhandel", *Vossische Zeitung*, Berlin (23 July 1914).

816 Undated anonymous article. NFS:XIV,32.DFI, 104. Scrapbook.

817 "En Verdens-Filmstrust?", *Hovedstaden* (23 July 1914).

818 "Films-Krachet. Ole Olsen kom de franske Fabriker i Forkøbet", *Social-Demokraten* (19 July 1914).

819 "Kæmpe-Filmstrust i Anmarsch", *Folkets Avis* (22 July 1914).

820 "En Verdens-Filmstrust?", *Hovedstaden* (23 July 1914); "En Films-Sammenslutning? Er det mere end Varmerygter?", *Nationaltidende* (22 July 1914).

go up in early August. I have not succeeded in producing any proof in the Nordisk Collection or from other sources of plans of a trust. The rumour was most likely circulated by a stockjobber with the aim of making the prices go up again. The rumour of an international trust among Pathé, Gaumont and Nordisk resurfaced again in 1920.[821]

The 50 per cent price reduction in Germany was indeed Nordisk's reaction to yet another emerging overproduction of film on the world market. Constantin Philipsen believes there was an overproduction of 50,000 metres a week, most of which were "poor films" made for the local markets.[822] In Europe, the market shares were divided among the big companies, and one way to increase sales of your films was to compete on prices. However, a price reduction on the German market, where Pathé and Gaumont maintained their market shares, would hardly change much.

Both Olsen and Stæhr chose to ensure themselves financially at a time when things were looking good for Nordisk. Olsen's motivation is obvious; he sold off when the price of shares were at its highest, but Olsen's and Stæhr's knowledge about the development of the international market probably played a part as well. In March 1914, Stæhr purchased the company A/S Dansk Skinkekogeri (Danish Canned-Ham Factory Ltd.) in Ingerslevsgade on Vesterbro, Copenhagen.[823] The characteristic ham-shaped can (later known as Jaka-bov) was invented by the company. Stæhr probably intended his interest in the cannery as a side-line activity, but in view of the emerging world war and the rising demand of canned goods, his interest in a cannery was perfectly timed.

In Europe, the leading film companies had divided the market shares in Europe among themselves and the opportunities for growth were limited, but the situation in the US had begun to change, and this opened new opportunities for Nordisk. Traditionally, Nordisk is seen as one of the few foreign companies that did well in the United States in spite of being outside the MPPC. "Great Northern joined the anti-Edison trust and did fine", writes Neergaard.[824] This view is shared by both Tybjerg[825] and Eileen Bowser who mentions:

> Great Northern, founded in January 1908 [sic] as the U.S. representative of Nordisk in Denmark and the one manufacturer of any strength on the American market outside the Patent Company group [...][826]

From a status report of the countries from which the United States imported the most films in the period from 6 August 1909 to 30 June 1910 it appears that the USA imported 2,759,485 metres of film from France, 383,565 metres

821 "Alle Filmsfabriker i hele Verden skal sluttes sammen", *Folkets Avis* (19 July 1920).

822 "Lille Films-Interview", *Politiken* (12 April 1914).

823 See Theodor Green, *Greens danske Fonds og Aktier*, vol. 1914 (Copenhagen: Børsen), 336.

824 Neergaard, *Historien om dansk film*, 32.

825 Abel (ed.), *Encyclopedia of Early Cinema*, 483.

826 Eileen Bowser, The Transformation of Cinema, 1907–1915 (New York: Charles Schribner's Sons, 1994), 73.

from Britain, 358,151 metres from Italy and 330,646 metres from Denmark.[827] The Danish figures are all from Nordisk since Nordisk was the only company exporting to USA at the time.[828] It is quite impressive that the number of metres which Nordisk exported to USA is so close to the amount imported from Italy and Britain. In the American trade press, Oes was considered one of the prominent members of the *Independents*. Through interviews and articles, Oes himself helped create the impression of Nordisk's American success.[829]

However, as Mottram has pointed out, the sales to the USA were never what Nordisk had hoped for. The company sent many films to its American branch that were never sold. In the New York correspondence, Nordisk complained time and again that "the profit of the branch is little compared to sales and risk".[830] Olsen stated in 1911 that the "American branch yields almost no profit at all",[831] and in 1913, Frost ascertained that there were indeed no profits from the New York branch.[832] The overall problem was that the films sent to America did not sell, and the problem became so big by the end of 1913 that Nordisk refused to send more samples to America before they had exhausted their stock of unsold films.[833] Oes suggested that Nordisk could begin producing in USA, and Nordisk was not averse to the idea, but these plans never materialized.[834] Another unrealized initiative was that Nordisk and the Italian company Cines, also outside the MPPC, should form a distribution company that would cover the USA, Mexico and Canada.[835]

The competitive advantage which Nordisk had acquired in Europe by being the first company to reorganize its production for making feature films did not apply in the USA. "The time is not ripe for feature films, if it will ever be", was what producer Adolph Zukor was told by the MPPC when he applied for permission to make longer films.[836] The MPPC insisted on one-reelers as the industrial standard, and the feature film did not emerge in USA until some years later.

Cadance Jones writes that the persistent scepticism concerning long films among the MPPC members eventually prevented them from holding their

827 *Moving Picture World* (18 March 1911), quoted from Mottram, "The Great Northern Film Company", 86.

828 See Mottram, *The Danish Cinema before Dreyer*, 8.

829 E.g. Ingvald C. Oes, "Growth of the Feature Film", *Moving Picture World* (23 November 1912), quoted from Bergsten, *Ole Olsen*, 25.

830 NFS:II,12.DFI, 179–180. Letter from Wilhelm Stæhr to Ingvald C. Oes, New York (1 February 1910).

831 NFS:II,11.DFI, 744. Letter from Nordisk (probably from Ole Olsen) to Ingvald C. Oes, New York (14 January 1911).

832 NFS:II,23.DFI, 591. Letter from Harald Frost to Ingvald C. Oes, New York (10 January 1913).

833 NFS:II,29.DFI, 31. Letter from Harald Frost to Ingvald C. Oes, New York (6 December 1913).

834 NFS:II,12.DFI, 573. Letter from Wilhelm Stæhr to Ingvald C. Oes, New York (1 April 1910).

835 NFS:I,87:19.DFI. Draft for agreement between A/S Cines and A/S Nordisk Films Co., ca. 1911/1912.

836 Jones, "Co-evolution of Entrepreneurial Careers", 932, quoted from Neal Gabler, *An Empire of Their Own. How Jews Invented Hollywood* (New York: Anchor, 1988), 30.

share of the market. The MPPC members who had tried to monopolize the American film industry by virtue of their patents did not manage the shift to the new type of product. Like Jones, Robert Anderson sees this as one of the MPPC's biggest mistakes and what caused their members to lose influence.[837] By the end of World War I, only four members of the MPPC were still active.[838] Film producers like William Fox, Carl Laemmle and Adolph Zukor, who opted for feature films, came out as the winners and became the future tycoons of the American film industry.

Already before the war, the MPPC was losing control of the American market. A string of law suits caused the monopoly situation in America to dissolve. In 1912, the Supreme Court ruled against the cartel's monopoly on raw stock, and in October 1915, the Federal government announced the anti-monopoly verdict that spelled the end of the MPPC. Nordisk's management and Oes debated the possibilities that arose when the MPPC ceased to control the market. One solution was to switch to direct distribution on the American market as it was done in Europe. Olsen planned to travel to the United States in the fall of 1914, and Nordisk hoped that the American market would grow;[839] in September 1914, Nordisk opened a distribution office in Minneapolis.[840] However, Olsen's planned trip was cancelled "due to the unstable circumstances".[841] The outbreak of World War I thwarted plans for Nordisk's expansion in the USA, but the war became the outward influence that created the opportunity for expansion in Europe and launched the next major reorganization of the company.

837 See Anderson, "The Motion Picture Patents Company", 150.

838 See ibid., 152.

839 NFS:II,34.DFI, 794. Letter from Harald Frost to Ingvald C. Oes, New York (16 January 1915).

840 NFS:II,33.DFI, 373. Letter from Harald Frost to Ingvald C. Oes, Great Northern Film Co., New York (22 September 1914).

841 NFS:II,32.DFI, 940. Letter from Rotkjær to Ingvald C. Oes, Great Northern Film Co., New York (3 August 1914).

1914–1917

The Growth of the Polar Bear

On 28 July 1914, the Austro-Hungarian Empire declared war on Serbia in response to the murder of Archduke Franz Ferdinand a month earlier. Very few could predict that the declaration would lead to an extensive, lengthy war that would take a toll on most of the world. All the same, World War I created the conditions for Nordisk's second major reorganization. Denmark's neutrality put the company in the favourable position of being able to maintain its export of films at a time when the French companies had to pull out of the Central Powers and Russia, leaving their market shares open. Nordisk could now launch a large-scale expansion in which one of the targets was to be vertically integrated on the German and Central-European markets.

Olsen was in Berlin when war was declared, and upon his return to Copenhagen, he told the press:

> I was walking down Unter den Linden when the message arrived that Serbia's answer had been unsatisfactory. What enthusiasm! People were cheering in the streets. In the cafés, everybody stood up and sang the national anthem, and God have mercy on the poor foreigner who didn't understand what had happened and remained sitting. He was kicked out the door before you could say knife.[842]

The experience in the German capital gave Olsen a clear notion of the nationalistic feelings that the war had set in motion, and through which Nordisk now had to navigate. In early August 1914, a Danish newspaper reported that "the managers of the French companies Pathé Frères and Gaumont's branches in Berlin have fled, taking along all petty cash, and without paying outstanding bills".[843] Under the slogan: "No more French films", German cinema owners decided to boycott films produced by their enemies.[844] Public opinion was so strong that Nordisk feared for the fate of REVOLUTIONSBRYLLUP because the film was set in France.[845]

Olsen was well aware of the importance of making and maintaining relations to decision makers in Denmark and the belligerent countries. One of the means doing so was through strategic donations, first in Denmark and then, as the war progressed, in the countries in which Nordisk had expanded. During

842 "Ole Olsen vender hjem fra Berlin", *Ekstra Bladet* (1 August 1914).

843 "Pathé frères og Gaumonts Repræsentanter flygter", *Nordsjællands Social-Demokrat* (7 August 1914).

844 E.g. untitled article, *Hamburger Fremdenblatt* (11 August 1914).

845 NFS:II,33.DFI, 380. Letter from Harald Frost to Nordische Films Co., Berlin (22 September 1914).

the first weeks of August 1914, Olsen donated six cars to the Danish Army, at a total cost of 50,000 kroner.[846] The cars were bought at Mammen & Drescher's.[847] To Copenhagen's Rifle Association, Olsen donated 1,000 kroner for ammunition,[848] and, finally, he donated 10,000 kroner to *Centralkomiteen, Dronningens Indsamling* (The Central Committee, the Queen's Collection). This contribution in particular made the headlines because the amount equalled what the Danish King and Queen had donated.[849]

Germany, too, came to feel the generosity of Olsen and Nordisk Films Co. Under the headline: "The Danes, Our Sincere Friends", the German newspaper *Leipziger Blätter* stated that Olsen had given 15,000 marks to "the national foundation for the bereaved of those killed in the war".[850] The company also provided film free of charge to different charity organizations and gave special privileges to its employees in Germany who participated in the war.[851] 5,000 German marks were donated by Olsen to the German Red Cross, [852] and an additional 5,000 marks by the German branch of Nordisk: "For the benefit of East-Prussian cinema people who in one way or another have suffered from the war."[853] The war and nationalism also came to play a part in Nordisk's promotion in Germany. One of the German ads for the company stated:

> Cinema has a mission in these hard times of war. Comforting and uplifting the many thousands of people, who, low in spirits, worry about the Fatherland and of the loved ones at the front. Therefore cinema owners: show only good first class films![854]

Actualities from the front were in demand, but hard to get. Nordisk's New York branch had asked for films from the front in late August, but Nordisk had to answer that filming at the front was strictly prohibited.[855] The German branch of the American Biograph Company had applied in vain for permission to film at the German front, and a few German film companies had sent cameramen to the front, but due to the fear of espionage, the military command immediately sent them back.[856]

The German general staff hired Oskar Messter as film adviser in October 1914, and among his first assignments was laying down the rules for gaining permis-

846 Letter of thanks from Minister of Defence P. Munck to Ole Olsen (8 August 1914). Ole Olsen's private archives.

847 "Ole Olsen og Krigen", *Vort Land* (7 August 1914).

848 Untitled article, *København* (9 August 1914).

849 "Centralkomitéen. Ole Olsens Bidrag lig Kongens og Dronningens", *Politiken* (1 September 1914).

850 "Die Dänen, unsere aufrichtigen Freunde", *Leipziger Blätter* (25 October 1914).

851 "Geschäftliches", *Der Kinematograph*, no. 409 (28 October 1914).

852 NFS:II,33.DFI, 545. Letter from Ole Olsen to Nordische Films Co., Berlin (9 October 1914).

853 NFS:II,33.DFI, 546. Letter from Ole Olsen to Nordische Films Co., Berlin (9 October 1914).

854 *Der Kinematograph*, no. 401 (2 September 1914).

855 NFS:II,33.DFI, 91. Letter from Harald Frost to Ingvald C. Oes, New York (22 August 1914).

856 See Wolfgang Mühl-Benninghaus, "Newsreel Images of the Military and War, 1914–1918", in Thomas Elsaesser (ed.), *A Second Life. German Cinema's First Decade*, 176.

sion to film at the front. The demands favoured German companies and excluded all foreigners.[857] Wolfgang Mühl-Benninghaus has identified the following four companies as those who obtained official permission: Messter-Film, Eiko, Express-Film and Martin Knopf.[858] In view of the fact that only a few official permissions were granted, and that Nordisk was not a German company, it is remarkable that Nordisk was actually given permission as early as September 1914.[859] The reason was probably Denmark's neutrality. The German trade paper *Der Kinematograph* wrote that Nordisk had sent cameramen to the German front, and the footage shot included the horrible moment when the church tower in the East-Prussian town of Tapiau collapsed; in spite of the Red Cross flag being visible, the Russian forces continued shooting at the brave nurses. The article even stated that Olsen, who was in Berlin, had given orders that the film should be distributed to all of the company's branches. The first copy of the film was to be sent to the United States, and *Der Kinematograph* reported of Nordisk's intentions: "Through this reliable document, the company hopes to uncover to all neutral nations the atrocities committed not by German soldiers but by our enemies."[860] The intention of showing the truth about the campaigns at the front also appears in Nordisk's German ads for the films:

> "Nordisk Films Co. *will ensure* that the aforementioned films *are going to be shown* in all the *neutral nations* (America, Australia, Italy, Spain etc.) in the course of the following days to demonstrate the truly correct behaviour of our German troops."[861]

Olsen's pro-German statements were published in the German media, and Harald Frost immediately wrote to the German branch that the content of the article was not in accordance with Olsen's or the company's neutrality. In the future, the branch was supposed to market itself by its German name, Nordische Films Co. G.m.b.H., and remove "Kopenhagen" from the company's trademark. This never happened, but when preparing ads and commercials, the Berlin branch was instructed never to forget that both Olsen and Nordisk belonged to a neutral country.[862] Yet a letter to the London branch illustrates a very different approach Nordisk pursued at the same time: "We agree with your suggestion of putting our name on all titles and subtitles of the films we send you, in order to avoid confusion between our films and German productions."[863]

Nordisk's reasons for making German propaganda films were blatantly commercial. The films had great market value, and the company proudly informed

857 See ibid., 176–177.

858 See ibid., 177.

859 NFS:II,33.DFI, 419. Letter from Harald Frost to Nordisk Films Co. Ltd., Berlin (26 September 1914).

860 "Aus der Praxis", *Der Kinematograph*, no. 406 (7 October 1914).

861 Ibid.

862 NFS:II,33.DFI, 592–593. Letter from Harald Frost to Nordische Films Co., Berlin (10 October 1914).

863 NFS:II,33.DFI, 813. Letter from Harald Frost to Nordisk Films Co., London (28 October 1914).

its branches and agents "that we have succeeded in shooting some interesting footage of the destruction caused by the war in East Prussia."[864] Nordisk released seven films from the Eastern front and Northern France. They were sold to most of the world, and the first one was even sent to Britain, France and Russia. In Denmark, the films were shown under relatively neutral titles such as KRIGSBILLEDER I-VII (WAR PICTURES I-VII, 1915), but in Germany the same films were shown with propaganda-like titles: RUSSISCHES SCHRECKENSREGIMENT AN DER OSTGRENZE (Russian Terror Regime on the Eastern Border, 1915) or WIE DEUTSCHE SOLDATEN KRIEG FÜHREN (How German Soldiers Fight, 1915). Nordisk even showed its gratitude towards the German administration: in a confidential letter, Frost asked the German branch to give the film VON DEN RUSSEN VERWÜSTETE STÄDTE UND ORTSCHAFTEN OSTPREUSSENS (East-Prussian Towns and Villages Destroyed by the Russians, 1915) as a gift to the German Military Command.[865]

I have not been able to find anything about Denmark's official view of these films in the National Archives, but that the Danish Ministry of Justice and the Ministry of the Interior approved the films while setting certain limits for their use is evident from a letter which Nordisk sent to its foreign branches and agents to emphasize that no alterations of the films were allowed. Frost wrote in a letter to Fotorama:

> As Director General Olsen and I told you over the telephone today, the titles of these and later war films may not be subject to any changes, regardless of where they are shown, be it Denmark, Norway or Sweden. We have had to promise this on our word of honour to the Justice Department and the Home Office in order to avoid confiscation of the negatives.[866]

Nordisk's manoeuvres with the films from the German front show that the company wished to be on good terms with the administration in one of the company's largest export markets. In addition, it indicates that the company trusted the Central Powers to win the war. This was never explicitly stated by the company, but board member Lamm recalls that "Ole Olsen believed firmly in the future of Germany [...]".[867] The incident surrounding the films from the war zone also gave Nordisk a clear impression of the balancing act which the company would have to perform to maintain its identity as a neutral company while simultaneously being forced conforming and ingratiating itself with different national interests in order to establish the best possible business.

All international mail was withheld for a while when the war broke out,[868] and

864 NFS:II,33.DFI, 479. Letter from Harald Frost to A/S de Giglio, Havnegade (5 October 1914). Almost identical letters to other foreign branches, agents and distributors in NFS:II,33.DFI, 480 up to NFS:II,33.DFI, 495 and NFS:II,33.DFI, 501 up to NFS:II,33.DFI, 504.

865 NFS:II,33.DFI, 555. Letter from Harald Frost to Fritz Knevels, Berlin (9 October 1914).

866 NFS:II,33.DFI, 557. Letter from Harald Frost to A/S Fotorama (9 October 1914). Almost identical letters to branches and agents in NFS:II,33.DFI, 561, NFS:II,33.DFI, 562, NFS:II,33.DFI, 591 and NFS:II,33.DFI, 605.

867 Lamm, *Erindinger og Tanker*, 190.

868 NFS:II,32.DFI, 949. Letter from Harald Frost to Nordisk Films Co. Ltd., London (4 August 1914).

Nordisk had to stop all shipping of films.[869] Even though Nordisk's contracts with its actors had a *force majeure* clause which relieved the company of all obligations in the event of war, Nordisk chose to continue production after the outbreak of World War I. However, on 24 August 1914, the management requested the actors to annul their contracts and continue on daily wages.[870] All of the actors except for Olaf Fønss and Betty Nansen agreed to do so. The season being almost over, it would have been difficult for most actors to find other employment on such short notice. It was widely assumed that Nordisk was short of money. Olsen explained that all film trade had come to a halt at the outbreak of the war, and Nordisk continued to make films in the hope that the war would not last long. When the war appeared to drag out, the solution of hiring actors on daily wages was implemented, although Nordisk felt obliged to keep up business as usual in the case of other employees.[871] From Olsen's statement that Nordisk hoped for a quick end to the war we may get the impression that the company was biding its time to decide how to tackle the situation. However, on 26 August 1914, less than a month after the war began, Harald Frost answered the question "What now, after the war?" in a newspaper interview:

> - Yes, hopefully we're going to earn lots and lots of money. You have to take national feelings into consideration. In Germany and Austria they won't buy French and Italian films; similarly, France, Russia, Britain, Belgium won't watch German films – therefore all countries will meet in neutral Denmark. And our films can be sold everywhere; to begin for now we only have American competition, but more competitors will surely emerge.
>
> - Do you have enough films in store?
>
> - Yes, we have so much that we can supply half of the world for many months. And we will continue to shoot.[872]

During winter, the company's shares rose steadily and reached an exchange rate of 150 kroner per share. The expectations still were that the war would soon be over and that Nordisk, being a company based in a neutral country, was going to do big business in Germany and Austria-Hungary as films from the Entente Powers were going to be banned for many years to come.[873]

On 6 February 1915, at an extraordinary general meeting of the company, a motion concerning a doubling of Nordisk's share capital from two to four million kroner passed with 1,213 votes against 80. The bank syndicate stood surety for one million while the other million was offered to the shareholders at an exchange rate of 105 – a good offer since Nordisk's shares were selling at an exchange rate of 120. Several of the shareholders asked what the money was

869 NFS:II,32.DFI, 958. Letter from Harald Frost to Great Northern Film Co., New York (6 August 1914).

870 Many of the actors' contracts in Nordisk Film Collection have addenda dated 24 August 1914, when the actors accepted daily wages.

871 "Nordisk Film og Skuespillerne", *Social-Demokraten* (26 August 1914).

872 "Filmsindustrien", *Viborg Stifts Folkeblad* (26 August 1914).

873 "Nordisk Films Co.", *Børs Referenten* (20 January 1915).

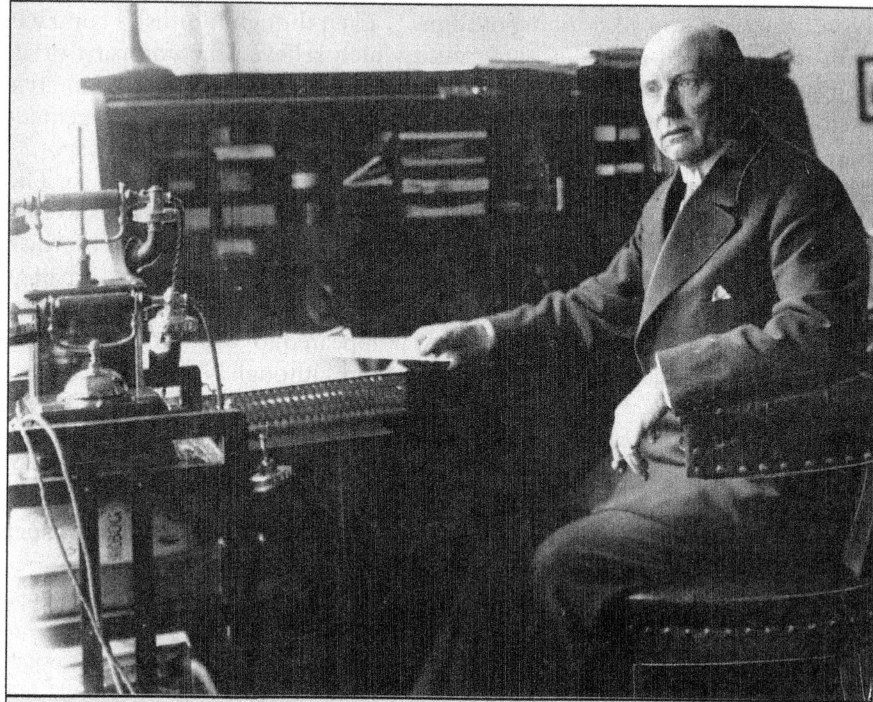

Figure 33. "Nordisk Films Kompagni will now become the biggest in the world." Ole Olsen at his desk about 1916–1917. Courtesy of DFI/Stills & Posters Archive.

for, but Olsen maintained that competition made it impossible to unveil the company's plans.[874] Olsen's vague explanation started the rumour that this was a trick to enable Olsen to buy back the shares he had sold at an exchange rate of 350, now down to 105 kroner per share. Or had Nordisk perhaps bought fifty cinemas in France?[875] In fact, Olsen had given the true answer in an interview published in *Filmen* on 1 February and republished in *Berlingske Tidende* on 27 February. Olsen had been asked whether a capital expansion would not be unwise in view of the world war.

> "No, in no way", responds Mr. Ole Olsen. "What we are doing now is sound, and it will profit the shareholders, I know that for a fact. You see, the war cannot last forever, peace must come; we have to count on that. As long as the war lasts, we'll manage, and when peace comes, we are where we want to be, and ready. That's the point: we will have our affairs in order like no one else. This is why it is prudent to act now. And it will pay off, I've looked into that." Mr. Olsen tilts his head and looks into the future: "Nordisk Films Kompagni will now become the biggest in the world. We are already the finest film producers, and I'm actually rather proud of this."[876]

874 "2 Mill. til 'Nordisk Film'", *Ekstra Bladet* (6 February 1915).

875 "Hvad Nordisk Film gemmer i sit Bryst", *Folkets Avis* (8 February 1915).

876 Mr., "Generaldirektør Ole Olsen udtaler sig om Situationen", *Filmen*, no. 8 (February 1915): 71.

Nordisk was going to be the biggest film company in the world. Olsen did not specify how Nordisk would obtain this position, but it was not mere rhetoric from the Director General. The first visible effect of the capital expansion was that the board decided to launch the building of a new and bigger printing laboratory in Frihavnen,[877] which was completed in 1917. In Valby, the company bought about 6,000 additional square metres of land. This made room for more workshops and an extra studio, which meant simultaneous shooting on five stages at a time.[878] Once more, Nordisk combined additional production facilities with large-scale organizational change.

Nordisk's film production increased so much during the war that the Valby studios were not sufficient, so in 1916, the company rented the two studios at Benjamin Christensen's A/S Dansk Biograf Kompagni studio at Taffelbays Allé in Hellerup, at a cost of 40,000 kroner per year. Part of the bargain was that Nordisk could employ actress Karen Sandberg and cameraman Johan Ankerstjerne.[879] The deal was for one year to begin with, and was later prolonged for 1917.[880]

Nordisk's production peaked in 1915 with a negative film total of 116,013 metres or 174 films, of which 96 were multi-reel films. This roughly corresponds to producing two feature films a week. The company strategy was to maintain and expand film production and exploit the advantages of being a company from a neutral country that could still export its products. However, an additional strategy became obvious during the war, but which had already been part of the plan when Nordisk expanded their share capital.

In January 1915, Olsen informed his board that he was negotiating with Fotorama about a possible takeover of the Aarhus company. Olsen therefore gave the following reasons for an expansion of the share capital: "To carry through such plans and possibly to purchase other companies, the possession of which will be of interest to our company."[881] Nordisk was at an advantage because Fotorama's distribution contract for film from Nordisk in Sweden would expire on 1 May 1915, and the contracts for Denmark and Norway expired on 1 May 1916. The takeover did not succeed, but instead the two companies together formed Fotoramas Filmsbureau A/S with a share capital of 130,000 kroner, of which each company owned half. The film rental company would be in charge of renting out Nordisk's films in Scandinavia. Through this deal, Nordisk achieved a greater share of the profit of its films.

While negotiating a takeover of Fotorama, Olsen also attempted to buy the Swedish company A/B Svenska Biografteatern's "Film Factory and Rental

877 NFS:I,25.DFI. Unpagn. Minutes of the Board of Directors Meeting (10 June 1915).

878 NFS:II,34.DFI, 732. Letter from Harald Frost to Barrister Børge Jacobsen (12 January 1915).

879 NFA. Nordisk's copy of contract between A/S Dansk Biograf Kompagni and Nordisk Films Kompagni (11 April 1916).

880 NFA. Letter from Harald Frost to A/S Dansk Biograf Kompagni (28 April 1917).

881 NFS:I,25.DFI. Unpagn. Minutes of the Board of Directors Meeting (21 January 1915).

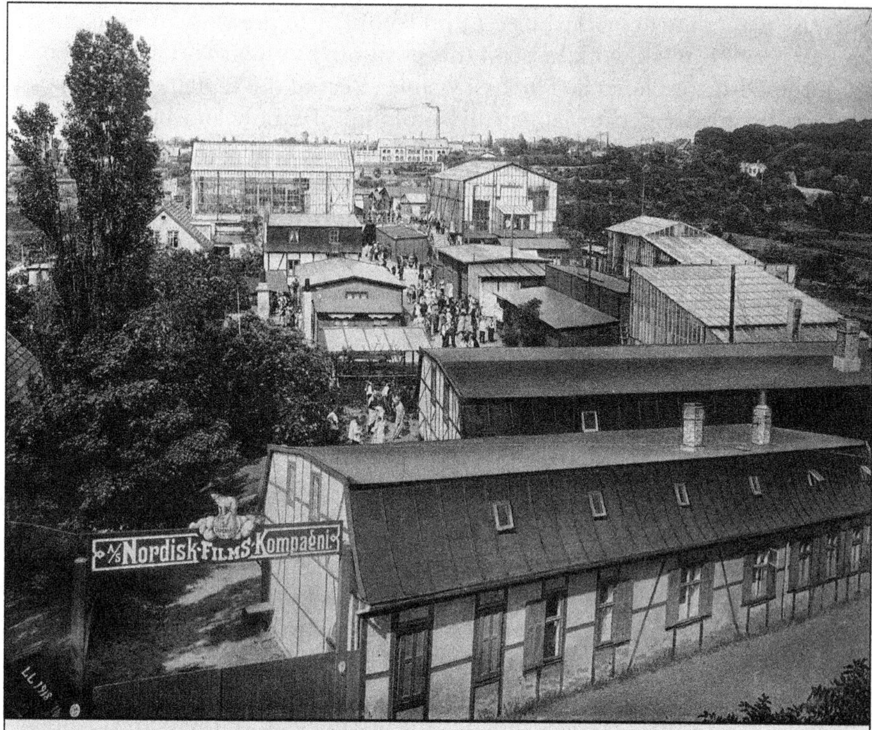

Figure 34. A view of the "Film Factory" in Valby. The front building has been copied to give an impression of a larger studio. Courtesy of DFI/Stills & Posters Archive.

Agency",[882] run by Charles Magnusson.[883] The purchase of Svenska Biografteatern was not realized either but the attempt brought about the result that Nordisk purchased half of the share capital in the following Swedish film companies:

A/B Svenska Biografteaterns Filmsbyrå, Stockholm	Kr.	50,000
A/B Nordisk Filmsfabrik, Stockholm	Kr.	81,500
A/B Fribergs Filmsbyrå, Stockholm	Kr.	6,000
A/B Svenska Biografteatern's distribution in Scandinavia in Nordisk shares.[884]	Kr.	180,000

882 NFS:I,25.DFI. Unpagn. Minutes of the Board of Directors Meeting (21 January 1915).

883 According to Swedish writer and journalist Bengt Idestam-Almquist, there had been a veritable "Dano-Swedish war" in 1912–1913 between Svenska Biografteatern and Nordisk. A Danish coalition consisting of Nordisk, Fotorama and Biorama tried to win market shares in Sweden from Svenska Biografteatern who collaborated with Pathé Frères, and the market shares were for distribution as well as production. See Bengt Idestam-Almquist, "Nordisk Tonefilm och dess fäder", in *Ur en Isbjörns memoarer: Nordisk tonefilm 1929–1954* (Stockholm: Nordisk Tonefilm, 1954), 118–145. Swedish research in silent pictures has mainly been focused on the golden age of Swedish film production, from the mid-1910s and into the 1920s, for which reason we have no research to shed light on this subject in Scandinavian film history. In the Nordisk Film Collection, the best evidence of a connection between Nordisk and Svenska Biografteatern in 1912–1913 is a letter stating that Olsen had bought shares for 10,000 kroner in A/B Svenska Biograf Kompagniet. NFS:II,21.DFI, 62. Letter from Ole Olsen to A/B Svenska Biograf Kompaniet, Stockholm (20 July 1912).

884 NFS:I,25.DFI. Unpagn. Minutes of the Board of Directors Meeting (22 February 1915).

The deal gave Nordisk the rights to distribute Swedish films, and Nordisk now sat more firmly on the Scandinavian market than ever before. Its acquisition of companies had only just begun, and the next target was Germany where Nordisk benefited from goodwill due to their earlier donations and production of propaganda films.

Foreign film companies had dominated the German market before the war. Eighty per cent of all films shown in Germany – and in some years as much as 90 per cent – were foreign. Films from France led the field with a share of 30 per cent, the USA came second with 25 per cent, Italy with 20 per cent and the Scandinavian countries with 15 per cent.[885] German film production was by no means large; in 1913, the entire German production was 353 films, while in that same year Nordisk alone had produced 98 films.[886] The months immediately before and after the outbreak of the war were turbulent for the German film trade, and Nordisk's reduction of prices in 1914 had added to the chaos. The business was characterized by mergers, divisions and new formations as everyone was trying to get a share of what was left of the market after the French companies had withdrawn.[887]

In March 1915, Nordisk began its expansion in Germany. For 700,000 marks and 300,000 kroner of shares in Nordisk, the company took over David Oliver's film distribution network and cinemas: one cinema in Berlin, five in Leipzig and two in Halle.[888] Proprietor David Oliver had been running cinemas in Germany since 1905. In May 1914, Olsen and Oliver had plans of collaboration which entailed that Oliver would manage a string of cinemas in Germany, and possibly elsewhere in Europe, for ten per cent of the profits.[889] Now the collaboration materialized. Oliver's experience with the German film industry was one reason that he became the manager of the rental agency Nordische Film G.m.b.H., which was to become a crucial part of the business network that Nordisk was about to establish.

Through its purchase of companies and cinemas, Nordisk had become a multinational as well as a vertically integrated company. Geoffrey Jones defines a multinational company as an enterprise "that controls operations or income-generating assets in more than one country".[890] A company whose sole interest

885 See Hans Traub, *Die Ufa. Ein Beitrag zur Entwicklungsgeschichte des deutschen Filmschaffens* (Berlin: UFA-Buchverlag, 1943), 9–10.

886 See Klaus Kreimeier, *The UFA Story. A History of Germany's Greatest Film Company 1918–1945* (New York: Hill and Wang, 1996), 17.

887 See Evelyn Hampicke, "The Danish Influence: David Oliver and Nordisk in Germany", in Thomas Elsaesser (ed.), *A Second Life: German Cinema's First Decade*, 72.

888 NFS:I,25.DFI. Unpagn. Minutes of the Board of Directors Meeting (8 March 1915). Several sources report that Nordisk owned and ran cinemas in Germany before the outbreak of the war, see e.g. Jerzy Toeplitz, *Geschichte des Films*, vol. 1: *1895–1928* (Berlin: Henschel, 1992), 70. No evidence in the Nordisk Film Collection indicates that Nordisk owned cinemas in Germany prior to 1915.

889 NFS:II,31.DFI, 592–593. Letter from Ole Olsen to Direktor David Oliver, Leipzig (4 May 1914).

890 Geoffrey Jones, *Multinationals and Global Capitalism* (Oxford: Oxford University Press, 2005), 5.

is to export goods from its homeland is not a multinational company according to Jones. Until its purchase of shares in the Swedish film companies and Oliver's company, Nordisk's foreign enterprises had been limited to three branches which, for all intents and purposes, were merely sales offices. Jones argues that in order to become multinational, a company has to make one or both of the following investments: direct investments connected with managerial control of capital in a foreign company, or portfolio investments such as private loans or purchase of foreign securities like bonds or shares without taking an active part in the management of the foreign business.[891] The purchase of Oliver's business was Nordisk's first direct investment in a foreign company, and it gave Nordisk direct control of the management of the company. With the Oliver takeover, Nordisk made a "forward integration". From controlling production, Nordisk now also controlled distribution and exhibition, and by gaining control over production, distribution and exhibition, Nordisk had become a vertically integrated company in Germany. The advantage of being vertically integrated was that the company now had a share in the profits at all stages of the business, and moreover that the transaction costs were reduced because all expenses were kept inside the company.

The choice of Oliver as the manager of Nordisk's German business was partly based on his experience, but another important reason was his German citizenship. The war had made the situation politically precarious for Nordisk, as the company had to act as a foreign firm in a country at war. To avoid governmental interference in a country where a multinational company does business, Ring, Lenway and Govekar consider it a necessity to install native management. If a multinational company directs management from home, it will be perceived as an alien agent and may incur far greater governmental interference.[892] Evelyn Hampicke even suggests that Nordisk's German organization was constructed in such a way that if a break-up should take place between the mother company in Copenhagen and Nordische Films Co. in Germany, Oliver would be able to step in and take control of the German part of the company as an independent firm.[893] Therefore, Oliver was well-suited to be the manager of the German network that Nordisk established during the war. Nordisk subsequently followed similar strategies in Russia and Central Europe. However, the strategy of selecting local managers to run its business abroad and making a horizontal integration through investments in film companies in the various countries only succeeded to a certain degree. To some extent, Nordisk avoided governmental interference, but was still perceived as foreign and at times even as a hostile company in the countries where it operated as a multinational.

891 See Jones, *Multinationals*, 5; Boje, *Danmark og multinationale virksomheder før 1950*, 12.

892 See Peter S. Ring, Stefanie A. Lenway, and Michelle Govekar, "Management of the political imperative in international business", *Strategic Management Journal*, vol. 11, no. 2 (1990): 145–147.

893 See Hampicke, "The Danish Influence", 77.

During the summer of 1915, Nordisk entered into collaboration with Germany's largest film company, Projections-Aktiengesellschaft Union (PAGU), as well as with the smaller Luna-Film-G.m.b.H. Under the enterprising Paul Davidson, PAGU had established a chain of large, luxurious cinemas that appealed to upper middle class patrons.[894] Together with the cinemas formerly owned by Oliver, Nordisk thus gained access to many of the most attractive cinemas in Germany. Another advantage in the collaboration with the new partner was that the company had signed a contract with Asta Nielsen in 1911, and in 1912, PAGU had moved its main office to Berlin in order to establish a studio for the specific purpose of making Asta Nielsen films. Nordisk now obtained the rights to distribute these films. In July 1914, PAGU had made an agreement with Pathé Frères to the effect that the French company was to supply raw stock to PAGU in return for the distribution rights of the products from the German company. The agreement with Pathé collapsed when the war broke out, and it was highly convenient for PAGU that Nordisk could step in with capital.

Luna was a small company, which Olsen was offered for purchase in September 1914.[895] Frost asked Fritz Knevels and Richard Seemann, who managed the Berlin branch, to discreetly investigate Luna's business and give a personal assessment of the company.[896] At first, Olsen turned the offer down,[897] but in August 1915, Nordisk went public with the news that the Nordisk-Oliver-PAGU company had been formed "on the quiet".[898] Nordisk and PAGU exchanged offices so that Nordisk now moved into Zimmerstrasse 16–18, while PAGU moved into Friedrichstrasse 225. PAGU maintained its film production, while Nordisk took over the rental of PAGU's films in Germany.[899] "The group", as the German trade press chose to call the outcome of the merger, caused quite a stir. Germany had introduced a general ban on the export of German films a month earlier. The costs of German films had hitherto been covered by sales in Germany, Austria-Hungary and the Balkans, and the profit had come from sales to Scandinavia, Holland and Switzerland. The export ban applied to Austria-Hungary and the Balkans, so now some German film producers could not even cover their costs.[900] The group, with Nordisk in the lead, had emerged at an inopportune moment in the German film industry and aroused the antagonism of its peers.

In Berlin, approximately 80 distributors, film producers and cinema owners gathered on 5 August 1915 at the Admiralspalast to protest the merger. The

894 See Lähn, "Paul Davidson", 82.

895 NFS:II,33.DFI, 197. Letter from Harald Frost to Luna-Film-Gesellschaft m.b.H., Berlin (2 September 1914).

896 NFS:II,33.DFI, 198. Letter from Harald Frost to Seemann & Knevels, Berlin (2 September 1914).

897 NFS:II,33.DFI, 380. Letter from Harald Frost to Nordische Films Co., Berlin (22 September 1914).

898 "Der neue Filmkonzern", *Der Kinematograph*, no. 449 (4 August 1914).

899 Hampicke, "The Danish Influence", 74.

900 Filmeur, "Den tyske Filmsindustri", *Politiken* (8 August 1915).

assembled protesters adopted a resolution expressing their conviction "[...] that this so-called merger has been made with the aid of foreign and possibly even hostile capital".[901] "The group" was seen as a threat to good taste as well as open competition on the German film market, so the protesters appealed to the government and audiences to support "the livelihood of thousands of people in the German film industry".[902] The protesters formed a commission, and already on the following morning, passed a resolution with seven points. One of the points campaigned for the black-listing of cinemas that showed films from Nordisk.[903] In *Der Kinematograph,* journalist Horst Emscher soberly summed up the situation in his article "It's Not That Bad!". Emscher found that the German film industry had been caught napping. Pathé had been Nordisk's greatest obstacle to the expansion on the German market, and the war had freed up many market shares when Pathé and Gaumont had withdrawn from Germany in August 1914. Emscher was reproachful: "A whole year has passed since then, and the German film industry did not lift a finger to exploit the financial situation and secure the German market in the future".[904] As for the allegation that hostile capital was behind the merger, Emscher wrote that this could not be entirely discarded, but noted Olsen had a thriving business and did not need money from Pathé at all. Emscher further argued that the money that Oliver and PAGU made stayed in Germany, so the German film industry should keep their shirts on.[905]

However, "the group" took the accusation very seriously and placed a series of double-paged ads in the German trade press. In response, under the headline "Clarification" Oliver made it clear that the company was operating solely with German capital.[906] "In Defence" was the title of PAGU's ad, which emphasized that the company was German through and through, and relied solely on "its own and exclusively German capital".[907] In yet another full-page ad, PAGU addressed "the cinema owners of Germany!" and declared that its first-class films expressed the "makings of the true German spirit".[908] Finally, Nordisk refuted the rumour that the company was subsidized by Pathé, and announced a reward of 300,000 marks to anyone who could prove the allegations. The company offered a similar sum to anyone who could prove the false rumour that Nordisk had purchased the Union Cinemas.[909]

901 "Protest-Versammlungen gegen den Union-Nordisk Konzern", *Der Kinematograph*, no. 450 (11 August 1914).

902 Ibid.

903 Ibid.

904 Horst Emscher, "Es ist nicht so schlimm!", *Der Kinematograph*, no. 450 (11 August 1914).

905 Ibid.

906 *Der Kinematograph*, no. 450 (11 August 1914).

907 *Der Kinematograph*, no. 450 (11 August 1914).

908 Ibid.

909 Ibid.

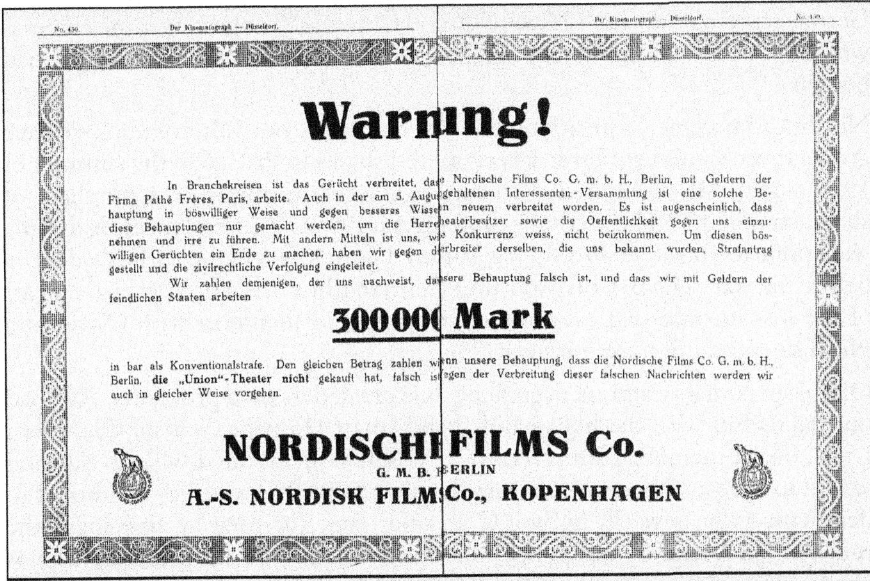

Figure 35. Double page ad from *Der Kinematograph* (no. 450, 11 August 1914) in which Nordisk offers a reward of 300,000 marks to anyone who could prove the company was backed by French capital.

In spite of the lucid commentary from Emscher and the group's ads, the protests continued, and on 9 August another meeting was held in Berlin where Oliver and his attorney, Dr. Frankfurter, put in an appearance to answer questions and to defend the nationalist nature of the group.[910] On 28 August, the anti-trust society "Deutsche Filmtrustabwehr" presented four "terms of peace" to the group:

I. 'Nordisk-Oliver-Union Konzern' will be obliged to make no long-term agreements with cinema owners, and, moreover

II. Make no agreements concerning a percentage share in sales.

III. 'Nordisk-Oliver-Union Konzern' will be obliged also to exhibit films from other companies in the cinemas in question.

IV. 'Nordisk-Oliver-Union Konzern' will refrain from purchasing further cinemas.[911]

And so, over the course of three weeks, the protests had gone from making serious accusations of subsidies from hostile nations to demands intended to protect German companies outside the group. The group agreed to the first three demands, but Nordisk rejected the fourth; the company was far from having concluded its acquisition plans. In October, Olsen could inform Nordisk's board that he had spent one million German marks to acquire 19

910 "Nordisk-Union-Konzern und Theaterbesitzer I", *Der Kinematograph*, no. 451 (18 August 1915); "Nordisk-Union-Konzern und Theaterbesitzer II", *Der Kinematograph*, no. 452 (25 August 1915).

911 "Deutsche Filmtrustabwehr", *Der Kinematograph*, no. 455 (15 September 1915).

German cinemas of which 16 were Union Cinemas[912] – the very same cinemas which Nordisk had previously challenged the public to prove that Olsen had bought.

Nordisk's strategic acquisitions did not end here, but Olsen seems to have grown more cautious. Nordisk was offered shares in PAGU in the summer of 1916, which Olsen advised the board against acquiring, so the purchase of shares stranded.[913] The accounts presented at PAGU's general meeting in June were none too positive. PAGU had suffered great losses in the Pathé deal made before the war. The ban on exporting German films made up such a great part of the lost income that even the distribution collaboration with Oliver and Nordisk could not make up for it.[914]

Olsen's personality and management style created its own problems. "We had our hands full with the high-handed and smart Director General Ole Olsen [...]", board member Lamm recalls.[915] Olsen alone decided what to buy and where to invest. Olsen was repeatedly given 500,000 kroner by the board to deal with as he saw fit; he would account later for how he had spent the money.[916] Because of this policy, the minutes of the board meetings do not always give a clear account of which transactions Olsen made on his trips, and the turbulent political situation meant that German companies had to keep a low profile if they made deals with Nordisk. Sources indicate that Nordisk also made deals with Carl Gabriel Film Distribution Munich in December 1915,[917] Deutsche Bioscop G.m.b.H. in January 1916,[918] and Continental-Projection.[919]

After the outbreak of the war, Nordisk established three additional branches in Germany: in November 1914 in Munich, in May 1915 in Leipzig and in June in Breslau.[920] Together with the branches in Berlin, Frankfurt am Main and Düsseldorf, Nordisk now had six branches in Germany.

Expansion in Germany was not the only focus of Nordisk's strategy. The company's correspondence after February 1915 is largely missing, but two surviving letters indicate that Nordisk surveyed the markets in Britain and Russia with the aim of buying up cinemas.[921] Nordisk also contemplated

912 NFS:I,25.DFI. Unpagn. Minutes of the Board of Directors Meeting (18 October 1915).

913 NFS:I,25.DFI. Unpagn. Minutes of the Board of Directors Meeting (19 July 1915).

914 "Projektions-Akt-Ges. 'Union', Berlin", *Berliner Börsen-Zeitung* (18 June 1916).

915 Lamm, *Erindringer og Tanker*, 190.

916 NFS:I,25.DFI. Unpagn. Minutes of the Board of Directors Meeting (28 June 1915 and 6 September 1915).

917 See Karl Zimmerschied, *Die deutsche Filmindustrie, ihre Entwicklung, Organisation und Stellung im deutschen Staats- und Wirtschaftsleben* (PhD-thesis, Frankfurt a.M.: Universität Frankfurt, 1922), 58; *Jahrbuch der Filmindustrie 1922/23* (Berlin: Verlag der Lichtbild-Bühne, 1923).

918 NFS:I,25.DFI. Unpagn. Minutes of the Board of Directors Meeting (5 January 1916).

919 See Engberg, *Dansk stumfilm*, 593.

920 It is difficult to give an exact date for the opening of the foreign branches. The dates are set according to when they first appear in Nordisk's ads and commercials in *Der Kinematograph*.

921 NFA. Letter from unidentified person to Ole Olsen (1 June 1915); NFS:II,58:22.DFI. Letter from Mollerup Thomsen, Petrograd to Harald Frost (22 April 1915).

buying other cinemas in Denmark. In the summer of 1915, Skaarup and Olsen made plans for converting a large department store in Frederiksberggade in the centre of Copenhagen into a cinema.[922] However, as Sandfeld reports, the Justice Department had not yet forgotten the scandal over LØVEJAGTEN, and Olsen was still blacklisted with the minister. The Justice Department's bias against Olsen manifested itself again when in 1915 Hjalmar Davidsen tried to move his own license to a new cinema on Strøget in Copenhagen. The Department rejected his application on suspicion that Davidsen was Olsen's front man, and that Olsen's plan was to open a cinema that would show exclusively Nordisk films. Likewise, Skaarup tried to get a license in 1917 in order to open a cinema in his amusement centre National Scala, but was also denied by the Ministry, once again because Olsen was suspected of being behind the application.[923]

Russia was another target of Nordisk's expansionist plans. The war prevented French films from reaching Russia, and a shortage of raw stock traditionally imported from France and Germany posed a problem. Film production decreased, but at the same time attendance at the cinema increased by 25 per cent after the outbreak of war.[924] Frost wrote to Nordisk's Russian agent, Thiemann & Reinhardt, to say that Perskii, Khanzhonkov and other Russian film merchants had travelled to Copenhagen to purchase films directly from Nordisk.[925] As in Germany, Olsen made charitable donations in Russia. Ten thousand Russian roubles were given to the Russian Red Cross; 2,000 roubles to an infirmary for Russian film workers;[926] and in 1916, Olsen received the Order of St. Stanislaus.[927] The donations were not enough to soften public opinion, however. Nordisk was considered a German company because the owners of the company's Russian agency, Thiemann & Reinhardt, were of German descent. An anti-German mood escalated in May 1915 when houses inhabited by Germans or persons with German-sounding names were burned down. Thiemann & Reinhardt, who had tried to protect themselves against the hostility towards all things German by adding a third partner and the Russian name "Osipov" to their company name, were also attacked. Paul Thiemann was exiled to Ufa, a town in the Ural Mountains, while Reinhardt was allowed to stay in Moscow since he had been a resident of Russia for many years. The film studios of the company were spared during the riots, and Thiemann

922 "Nyt stort Biografteater i København. Direktørerne Ole Olsen og Skaarups Planer", *Social-Demokraten* (13 June 1915).

923 See Sandfeld, *Den stumme scene*, 52–54.

924 NFS:II,34.DFI, 112. Letter from Harald Frost to Thiemann, Reinhardt & Osipov (21 November 1915).

925 NFS:II,34.DFI, 63. Letter from Harald Frost to Thiemann, Reinhardt & Osipov (17 November 1915).

926 NFS:XIV,32.DFI, 137. Scrapbook. Russian article from *Sine-Fono*. Most likely from 1915.

927 "Stumper og Strimler", *Filmen*, no. 8 (1916): 78. The Order of St. Stanislaus was frequently awarded and of a lower order. Olsen also received Red Cross Medals and distinctions from Austria-Hungary, Prussia, Russia and Portugal. I am indebted to Sven Philip Jørgensen, The Society for the History of Orders, for this information.

succeeded in running the business through his wife who had stayed behind. In the spring of 1917 he was able to return from Ufa.[928]

Nordisk was accused of being backed by German capital, and popular Danish actors like Garrison (Valdemar Psilander's Russian name) and Asta Nielsen disappeared temporarily from Russian cinema programmes.[929] Thiemann & Reinhardt placed ads in August 1915 stating that Nordisk was a purely Danish company, and that the films were inspected by Russian authorities before entering Russia,[930] but this did not prevent a ban on all film imports from Nordisk in March 1916. The reason given for this ban was that the company imported German films under Nordisk's name.[931] However, the situation in Russia was so chaotic at the time that the ban was observed in the breach. Films from Germany had been imported into Russia since the outbreak of the war,[932] and Nordisk may have been guilty as charged. From the distribution protocols of Nordisk we can see that at least one film produced by Oliver was exported by the Danish company to Russia in February 1916.[933] Some Russian distributors released German films under the name of Nordisk to hide their German origin. At the beginning of the war, the Russian company Perskii was accused of exactly this sort of manipulation, and was forced to stop.[934]

Nevertheless, such hostilities towards Nordisk in Russia did not deter the company. In June 1916, Olsen commenced negotiations with Thiemann, Reinhardt & Osipov about buying half of the shares in the firm, and in October or November, Nordisk secured a solid foothold in Russia.[935] For 200,500 roubles, it acquired half of the Russian company which also owned the production company Era and the Electro cinema in Moscow. [936] How Nordisk developed on the Russian market is uncertain;[937] evidence suggests that Thiemann, Reinhardt & Osipov was divided into smaller companies in April/May 1917, and that Nordisk was planning to open its own branch in Petrograd in

928 See Rashit Yangirov, "Pavel Gustavovich Thiemann", in *Testimoni silenziosi: Film Russi 1908–1919*, research and co-ordination by Yuri Tsivian, 590.

929 See Leyda, *Kino*, 83.

930 *Sine-fono*, no. 19–20 (1915): XXIX. I am indebted to Lauri Piispa for the reference.

931 "Ingen dansk Films til Rusland", *Politiken* (9 March 1916).

932 "Film-Industriens Vanskeligheder", *Ekstra Bladet* (13 March 1916).

933 NFS:XII,34.DFI, 138. Distribution Protocol. The exported copy of the Oliver film could of course be a sample copy, but given the political circumstances and the general ban on German films in Russia it seems unlikely.

934 *Kine-Zhurnal*, no. 21–22 (29 November 1914): 54–55. I am indebted to the late Rashit Yangirov for the reference.

935 NFS:I,25.DFI. Unpagn. Minutes of the Board of Directors Meeting (26 June 1916).

936 NFS:XII,31:33.DFI. Translation of contract between the trading company Thiemann, Reinhardt & Osipov and A/S Nordisk Films Kompagni (13 November 1916).

937 The time leading up to the Russian Revolution was turbulent, and exact information is hard to come by. Moreover, research in early Russian film production is insufficient. Russian film researcher Rashit Yangirov was one of the few who researched the early years, and he has been a great help in the mapping out of Nordisk's activities in Russia in these years. Yangirov died after a long illness on 14 December 2008, and it has not been possible to obtain more data concerning the dissolution of Thiemann, Rheinhardt & Osipov or of Nordisk's plans of opening a branch in Russia.

order to launch direct distribution of its films, but Thiemann, Reinhardt & Osipov were still advertising films from Nordisk as late as August 1917.[938]

As the war ground on, Nordisk's many transactions in Germany began to cause problems for the company in other belligerent countries. On 7 November 1914, Britain had issued a decree that goods from Denmark should be supplied with a certificate of origin and a declaration.[939] Before Nordisk's films were admitted into Britain, they had to pass the Danish Industrial Council in Copenhagen and be declared an entirely Danish product. After being approved as such, the British Council had to issue a certificate of origin before the film could be shipped off. According to Frost, the British authorities feared two possibilities: firstly, that German films might be supplied to British cinemas via Denmark; second, that films shown in Britain might be copied on raw stock produced in Germany, and that Britain in this manner would indirectly support the German industry.[940] In August 1915 Frost told the press about these difficulties:

> We cannot be accused of selling German films to England. Even if we should attempt this, which would never occur to us, it would be essentially impossible. For each film we ship to England, we have to produce a certificate of origin, and we even have to guarantee that the raw stock is not German or from some other nation at war with England. The British Consul in town has been through our factory with a fine-toothed comb – and we have even been asked if we employ German actors.[941]

The suspicion that Nordisk had tried to evade British trade restrictions was reinforced by a speculative article in the Copenhagen newspaper *Politiken*. The article stated that negotiations were ongoing between Danish financiers and German film producers about moving German film production to Denmark. German cameramen, technicians and actors were said to be allowed to rent Danish studios and shoot films there, the article surmised: "[...] in the hope of being able to sell such films, at least after the war, made in Denmark and with a partly Danish cast, to the countries now at war with Germany". The article ended by claiming that German film producers were already in town to investigate the facilities.[942] The contents of the *Politiken* article reached the British newspapers, and the information was taken as fact.[943] In *Politiken* on 13 August, Frost officially denied the allegations which, according to him, were arbitrarily targeting Nordisk. Frost ended his denial:

938 *Kine-zhurnal*, no. 7–10 (1917): 72. I am indebted to Lauri Piispa for the reference.

939 Rigsarkivet/Udenrigsministeriet (RA/U.M.) (The Danish National Archives/Ministry of Foreign Affairs) 72.H.3. Article from Ritzau's Bureau (21 November 1914).

940 'Meis', "Nordisk Films Co. i Tyskland", *Berlingske Tidende* (13 August 1915).

941 Ibid.

942 Filmeur, "Den tyske Filmsindustri", *Politiken* (8 August 1915).

943 Freddy, "En stor Films-Løgn stoppet!", *Ekstra Bladet aften* (11 August 1915).

> This request for a retraction is mostly due to the fact that the British film market has quoted your article from English newspapers in order to throw suspicion on our company with the intention of harming our business.[944]

The attempts to cast suspicion on Nordisk and the Danish film industry were successful. In November, the entire Danish film industry became subject to an export ban in Great Britain and its colonies, due to the rumour that German films had reached Britain under a Danish certificate. The British Consulate reported that "[...] it was under orders from the Home Office, and that the ban applies not only to one but all Danish companies".[945] In Nordisk's case the ban involved a shipment of films which were going to Italy and Australia via Britain, and which the British consul would not approve.[946]

The Danish Foreign Ministry asked its envoy in London to make contact with the Foreign Office, and by the end of November it was declared that the issuing of certificates could be resumed in return for a guarantee that "the films do not contain hostile material or work from hostile countries that exceeds 25 per cent".[947] The crisis had lasted a month and may be seen as a warning to Nordisk and its many enterprises in Germany. This is how *Berlingske Tidende* interpreted the brief ban:

> It has been suggested that England is sceptical and suspicious of Danish films because of Nordisk's merger with German companies since England has now concluded that Nordisk is a partly German company.[948]

The ban may simply have been harassment. *Filmen* reported that Russia and Britain had been averse to films copied in Germany, but in fact Nordisk was the only Danish film company that did not have its films copied in Germany because they owned their own printing laboratory.[949] In October and November 1915, British authorities time and again impounded Nordisk's shipments.[950] Joachim Nielsen, who worked as a clerk at the Nordisk main office in Copenhagen, was convinced that the British authorities were harassing the company.[951] Raw stock from Eastman came on ships from the United States and made a stop at Kirkwall in Scotland where the shipments were opened and examined, and several times Nordisk's shipments of raw stock were detained and sent with the next ship. The supply of raw film became a problem as the war progressed, and in a letter to the Danish Foreign Ministry, Nordisk wrote that British authorities had actually forbidden Eastman to sell raw film to the

944 "Filmsindustrien. En Erklæring fra Nordisk Films Ko.", *Politiken* (13 August 1915).

945 "Forbud mod danske Films i England", *Politiken* (20 November 1915).

946 RA/U.M.72.H.3. Letter from Harald Frost to the Ministry of Foreign Affairs of Denmark (8 November 1915).

947 RA/U.M.72.H.3. Letter from the Royal Legation in London to the Ministry of Foreign Affairs of Denmark (2 February 1915).

948 'Mr', "Et Filmsforbud. De engelske Myndigheder forbyder Udførslen af danske Films til England og de engelske Kolonier", *Berlingske Tidende* (20 November 1915).

949 "Kopierings-vanskeligheder", *Filmen*, no. 20 (1915): 168.

950 NFS:II,58:27-30.DFI. Letters from DFDS (The United Steamship Company) to Nordisk (28 October, 1, 9 and 17 November 1915).

951 Interview with Joachim Nielsen II. DFI.

Danish company.[952] In March 1916, two tons of fixing natron which Nordisk had bought in New York were confiscated in Kirkwall.[953] The natron was not released until 1920. And in the spring of 1917, British authorities stopped shipments of film from Nordisk to Iceland.[954] In both cases, the Danish Foreign Ministry received only vague and unsatisfactory answers from the British Government.[955] "They thought we were German", Nielsen later stated, recalling the British impression of Nordisk.[956]

Nordisk was not actually blacklisted on the official British lists.[957] Both Britain and France had made blacklists of companies or individuals who collaborated with the Central Powers and therefore should be boycotted. But as early as 8 June 1916, Nordisk was put on a confidential British blacklist, with a "P" classification meaning that "[...] their inclusion in Class A is for the time being provisional. Facilities for these firms are not, as a rule, definitely refused, but held in abeyance."[958] Nielsen's suspicions were correct: Nordisk was indeed harassed by the British port authorities with the consent of the British Government. It appears from the distribution protocols of Nordisk that export to Britain dropped from 441 titles in 1915 to 81 the following year.[959] The "P" entry on the confidential British blacklist had not only influenced Nordisk's import of raw materials but probably also the company's export to Britain and its colonies.

We can get an impression of the size of Nordisk's organization in Germany from a commercial article in which Nordisk presents the main office in Zimmerstrasse floor by floor. The management was on the top floor, along with the correspondence department, accounts, box office, archives and the telephone exchange. The top floor also housed two other important departments: the large screening room and statistics which was seen as the heartbeat of the company. The article states that "[...] here it is ascertained what raises or slows the pulse of the business at any given moment." The floor under the top floor was home to the literary department where scripts and souvenir programmes were written. The public relations department was attached to this office. Everyone is familiar with Nordisk's great commercial campaigns,

952 RA/U.M.70.T.92. Letter from Harald Frost to the Ministry of Foreign Affairs of Denmark, 2nd Department (17 July 1918).

953 RA/U.M.17.N.185. Fixing natron is part of the development process of film. Letter from Albert Gøte to the Ministry of Foreign Affairs of Denmark (6 April 1920).

954 RA/U.M.70.T.92. Letter from the Royal Legation in London to the Ministry of Foreign Affairs of Denmark (14 November 1918).

955 RA/U.M.70.T.92. Letter from the Ministry of Foreign Affairs of Denmark to Nordisk Films Kompagni (30 November 1918).

956 Interview with Joachim Nielsen, II. DFI.

957 RA/U.M.70.T.17. "Consolidating Statuary List of persons and firms in countries, other the enemy countries, with whom persons and firms in the United Kingdom are prohibited from trading" (12 October 1917).

958 RA/U.M.70.T.17. "Confidential: Denmark General Blacklist. November 27th 1916". Class A consisted of the names of blacklisted individuals or companies.

959 See note for Table 1.

the article informs us, and continues: "According to many successful businessmen, advertising is the soul of any business." This floor also housed the censors and the music department, and it had three small screening rooms. On the bottom floor was the storeroom with films and commercial material. This was the organization in Zimmerstrasse which kept up "a production of more than 4,000 metres a week".[960] The Berlin branch of Nordisk had developed into the heart of a large business network. Olsen later estimated the number of employees in Germany to be either 700[961] or 1,000.[962]

Wolfgang Mühl-Benninghaus writes that Nordisk had influence on about 60 per cent of the German film industry.[963] The German trade press claimed that, through co-operation with German companies, Nordisk controlled 60 cinemas.[964] Nordisk claimed to own only 30 cinemas, which number roughly matches the details of the company's possessions in Germany held at the Bundesarchiv in which the number is given as 31.[965] However, through alliances with other German companies such as PAGU, it is likely that Nordisk did in fact control around 60 cinemas.

Of the 1,316 films censored in Germany in 1916, 477 were foreign, and 180 of the foreign films came from Nordisk. At first glance this may not sound like much, but in addition, Nordisk had stock from PAGU and Oliver. Furthermore, Nordisk distributed Swedish films from Svenska Biografteatern, American films from Kalem, and a few other films such as Benjamin Christensen's HÆVNENS NAT (BLIND JUSTICE, Benjamin Christensen, Dansk Biograf Compagni, 1916) and Alfred Lind's Italian ULTIMA RAPPRESENTAZIONE DI GALA DEL CIRCO WOLFSON (THE LAST GALA NIGHT OF CIRCUS WOLFSON, Alfred Lind, Vay-Film, IT 1916). In a vertically integrated film company, it is not out of the ordinary to show films from rival companies in your own cinemas as long as there is a chance that they make more money than your own productions.[966]

Alfred Kallmann estimates that between a fifth and a fourth of the films shown in Germany had a connection to Nordisk's distribution organization. Kallmann has compiled the following list of companies connected to Nordisk and the companies' number of films on the German market in 1916:

960 "Die 'Nordische Films Co. G.m.b.H.'", *Der Kinematograph*, no. 500 (28 July 1916).

961 "Hvordan de skabte deres Livs Værk VII. Ved Leo Tandrup. Fhv. Generaldirektør Ole Olsen, skaberen af den første dramatiske film i verden siger: FORSTAA UNGDOMMEN!", *Berlingske Søndag* (10 February 1935).

962 See Olsen, *Filmens Eventyr og mit eget*, 138.

963 See Wolfgang Mühl-Benninghaus, *Vom Augusterlebnis zur UFA-Gründung* (Berlin: Avinus-Verlag, 2004), 217.

964 See Alfred Kallmann, *Die Konzernierung in der Filmindustrie, erläutert an den Filmindustrien Deutschlands und Amerikas* (PhD-thesis, Würzburg: Universität Würzburg, 1932), 11. Behn estimates the number of Nordisk cinemas at 56. See Manfred Behn "Großeinkauf", in Hans-Michael Bock and Michael Töteberg (ed.), *Das Ufa-Buch. Kunst und Krisen, Stars und Regisseure, Wirtschaft und Politik* (Frankfurt am Main: Zweitausendeins, 1994), 36.

965 Bundesarchiv-Filmarchiv R109–139. Deutscher Besitz, Nordisk Kopenhagen.

966 See Sedgwick and Pokorny (ed.), *An Economic History of Film*, 7.

Nordisk	180 films
Svenska Biografteatern	53 films
Union	41 films
Oliver	48 films
Luna	15 films
Total	**337 films**

Kallmann overlooks the 49 films which Nordisk distributed through Kalem in 1916,[967] which if added to this total, means that 386 out of the 1,316, or around 30 per cent of the films that went through censorship in 1916, were part of Nordisk's distribution. The quantity of films is one way to estimate the company's position on the German market; another way to is to consider their control of some of the best and most prestigious cinemas. In the year 1916/1917, the returns from Nordisk's German cinemas were 6,597,479.84 marks.[968]

In March 1916, Nordisk's position was apparently weakened when the German chancellor issued a "decree on the import of luxury goods".[969] The decree was an import ban that was to relieve Germany's foreign currency reserve, and it applied to film imports as well. "For foreign countries, and Denmark in particular, the ban will probably have serious consequences", wrote *Der Kinematograph*.[970] The German film industry saw the ban as a happy rehabilitation which could strengthen the national industry.[971]Nordisk was the only foreign company to obtain an extraordinary licence allowing them to export to Germany 1,800 kilos before July and 1,000 kilos before September 1916, a total of 2.8 tons, or 500,000 metres of film.[972] To no one's great surprise, the German film industry protested once again, this time by sending a direct complaint to the chancellor.[973] In March 1916, hostilities against Nordisk made Luna cancel its connection to Nordisk, which decision was announced in a double-page ad in *Der Kinematograph*.[974] In a short article about the first 20 years of German cinema in *Lichtbild-Bühne* Nordisk was mentioned negatively: "[...] als jüngstes Schreckgespenst spukt die Nordische Gefahr" (the latest ghost to haunt us is the danger from Nordisk).[975] The fear of Nordisk's expansion policy spread to Sweden, when a 45-page book was published with the title *Faran från Nordisk Films Co. Et varningsrop fran Tyskland* (The Danger from Nordisk Films Co. Words of Warning from Germany). The book is an

967 See Kallmann, *Die Konzernierung*, 12.

968 Bundesarchiv-Filmarchiv R109–139. Deutscher Besitz, Nordisk Kopenhagen.

969 "Das neue Filmeinfuhrverbot", *Der Kinematograph*, no. 480 (8 March 1916).

970 Ibid.

971 "Resolution zum Filmeinfuhrverbot", *Der Kinematograph*, no. 481 (15 March 1916).

972 "Die 'Nordische' führt Films ein!", *Lichtbild-Bühne*, no. 15 (15 April 1916).

973 "Aus der Praxis", *Der Kinematograph*, no. 489 (10 May 1916).

974 *Der Kinematograph*, no. 483 (29 March 1916).

975 "20 Jahre deutsche Kinematographie", *Lichtbild-Bühne*, no. 15 (15 April 1916).

anthology of articles from *Lichtbild-Bühne* about Nordisk's expansion in Germany, and a warning to the Swedish film companies to be on their guard against the Danish competitor.[976]

German film historian Manfred Behn suggests that Nordisk must have had some very good lobbyists in the Reichstag to obtain its special license.[977] This may have been the case, but Nordisk also had other good connections. When the news of the ban was debated among the board members at Nordisk, it was decided,

> [...] to form a committee consisting of the chairman, Manager Paulsen and Manager Fabricius for the purpose of negotiating with the Minister of Trade and the Foreign Ministry of assistance in obtaining a dispensation from the import ban.[978]

Fabricius was the manager of Revisionsbanken, and he was by no means a random choice for the committee that was to negotiate with the Minister of Trade in the social-liberal government led by Prime Minister Carl Theodor Zahle, Jens Hassing-Jørgensen. In 1903, Hassing-Jørgensen had founded Revisionsbanken, and it was he who led the negotiations with Nordisk's board in 1912 when the bank stood surety for Nordisk's two million kroner share expansion.[979] In other words, the Minister of Trade had close ties to Nordisk and a personal interest in one of the banks that had guaranteed the expanded share capital the previous year.[980]

In the archives of the Foreign Office is a letter from Olsen dated 9 March 1916, in which he requests assistance in the case and complains that the Berlin branch had approached the German authorities in vain. The German envoy in Copenhagen, Count Brockendorff Rantzau, wanted to help Nordisk, but he had let Olsen know that a request from the Foreign office would have more clout. No papers reveal whether the Foreign Office actually gave the envoy such intimation. Olsen ended his letter by stating that Nordisk's export to Germany in 1915 amounted to approximately 822,000 metres of film or 5,750 kilo film,[981] so, according to Olsen, a dispensation would guarantee around half of the company's sales in Germany. Officially, the dispensation was a one-off, but it appears from Nordisk's distribution protocols that the company maintained its exports to Germany throughout the war.

Nordisk did not manage to send its entire quota of film before 18 September 1916, and applied for a continuation of the export licence in order to send the

976 Anonymous (1916). I am indebted to Anna Bachmann for having found and copied this pamphlet in the Swedish Film Institute's library.

977 See Manfred Behn, "Reaktionen auf die Nordisk in Deutschland zwischen 1914 und 1917". Unpublished lecture held at the seminar Danish-German Relations and Interactions in Film, Københavns Universitet/Goethe Institut Kopenhagen (3–4 November 1995), 6.

978 NFS:I,25.DFI. Unpagn. Minutes of the Board of Directors Meeting (6 March 1916).

979 NFS:I,25.DFI. Unpagn. Minutes of the Board of Directors Meeting (5 June1912).

980 I have not been able to find any files from the Ministry of Trade concerning the dispensation, and Jens Hassing-Jørgensen's memoirs make no mention of Nordisk. National Archive/Private archives.

981 RA/U.M.79.L.25. Letter from Ole Olsen to the Ministry of Foreign Affairs of Denmark (9 March 1916).

remainder. In November, Nordisk was granted permission to maintain its exports to Germany, as long as the films were produced in Denmark or Sweden.[982] Concerning the first dispensation of 2.8 tons, Mottram states: "Since this figure included negatives from which copies not under the quota could be made, the actual number of feet of film that Nordisk could sell was many times higher than the initial figure."[983] Mottram's point is that Nordisk could ship negatives from the printing laboratory in Frihavnen to Germany, after which a film could be copied as many times as desired; thus, only the length or weight of one film would be entered in the quota and appear. In fact, Nordisk later used this solution to maintain its exports to Austria-Hungary.[984] Moreover, the import ban could not prevent Nordisk from earning profits from its distribution and cinemas, regardless of whether the films were Danish or not.

Nordisk's privileged position on the German market also caused uproar in the Danish film industry. Its competitor Kinografen addressed the Foreign Office in bewilderment, demanding an explanation for how Nordisk could get its films into Germany in spite of the import ban.[985] The Foreign Office replied that it was a matter of a temporary license and sent Kinografen to Engineer Erik Bang Cruse, the deputy of the Danish Industrial Council in Berlin.[986] Cruse replied:

> According to what the authorities inform me, import permission has been granted Mr Ole Olesen [sic] for one single time by persuasion, but if the unpleasantness it entailed had been foreseen, I believe the permission would not have been given. Moreover, it was decided that no other import permits will be given since the German film industry works under a severe strain and must be protected. In this case, foreign currency played a minor part, so it could not change the outcome even if the money were not paid until the war ended.
>
> I cannot vouch for the truth of the above; I can only relate what I myself have been told. For instance, I might imagine that Mr Ole Olesen [sic] has been given the import permission against an obligation to sign up for war loans from the profits.[987]

The suggestion that Nordisk had signed up for German war bonds in order to maintain its exports to Germany cannot be verified; nothing indicates that Nordisk had anything to do with war bonds, but Oliver had: he signed up for 1.25 million marks.[988] And Cruse was wise to doubt the veracity of the

982 *Jahrbuch der Filmindustrie 1922/23*, 23.

983 Mottram, *The Danish Cinema before Dreyer*, 210.

984 RA/U.M.79.T.103. Letter from the Royal Danish Legation, Vienna to the Ministry of Foreign Affairs of Denmark (25 January 1917).

985 RA/U.M.79.L.25. Letter from Oscar Philip to Head of Office K. Styhr Hr. at the Ministry of Foreign Affairs of Denmark (22 June 1918).

986 RA/U.M.79.L.25. Letter from the Ministry of Foreign Affairs of Denmark to Engineer Erik Bang Cruse, Berlin (29 June 1918).

987 RA/U.M.79.L.25. Letter from Erik Bang Cruse to Head of Office K. Styhr Hr. at the Ministry of Foreign Affairs of Denmark (8 July 1918).

988 See Hampicke, "The Danish Influence", 77.

information he had been given. If one counts the amount of positive film that Nordisk exported to Germany from April 1916 to October 1918, it adds up to 1,490,549 metres of film, or nearly three times as much as allowed in the original dispensation.[989] The astoundingly high number indicates that Nordisk maintained its export to Germany, either because control of film imports was insufficient, because Nordisk cheated on the amount, or because of a secret agreement between Nordisk and German authorities in which Oliver's war bonds may have played a part. Such a clandestine agreement, officially denied, did in fact exist between Germany and Austria-Hungary, and it secured the free trade of films between the two countries.[990] Consequently, the German restrictions of import were of no great consequence to Nordisk.

In the autumn of 1916, Olsen approached the Board of Directors with the following proposal:

> As it turns out, it has been still more compelling to abort the exploitation of the company's fabricata, the sale of finished positives, and instead resort to direct distribution to cinemas, those of others and our own. In order to carry through such a change, for the time being especially in Germany, Austria-Hungary and Russia, the share capital available will not suffice. Consequently, at an extraordinary general meeting, the chairman will move that our share capital be increased with 4 million kroner.[991]

The board granted his wish, and this presented the opportunity of raising the share capital to eight million kroner, which sum could be enlarged to ten million if the need should arise. On 6 November, the share capital expansion was approved at an extraordinary general meeting. Old shareholders were given the privilege of buying further shares corresponding to the number of shares they already possessed, at exchange rate of 140. The rate of a Nordisk share was 208 kroner in October 1916. Revisionsbanken and Diskontobanken stood surety for the expansion of that part of the share capital which was not purchased by the old shareholders, and once again, they signed for the transaction. The banks received a commission of ten per cent of the premium, 400,000 kroner, and the remaining 1.2 million kroner of the premium was transferred to a reserve fund.[992] Olsen accounted for the expansion of the share capital to the press as follows:

> The fear that the American system will gain power over the European market after the war has forced Nordisk Films Co. into these measures. For the time being, America possesses a large quantity of finished negatives, and will, at the first opportunity, throw these out on the European market at prices that will exclude

989 NFS:XII,34-39.DFI. Distribution protocols. The counted films are produced between 1914 and 1918, and the figure includes the films Nordisk distributed from other companies such as Svenska Biograftheatern, Kalem or Benjamin Christensen's BLIND JUSTICE and Alfred Lind's ULTIMA RAPPRESENTAZIONE DI GALA DEL CIRCO WOLFSON.

990 RA/U.M.79.T.103. Letter from the Royal Danish Legation, Vienna to the Ministry of Foreign Affairs of Denmark (25 January 1917).

991 NFS:I,25.DFI. Unpagn. Minutes of the Board of Directors Meeting (13 October 1916).

992 NFS:I,25.DFI. Unpagn. Minutes of the Board of Directors Meeting (13 October 1916).

> all European competition. This will mean the death of the European film industry, which is what we are trying to prevent by taking this course of action.[993]

This interview with Olsen was published in several media in Germany,[994] and Mühl-Benninghaus interprets Olsen's manoeuvre as a tactical move. The expansion of the share capital might be construed as a threat to the German film industry, and, to avoid repercussions as in the case of the Nordisk-Oliver-PAGU-Luna merger, Nordisk chose to focus on a common threat, i.e. the American film industry.[995] All the same, a reaction from the German film industry was not prevented. This time, the film industry "appealed to the government for protection".[996]

Olsen's prophecy concerning the future of the European film industry was amazingly prescient, and Nordisk was the only European company preparing for a new power balance in the international film industry. The Americans had exploited the weakness of the European film companies during the war. Kristin Thompson writes that in 1917, the U.S. had gained control of all film markets save those in Central and Eastern Europe, Russia and the Middle East.[997] Apart from the Middle East, Nordisk dominated the last markets not yet under American control. In the magazine *Filmen,* Olsen's plan of buying up cinemas was considered prudent: "On the whole, Europe is severely handicapped and, in fact, among all the European film factories, only one emerges strong, and that is Nordisk Films Co [...]."[998]

Both before and after the expansion of the share capital in October 1916, Nordisk had maintained its expansion in Central Europe. The company established three branches in Austria-Hungary: two in Vienna and Prague in July 1916, and one in Budapest in December that same year.[999] The establishing of the branches was accompanied by donations to the Red Cross in Austria-Hungary.[1000] Moreover, Nordisk started collaborating with the company's agent in Austria-Hungary, Projectograph, in which connection Nordisk bought shares in the Austro-Hungarian company.[1001]

According to Kallmann, Nordisk took over two distribution companies in Switzerland: Franzos in Geneva and Lang in Zurich, and in October 1916, the

993 "Interview med Ole Olsen", *Filmen*, no. 3 (1916): 25–26.

994 *Berliner Zeitung am Mittag* (6 November 1916), reprinted in *Der Kinematograph*, no. 515 (8 November 1916).

995 See Mühl-Benninghaus, *Vom Augusterlebnis*, 221.

996 "Nordisk Films Kompagni og den tyske Filmindustri", *Statstidende* (3 November 1916).

997 See Kristin Thompson, "The Rise and Fall of Film Europe", in Andrew Higson and Richard Maltby (ed.), *"Film Europe" and "Film America". Cinema, Commerce and Cultural Exchange 1920–1939* (Exeter: University of Exeter Press, 1999), 56.

998 "De amerikanske Films", *Filmen*, no. 11 (June 1917): 165–166.

999 Bundesarchiv-Filmarchiv R-109–464. Nordisk Films Co., G.m.b.H. Wien und Budapest; R-109-463. Nordisk Film Co., Prag.

1000 NFS:I,25.DFI. Unpagn. Minutes of the Board of Directors Meeting (15 May 1916).

1001 See Kallmann, *Die Konzernierung*, 11.

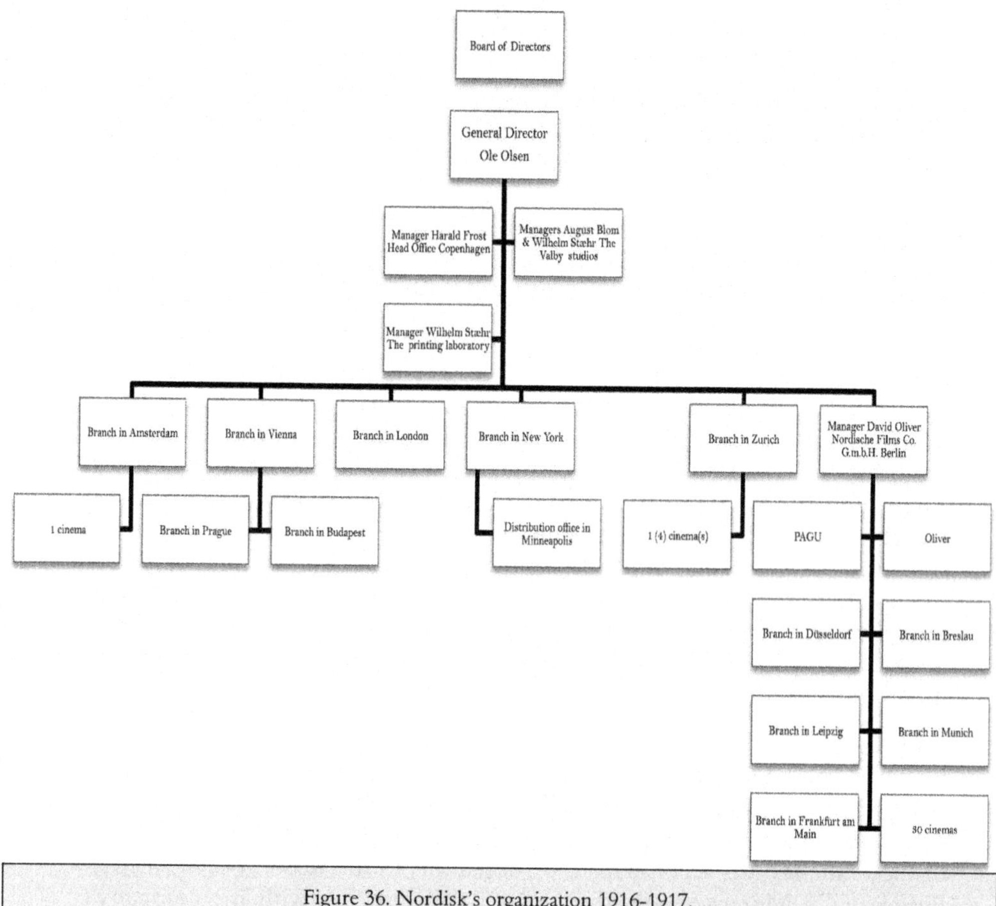

Figure 36. Nordisk's organization 1916-1917.

company bought Switzerland's biggest cinema, Orient-Kino in Zurich. Furthermore, Nordisk purchased three cinemas in Zurich, St. Gallen and Lucerne.[1002] Only the Orient-Kino and the branch later established in Switzerland are listed on the inventory of the company's possessions in the Bundesarchiv. These acquisitions were carried out in 1916/1917, and Nordisk probably used subterfuge with these investments, for which reason they are not listed in the official records. On 23 March 1917, Nordisk Films Co. bought the cinema Maatschappij Union in Amsterdam, and this business became a branch under Nordisk in Copenhagen.[1003] Eight branches, a distribution office and 33 cinemas mainly concentrated in Germany and Central Europe were the results of Nordisk's strategy (see Figure 36).

Furthermore, Nordisk also invested in the following national and international companies:

1002 *Jahrbuch der Filmindustrie 1922/23*, 23. See also Kallmann, *Die Konzernierung*, 11.

1003 Bundesarchiv-Filmarchiv R-109-476. N.V. Nordisk Films Co., Amsterdam.

Fotoramas Filmsbureau A/S
A/B Svenska Biografteaterns Filmsbyrå, Stockholm
A/B Nordisk Filmsfabrik, Stockholm
A/B Fribergs Filmsbyrå, Stockholm
A/B Svenska Biografteaterns distribution in Scandinavia
Thiemann, Reinhardt & Osipov, Moscow
Era-production company, Moscow
Electro cinema, Moscow
Projectograph, Vienna/Budapest

Finally, as shown above, sources indicate that Nordisk had interests or investments in the following companies, but this has yet to be verified:

Carl Gabriel Filmverleih, Munich
Deutsche Bioscop G.m.b.H., Berlin
Continental-Projection, Leipzig
The distribution company Franzos, Geneva
The distribution company Lang, Zurich
Cinemas in Zurich, St. Gall and Lucerne

Thus, halfway through the First World War, Nordisk had become a multinational, vertically integrated company in Germany and Central Europe, and the neutrality of Denmark still made it possible for Nordisk to fulfil the distribution contracts arranged before the war.

In November 1916, at the same time as Nordisk was expanding its share capital, the company lost contact with its French agent, Louis Aubert. Every attempt to get in contact with Aubert was prevented by French censorship. Aubert owed Nordisk 35,000 French francs, and the company had addressed the Danish legation in Paris, the Danish Vice Consulate in Geneva and the Confederation of Danish Employers for help, all in vain.[1004]

From correspondence in February 1918 between the Confederation of Danish Employers and the Ministry of Foreign Affairs, it appears that Nordisk was on the French Ministry of Blockade's confidential blacklist no. 4, as of December 1917, and that the company's outstanding debts from Aubert were deposited in the Caisse des dépôts et consignations,[1005] which is where money sent from French subjects to Germany or Austria-Hungary ended up, since such transactions were prohibited by a decree of September 1914. The same decree further stated that the prohibition also included persons who were presumed to serve German or Austro-Hungarian interests.[1006] Nordisk was now blacklisted by France due to the company's German interests. Up until that point in the war, Nordisk had traded extensively with French companies – not only

1004 RA/U.M.79.H.79. Letter from Harald Frost to Confederation of Danish Employers (31 January 1918).

1005 RA/U.M.79.H.79. Letter from Confederation of Danish Employers to the Ministry of Foreign Affairs of Denmark (13 February 1918).

1006 RA/U.M.79.H.79. Letter from the Royal Danish Legation, Paris to the Ministry of Foreign Affairs of Denmark (11 September 1918).

with Aubert, but also with Pathé Frères. A possible reason that the trade continued is that it had passed unnoticed. It was only when it became known that France and Germany were still trading with Nordisk as an intermediary that the company was blacklisted.

The German magazine *Lichtbild-Bühne* published an article on 14 October 1916 in which Nordisk was accused of using contraband French raw stock for the copying of films brought into Germany. Deliveries from the American company Eastman had ceased five months earlier, at which time Pathé Frères' sales in Scandinavia had increased by three million metres of raw film compared to the year before.[1007] Nordisk rejected the accusation as "evil gossip".[1008]

The French Ministry of Trade and Industry asked Edmond Pabst, the French trade attaché in Copenhagen, to investigate the accusation, and Nordisk promptly volunteered to cooperate. In September 1917, Pabst could report that Pathé Frères had indeed shipped 2,027,560 metres of film to Nordisk, of which 1,761,997 metres were within the quota that Pathé Frères was allowed to ship to the Danish company. Of these, 1,303,380 metres were used for films exported to the Entente Powers; 167,714 metres went to neutral countries; and 135,619 metres were exported to the Central Powers. The rest, approximately 400,000 metres, had gone to Russia where it had been used for titles, had vanished, or had not yet been sold. Since Eastman was the only company which marked their own film stock, Pabst found it mathematically impossible to decide if the decree had been breached.

In connection with the charges in *Lichtbild-Bühne*, Pabst reported the following story: when he heard of the accusation from the German trade journal, a worker at Nordisk's copying lab had spliced 130 metres of French film stock into a shipment for the Central Powers. Luckily, Nordisk had discovered the deed and sacked the man. The worker's intention was to "discover" the spliced-in section of film himself and thereby expose the hypocrisy of Nordisk.[1009] This rather contrived tale sounds like a fabrication made to prove that Nordisk had full control over its production and discovered the irregularities itself. Or perhaps the story is true. If the worker's intention was really to expose the double-dealing of Nordisk, it may have been a rule rather than an exception to use contraband French film stock for copies sent to Germany.

An interesting point of Pabst's investigation is that he still did not know why film from Nordisk was being stopped by the French customs, a puzzle he hoped the French Government could shed some light on.[1010] In other words, in September 1917 neither Pabst nor Nordisk apparently knew that the company was on the confidential French blacklist. In fact, however, Olsen had

1007 "Auf welchem Material kopiert die 'Nordische'?", *Lichtbild-Bühne*, no. 41 (14 October 1916).

1008 "Ondsindet Vrøvl i 'Aftenbladet'", *Social-Demokraten* (20 October 1916).

1009 RA/U.M.79.H.79. Copy of letter from Edmond Pabst, Apppointed Envoy Extraordinary and Minister Plenipotentiary of France at Copenhagen to the Minister (19 September 1917).

1010 RA/U.M.79.H.79. Copy of letter from Edmond Pabst, Apppointed Envoy Extraordinary and Minister Plenipotentiary of France at Copenhagen to the Minister (19 September 1917).

been warned early in the war about the risk of buying film from both the Entente and the Central powers. Home from Berlin in June 1915, Olsen could inform the board that he had led negotiations about the purchase of Asta Nielsen negatives, a shipment of Pathé film and Union negatives. Nordisk's board decided on the following:

> The board authorizes the manager to bring these negotiations to the conclusion that is most beneficial to the company and to handle the purchase of the Pathé film with the utmost caution to avoid unpleasantness for the company in the future.[1011]

In the last two years of the war, Nordisk came to feel the political consequences even further. Their branch in Zurich was blacklisted by France in November 1917,[1012] and the Danish consul in Switzerland could inform the Foreign Office that the Swiss press reported how Nordisk was spreading propaganda for the Central Powers through its business.[1013]

The loss of contact with its French agent, Aubert, was a major blow for Nordisk because Aubert also had the agency for the important South American market. Another overseas market closed for Nordisk in October 1916 when the company shut down its branch in New York.[1014] The exact reason is unknown, but American filmgoers began to prefer American films to European ones, and the share of European films on the American market, which had been in decline since 1910, fell to about 5 per cent during the war.[1015] In fact, Nordisk's New York branch had never been successful, and the difficult trading conditions must have given the branch the deathblow. Olsen later claimed that Nordisk's exports to America ceased around 1 November 1916.[1016]

On 1 January 1917, a general import ban on films was passed in Austria-Hungary, but Nordisk obtained a dispensation when the company agreed to freeze its present and future earnings in the country up to two years after an armistice.[1017]

At a board meeting on 30 March 1917, Olsen could report:

> [...] there are plans for a company of grand-scale, international cinema operation. The intention is to form a company, based in Copenhagen, with a share capital of ten million kroner which sum is expected to be readily available from Danish interested parties so that it will not be necessary to put shares out for sale at all.[1018]

Olsen told the other board members that he was already negotiating with Skaarup and others, and that he counted on closing an advantageous deal for

1011 NFS:I,25.DFI. Unpagn. Minutes of board of directors (19 July 1915).

1012 *Jahrbuch der Filmindustrie 1922/23*, 26.

1013 RA/U.M.70.T.92. Letter from the Danish Consul, Switzerland to the Ministry of Foreign Affairs of Denmark (13 April 1918).

1014 See Mottram, *The Danish Cinema before Dreyer*, 215.

1015 See Bakker, *Entertainment Industrialised*, 187 and 192.

1016 NFS:IV,52:38.DFI, 6. Ole Olsen's confidential testimony undated (1917/1918), 6.

1017 NFS:I,25.DFI. Unpagn. Minutes of the Board of Directors Meeting (22 January 1917).

1018 NFS:I,25.DFI. Unpagn. Minutes of the Board of Directors Meeting (30 March 1917).

Nordisk. Skaarup, who was waiting outside the conference room, was called in to shed more light on the upcoming company: the European Shareholding Company. The new company would buy up and run cinemas all over Europe, and Nordisk would get an exclusive deal through which the company's films would get top priority in the European cinemas, provided that "Nordisk is willing to sign up for a large part of the shares in the new company".[1019] The board at Nordisk agreed to sign up for one fifth of the share capital, two million kroner, and authorized Olsen to sign another contract on condition that the agreement above was kept.

From the accounts of the new company it appears the European Shareholding Company had fourteen shareholders. The ones who had signed up for more than 100,000 kroner were:

Frede Skaarup	Kr. 250,000
Ole Olsen	Kr. 500,000
Johan Ramm	Kr. 270,000
David Oliver	Kr. 100,000
Mammen & Drescher	Kr. 100,000
Nordisk Film	Kr. 500,000[1020]

The two biggest investors were Olsen and Nordisk with a million kroner between them, out of the 1,885,000 kroner that had been deposited on 7 May 1917. During the summer, Olsen negotiated further with the European Shareholding Company, and at a board meeting in July, Olsen reported:

> [...] that the board of the European Shareholding Company had proposed making the contract's duration dependent on the present board of directors at Nordisk's continued position in the management, so that the European Shareholding Company should be at liberty to annul the contract if Managing Director Olsen and Manager Frost should leave Nordisk, in which case the European Shareholding Company will purchase Nordisk's shares in the European Shareholding Company at par.[1021]

The board rejected this proposition and maintained that if a contract could not be agreed upon on the terms already laid out, Nordisk would pull out of the European Shareholding Company, which would then have to be liquidated or would have to pay back the sums received from the shareholders. Olsen requested that this decision be recorded in the minutes. Less than a month later, Olsen announced to the board that he had negotiated with European without being able to negotiate an agreement for which the board had given him a mandate. He now expected that European would go into liquidation. Board member Paulsen suggested that, in case the liquidation would become a fact, Nordisk should offer to take over the cinemas already purchased by European, and this motion was passed. However, European had never had time

1019 NFS:I,25.DFI. Unpagn. Minutes of the Board of Directors Meeting (30 March 1917).

1020 NFS:I,87:33.DFI. Unpagn. Accounts of Europæiske Kompagni Aktieselskab (European Shareholding Company) (17 November 1917).

1021 NFS:I,25.DFI. Unpagn. Minutes of the Board of Directors Meeting (6 July 1917).

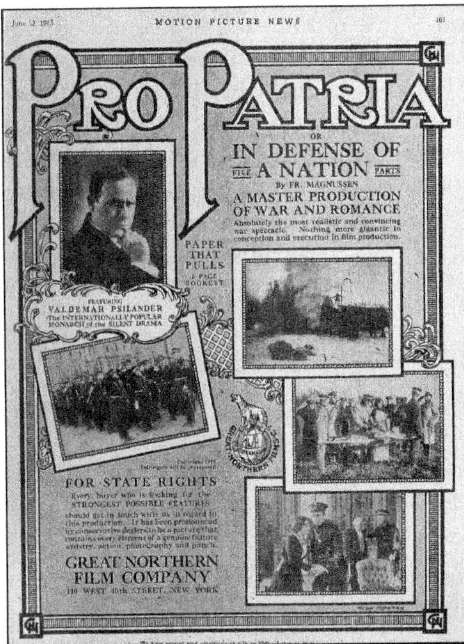

Figure 37. Great Northern ad in *Motion Picture News* (no. 23, 12 June 1915).

to buy cinemas and the company paid back the invested capital with interest on 14 August.[1022]

In fact, the European Shareholding Company venture would have been a good idea. Since the outbreak of the war, cinemas had experienced a colossal rise in turnover. In Denmark, the cinemas' earnings had increased: in the Copenhagen area by 330 per cent; in the cities by 350 per cent and in the provinces by 250 per cent.[1023] The clause to the effect that European could liberate itself entirely from Nordisk if Olsen and Frost left the company, however, may indicate that Olsen was hedging his bets. This suspicion is apparently to be supported by a handwritten note in the Nordisk Collection stating: "Secret executive committee Skaarup and Ole Olsen."[1024] One interpretation of these events seems to be that Olsen and Frost were planning to disconnect themselves from Nordisk and start, together with Skaarup among others, a European company running cinemas all over Europe. In spite of the fact that the war was in its third year, the plans of the European Shareholding Company suggest a great optimism and willingness to invest in the future European film industry.

While negotiations concerning the European Shareholding Company were going on, the war started to take its toll on film production in Valby. Shortages of coal and petrol meant a reduction in electricity, and in May 1917, Nordisk sacked two hundred part-time employees, since only one of the studios could be lit without lamps.[1025] In the following months, the shortage of supplies worsened, exports were further limited, and Nordisk chose to end the filming season on 1 September, a month earlier than usual. "A Catastrophe in the World of Film", wrote the newspaper *København*[1026] when word got out that

1022 NFS:I,87:33.DFI. Unpagn. Accounts of Europæiske Kompagni Aktieselskab (European Shareholding Company) (17 November 1917).

1023 See Ulff-Møller, *Biografvæsenets udvikling*, 74.

1024 NFS:I,87:20-36.DFI. Unpagn. Documents concerning the establishing of Europæiske Kompagni Aktieselskab (European Shareholding Company).

1025 "Nordisk Films Co. og Elektricitetsforbudet", *B.T.* (14 May 1917). "Nordisk Films Co. sætter 200 Mennesker paa Gaden", *Aftenbladet* (21 May 1917).

1026 "En Katastrofe i Filmsverdnen", *København* (20 July 1917).

one hundred full-time employees and between three and four hundred part timers were to be fired.[1027] Three actors felt unjustly dismissed with only eight days' notice, and they sued Nordisk. The case made the headlines; as rumours would have it, shortage of supplies was not the reason for the cutbacks – the true reason, according to the papers, was that Nordisk had been blacklisted by Britain and France. Olsen was confronted in court with the following allegations:

> Barrister Levinsen: Does the Director General know whether his company, Nordisk Films Co., is blacklisted in England and France?
>
> Ole Olsen: No!
>
> Barrister Levinsen: In answering this question, you are not under oath.
>
> Ole Olsen: If Mr. Levinsen knows more about the case in question than I do, he should not withhold this information.
>
> Barrister Levinsen: This is solely a matter of what Mr. Ole Olsen knows. I suggest the Director General consider his reply carefully.
>
> Ole Olsen: *Nordisk* is not on any *official* blacklist.[1028]

Olsen probably felt hard-pressed during the court case. The rumour that Nordisk was blacklisted was bad publicity. Considering Nordisk's business interests, Olsen requested leave to write a confidential document as testimony in the case. The document lists the difficulties which his company had suffered since the outbreak of the war and until December 1917. The document is to be regarded as evidence from one of the parties, as it renders Olsen's view of the company's tribulations. According to Olsen, Nordisk's exports to the United States, Britain and its colonies had terminated by the end of 1915. In December 1916, a ban on imports was imposed in Austria-Hungary, and at the same time the special license which Nordisk had obtained in Germany expired. Exports to France and hereby Spain and South America stopped by 1 February 1917 due to the German blockade which made the Danish postal service suspend its deliveries. Exports to the Russian market ended in March 1917 and were not continued after the October Revolution. It was only in Norway, Sweden, Holland and Switzerland that exports could proceed unaffected.[1029]

In his testimony, Olsen omits numerous events that had influenced the company's business, and his claim that Nordisk had not been able to export to Germany since December 1916 was a misrepresentation of fact. Finally, Olsen does not utter a word about the event that would break the backbone of Nordisk's business network, which will be described below. The court did not reach a verdict until 8 April 1918. The actors won the case on the grounds that the company's difficulties had not increased significantly since their contracts were signed, together with the fact that they would have been under contract for a very short time after their dismissal. The actors were awarded, respec-

1027 "Nordisk Film afskediger sit Personale til 1. September", *Nationaltidende* (19 July 1917).

1028 "Generaldirektør Ole Olsen som vidne", *Politiken* (28 November 1917).

1029 NFS:IV,52:38.DFI, 6. Ole Olsen's confidential testimony undated (1917/1918), 1 and 6.

tively, 1,406.25 kroner, 712.50 kroner and 1,928.58 kroner – and Nordisk had to cover the costs of the case.[1030]

Even if the export markets had closed to Nordisk in the course of 1917, the idea of a European Shareholding Company still indicated Olsen's trust in the future. In Germany and Central Europe, Nordisk's solid and far-flung network still remained until the day the war ended. But there were others who had plans for those networks. In his memoirs, the German General Erich Ludendorff writes about German propaganda during the war:

> Our political aims and decisions often seemed brutal and haphazard because they took the world by surprise. This might have been prevented by a grand-scale and far-sighted propaganda campaign. Not only did we lack the will to propagandize in peacetime, we also lacked the proper media.[1031]

Together with General Paul von Hindenburg, Ludendorff made up the General Staff which had de facto ruled Germany since August 1916. Ludendorff calculated that if Germany was going to win the war, the spirit of the German people had to be changed by means of propaganda. The summer of 1916 would prove to be a turning-point in the general staff's view on propaganda; a military department was established in the Foreign Office to take care of this matter in the neutral countries. In charge of the office was Colonel Hans von Haeften who was assigned to systematize the propaganda, and film would be crucial to his plans. "In the neutral countries, Colonel v. Haeften tried to make his point through words and images, but first and foremost through films", Ludendorff reports.[1032]

Scandinavia was selected as a place where German film could gain a foothold, and this led to the establishment of the "Central Office for German Propaganda in Scandinavia", based in Stockholm, and the branch office *Nordstjernen* (The North Star) in Copenhagen. The attempt to promote German films in Denmark was not successful. It was difficult to get into the Scandinavian distribution markets which were controlled by the big companies; the public was tired of films about the war, and German films could not compete with the American films shown in Copenhagen cinemas.[1033] On 4 July 1917, a memo was sent to the general staff, signed by Ludendorff but in all likelihood written by von Haeften and Major Alexander Grau. "The war has seized upon the colossal power of pictures and films as a means to elucidation and influence", Ludendorff states and continues:

> The Nordisk Company is therefore considered a power by German propaganda as they might cause great damage if they should choose to act with hostility against

1030 "Nordisk Film Co. dømt i dag", *B.T.* (8 April 1918).

1031 Erich Ludendorff, *General Ludendorffs Krigserindringer 1914–1918* (Copenhagen: H. Aschehoug og Co., 1919), 259.

1032 Ludendorff, *General Ludendorffs*, 260.

1033 See Jeanpaul Goergen, "'Neue Filme haben wir nicht erhalten.' Die deutsche Filmpropaganda 1917/18 in Dänemark", in Manfred Behn (ed.), *Schwarzer Traum und weiße Sklavin. Deutsch-dänische Filmbeziehungen 1910–1930*, 30–37.

> Germany. In addition, Nordisk has the possibility to send films to Russia. What this influence, when used in a German-friendly way, might occasion with the volatile disposition of the Russian population today, is difficult to assess.[1034]

The memo outlines a new, national film company under government control. Ludendorff was fully aware of Nordisk's dominant position on the German market and the damages which the Danish company could cause if it turned against Germany. Buying shares in Nordisk would not be enough; all the German assets of the company had to be purchased.

In the early spring of 1917, the German administration tried to gain influence over Nordisk by buying up shares on the free market but only succeeded in obtaining 600,000 kroner worth of shares through the free stock market, which equalled five per cent of the total share capital of the company.[1035] The manoeuvre failed, and influence over Nordisk had to be obtained in another way, namely through acquisition. Ludendorff estimated the price of Nordisk at 20 million German marks, but it was of the utmost importance that the German state was not identified as the buyer. A syndicate of German banks and businessmen was to act as puppet for the German Military Command. Among the members of the syndicate were Bosch, AEG, Deutsche Bank and Dresdner Bank.[1036]

At a board meeting on 15 November 1917, Olsen presented an offer from the German syndicate which was represented by the general manager of Deutsche Bank, Emil Georg von Stauss. The syndicate wished to form a company with a capital of 20 million marks, and Nordisk was to hand over all its interests in Germany, Austria-Hungary, Holland, and Switzerland to the new company in return for ten million German marks, out of which the seven million marks would be paid to Nordisk as shares in the new company, and three million would be paid in cash. The terms of the takeover was a mutual agreement of film distribution, and the share capital would be spent on purchasing similar companies. Olsen's suggestion was to "[…] accept the offer, inasmuch as he had personally promised the syndicate to recommend the offer to his board".[1037] The board decided that a committee should conclude the agreement with the syndicate, and in February 1918, Olsen could announce to the board that the agreement with the German syndicate, now bearing the name of Universum Film Aktiengesellschaft (UFA), had been closed.[1038] In his memoirs, Olsen states: "We had no choice – as foreigners in a country at war, we had to make the most of the deal."[1039]

1034 Manfred Behn, "Der Ludendorff-Brief", in Hans-Michael Bock and Michael Töteberg (ed.), *Das Ufa-Buch*, 34.

1035 See Wolfgang Mühl-Benninghaus, *Vom Augusterlebnis*, 281.

1036 See Behn, "Der Ludendorff-Brief", 35.

1037 NFS:I,25.DFI. Unpagn. Minutes of the Board of Directors Meeting (15 November 1917).

1038 NFS:I,25.DFI. Unpagn. Minutes of the Board of Directors Meeting (12 February 1918).

1039 Olsen, *Filmens Eventyr og mit eget*, 139.

1918–1924

The Fall of the Polar Bear

Olsen characterized the years after the outbreak of the war in this way:

> The great years of Nordisk Films Company were *before* the war, and what followed in the decade from 1914 to 1924 – the year when I left for good – was very hard work in which both I and my board of directors had to watch our step and make sacrifices.[1040]

It is striking how Olsen plays down Nordisk's role during the war by emphasizing that the company was in its prime before 1914. Olsen would make similar statements in the years after the war, such as in an interview from 1921 in which he said: "We had great assets in German theatres and film companies that we were forced to sell at the beginning of the war."[1041] In the interview Olsen clearly claims that Nordisk was compelled to sell out at the outbreak of the war rather than around 1917/1918, and the close connection Nordisk would make with UFA in the years after the war is left entirely out of the equation.

World War I was a turning point in the development of Nordisk. After the war, the company started the decline that would eventually lead to suspension of payments and liquidation in 1928. Several Danish film historians explain the crisis by a deterioration of the quality of Nordisk's films, but this argument simplifies the facts. A series of crucial circumstances had changed. Due to the war, Nordisk had incurred substantial losses, and the company's close alliance with the Central Powers influenced Nordisk's opportunities. The trade situation in which Nordisk was to act changed consistently – the free trade that had existed before the war was now subject to custom duties and taxation, and at the same time, the European film industry lost its position on the world market to American film companies.

Nordisk's grand expansion plans suffered defeat at the end of 1917, but the board's and the management's eagerness to invest persisted after the war, as did their hopes of resuming their former position on the international market. Nordisk reacted to the new situation by reorganizing thoroughly. Film production was scaled down, and the company invested large sums in becoming

1040 Ibid., 150–151.

1041 Lars, "Sandheden om Nordisk Films Co.", *B.T.* (5 July 1921).

a centre of film-trade that would purchase and distribute films from other companies, and in time be partners in a large-scale Danish-German-American collaboration.

As mentioned, the widespread belief that the cause of Nordisk's post-war misfortune was the artistic quality of the productions is a misconception that took shape in the late 1910s and early 1920s. In 1920 Carl Theodor Dreyer pronounced his verdict on Danish film, and indirectly on Nordisk, when he stated that Danish film had all the opportunities but lacked the key person with "authority, taste and culture" who could "raise film to a higher sphere". The Danish film factories went on as usual but by now, Danish products had gained an alarmingly bad reputation:

> A dubious odour hung about Danish films and scared off the cultural elite – this odour is so persistent that audiences in our more fastidious neighbouring countries still turn up their noses at the mere sight of a Danish film poster.[1042]

In an unsigned article from 1921, "An anonymous specialist" said to *Politiken* that the cause of Nordisk's post-war crisis was that Olsen's interest in gaining wealth eclipsed his ability to see film as an art form; according to the reviewer, the war and the post-war financial climate had no hand in the decline of the company. Nordisk had failed to keep up with the times; the company's artistic level had plummeted, he stated, and now Nordisk and Danish film was in ill repute on the world market:

> The management is solely to blame. Under the auspices of the Director General, it has hindered a certain level of quality. It is in fact a shame that Nordisk has thus brought infamy on Danish film, and that Danish film's potential has remained latent for several years. There is a possibility that Nordisk may resume its former reputation on the world market; the opportunities and the technical circumstances are present, but to pull this off, a different spirit is needed in the management. To be precise, a cultured spirit.[1043]

Dreyer's polemic statements and the anonymous attack on Olsen are in line with the widespread explanation of Nordisk's and also Danish film's crisis which we find in the years after the war. I will later include statements from the directors Urban Gad and Benjamin Christensen which are further examples from the period of this general discourse.

Especially in the older Danish film historiography the artistic decline is the explanation for Nordisk's crisis in the post-war years. Although Erik Ulrichsen does mention in his article "La belle époque" that World War I interfered with Nordisk's foreign export, his overall argument is that the artistic quality of the films was mainly to blame for the crisis.[1044] Ulrichsen quotes a letter from director August Blom to the management at Nordisk. Blom argues that the "factory-like production of films" has caused 90 per cent of the films to fall

1042 Carl Th. Dreyer, "Svensk Film", *Dagbladet* (20 January 1920).

1043 "Nordisk Films Co. Det slette Regnskab. Interview med Ole Olsen", *Kinobladet*, no. 15 (1921): 589–595.

1044 See Erik Ulrichsen, "La belle époque", in Svend Kragh-Jacobsen, Erik Balling and Ove Sevel (ed.), *50 Aar i dansk film*, 30.

short of what the company might have achieved.[1045] A similar view on the company's films is shared by director A.W. Sandberg in a letter to Olsen:

> Cannot the Director General see that 'Nordisk films Co.' – in spite of the great work you have done to raise the level of the films, – has declined thanks to the 'factory films' which have been left without head and tail in 'Frihavnen', – and they are still poor films.[1046]

Ulrichsen believes that this explains why the "polar bear is no longer *going strong*".[1047] In *Historien om dansk film*, Ebbe Neergaard writes that the outbreak of the war and the subsequent reduction of foreign export was what caused the decline, but Neergaard still ends by stating: "However, external obstructions such as these are not a sufficient explanation for the crisis that followed. There must have been internal causes – and these causes must have to do with the films themselves."[1048] Engberg argues in a similar way:

> It has often been stated that World War I was the cause of the decline in Danish film. This, however, is only part of the truth. The decline was due to the drop in artistic quality, begun before the outbreak of the war, and it might have been stopped if Nordisk and others had tried to learn something from the competitors whose films were shown in Danish cinemas, too, such as Sjöström's INGEBORG HOLM (1913) and Griffith.[1049]

Ulrichsen, Neergaard and Engberg all agree that the financial crisis Nordisk faced after World War I may be explained by the outbreak of the war and the limitations of export, but they all lean towards the deterioration of artistic quality as the true cause. They base their analyses of Nordisk's development on a series of circumstances which deserve modification. One such circumstance is the claim that Nordisk's foreign export stopped at the outbreak of the war. "World War I broke out and closed the borders",[1050] writes Engberg, marking 1914 as the end of the Golden Age in Danish film. However, the outbreak of the war did not limit Nordisk's export, quite the contrary. As previously stated, the war presented the company with an opportunity for large-scale foreign export.

Engberg further reports that a great part of Nordisk's films had become unsellable as early as 1914, for which reason the value of the negatives were written down with nearly 67,000 kroner, and written further down with 823,776 kroner in 1915. "These figures testify to dead capital", writes Engberg.[1051] How Engberg has reached this conclusion is not quite clear. The

1045 Letter from August Blom to Ole Olsen (24 January 1917), quoted from Ulrichsen, "La belle époque", 30. I have not succeeded in finding the mentioned letter in the Nordisk Film Collection.

1046 NFA. Letter from A.W. Sandberg to Ole Olsen (24 November 1918).

1047 Ulrichsen, "La belle époque", 30.

1048 Neergaard, *Historien om dansk film*, 75.

1049 Engberg, *Dansk stumfilm*, 510.

1050 Ibid., 7.

1051 Ibid., 592.

figures on which Engberg bases her assumption must be from Nordisk's 1911–1915 ledgers in which the first pages list annual income from stocks.[1052] That the inventory increased and decreased does not mean that the value of the assets declined, as Engberg surmises. With a sale of about four million metres of positive film a year from 1912 to 1915, the company had large reserves of film, and that this stock varied from year to year does not mean that Nordisk wrote off the value of the films. A writing-off of 800,000 kroner's worth of useless film would appear in the annual financial statement, such as it does in the books from 1918, when the company wrote off 492,609.95 kroner's worth of old and useless negatives, but such a manoeuvre has nothing to do with the quality or saleability of the company's films. Older films which had served their purpose were written off, as were inventory and machines. In general, the listed expenses for a film were written off in the year when the film was released. The practice of not writing off the value of a film until 18 months after its release was not introduced before the 1920s.[1053]

Engberg states in a later article: "Already from 1913, a growing number of unsold films had been accumulating on the shelves of the factory [...]", and she believes that these films were unsellable after the war.[1054] In his confidential letter in the court case between the actors and Nordisk, Olsen touches upon the saleability of Nordisk's extensive production during the war. Olsen mentions a big, unnamed film as one of the reasons for stopping other productions in September 1917, and adds that this film was scheduled for release after the war, "whereas ordinary films, due to changing fashions, could easily appear out of style and unprofitable if they were released much later than they were made".[1055] In other words, Olsen makes a distinction between big and durable productions that will sell for a good many years, and what may be termed standard films with a short shelf life. This means that the company was indeed conscious about adjusting their productions to alterations on the market.

The films which Nordisk produced during the war were not dead capital soon to be shelved – they were in fact sold. If we look at the average of films sold from 1912 to 1924 (see Figure 38), we note a drastic decline in sold copies per title from 69 to 39 in 1914.

Part of this decline reflects the fact that the important German and British markets went from regular sales to monopoly rental by which a single copy could reach a wider audience. During the war, when Nordisk could show its own films in its own cinemas, the demand for copies was further reduced. On the average, 27 copies of each film made during the war were sold. We must

1052 NFS:III,46.DFI, 8. Balance sheet and ledger. The figures in the ledger correspond with Engberg's but the amount 67,000 kroner is listed 66,844 kroner in May 1914, and it is not clear where her figures from 1915 originate from.

1053 See Bakker, *Entertainment Industrialised*, 182.

1054 Marguerite Engberg, "Nordisk in Denmark", in Karel Dibbets and Bert Hogenkamp (ed.), *Film and the First World War* (Amsterdam: Amsterdam University Press, 1995), 43.

1055 NFS:IV,52:38.DFI, 5–6. Ole Olsen's confidential letter in the court case in 1917/1918, undated.

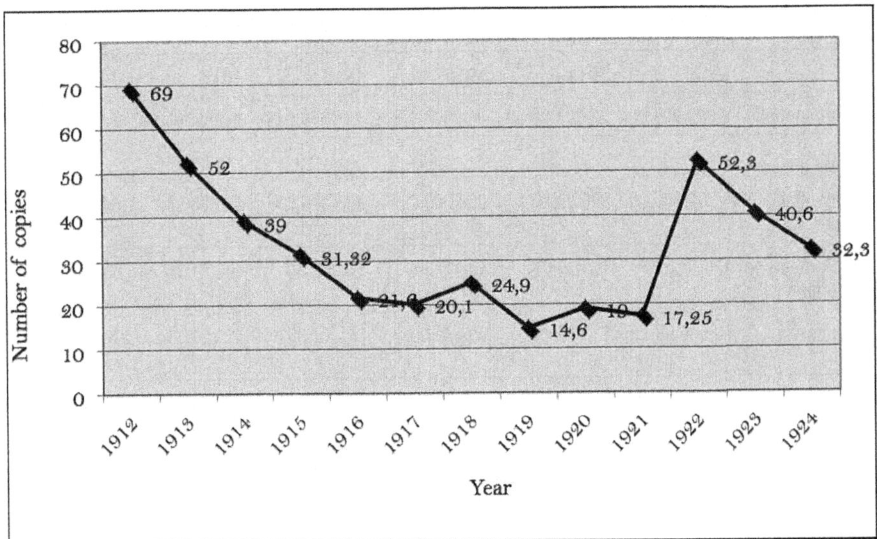

Figure 38. Average number of sold copies 1912–1924.
Note: Films for which there are no distribution figures are not included here. This goes for 17 films from 1913 to 1917, most of which made for special occasions, such as the Psilander film GREV DAHLBORGS HEMMELIGHED. 37 films from the first part of 1912 are excluded as well since the distribution protocols from around 1908 to the beginning of 1912 have been lost. The high sales average in the early 1920s is due to the fact that Nordisk produced very few films in these years: three films in 1922, four films in 1923 and seven films in 1924.
Source: see note for Table 1 (on page 30).

also consider that Nordisk's production peaked during the war, and even if the number of copies of each film went down, this was balanced by a considerable larger volume of production.

Engberg's interpretation of Nordisk's post-war decline is most evident in the conclusion of her English summary where she argues that Nordisk's sales went down before the outbreak of the war: "I feel that the economic conditions imposed by the world war accelerated a decline of which roots had been manifested earlier in the Golden Age."[1056] However, nothing indicates that Engberg's feelings are right in supposing that Nordisk's crisis started already in the early 1910s. The big share payments before the war testify to profits in the company, and throughout the war Nordisk was able to pay dividends to its shareholders. The dividends were not as large as in 1913 and 1914, but they were still paid all the way up to 1918 (see Table 7). Of course, the profits must be seen in relation to the fact that the share capital was quadrupled in the years from 1913 to 1918.

1056 Engberg, *Dansk stumfilm*, 619.

Table 7: Nordisk's dividends, emoluments and staff bonuses 1913–1918

	1913	1914	1915	1916	1917	1918
Share capital	2,000,000.00	2,000,000.00	4,000,000.00	4,000,000.00	8,000,000.00	8,000,000.00
Dividend in %	60	33	10	10	7 (3½)	8
Dividend in kroner	1,200,000.00	660,000.00	200,000.00	400,000.00	420,000.00	640,000.00
Emoluments to the board	179,017.76	119,304.59	49,417.08	90,902.58	42,791.76	83,583.31
Bonuses to staff	60,500.00	67,988.78	60,000.00	50,771.38	41,124.60	49,971.30
Total	**1,439,517.76**	**847,293.37**	**309,417.08**	**541,673.96**	**503,916.36**	**773,355.61**

Source: NFS:I,25.DFI and III,36:1-9.DFI. Printed annual reports 1913–1918.
Note: Due to the expansion of the share capital in the middle of the term 1916/1917, the board chose to pay seven per cent on old shares and 3.5 per cent on new shares.

The assumption that the artistic quality of the films deteriorated and that Nordisk's management was unable to change this is another hypothesis that deserves to be nuanced. Ron Mottram views Neergaard's and Engberg's criticism of the films as largely correct but adds that "[...] this is a vague criticism, and it should also be considered a highly tentative one since very few of Nordisk films have survived from the 1915–17 period".[1057] As mentioned in the introduction, Thomas C. Christensen has argued against explaining financial matters by aesthetics, and Christensen further states that since only a small number of films have survived, any analysis of their quality must remain conjectural. I would not put it as simply as that. We do have materials such as programmes, film stills, letters, reviews etc. which may give us an impression of the quality of the lost films. This means that the opportunity of examining the artistic development more closely is still present, but I agree with Christensen that an explanation of the company crisis based only on the decline of the quality of the films must be considered facile.

A review of EN FARE FOR SAMFUNDET points out another circumstance to take into consideration in the judgement of the artistic quality of the company's films:

> EN FARE FOR SAMFUNDET differs significantly from Nordisk Co.'s earlier productions. You get the impression of great effort, and that not a single scene has been rushed through with the usual Danish sloppiness.[1058]

The review's judgement of the film is tied to the general discourse of the company's declining artistic quality in the post-war years, but also highlights the qualities of EN FARE FOR SAMFUNDET. What makes guessing about Nordisk's productions highly dubious, is the overall varying quality of the

1057 Mottram, *The Danish Cinema before Dreyer*, 212.

1058 Kinomand, "En fare for samfundet", *Aftenposten* [January 1918]. NFS:XIV,35.DFI, 56. Scrapbook.

films. The management was well aware of this. In 1910, Stæhr estimated that not all the films were "gold",[1059] and Olsen also judged the production as highly uneven: "Of course we cannot, and nor can other companies, always make attractive pictures, and when substandard films are the result, we have to make an extra effort to sell them."[1060] Mottram also points to variations in Nordisk's efficient and standardized production:

> [...] the early Danish cinema was diverse in its artistic accomplishments. Even within Nordisk Films Kompagni, where a certain stylistic coherence pervaded production, certain distinct directorial personalities emerged.[1061]

Bordwell supports Mottram's notion of diversity in artistic accomplishments when he writes: "Nor did the studio's talent work at a consistently high level."[1062] Even within a single season, the films from one director could vary greatly. A case in point could be two films directed by August Blom in 1911, EKSPEDITRICEN and UNGDOMMENS RET (THE RIGHT OF YOUTH, August Blom, 1911). EKSPEDITRICEN is the story of a shop assistant who has an affair with the son of a counsellor. Much as they love each other, the counsellor forbids them to marry. Unfortunately, the shop assistant gets pregnant and is fired. She dies in childbirth, miserable and alone. The visual composition of the film is thorough and exhibits a careful use of light and shadow, and the interaction between the two main characters, played by Clara Wieth and Carlo Wieth, is subtle and moving.

UNGDOMMENS RET is about a rich man who hires a young woman, Miss Engelke, to look after his daughter. The rich man's grown-up son falls in love with Miss Engelke who used to be the mistress of the neighbour's son. After a series of entanglements, the rich man sends Miss Engelke away and harmony is restored to the family. Mottram's verdict on UNGDOMMENS RET is as follows: "Although the film is beautifully photographed, it is ultimately less interesting than most other Blom films. The plot is contrived, and the narrative points are made in the most obvious ways."[1063] The two films exemplify the variations in the work of one director within the same year, and also exemplify the difficulties in ascertaining the overall artistic development of Nordisk on the basis of the few films still in existence.

Besides, artistic quality has not always meant commercial success. Nordisk was, by and large, a business, and its aim was to make the largest possible profit. If changes in the content and style of the films would improve their commercial potential, Nordisk's management intervened and insisted on the necessary changes. The guidelines for scriptwriters and the censorship memoranda constituted efforts to ensure productions that would meet the demands of the

1059 NFS:II,12.DFI, 179. Letter from Wilhelm Stæhr to Ingvald C. Oes, New York (1 February 1910).

1060 NFS:II,18.DFI, 413. Letter from Ole Olsen to Richard Seemann, Berlin (20 January 1912).

1061 Mottram, *The Danish Cinema before Dreyer*, 7.

1062 Bordwell, "Nordisk and the Tableau Aesthetic", 89.

1063 Mottram, *The Danish Cinema before Dreyer*, 142.

distribution contracts Nordisk had signed, but also tools to control and adjust the content of the company productions. *Autorenfilms* are another example of a management initiative to change and improve the artistic quality of the films. Just as Nordisk followed the technical development of the market and the various alterations in the international censorship regulations, the company also paid close attention to new artistic trends in the world.

Several contemporary sources and later film historians use the works of Griffith and the films from the Swedish Golden Age as a comparison to show the poor state of the artistic quality of the films from Nordisk. From the company correspondence it appears that Nordisk was aware of the new artistic currents in films such as BIRTH OF A NATION (David Wark Griffith, David W. Griffith Corp., Epoch Producing Corporation, USA 1915)[1064] and the Swedish TERJE VIGEN (A MAN THERE WAS, Victor Sjöström, Svenska Biografteatern, SE 1917).[1065] In the spring of 1918, Nordisk actually showed INTOLERANCE (David Wark Griffith, Triangle Film Corporation, Wark Producing, USA 1916) at a special screening for the company's directors.[1066] The screening left the director Holger-Madsen disheartened, in his own words.[1067] But one might argue that it is unfair to compare the films from Nordisk with single films which many consider milestones in film history. A fair comparison would hold the films from Nordisk up against, for example, several of the films directed by Griffith or the production of A/B Svenska Biografteatern, the company behind TERJE VIGEN. The aforementioned anonymous specialist's claim in *Politiken* that Olsen lacked artistic flair is not altogether justified, and neither is Engberg's subsequent statement:

> Ole Olsen was a great businessman with a sense of the organisational, technical and distributional side of the matter, but for film as art he did not have the same awareness as e.g. his Swedish colleague Charles Magnusson.[1068]

Evidence shows that Olsen and the management were aware of the changing artistic currents, and he acted on this awareness. In June 1916, he apparently sent the same letter to all of the directors in Valby of which only those copies sent to Alexander Christian and Robert Dinesen still exist.[1069] Hending refers to the letter as a "memo to be sent to the trusted employees of the firm, first and foremost the directors",[1070] and the tone of the letter indicates as much. "With growing apprehension, the management has witnessed how the company's productions have become weaker than ever before", Olsen starts off the memo. Olsen explains that the stock of new films is now so large that it can

1064 NFS:II,57:15.DFI, 5. Letter from Marie Louise Droop to A/S Nordisk Films Kompagni (13 April 1918).

1065 NFS:II,57:8.DFI, 1. Letter from Harald Frost to Nordische Films Co., Berlin (20 October 1916).

1066 See Schröder, *Ideale Kommunikation*, 931.

1067 NFA. Letter from Holger-Madsen to Nordisk Films Kompagni (15 March 1918).

1068 Engberg, *Dansk stumfilm*, 9.

1069 NFS:IV,78.DFI. Letter from Ole Olsen to Alexander Christian (10 June 1916); NFA. Letter from Ole Olsen to Robert Dinesen (10 June 1916).

1070 Hending, "Det københavnske Hollywood", 666–667.

cover Nordisk's needs far into the future. In spite of the difficulties caused by the war, Nordisk had upheld its production level, but the management could no longer sit by and witness that the stock increased with films "[...] that stand a poor chance on the world market, to the detriment of our reputation as a leading company". Olsen was prepared to sack the entire staff, "[...] unless the directors henceforth produce considerably better work, worthy of the company standards". The Swedish BALLETPRIMADONAEN/WOLO CZAWIENKO (ANJALA THE DANCER, Svenska Biografteatern, SE 1916) directed by Mauritz Stiller, Benjamin Christensen's HÆVNENS NAT, and Alfred Lind's Italian film ULTIMA RAPPRESENTAZIONE DI GALA DEL CIRCO WOLFSON (THE LAST GALA NIGHT OF CIRCUS WOLFSON, Vay-Film, IT 1916) are described by Olsen as "films of the highest quality", even though the scripts are slight and trivial:

> [...] the directors have secured the quality from scratch. It is this very ability in a director, to create from nothing or very little a film that audiences wish to see, by adding ideas of his own invention to arouse interest and improve the film's saleability – this ability alone justifies the high salaries paid to the director by the company.

Olsen asserts the right to rework films that are substandard, and he ends his letter by expressing hope that his appeal will have an effect so that he may avoid "[...] resorting to the measure of firing the theatrical staff".[1071] The memo smacks of a threat clearly aimed at the directors.

The timing of Olsen's circular is no coincidence. Since 1913, American films had begun to gain a foothold in European cinemas, and they brought new artistic tendencies in their wake. Bordwell has accounted for the persistent tableau aesthetics that characterized the Nordisk as well as the rest of Europe's film production.[1072] The tableau aesthetics contrast with the faster cuts of the American style, which were to become dominant after the war. From the positive examples mentioned by Olsen, only HÆVNENS NAT and a 12-minute fragment of BALLETPRIMADONAEN have survived, and common these two is their use of parallel editing as an integrated part of the film's narrative.[1073] For instance in HÆVNENS NAT, when "Strong Henry" breaks into a villa at a New Year's Eve party, the film cuts from Henry moving about to the party guests. Very little remains of BALLETPRIMADONAEN, but in the preserved fragments parallel cutting is used, for instance in the scene in which the girl Anjuta is at an audition at the ballet school and her anxious admirer Wolo waits outside the dance hall. Neither of these two films uses particularly fast cutting; the fragment from BALLETPRIMADONAEN has an average shot length (ASL) of 10.95 seconds, and HÆVNENS NAT's ASL is at 14. The average ASL for an American film in 1916 was between five and seven seconds.[1074] ULTIMA

1071 NFS:IV,78.DFI. Letter from Ole Olsen to Alexander Christian (10 June 1916); NFA. Letter from Ole Olsen to Robert Dinesen (10 June 1916).

1072 See Bordwell "Nordisk and the Tableau Aesthetic", 93.

1073 I am indebted to Thomas C. Christensen and Jon Wengström for having brought BALLET-PRIMADONAEN/WOLO CZAWIENKO to Copenhagen.

RAPPRESENTAZIONE DI GALA DEL CIRCO WOLFSON is lost, but if it resembles Alfred Lind's other Italian films, such as IL JOCKEY DELLA MORTE (THE JOCKEY OF DEATH, Alfred Lind, IT 1915), it was most likely a fast-paced sensation film.

In his letter, Olsen does not place the blame with Nordisk's organization or the way the films were produced; he only blames the directors. The reason is most likely that Olsen was aware that Nordisk's financial success was largely dependent on the factory-like assembly-line production which enabled the company to churn out a lot of films that were sold in a great many copies. Nordisk's organization, as well as the bureaucracy it entailed, is sure to have limited artistic, innovative ideas in the company. Photographer Helvig Ferdinand Rimmen relates that during the shoot of TROEN, DER FRELSER (THE LANTERN OF FATE, Alexander Christian, 1917), he wanted to experiment with evening takes of a boat sailing out on a lake only lit by Japanese lanterns. Rimmen had previously had an altercation with Stæhr because the cameraman used too little light on the shoots. To carry through his night-shoot experiment, Rimmen had to violate Nordisk's usual, bureaucratic work schedules. He surreptitiously bypassed the standard film development process, and the following day the film was shown to Olsen, Frost, Stæhr and all the directors. Stæhr was furious that Rimmen had deviated from standard procedure, but after seeing the result, everybody was delighted – the light from the Japanese lanterns reflected beautifully in the lake. Olsen stated: "I think we're on to something good" and rewarded Rimmen with a bonus of 300 kroner. Rimmen was subsequently dubbed "First Prize Cameraman" at Nordisk.[1075] In Rimmen's story, Olsen acknowledged the value of Rimmen's initiative as well as his disregard of the bureaucracy that Stæhr represented. Statements from Stæhr such as "You can go to the loo and s... art",[1076] may not have motivated independent initiatives among Nordisk's artistic staff.

Another management initiative which must be viewed as an incentive for the directors to focus their attention on the quality of the films, and one which was an extension of Olsen's letter, was an arrangement that rewarded the best films of the season with a financial bonus.[1077]

Engberg further argues that Nordisk's loss of position on the world market was due to Olsen's failure to attach talent to his company, first and foremost talented directors "[...] who wished to achieve something with their films, directors with a message and the skills to express it".[1078] Engberg mentions Asta Nielsen, Alfred Lind and Valdemar Psilander as talents whose fees became so high that Olsen let them go. Benjamin Christensen was not employed by Nordisk in spite of his gifted work, Engberg continues.[1079] In addition to

1074 See Bordwell, Staiger and Thompson, *The Classical Hollywood Cinema*, 61.

1075 Interview with H.F. Rimmen. DFI.

1076 NFA. Letter from A.W. Sandberg to Ole Olsen (24 November 1918).

1077 NFS:XIV,35.DFI, 111. Scrapbook. Untitled paragraph, *Dagbladet* (31 December 1918).

1078 Engberg, *Dansk stumfilm*, 595–596.

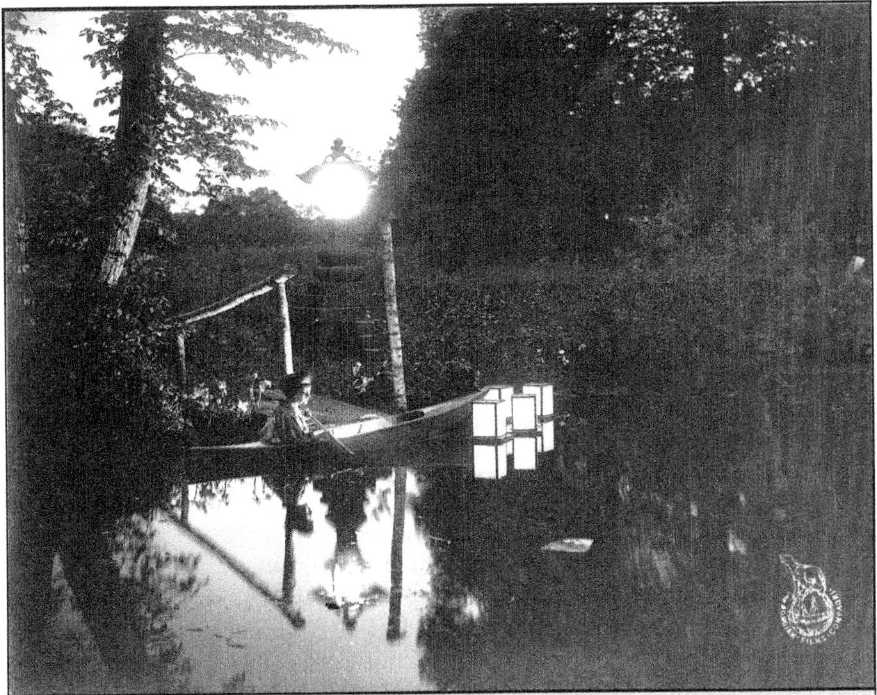

Figure 39. The light from the Japanese lanterns reflected beautifully in the lake in TROEN, DER FRELSER. Courtesy of DFI/Stills & Posters Archive.

Engberg's list one may add talented directors like Robert Wiene[1080] and Mauritz Stiller,[1081] both of whom offered their services to Nordisk but were never hired. Alfred Lind worked for Olsen in 1906 before he started directing, but his employment ended in a disagreement with Olsen.[1082] As mentioned, Asta Nielsen and Urban Gad were both briefly under contract at Nordisk but chose to move to Berlin to work. It does not appear likely that the maverick Benjamin Christensen would ever have put up with the working conditions in Valby: "Factory production of films is a thing of the past. The factory principle may work well enough when it comes to automobiles and lighting bulbs, but as for film, everything depends on the artist", said Christensen in 1918 in an interview about the future of Danish film.[1083] HÆVNENS NAT had taken him half a year to make, and Nordisk would never have suffered such a time-consuming production. Frost did in fact correspond with Christensen in January 1923 about potential employment with Nordisk, but it never materi-

1079 See Engberg, *Dansk stumfilm*, 596.

1080 NFS:II,30.DFI, 665. Letter from Harald Frost to Robert Wiene, Berlin (5 March 1914).

1081 NFS:II,37.DFI, 271. Letter from August Blom to Instruktør [Director] Stiller, Stockholm (17 April 1915).

1082 Interview with Alfred Lind. DFI.

1083 "Benjamin Christensen om dansk Films Fremtid", *Dagens Ekko* (10 April 1918).

alized since Nordisk subsequently chose to cut down production that year.[1084] Even if these directors had been permanently employed by Nordisk, it is doubtful whether they would ever have accepted the working conditions of Nordisk's regular staff of directors.

On the other hand, Tybjerg points out that Swedish producer Charles Magnusson did exactly what Engberg blames Olsen for not doing. Magnusson hired talented directors who wished to make something other than entertainment – Dreyer and Christensen. "Two superb films were made, but it cannot be said that it was a commercially astute decision", writes Tybjerg. Dreyer's PRÄSTÄNKAN (THE PARSON'S WIDOW, Svensk Filmindustri, S 1921) was a moderate financial success, and HÄXAN (HÄXAN WITCHCRAFT THROUGH THE AGES, Svensk Filmindustri, S 1922), which Christensen directed for Magnusson, cost between a million and a half to two million kroner, but only brought in a percentage of the expenses.[1085]

Mottram points to "the constant erosion of Nordisk's artistic base"[1086] as a reason for the artistic apathy of the company's productions. However, Nordisk's production mode incorporated an automatic selection process: directors like Gad, who could not tolerate the factory-like work, soon left, and the director William Augustinus was sacked because he lacked the ability to deliver good films.[1087] For directors like Dinesen and Leo Tscherning, having worked for Nordisk, became a recommendation that secured them jobs with other companies. In the heyday of Nordisk, the company had a handful of very prolific directors who accepted the conditions and only left when Nordisk's film production had become so meagre that there was no work for them anymore.

Ulrichsen, Neergaard and Engberg may be right in arguing that Danish film was in an artistic slump around 1916 and continued to be in the post-war years, but to point to this crisis as the root cause of the end of Nordisk and the Golden Age of Danish cinema is misleading. "If anyone thinks that we have become less efficient in our artistic or technical aspirations in Denmark, they better think again", wrote *Kinobladet* in 1919. The article's author Fritz Magnussen pointed to the difficulties with export and the impossible conditions for cinemas at home as the true causes of the crisis in Danish film.[1088]

Throughout most of the nineteenth century and up to World War I, an almost "borderless" trade thrived among all countries, and Denmark was an avid participant. Nordisk's Golden Age was the product of a period in the history of western world economy in which "[...] the economic importance of

1084 NFS:IV,74.DFI. Telegramme from Harald Frost to Benjamin Christensen (10 January 1923); Letter from Benjamin Christensen to Harald Frost (17 January 1923).

1085 See Tybjerg, *An Art of Silence and Light*, 267.

1086 Mottram, *The Danish Cinema before Dreyer*, 212.

1087 NFS:II,16.DFI, 334. Letter from Wilhelm Stæhr to William Augustinus (9 July 1911).

1088 Fritz Magnussen, "Den danske Filmsindustri gaar til Grunde", *Kinobladet*, no. 14 (1919): 173–177.

multinational activities at the turn of the century, when seen in a socio-economic perspective, did not reach the same level until the 1980s".[1089] World War I brought an increased governmental control which led to a decline in international trade, and this affected the film industry as well.

As both Rønn Sørensen and Mottram have pointed out, post-war film trade was hampered by customs and import regulations.[1090] Denmark placed no charges on import, and this created uneven competition for Nordisk. In 1922, 85 per cent of the films shown in Danish cinemas were American, and only three to four per cent of the films were Danish or Swedish.[1091] Olsen appealed to the Danish authorities:

> I wish 'Nordisk Films Co.' would be regarded as business, as an important Danish industry in need of support. If only people could forget that it is also an art form we are trading in, and if only this short-winded theatre fascination would yield to a sound and wholesome interest in the business, then the management would do all in its power to better the conditions. What we need is protection from foreign competition – and a new approach to the film industry. It is downright insane that a company like ours must beg to have our costly films shown in one of the big Copenhagen cinemas because the Germans, the Swedes and the Americans dominate the best screens.[1092]

Not only had the economic climate changed; without naming names, Benjamin Christensen said the following as early as in April 1918:

> Especially in 1914–15, many Danish film-makers believed that neutral films would be an excellent commodity after the war. But who is still so sanguine as to hope that the warring nations harbour any warm feelings toward the neutrals?[1093]

To be sure, the poor reputation which Nordisk had acquired with the Entente lasted after the armistice. In June 1920, the French occupation committee in Constantinople banned films from Nordisk and gave as their reason that the films were German and that Psilander, who starred in some of the films, was German.[1094] However, the Danish Ambassador in Turkey managed to lift the ban.[1095] The shipment of chemicals that had been seized by the British authorities in Kirkwall in 1916 was not released until June 1920, one year after the signing of the Versailles Treaty,[1096] and in Belgium in January 1922,

1089 Boje, *Danmark og multinationale virksomheder før 1950*, 11.

1090 See Sørensen, *Den danske filmindustri*, 98–100 and 116; Mottram, *The Danish Cinema before Dreyer*, 213–216.

1091 See H. Andersen, *Filmen. I social og økonomisk belysning* (Copenhagen: C.E.C. Gad, 1924), 40.

1092 "Nordisk Films Co. Det slette Regnskab. Interview with Ole Olsen", *Kinobladet*, no. 15 (1921): 589–595.

1093 "Benjamin Christensen om dansk Films Fremtid", *Dagens Ekko* (10 April 1918).

1094 RA/U.M.17.R.398. Letter from Harald Frost to Ministry of Foreign Affairs of Denmark (17 June 1920).

1095 RA/U.M.17.R.398. Letter from the Royal Danish Legation in Constantinople (2 September 1920).

1096 RA/U.M.17.N.185. Letter from Harald Frost to the Ministry of Foreign Affairs of Denmark (20 June 1920).

filmgoers and press accused Nordisk of presenting German films disguised as Danish productions.[1097]

In November 1918, the allies blacklisted Revisionsbanken.[1098] The reason is not apparent from the files in the Danish Foreign Office, but in all likelihood, it had to do with the bank's German transactions during the war.[1099] The bank was taken off the blacklist in March 1919.[1100] In the confidential 1925 files of the Banking Supervision, it appears that the bank was taken off the blacklist because Olsen and Lamm, both board members at Nordisk, left Revisionbanken's board.[1101]

Not only did Nordisk have to face disrepute and a changed economic climate after the war, the company had also lost substantial investments. Thiemann, Nordisk's Russian partner, managed to pay 180,000 Russian roubles to the Danish Consulate in Moscow before he fled from the "Bolshevik disturbance".[1102] The Red Cross brought 36,000 roubles from Moscow to Nordisk in 1919,[1103] but the money never reached the company.[1104] Even if the money had found its way to Nordisk, the massive inflation of the rouble would still have nullified its value. In 1935, Olsen told, "[...] I have 400,000 kroner lying in worthless Russian bonds from the days of the Tsar".[1105] It is hard to estimate the extent of Nordisk's Russian losses, but we may form an impression from the accounts of Thiemann, Reinhardt & Osipov in January 1919, when Nordisk's assets in Russia amounted to 832,546.74 kroner.[1106] From March to August 1919, Hungary was briefly a Communist republic, and rumours had it that the Austrian krone would lose value. In order to maintain export to Austria-Hungary, Nordisk had agreed to freeze its assets in the country for two years after the end of the war, and the company now had 532,149.70 Austrian

1097 RA/U.M.70.U.30. Letter from the Royal Danish Legation, Brussels to the Ministry of Foreign Affairs of Denmark (28 January 1922).

1098 RA/U.M.70.T.156. Letter from British Legation, Copenhagen to Ritzau (15 November 1918).

1099 RA/U.M.70.T.156. Cypher telegramme from Ministry of Foreign Affairs of Denmark to the British Legation, London (7 November 1918).

1100 RA/U.M.70.T.156. Letter from the Royal Danish Legation, Paris to the Ministry of Foreign Affairs of Denmark (6 March 1919).

1101 The Danish National Archive. Ministry of Economy and Business. Beretning om Banktilsynets undersøgelse i Københavns Diskontobank og Revisionsbank 1924/25. (Report on the investigation into the affairs of Diskontobank and Revisionsbank 1924/25, conducted by the Inspectorate of Banks, Copenhagen.)

1102 RA/U.M.6.U.59a. Letter from Harald Frost to the Ministry of Foreign Affairs of Denmark (5 August 1921).

1103 RA/U.M.6.U.59a. Letter from Red Cross to the Ministry of Foreign Affairs of Denmark (21 August 1919).

1104 RA/U.M.6.U.59a. Letter from Harald Frost to the Ministry of Foreign Affairs of Denmark (6 January 1922).

1105 "Hvordan de skabte deres Livs Værk VII. Ved Leo Tandrup. Fhv. Generaldirektør Ole Olsen, skaberen af den første dramatiske film i verden siger: FORSTAA UNGDOMMEN!", *Berlingske Søndag* (10 February 1935).

1106 NFS:XII,88:56.DFI. Unpagn. Statement from Thiemann, Reinhardt, Osipov & Cie.

crowns in a bank in Vienna and 40,886 in Budapest.[1107] These assets were not all Nordisk's interests in Austria-Hungary since three branches still belonged to Nordisk even if they had been transferred to UFA. This ensured their position as belonging to a neutral country, so they were not subject to paying war damages or being seized. Nordisk appealed to the Foreign Office for help when the Budapest branch was in danger of being "socialized".[1108] A few weeks later, Nordisk could report that before it was seized by the Communists, an agreement had been made with the Hungarian Republic to the effect that Nordisk would receive its dues as well as compensation for the branch.[1109] Nordisk salvaged some of their assets in Austria-Hungary, but post-war inflation took its toll. Nordisk's accounts for 1919 show losses of 1.5 million kroner.[1110] The main course was the low rate of exchange, especially of German marks and Austrian crowns.

The offices in Germany and Central Europe were taken over by UFA. The New York branch closed in October 1916,[1111] and in June 1920, Nordisk handed over its last office in London to its manager, Axel Severin Paulsen.[1112] Most of the distribution contracts that had ensured sales had expired during the war, and export to the important South-American market stopped when the company lost contact with Aubert and was blacklisted by France. After the war, Nordisk was left with the distribution contract for Fotorama for Scandinavia and its partnership with UFA. The latter in particular would play a decisive role in Nordisk's post-war development.

World War I meant a turning point in the European film industry at large. During the war, French film production dropped from 9,000 metres a week to 4,075 metres in 1916, whereas the import of foreign films went up from an average of 14,800 metres to 18,200 metres a week.[1113] The war had such an impact on Pathé Frères and Gaumont, the two big French film companies, that they sold all their international interests after 1918, abandoned film production and concentrated on film distribution in France. In 1922, the American company MGM bought Gaumont, and the third big French company, Éclair, went bankrupt in 1920. In 1919, the eleven biggest Italian companies formed the *Unione Cinematografica Italiana*, a trust that flopped dismally, and one by one, the Italian film companies faced financial disaster. Poor finances deprived

1107 RA/U.M.17.n.95. Letter from Albert Gøte to the Ministry of Foreign Affairs of Denmark (25 March 1919).

1108 RA/U.M.17.n.95. Letter from Albert Gøte to the Ministry of Foreign Affairs of Denmark (7 April 1919).

1109 RA/U.M.17.n.95. Letter from Albert Gøte to the Ministry of Foreign Affairs of Denmark (23 April 1919).

1110 NFS:I,25.DFI. Minutes of the Board of Directors Meeting (10 July 1919).

1111 See Mottram, "The Great Northern Film Company", 215.

1112 NFS:XII,31:85.DFI, 1–7. Agreement between Nordisk Films Kompagni and A.S. Paulsen (5 May and 2 June 1920).

1113 See Kallmann, *Die Konzernierung*, 9.

British producer Cecil Hepworth of the control of his estate in 1923, and by 1924, virtually no film production existed in Britain.[1114]

The decline of the European film industry spelled success for the Americans. The MPPC had initially thwarted Nordisk's potential opportunities on the lucrative American market, but the MPPC can also be seen as a blessing to Nordisk and European film as such. The American film industry tied up its resources in the struggle between the MPPC and the Independents, and relieved the European market of American competition. It was not until the law intervened and reduced the influence of the MPPC through its verdicts on patenting that the American film industry gained a foothold in Europe. A report from Secretary of Commerce, Herbert Hoover, to the Senate in 1922 states that the import of film into the United States dropped from 20,057,000 feet in 1915 to a mere 6,233,000 feet in 1920, while the export went up from 192,000 feet in 1913 to 175,233,000 feet in 1920.[1115] These figures speak rather clearly of the growth in the American film industry due to its export to foreign countries.

As economist Gerben Bakker writes, the post-war turbulence in the film industry is unique in the history of finance: "Few industries experienced such an extreme shift in both industrial and geographical concentration."[1116] In his analysis of this extreme shift from European to American supremacy on the film market, Bakker refers to economist John Sutton's theory of "sunk cost". Sunk cost is an investment which has already been incurred and cannot be recovered. Often spendings on marketing, research and development is considered as sunk cost. Bakker argues that the European film industry could not keep up in the "quality race" that America started in the 1910s.[1117] Bakker writes that the number of films produced in Europe did not fall but that American film production escalated. As production increased, it became still more important how much the companies invested in their productions, and when trying to recover sunk cost investments, the size of the market is paramount. By the end of the war, the American film industry had conquered the international market. Bakker points to Nordisk as a company that invested in marketing, research and development, and acquired market shares through horizontal and vertical integration, precisely the strategy which the Hollywood studios would later pursue. However, the loss of the German and Central European distribution networks barred Nordisk from capitalizing on its investments.[1118] Olsen acknowledged the problem in 1919:

1114 See Bakker, *Entertainment Industrialised*, 227.

1115 See Marguerite Engberg, "Danske stumfilm i USA", in Kaare Schmidt (ed.), *Sekvens. Filmvidenskabelig Årbog 1980* (Copenhagen: C.A. Reitzels Boghandel A/S, 1980), 110. Quoted from *Moving Picture World* (7 January 1922).

1116 Bakker, *Entertainment Industrialised*, 186.

1117 See ibid., 185.

1118 See ibid., 333.

> In Denmark, we have already embraced the American productions, and for us to produce our own films is no longer profitable. Prices have gone up, and we lose half a million a year. We cannot go on like this, and the future is uncertain since we cannot count on the value of money. By contrast, America has an overproduction, and they can easily beat us.[1119]

Bakker bases his analysis on studies of the French and the British film industry, but things were different at Nordisk, and Bakker's thorough analysis needs to be modified. First of all, through its collaboration with UFA, Nordisk was in a considerably better position than most other European film companies. Before proceeding to consider the UFA partnership, which was extremely important to Nordisk, it will be wise to look at the changes that Nordisk made in its film production in Valby.

On 1 April 1918, Nordisk resumed its film production, albeit on a smaller scale than before. Shortages of coal, gasoline and raw stock automatically limited the production, and the management issued new directives which entailed a decisive change in the organization. In "Working Rules for the Studios" from February 1918, Olsen stipulated that the film director had to supply the scripts, either by searching through unused scripts in the archives or by finding them elsewhere. Nordisk's script department was phased out in the years from 1917 to 1920.[1120] Olsen now personally approved the scripts. Planning the productions became the director's responsibility, as were the budgets, and as for the latter, the director was personally held responsible if he exceeded the budget or spent more time on the film than planned. The director also had to edit the films. The new organization gave the director more authority and resembled the *director-unit* system previously used by Pathé Frères and Gaumont. Production continued with five permanently employed directors, August Blom, A.W. Sandberg, Holger-Madsen, Emanuel Gregers and Lau Lauritzen, whereas actors were no longer employed for a season at the time but on an *ad hoc* basis, from film to film. Production dwindled drastically after the war (see Figure 40).

In 1918 and 1919 Nordisk produced, respectively, 65 and 52 films, after which production fell to twelve films in 1920 and eleven in 1921. From here and until 1928, Nordisk produced between seven and one films a year. The drastic drop in production from 1919 to 1920 reflects Lau Lauritzen's exit from Nordisk. Lauritzen directed 30 short comedies in 1918 and 22 in 1919, which amounts to about half of Nordisk's productions in those years.

Grand American films like D.W. Griffith's BIRTH OF A NATION and INTOLERANCE premiered in Denmark in 1918 and received rave reviews from critics and audiences alike.[1121] Influenced by both American films, and, as Tybjerg

1119 "Nordisk Filmskompagni opsiger sine Funktionærer", *Berlingske Tidende* (1 September 1919).

1120 See Schröder, "Screenwriting for Nordisk 1906–1918", 105.

1121 See Sandfeld, *Den stumme scene*, 177; Tybjerg, *An Art of Silence and Light*, 253.

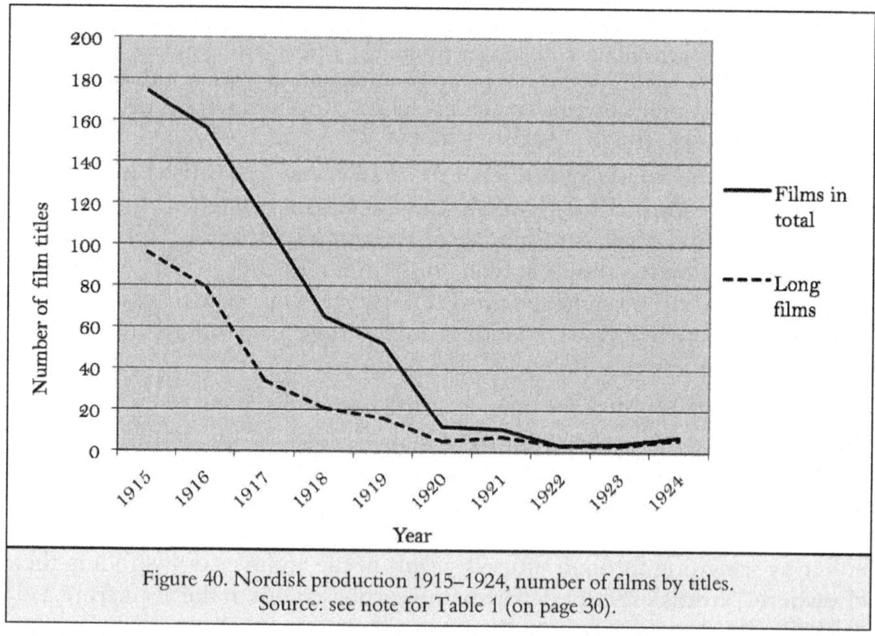

Figure 40. Nordisk production 1915–1924, number of films by titles.
Source: see note for Table 1 (on page 30).

emphasizes, the highly successful Swedish films, Nordisk decided to make fewer but bigger films.[1122]

In early September 1919 Nordisk fired its entire staff with effect from 1 December, "[...] apart from a few who can keep things together in Valby", as Olsen explains.[1123] The reduced production and the new organization meant that the number of permanent staff members became even smaller. According to Stæhr, they were now down to fourteen or fifteen.[1124] The film factory in Valby was now dubbed "the Ghost Town".[1125] Urban Gad commented on Nordisk's "shutdown": "What is happening now should have happened years ago. Nordisk Films Co. has long been an unsound enterprise." Gad blamed Nordisk's management and their "reprehensible policy" for the closure, but never clarified what exactly he found reprehensible. That Nordisk was trying to compete with the Americans was tremendously foolish, said Gad, for even though massive amounts were invested in Danish films, they could never be more than "[…] a small steamship on a lake compared to the American ocean liner".[1126]

In 1919 Nordisk produced films to the total value of 1.5 million kroner.[1127] Halfway through 1920, Olsen could report that a profit of 7.2 million marks

1122 See Tybjerg, "Et lille lands vagabonder", 69.

1123 "Nordisk Filmskompagni opsiger sine Funktionærer", *Berlingske Tidende* (1 September 1919).

1124 Ibid.

1125 "Den døde By", *Aftenbladet* (3 September 1919).

1126 Jernmasken, "Urban Gad udtaler sig om Nordisk Films-Comp.'s Forhold", *B.T.* (2 September 1919).

1127 NFS:I,25.DFI. Unpagn. Minutes of the Board of Directors Meeting (26 February 1920).

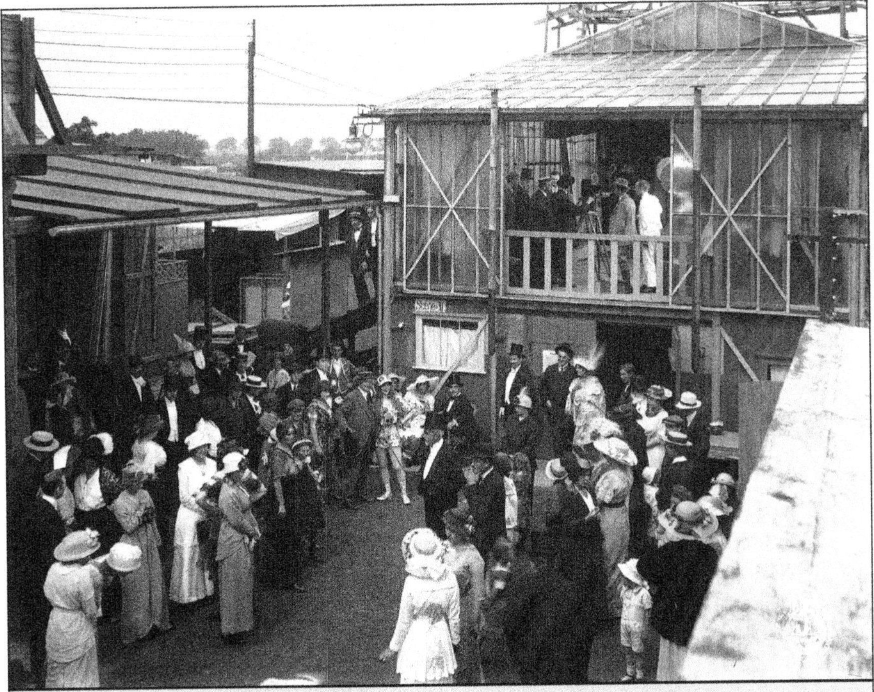

Figure 41. The lively "Film factory" in Valby was now dubbed "the Ghost Town". Courtesy of DFI/Stills & Posters Archive.

had been achieved from the Central Powers and the Balkans, roughly one million kroner, and he hoped that sales in the rest of the world would bring home a profit. However, the chance of covering the costs was rather small.[1128]

Tybjerg writes that the one million kroner made on the expansion of shares in 1920 was to be spent on prestige films.[1129] However, the shares were not expanded until 1921 as part of Nordisk's agreement with UFA, and finances were now so strained that the million was not spent exclusively on film production. In the 1920 season, the company set aside half a million kroner for the production of a long serial and three feature films.[1130] A similar amount was set aside for film production in 1921.[1131] As means were so scarce, it was difficult to keep up in any "quality race" with American films. The strained economy forced Nordisk to reuse outtakes from FOLKETS VEN (A FRIEND OF THE PEOPLE, Holger-Madsen, 1918) in the new film LYKKENS GALOSCHER (THE GIFT OF HAPPINESS, Gunnar Sommerfeldt, 1921).[1132] Financially speaking, competition with the Americans was futile.

1128 NFS:I,25.DFI. Unpagn. Minutes of the Board of Directors Meeting (14 June 1920).

1129 See Tybjerg, "Et lille lands vagabonder", 69.

1130 NFS:I,25.DFI. Unpagn. Minutes of the Board of Directors Meeting (26 February 1920).

1131 NFS:I,25.DFI. Unpagn. Minutes of the Board of Directors Meeting (16 February 1921).

1132 See Tybjerg, "Et lille lands vagabonder", 69.

Another artistic trend which Nordisk tried to emulate was found in the Swedish films, which had entered their Golden Age from around 1917. Swedish films were often based on literary works and the stories often set in nature. However, Nordisk did not have much luck with this enterprise. Tybjerg notes that a film like BORGSLÆGTENS HISTORIE (SONS OF THE SOIL, Gunnar Sommerfeldt, 1920) was perceived as a lamentable attempt to copy the Swedes, quoting a review of the film:

> It was a disservice to Nordisk Films Co. that Paladsteatret showed the big Icelandic drama "Borgslægten". Poorer film art [...] has not been seen in a long time, and it cannot hold a candle to the Swedish Selma Lagerlöf films, as was the intention.[1133]

Nordisk seemed to have more luck with director A.W. Sandberg's dramatizations of Charles Dickens, starting with VOR FÆLLES VEN (OUR MUTUAL FRIEND, A.W. Sandberg, 1921) which was "[...] the longest and most expensive Danish film to date".[1134] It was followed by a string of other Dickens films such as STORE FORVENTNINGER (GREAT EXPECTATIONS, A.W. Sandberg, 1922), DAVID COPPERFIELD (A.W. Sandberg, 1922) and LILLE DORRIT (LITTLE DORRIT, A.W. Sandberg, 1924). The company's film production was now so modest that the board alone decided which films to make, and with a production that small, Nordisk was unable to keep its contractual obligations. Even though the average number of sold copies of each film was 52,3 in 1922, with only three films produced that year it was not sufficient to keep a film production running for a company with international ambitions (see Figure 40). The chairman of Fotorama's board, Drescher, who had also been a member of Nordisk's board since 1921, objected that Nordisk should make ten to twenty films a year instead of just three, but Frost and Olsen maintained that the international market was still so unstable that expanding production would be too much of a risk.[1135] After the war, Nordisk would no longer invest its money in film production.

Regrettably, the original contracts to UFA's takeover of Nordisk's network in Germany and Central Europe no longer exist, but transcripts of two agreements between UFA and Nordisk still do.[1136] One is a transfer agreement from June 1918, the contents of which correlate with the information in the minutes from a board meeting at Nordisk.[1137] UFA took over the entire network that Nordisk had built in Germany and Central Europe: a distribution company, eleven branches, a production company and 33 cinemas. Nordisk received 8.4

1133 "Borgslægten", *Københavns Amts folkeblad* (17 September 1920), quoted from Casper Tybjerg, "Dreyer and the National Film in Denmark", *Film History*, no. 1, vol.13 (2001): 26.

1134 NFS:XIV,35.DFI, 129. Scrapbook. Untitled paragraph, presumably the newspaper *B.T.* (3 May 1919). The year is wrongly stated as 1916.

1135 NFS:I,25.DFI. Unpagn. Minutes of the Board of Directors Meeting (29 August 1923).

1136 Joachim Nielsen states that in the 1970s, he collected all documents concerning UFA in Valby. However, there is very little material on UFA in the Nordisk Film Collection and the Nordisk Archives in Valby. Interview with Joachim Nielsen II. DFI.

1137 Bundesarchiv-Filmarchiv R109.139. Deutscher Besitz, Nordisk Kopenhagen.

million marks in UFA shares and 1.6 million marks in cash, thus ten million marks altogether.[1138] Since UFA's collected share capital was 25 million marks, this deal gave Nordisk a considerable influence in the new company. At the same time, UFA committed itself to buying one million kroner of shares in Nordisk, at the rate of 150 kroner per share. Nordisk's share capital would then be expanded to nine million kroner, which was made possible by the decision concerning expansion of shares in 1916. However, UFA's investment of 1.5 million kroner would be made at a later time, but UFA would still be entitled to dividends already as of 15 December 1917.[1139]

Nordisk was not the only company to be included in UFA; Messter Film and PAGU were among a string of German companies bought by UFA, but Nordisk's former network was indeed the backbone of UFA's organization. Nordisk's building in Zimmerstrasse became UFA's headquarters, and UFA divided Nordisk's efficient network into a distribution company, Universum-Filmverleih G.m.b.H., and into UFA-Theater-Betriebs-G.m.b.H., which was to run the cinemas and expand their number. Several of Nordisk's former business partners were employed by UFA. David Oliver was appointed manager with an annual salary of 44,000 marks and a share in the profits, and Paul Davidson from PAGU was paid 30,000 marks a year to be the "adviser on camerawork".[1140] This meant that, to a great extent, UFA was based on Nordisk's organization, and Olsen's know-how came in handy as well. Already in August 1918, during the war, a confidential meeting was held at *Auswärtiges Amt* (Foreign Office) at which the possibility of capitalizing on Nordisk's lack of raw stock was discussed. The idea was to supply Olsen with raw stock in exchange for his know-how, which could then be used for propaganda, as well as his experience with getting funding abroad. Olsen's connections in the film industry in the Entente countries were also useful.[1141]

The other transcript of an original contract is an agreement between Nordisk and the company Schwarz, Goldschmidt & Co. and Carl Lindström Aktiengesellschaft who acted as front men for UFA. The contract informs us about the distribution agreement which tied the two companies together after the war.[1142] During the negotiations with UFA in November 1917, Olsen had imposed the condition before signing an agreement that UFA would buy Nordisk's films.[1143] Nordisk handed over the distribution of its films, along with those of Svenska Biografteatern, to UFA in Germany, Austria-Hungary, the Netherlands, Switzerland and Luxemburg. The agreement left room for

1138 NFS:I,25.DFI. Unpagn. Minutes of the Board of Directors Meeting (12 February 1918).

1139 NFS:I,25.DFI. Unpagn. Minutes of the Board of Directors Meeting (12 February 1918).

1140 See Kreimeier, *The UFA Story*, 30.

1141 See Goergen, "Neue Filme", 38.

1142 Bundesarchiv-Filmarchiv R109.139. Deutscher Besitz, Nordisk Kopenhagen.

1143 Bundesarchiv-Filmarchiv R109.139. Deutscher Besitz, Nordisk Kopenhagen.

expansion to Belgium, Poland, Courland, Lithuania and the Balkans. UFA should buy at least 16 copies of each film, although the annual quantity of negatives should not exceed 50,000 metres.

UFA paid Nordisk according to the production costs of the films. If a film cost 40,000 kroner to produce, UFA would pay one mark per metre; if 60,000 kroner, UFA paid 1.25 marks; a 100,000 kroner film would cost 1.50 marks per metre; and if the costs exceeded 100,000 kroner, UFA would pay two marks per metre. On top of this, Nordisk obtained part of the profits according to a carefully calculated system, and between 45 and 55 per cent of the earnings would be added to the price per metre.[1144] Moreover, UFA was committed to redistributing that part of Nordisk's productions from 1915 and 1916 which had not yet been marketed in Austria-Hungary. The agreement guaranteed Nordisk sales of new films as well as some of the films produced during the war. Germany was subject to a ban on imports, but Nordisk acquired a special permission from the military to import 50,000 metres of negative film in 1918, and UFA guaranteed the import of a similar amount of negative film or 450,000 positive metres in the next nine years.[1145] UFA's close ties to the German government opened opportunities to Nordisk after the war.

Nordisk was committed by the UFA agreement to form a Danish company with the purpose of renting out films and running cinemas in Scandinavia. This new company was called Skanlandia, and it was to buy at least 30,000 metres of negative film from UFA in as many copies as possible.[1146] In 1943, German film historian Hans Traub wrote about UFA's takeover of Nordisk's businesses: "After the attempts at expansion in Austria, Hungary, Switzerland, the Netherlands and Sweden, UFA saved the company from financial danger."[1147] Traub describes UFA as a blessing to Nordisk, and Nordisk was indeed saved from the dangers of its own expansion attempts. Klaus Kreimeier has called Traub "a conscientious chronicler of UFA's history" but adds that Traub had an interest in presenting UFA in a favourable light.[1148] We must not forget that Traub's book is from 1943. The first page of it exhibits a colour photo of Joseph Goebbels, Propaganda Minister of the Third Reich, and Traub must be read in the proper political context. By claiming that Nordisk was relieved by UFA, Traub tones down Nordisk's dominant role in Germany. Traub's interpretation is partly shared by Manfred Behn when he claims that UFA chose the most opportune moment to buy, because Nordisk was in financial trouble. The company's dividend had dropped from 16 per cent in 1912 to 8 per cent in 1917, and the UFA capital enabled Nordisk to consolidate.[1149] However, to claim that Nordisk consolidated with the UFA money

1144 Bundesarchiv-Filmarchiv R109.139. Deutscher Besitz, Nordisk Kopenhagen.

1145 Bundesarchiv-Filmarchiv R109.139. Deutscher Besitz, Nordisk Kopenhagen.

1146 Bundesarchiv-Filmarchiv R109.139. Deutscher Besitz, Nordisk Kopenhagen.

1147 Traub, *Die Ufa*, 34.

1148 Kreimeier, *The UFA Story*, 24.

1149 See Behn, "Großeinkauf", 36.

is a stretch, since the majority of the capital was tied up in UFA shares. Apart from getting the dividends wrong (see Table 6) Behn also overlooks that the expansion of shares in 1916 and the whole idea of establishing the company European Shareholding Company at the end of the war are signs that the board at Nordisk, helped by their connections, could quickly raise more capital, and it would not be the last time they raised a couple of millions in the course of a few hours. Tybjerg objects to Traub's allegation that by selling out to UFA, Nordisk lost the leading position which Olsen needed in order to withstand the American film industry.[1150] Tybjerg's interpretation is correct, but by collaborating with UFA, Nordisk was still strong in Europe. Thomas C. Christensen surmises that through its business network with Oliver and PAGU, Nordisk was well-equipped to resist the American pressure which was expected to arrive at the end of the war:

> [...] yet it was not to be Nordisk but UFA which would benefit from Ole Olsen's plan. It was not the war, but the German government and their efforts to protect national interests that brought Nordisk Films Kompagni and the Golden Age of Danish film to an end.[1151]

However, this conclusion is still a simplified version of the circumstances surrounding UFA's takeover of Nordisk's interests. Christensen overlooks the investments which Nordisk lost at the end of the war and which changed the economic situation. He also forgets the impact of American films in Europe, and he neglects to notice the advantages on the European market which Nordisk actually achieved from the deal – although things did not turn out as planned. What really brought Nordisk down was the failed investments made by Nordisk in collaboration with UFA.

One may get the impression from the minutes of the board meetings at Nordisk that Olsen carried on with business as usual in the spring of 1919, at least as much as he could, considering the conditions to which his company was now subjected. On a trip to Germany, Olsen purchased the Colosseum in Flensburg for 1,050,000 marks, a large building containing a restaurant and two dance halls which could seat, respectively, 1,900 and 1,400 guests. Olsen's intention was to convert the place into cinemas. Furthermore, Olsen bought two small cinemas for 190,000 marks. In fact, according to the UFA agreement, Nordisk was not at liberty to own and run cinemas in Germany, but Olsen must have felt that he could square things out with UFA's managing director, Karl Bratz. Also, there was a chance that Flensburg would not remain German after the new borders were introduced, as Olsen surmised.[1152] Together with Oliver, Olsen had plans to take over a film distribution business and some cinemas in Warsaw, and to found a new company in Poland. Nordisk would invest one million marks in the Polish enterprise, which was to have a share

1150 See Tybjerg, *An Art of Silence and Light*, 240.

1151 Christensen, "Isbjørnens fald", 238.

1152 NFS:I,25.DFI. Unpagn. Minutes of the Board of Directors Meeting (30 April 1919).

capital of three million marks. The plans for the Polish company seem to have foundered.[1153] Olsen paid Oliver 340,000 kroner for the rights to distribute seven Swedish films from Svenska Biograftheatern in Germany, Austria, Hungary and the Balkans. The films were to be handed over to UFA, and the profits were to be shared between Nordisk and UFA.[1154] Olsen's projects and ventures indicate optimism and an eagerness to invest, but unfortunately, UFA turned out not to be the great partner Olsen had hoped for. In the spring of 1919, Olsen reported to the board at Nordisk:

> Regrettably, a series of mistakes and unwise decisions have been made, but I expect things to look up when UFA starts heeding his – the chairman's – advice, and also that UFA's management has gained some experience of their own.[1155]

UFA had lost huge investments in Romania and Ukraine, areas which the Central Powers had lost at the end of the war.[1156] Olsen told the board at Nordisk that he did not have a sufficient basis to ascertain how UFA was doing, but he suspected that things were unsatisfactory. In the middle of 1919, UFA had worked up a debt of 17 million marks besides sureties signed to the tune of 20 million marks.[1157] Due to a shortage of working capital, UFA could not proceed with the planned film production that year. The films had already been rented out at a good price, but the German banks refused to give UFA more credit. Olsen therefore suggested that the three groups of shareholders in UFA – the German shareholders, the German government and Nordisk – each chipped in with a loan of two million marks, six million marks in all, against a collateral consisting of UFA's distribution contracts which were valued at 30 million marks. The board at Nordisk authorized Olsen to make such a loan to UFA, even if the board referred to the UFA situation as "the German chaos".[1158]

In spite of UFA's chaotic situation, Nordisk did not fear lending money to UFA nor to enter into the collaboration with UFA, and this was to have serious consequences for both companies. In June 1919, Nordisk and UFA formed the company Danish American Film Corporation (DAFCO). DAFCO is a largely unexplored chapter in both Danish and German film history. Kreimeier briefly mentions the company without naming it.[1159] Otherwise, the most detailed account of DAFCO has been in an article by Thomas J. Saunders (see below).

DAFCO first had its address on 4 Hambroesgade and later on the familiar address of 45 Vimmelskaftet – Nordisk's offices. The board of the new

1153 Unfortunately, many archives were lost in Poland during World War II, for which reason it is difficult to verify or dismiss that the plans materialized.

1154 NFS:I,25.DFI. Unpagn. Minutes of the Board of Directors Meeting (30 April 1919).

1155 NFS:I,25.DFI. Unpagn. Minutes of the Board of Directors Meeting (30 April 1919).

1156 See Kreimeier, *The UFA Story*, 61–62.

1157 NFS:I,25.DFI. Unpagn. Minutes of the Board of Directors Meeting (10 July 1919).

1158 NFS:I,25.DFI. Unpagn. Minutes of the Board of Directors Meeting (10 July 1919).

1159 See Kreimeier, *The UFA Story*, 63.

company consisted of Olsen, Frost, Ingvald C. Oes, the former manager of Nordisk's New York branch and now the Danish representative of the American company Famous Players-Lasky, the UFA manager Karl Bratz, and finally Ove Davidsen, the manager of the Copenhagen cinema Kinografen and the film rental company Skandinavisk Films Union.[1160]

The purpose of DAFCO was to buy American films and distribute them on the European market via UFA's network. There was a great demand for American films throughout Europe, especially in Germany and Central Europe which had been cut off from American films during the war. DAFCO's share capital was 20,000 kroner of which Nordisk and UFA owned fifty per cent each. 20,000 kroner was hardly enough to run DAFCO, so Nordisk and UFA had created a credit syndicate that would initially make two million kroner available to DAFCO. DAFCO was expected to make a 50 per cent profit on the American films, and after administrative expenses and ten per cent commissions to DAFCO's board, the profit would be divided between Nordisk and UFA. DAFCO had already bought one hundred big Metro films and twelve Chaplin films from Ben Blumenthal in New York at the price of 1,331,000 dollars, and Nordisk had stood surety for half of this. Moreover, DAFCO had started negotiations with Famous Players about the purchase of films.[1161] Olsen cautioned his board:

> Even if the enterprise may yield a beautiful profit, the board is advised not to be too optimistic about finances this year, since the chaos concerning the countries formerly belonging to the Central Powers may lead to less favourable conditions and incur losses.[1162]

Olsen's misgivings notwithstanding, the idea of purchase and distribution was actually quite sound. A regular way for an MIE to ensure continued growth is through diversification, for instance by spreading its activities to other products. However, diversification may also be started by exterior influences such as technological innovation, economic depression or war. In the fundamentally altered state of the industry after the war, Nordisk was wise to diversify. The obvious choice for an MIE would be to exploit its production facilities to make new or different products. The snag about film production is that the facilities cannot easily be used for other things than film production since a film studio is nothing but a large and empty room. Nordisk's plan of action under the changed conditions was to exploit its expertise and try its hand

1160 See Goergen, "Neue Filme", 37. Skandinavisk Films Union had been purchased by UFA in the spring of 1918, as part of the dissemination of German propaganda in Scandinavia. Skandinavisk Films Union had bought the cinema Kinografen in which two out of three films would be German, and later, the company bought the majority of shares in the big Copenhagen cinema Kinopalæet. 60 per cent of the films shown at Kinopalæet were to come from Skandinavisk Films Union, and the majority of these should be German.

1161 NFS:I,25.DFI. Unpagn. Minutes of the Board of Directors Meeting (10 July 1919).

1162 NFS:I,25.DFI. Unpagn. Minutes of the Board of Directors Meeting (10 July 1919).

at film trade instead of film production. At the end of 1919 DAFCO had bought:

305 Triangle feature films
126 Triangle one-act films
168 Keystone films
12 Chaplin films
100 long Metro films
7 feature films from Sweden
156 Famous Players films
52 Kardinal films [sic]
35 comedies
1 Joan of Arc film[1163]

The films were the cream of the crop of what could be had of American cinema. Chaplin was a box-office draw and attracted moviegoers in droves, and the Triangle films featured, among others, the western hero William S. Hart and the swashbuckling Douglas Fairbanks. A film like Cecil Blount DeMille's JOAN THE WOMAN (Paramount Pictures, USA 1917) was at that time considered as outstanding as Griffith's BIRTH OF A NATION (1915) and INTOLERANCE (1916). The Triangle films were produced in 1915, 1916 and 1917, and the Metro films were from 1916, 1917, 1918 and 1919.[1164] The films were purchased by Ben Blumenthal who, together with his partner Samuel Rachman, ran Hamilton Theatrical Corporation, a company owned by the American company Famous Players.[1165] The price of the 962 films was 3,705,689.75 kroner of which Nordisk and UFA would each pay half.[1166] According to the agreement, Nordisk stood as guarantor.

Bratz, UFA's managing director, liked taking chances, and with DAFCO he violated a decree from UFA's management that contracts in foreign currency were to be avoided at all costs, since the deal with Blumenthal was made in dollars.[1167] A dollar was worth 14 marks when UFA and Nordisk signed the DAFCO contract in June 1919, but, due to inflation, the dollar stood at 42 marks at the end of the year.[1168] However, far worse was that the general ban on imports, which experts predicted would be lifted in the course of 1919, was actually kept. Saunders writes that UFA, which held the status of a semi-public institution, had hoped for a dispensation, but the German government found it hard to justify such a dispensation, because the German film industry knew

1163 Bundesarchiv-Filmarchiv R109.I.5379. Nordisk Films Co.

1164 NFS:XII,31:76.DFI, 1. Contract between Nordisk, DAFCO and UFA (29 October 1919).

1165 See Kristin Thompson, *Herr Lubitsch Goes to Hollywood* (Amsterdam: Amsterdam University Press, 2005), 22.

1166 Bundesarchiv-Filmarchiv R109.I.5379. Nordisk Films Co.

1167 See Kreimeier, *The UFA Story*, 63.

1168 See Thomas J. Saunders, "Von Dafco zu Damra", in Hans-Michael Bock and Michael Töteberg (ed.), *Das Ufa-Buch*, 71.

that Nordisk was involved in the DAFCO agreement.[1169] Since the ban was upheld and only partly lifted on 31 December 1920, and since UFA had to borrow the money for the DAFCO investment in the midst of inflation, the company amassed a debt of 47 million marks by purchasing the American films.[1170] Nordisk, the guarantor of the more than 900 films which would not be as lucrative as was hoped, was also in an unfavourable position. The DAFCO investments were now weighing down both companies.

In August 1919, Olsen returned after a trip to Berlin and told the board that he had examined UFA's actual position. Olsen had had a meeting with the UFA board, and he had refused to stand surety for the two million marks. Actually, he had demanded surety for the four million marks which UFA owed Nordisk for the rental of Nordisk films, and he had received a written guarantee which protected Nordisk's assets against inflation. On the whole, Olsen believed that UFA was a sound business which a proper management could bring to a profit of ten million marks a year. However, this would require that UFA got rid of some unprofitable companies such as Deutsche Lichtbild-Gesellschaft and Maxim-Film Gesellschaft, and, moreover, that UFA acquired some working capital.[1171] Olsen's reasoning exposes the core dilemma in the UFA construction. The Deutsche Lichtspiel-Gesellschaft e.V. (DLG) was formed in 1916 by the German military and may be seen as a forerunner of UFA.[1172] The company represented the part of UFA that was to propagandize and enlighten the population. As Olsen saw it, the Deutsche Lichtbild-Gesellschaft had no commercial potential and should be sold off, but to the German government, which owned a third of the shares in UFA, this unprofitable company was a chief interest.

To get the necessary working capital, Olsen presented the board with a new grand scheme: to interest an American company in a partnership. Nordisk would bring ten million marks to UFA and later hand over half of the shares to the American company on condition that the American company and Nordisk – which together would have the majority shareholding – always voted together.[1173] Olsen does not mention to the board which American company he had in mind, but there is little doubt that it was Famous Players where Aldolph Zukor was the manager.

Zukor's career in the film industry is much like Olsen's. In 1904, he began as the owner of a nickelodeon and proceeded to build a chain of nickelodeons. In 1912, he formed the company Famous Players-Lasky with Daniel Frohman and Edwin Stanton Porter; the company that was opposed to the MPPC from the start and played an important part in the introduction of feature-length

1169 See ibid., 70–71.

1170 See ibid., 70.

1171 NFS:I,25.DFI. Unpagn. Minutes of the Board of Directors Meeting (26 August 1919).

1172 Manfred Behn, "Krieg der Propagandisten", in Hans-Michael Bock and Michael Töteberg (ed.), *Das Ufa-Buch*, 28–29.

1173 NFS:I,25.DFI. Unpagn. Minutes of the Board of Directors Meeting (26 August 1919).

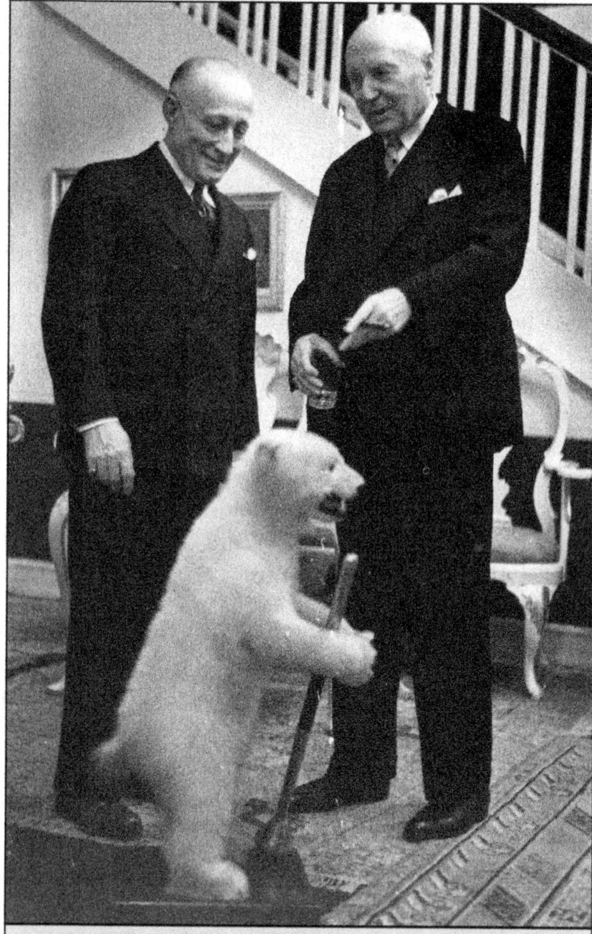

Figure 42. Adolph Zukor visiting Ole Olsen in his home in 1939. Courtesy of Bente Ole Olsen.

films in America. Zukor was involved in one of the first American feature film, THE SQUAW MAN (Oscar Apfel, Cecil Blount DeMille, Famous Players-Lasky Corporation, USA 1914), which was made in Hollywood, and by 1919, through his commitment in production, distribution and cinemas, Zukor had become one of the tycoons in the American film industry. One reason for Zukor to be interested in a European enterprise was of course winning market shares, and since UFA's first big films appeared to be professionally made, it would be attractive to American companies to start producing films in Germany where the currency was low.

One may wonder that one of the most influential men in the American film industry would bother about Nordisk at all, but Zukor could use Nordisk's connection with UFA as a lever to get inside the German company. Moreover, Olsen and Zukor quickly became friends. Olsen was the only European to be invited to the 25th anniversary of Zukor's company in Hollywood, and in 1939, after Olsen had retired, Zukor visited him in his home in Odsherred, Denmark. Zukor told the press: "Ole Olsen is my old friend. I have admired him since I got to know him a long, long time ago, and I look forward to seeing him again."[1174] Among the wreaths at Olsen's funeral in 1943, there was one from Zukor.[1175]

The board at Nordisk gave Olsen permission to pursue the plan with Famous Players. However, Olsen first had to find out if the necessary capital could be raised, and this could only be cleared up when board member Fabricius, the general manager of Revisionsbanken, returned from his vacation.[1176] Ten days later, both Diskontobanken and Revisionsbanken informed Olsen that they could not accept such a large credit. In fact, the banks wished to reduce Nordisk's credit. Olsen was convinced that if Nordisk were to maintain its influence in the German company, there was no time to waste. Olsen had received a telegram from Bratz stating that Bratz was trying to find another investor for UFA, and rumours had it that this investor was Pathé Frères.[1177] The board agreed that the future of UFA and Nordisk's future were closely connected, and it would spell disaster for Nordisk if UFA did not obtain the credit needed. Pathé Frères' possible involvement only made matters worse.

Olsen declared that he and Johan Ramm were personally willing to raise some of the capital required if Diskontobanken and Revisionsbanken would provide the rest. The banks turned the offer down, but when board members A.F. Lamm and Carl de Neergaard also offered to chip in, the banks acquiesced, and a credit syndicate was made. The investors and their deposits were as follows:

Olsen	Kr. 550,000
Ramm	Kr. 500,000
Neergaard	Kr. 250,000
Lamm	Kr. 150,000
Revisionsbanken	Kr. 500,000
Diskontobanken	Kr. 300,000
Total	**Kr. 2,250,000**[1178]

It took Olsen less than an hour to raise 2.25 million kroner. The money was to be spent solely on securing Nordisk's influence in UFA and was to be paid back as soon as Famous Players took over half the shares, which, according to the plan, were worth 9.2 million marks in UFA shares. It was paramount for Nordisk to maintain control of UFA and also to prevent further mistakes in the company.[1179]

1174 Rech, "27 Aar i Filmen og stadig mere Filmstosset", *Social Demokraten* (4 March 1939).

1175 "Generaldirektør Ole Olsens Jordefærd", *Berlingske Tidende* (9 October 1943).

1176 NFS:I,25.DFI. Unpagn. Minutes of the Board of Directors Meeting (26 August 1919).

1177 NFS:I,25.DFI. Unpagn. Minutes of the Board of Directors Meeting (5 September 1919).

1178 NFS:I,25.DFI. Unpagn. Minutes of the Board of Directors Meeting (5 September 1919).

Olsen's later version of what happened when the board raised the money differs somewhat from the above. In 1921, Olsen told the newspaper *B.T.* that Nordisk was on the brink of liquidation in 1919 because the company had debts of three million kroner. "But we were all heartbroken about ending Danish film in such a manner." With Olsen at the helm, the board raised two million kroner in a matter of ten minutes in order to get the company out of the crisis.[1180] In Olsen's memoirs, the board members' private deposits appear as a heroic gesture. Nordisk could not pay the Valby staff, and since the cash credit had grown to 3.2 million, the bank chose to stop further loans.[1181] Olsen immediately signed a check for the staff salaries, and at the subsequent board meeting, capital was raised to cover the deficit. Seven months later, Olsen paid back the banks and the board members.[1182]

The truth is that Olsen was embarking on an alliance between Nordisk and Famous Players with the aim of getting control of UFA. It was a grand scheme – the biggest European company and the biggest American company under the same management, and with Nordisk in a central role in the alliance.

In late September 1919, however, after a trip to Berlin, Olsen had to tell his board of directors that in his opinion, it would not help to expand the UFA share capital. Instead, Olsen presented the board with a new, grand scheme according to which UFA would gather its cinemas in Germany, Austria, Hungary, the Netherlands, Switzerland, Poland and Scandinavia in a new company. Nordisk could take over 60 per cent of the new company, possibly with the help of American investors, and the remaining 40 per cent would go to UFA shareholders. Nordisk would then write off outstanding debts, and UFA's credit banks would follow suit. The new company would be worth 40 to 50 million marks.

Olsen needed authorization from the board at Nordisk to use the credit syndicate's capital to realize this plan since Nordisk's entire working capital was tied up in UFA and in DAFCO investments. But the board members were worried; the DAFCO investments constrained Nordisk's freedom to manoeuvre, and board member Frederik Paulsen felt that everything depended on the DAFCO investments; exchange rates and import opportunities were so poor that it would be wise to try to get the contracts annulled. Olsen responded that indeed, if anyone could have foreseen the exchange rate disaster, those contracts would never have been signed. The DAFCO risk being so great, Paulsen assessed that Nordisk should get out of its obligations even if it meant a loss of investments already made. The board unanimously decided that the new German company should not take over UFA's commitments to DAFCO.[1183]

1179 NFS:I,25.DFI. Unpagn. Minutes of the Board of Directors Meeting (5 September 1919).

1180 Lars, "Sandheden om Nordisk Films Co", *B.T.* (5 July 1921).

1181 See Olsen, *Filmens Eventyr og mit eget*, 151.

1182 See ibid., 151–152.

1183 NFS:I,25.DFI. Unpagn. Minutes of the Board of Directors Meeting (30 September 1919).

The plans of the new company appear to have foundered, for the status Olsen gave his board in November only addresses the matters of repayments on the DAFCO films and UFA's outstanding debts to Nordisk. Nordisk had paid Blumenthal 200,000 dollars and made an agreement that Nordisk would then be released of its obligations as guarantor and its credit obligations to UFA. Nordisk would not be liable to make further payments until two months after the films had reached Germany. In the event that DAFCO went bankrupt, UFA and Nordisk would still hold the rights for the profits on the films. UFA was still obliged to buy the films and pay Nordisk 50 per cent of the profit. If UFA was unable to pay its share, Nordisk would join in with Blumenthal, and they would sell the films together. Nordisk had paid 200,000 dollars out of its own pockets, but the company still owed a repayment of 115,750 dollars, and this amount was two months overdue. The situation was critical, and Blumenthal would surely take legal action against UFA if he did not receive his money.[1184]

In early 1920, UFA could pay ten million marks of its debts to Nordisk, but the one million which was to be spent on the share capital of Nordisk was still missing. Olsen pointed out to UFA that the German company had not paid according to the agreed exchange rate, and, by way of compensation, Olsen had received 900,000 Austrian kroner worth of shares in Sascha Film-Industrie A.G. in Vienna, at the rate of 110 Austrian kroner per share. The managing director of Sascha Film had immediately offered to buy the shares of Nordisk at rate 200 Austrian crowns per share, but Olsen declined.[1185] In February 1920, Nordisk's outstanding assets at home and abroad were worth 2.5 million kroner, of which UFA's debts alone were 1.45 million kroner. Nordisk's total debts were 2,687 million kroner.[1186]

In March 1920, Olsen could inform his board that the plan on which he had been working over the last three years appeared to be succeeding; there had been a breakthrough in negotiations between himself, UFA and Famous Players.[1187] If everything went to plan, Nordisk would recover its outstandings from UFA. The DAFCO trade would also be solved, since UFA was to shoulder Nordisk's DAFCO debt of two million kroner. The plan was to collect all of UFA's interests abroad in a new company with a share capital of ten million Swiss francs of which Famous Players would own three million. UFA's old shareholders would get bonus shares in the new company, corresponding to what they owned in UFA shares. Nordisk would receive 840,000 Swiss francs in shares since the company owned 8.4 million marks worth of shares in UFA. UFA's own share capital would be raised from fifteen million marks to forty million marks, and ten million marks of the new share capital

1184 NFS:I,25.DFI. Unpagn. Minutes of the Board of Directors Meeting (7 November 1919).

1185 NFS:I,25.DFI. Unpagn. Minutes of the Board of Directors Meeting (26 February1920).

1186 NFS:I,25.DFI. Unpagn. Minutes of the Board of Directors Meeting (26 February1920).

1187 NFS:I,25.DFI. Unpagn. Minutes of the Board of Directors Meeting (31 March 1920).

would go to Famous Players at rate 147, while the last five million marks would go to German shareholders. The distribution of share capital would have the effect that 21.6 million marks stayed in German hands, and 18.4 million marks would be in foreign hands.

It was important to UFA that it would still appear to be a German company, but a special contract would ensure the foreign investors half the seats on the board of directors and the committees. Børge Jacobsen, the vice chairman of the board at Nordisk, objected that such a contract would be in violation of UFA's statutes, but Olsen believed that it would be possible to secure some German votes and thereby the majority of votes, and so maintain influence. Olsen deemed that if this plan succeeded, it would be a great combination with big foreign interests attached. Olsen was convinced that it would all pan out, and he was delighted that Zukor had personally asked him to settle the last details of the matter.[1188]

In April 1920, a telegram to Zukor from the chairman of UFA's board of directors, Max Stauss, shows that UFA's board was "impressed with combination of interest", and Stauss suggested that negotiations should continue in Copenhagen with Olsen and the representatives of Famous Players, Oes and Graham.[1189] And the plans progressed. In April 1920, Zukor arrived in Copenhagen and led negotiations with Olsen,[1190] and in May, several UFA people came to Copenhagen with Bratz to negotiate.[1191]

Eventually, the plans for the transatlantic alliance fell flat. The minutes of Nordisk's board meeting do not tell us exactly why, but the reason is probably that while Olsen and Zukor were planning, the German government was preparing to pull out of UFA. The German Ministry of Finance was no longer willing to subsidize UFA. In 1919, Deutsche Bank had taken over 30 per cent of the German state's shares in UFA,[1192] and in early 1921, Deutsche Bank bought the remaining UFA shares off the German state with the result that UFA was now a private enterprise with no connection to the state. Deutsche Bank spearheaded UFA's great expansion of share capital and would share influence in the company with neither Nordisk nor Famous Players. Nordisk was back at square one and faced the problem of how to recover its assets from UFA. When would UFA pay Nordisk the million they needed to expand the share capital? And what to do about Blumenthal concerning the DAFCO debt?

The DAFCO matter had to be settled, and Nordisk's legal counsellor in Berlin, Cohn, arrived in Copenhagen in January 1921 to advise the board at Nordisk. UFA had made a proposal which is not reported in the minutes, but it appears

1188 NFS:I,25.DFI. Unpagn. Minutes of the Board of Directors Meeting (31 March 1920).

1189 Bundesarchiv-Filmarchiv R109.I.5256. DAMRA-Film A.G.

1190 NFS:XIV,36.DFI, 49. Scrapbook. Anonymous undated article.

1191 Bundesarchiv-Filmarchiv R109.I.5379. Nordisk Films Co.

1192 See Lothar Gall, Gerald D. Feldman, Harold James, Carl-Ludvig Holtfrerich and Hans E. Büschgen, *Die Deutsche Bank 1870–1995* (München: Verlag C.H. Beck, 1995), 235.

that the board found it unacceptable. Legal action against UFA was considered, but Cohn advised against it. If Nordisk refused UFA's offer, UFA and Blumenthal would join forces against DAFCO, DAFCO would lose, and Nordisk's two million kroner would be lost. Conversely, if Nordisk accepted UFA's offer, the company would retrieve some of its money – perhaps even all of it.[1193] UFA's offer must have been the formation of a new syndicate, DAMRA, which was to take over the DAFCO films. DAMRA had been formed in December 1920 by UFA, Nordisk and Blumenthal.[1194] UFA remunerated Blumenthal with 12.5 million marks and a share in the profits on the films: 50 per cent on the Chaplin films and a third on the rest.[1195] Saunders reports that DAMRA made a reasonable profit on the Chaplin comedies whereas the rest of the American films were four to five years old and could no longer attract audiences.[1196] At the board meeting, Børge Jacobsen suggested that one way of getting out of the DAFCO problem was to call a general meeting and vote for an annulment of the contracts; in this way, the board would not be personally liable. With this in mind, Børge Jacobsen suggested that Nordisk should accept UFA's offer. At a general meeting held in the DAFCO office on 18 January 1921, the contracts between DAFCO and UFA were indeed annulled.[1197]

In a personal letter to Zukor, Olsen regretted the entire DAFCO debacle. Olsen felt he had been deceived by Cohn and Blumenthal and the latter's partner, Samuel Rachman, who had told Olsen that they were acting on behalf of Famous Players. However, the precise nature of this alleged deceit is not easy to discern from the letter. Olsen voices his dismay that his and Zukor's plans never materialized:

> I have struggled during the last two years to find a way in which my company could work satisfactorily together with your company […] You will therefore understand that personally it was a very big disappointment to see that I did not succeed in arriving at any arrangement with you.[1198]

However, Zukor was not entirely out of the picture. At a board meeting at Nordisk on 31 January 1921, everyone was happy to be out of DAFCO, and Olsen mentioned that Famous Players might buy the majority shareholding in DAMRA.[1199]

Olsen learned that at UFA's first ordinary general meeting on 22 March 1921, an expansion of the share capital to 100 million mark was to be announced. This move dwarfed Nordisk's influence, and Olsen therefore suggested selling

1193 NFS:I,25.DFI. Unpagn. Minutes of the Board of Directors Meeting (3 January March 1921).

1194 Bundesarchiv-Filmarchiv R109.I.489. Damra Konsortium 1922–1926. I have not been able to trace what Damra means or what the letters could be a possible abbreviation for.

1195 Bundesarchiv-Filmarchiv R109.I.489. Damra Konsortium 1922–1926.

1196 See Saunders, "Von Dafco zu Damra", 71.

1197 NFS:II,58:51.DFI, 1. Minute of General Meeting in DAFCO (21 January 1921).

1198 NFS:II,58:54.DFI, 4. Letter from Ole Olsen to Adolph Zukor, New York (29 April 1921).

1199 NFS:I,25.DFI. Unpagn. Committee meeting (31 January 1921).

Nordisk's UFA shares.[1200] Shortly before the general meeting, Olsen did indeed sell the shares to Deutsche Bank at the rate of 120 kroner per share. According to Olsen, Deutsche Bank ended up with roughly all 100 million worth of UFA shares after the share expansion.[1201] However, Olsen had guaranteed his right to buy back the shares since he was still negotiating with Zukor, and the shares could turn out to be necessary for Nordisk.[1202]

Zukor did not buy Nordisk's UFA shares but instead formed the production company *Europäische Film-Allianz* (EFA) in Germany in April 1921. The company was equipped with modern studios, and Zukor hired the former UFA managing director Karl Bratz and Paul Davidson who had been the manager of PAGU. Although EFA could boast of having director Ernst Lubitsch and actress Pola Negri, the company folded as early as 1922. When UFA landed in another financial crisis in the mid-1920s, Zukor attempted one further transatlantic alliance with the Parufamet deal. In 1925, Zukor's new company Paramount and the American company Metro Goldwyn Mayer provided UFA with a loan of four million dollars in return for a mutual distribution agreement which richly favoured the American companies. The Parufamet deal was loosened in 1927 when right-wing newspaper tycoon Alfred Hugenberg acquired UFA and was finally disbanded in 1932.[1203] After selling its UFA shares, Nordisk was left with eleven million marks. A competition clause in the UFA contract barred Nordisk from buying further businesses in Germany, and when Olsen had no success changing this clause, the board decided to sell the company's assets of German marks.[1204] The exchange rate was low, and Nordisk ended up with 993,000 kroner from the sale.[1205] Once the greatest business network in the European film industry, Nordisk now had less than a million kroner left. Nordisk's connections to UFA were not altogether severed, since Olsen continued as a member of UFA's Aufsichtsrat (Board of Representatives),[1206] but Olsen harboured no great hopes for the future. Through UFA, Nordisk could only export 15,000 metres of film into Germany.[1207] The exclusive role Nordisk had played in Germany vanished after the temporary break with UFA.

In June 1921, Nordisk could present accounts that showed a deficit of 4,534,219.90 kroner. The greater part of the deficit was due to the sale of the UFA shares as well as to the DAFCO investment of 2,170,785.11 kroner, which was now written off as a loss.[1208] The board prepared thoroughly for the

1200 NFS:I,25.DFI. Unpagn. Committee meeting (31 January 1921).

1201 NFS:I,25.DFI. Unpagn. Minutes of the Board of Directors Meeting (16 April 1921).

1202 NFS:I,25.DFI. Unpagn. Minutes of the Board of Directors Meeting (6 April 1921).

1203 See Kreimeier, *The UFA Story*, 127–129, 183–184.

1204 NFS:I,25.DFI. Unpagn. Minutes of the Board of Directors Meeting (16 April 1921).

1205 NFS:I,25.DFI. Unpagn. Minutes of the Board of Directors Meeting (19 August 1921).

1206 *Jahrbuch der Filmindustrie 1922/23*, 107.

1207 NFS:I,25.DFI. Unpagn. Minutes of the Board of Directors Meeting (16 April 1921).

1208 NFS:I,25.DFI. Unpagn. Minutes of the Board of Directors Meeting (25 June 1921).

general meeting at which the shareholders were entitled to a relatively clear picture of the company's finances over the past years. It was calculated that the board had 5,400 votes in their favour and 2,800 votes in opposition.[1209] A showdown between the board and the disgruntled shareholders was expected, but the board's majority of shares quickly decided the matter, and no revolt took place. After the general meeting, Børge Jacobsen resigned. He had been the vice chairman of the board since 1912, and he felt that he was getting too old for the task. Managing director in the Revisionsbanken, Fabricius, was the new chairman, and Olsen became the vice chairman but retained the authority to sign for the company. Felix Kallmann, placed by Deutsche Bank in UFA's management, became a new member of Nordisk's board because UFA's shares in Nordisk entitled the German company to a representative.[1210]

Nordisk's elaborate, international plans were scaled down. Considering the company's modest film production and the difficult international market, Nordisk decided to focus on Denmark and Scandinavia. Nordisk pursued two schemes of keeping and strengthening its position. One was to run cinemas, and the other was a closer connection to Fotorama. Cinema licensing laws in Denmark prevented Nordisk from buying or establishing cinemas, but the legislation left an opening: a company could run a cinema as long as the licensee was the manager of the cinema and owned half the shares in the enterprise. In 1921, Nordisk started collaborating with Sophus Madsen who ran Paladsteatret and was the manager of Metropolteatret. Olsen wanted to pay Madsen to move the license which cinema owner Walter Christmas had for Metropolteatret in Mikkel Bryggersgade to a new cinema to be established in Frederiksberggade. A new limited company was to be formed with a share capital of 700,000 kroner, and Sophus Madsen's remuneration for the license was 100,000 kroner in bonus shares. The project as such, including the purchase of real estate, re-building and inventory, would cost about four million kroner. Nordisk bought shares for 300,000 kroner in Metropolteatret.[1211] Through this transaction, and without owning a license, Nordisk gained influence in an attractive Copenhagen cinema situated in the centre of the city.

Nordisk had kept its ties to Fotorama. Fotoramas Filmsbureau A/S, which Nordisk and Fotorama owned together, was dissolved in February 1920. Nordisk had agreed to hand over its shares in Fotoramas Filmsbureau A/S, worth 130,000 kroner, to Fotorama in return for 600,000 kroner in Fotorama shares, mainly for tax purposes. Moreover, it was agreed that in the future Fotorama should buy an average of at least four copies of each film from Nordisk at a price of two kroner per metre.[1212]

1209 NFS:I,25.DFI. Unpagn. Minutes of the Board of Directors Meeting (19 August 1921).

1210 NFS:I,25.DFI. Unpagn. Minutes of the Board of Directors Meeting (19 August and 16 September 1921).

1211 NFS:I,25.DFI. Unpagn. Minutes of the Board of Directors Meeting (16 September 1921).

1212 NFS:I,25.DFI. Unpagn. Minutes of the Board of Directors Meeting (26 February 1920).

Alfred William Mammen had retired from Nordisk's board in 1918, and at Olsen's behest, Mammen's partner and chairman of the Fotorama board of directors, Martin Peter Drescher, joined Nordisk's board in 1921. Bringing the two companies together was the obvious move, and this plan was presented at a board meeting in December 1921.[1213] The two companies were hardly on a friendly footing. Although Nordisk, by virtue of its shares in Fotorama, was entitled to representation in the Fotorama board of directors, they had none, and Nordisk was dissatisfied with Fotorama's marketing of Nordisk's films. At a board meeting, Nordisk discussed whether or not to discard the cooperation altogether, but Olsen felt that Nordisk had to do something; the company could not just stand still. He did not rule out that the main objective, strengthening Nordisk's position in Scandinavia, might entail quitting Fotorama. An objection to this was that the Aarhus company then might resume its former film production. Drescher feared this might lead to a war of attrition on the Scandinavian market. In the short run, Nordisk consequently opted to pursue a new contract with Fotorama.[1214]

Negotiations went ahead, and in May 1922, the parties had agreed to the main lines of a contract between the two companies. Nordisk was to reduce its share capital to three million kroner, and Nordisk's and Fotorama's shares were to be converted into shares in a new company with a share capital of six million. The board of directors would consist of the members from the two boards, together with an advisory board consisting of Drescher, Fabricius, Olsen and Ramm. The management of the new company would be Eduard Schnedler-Sørensen, Frede Skaarup, Harald Frost, Albert Gøte (Head of Office from Nordisk) and Sophus Madsen. The merger was approved by the board of directors at Fotorama.[1215] Reducing Nordisk's share capital by six million kroner may seem drastic, but the company was still suffering from the losses of the DAFCO investments and the sale of the UFA shares, and Nordisk's shares were not subject to great confidence; it was at the rate of 40 kroner per share whereas a Fotorama share was at 120.[1216]

In spite of all these careful considerations, negotiations stopped in June. The two companies could not amalgamate legally; Fotorama also ran a hotel, and Danish law prohibited two companies from different professions to unite. The amalgamation was attempted in an alternative way; Fotorama could buy Nordisk with its assets and liabilities estimated at three million kroner, and after the amalgamation, the new company was to be called Nordisk Film & Fotorama Co.[1217] Negotiations concerning Fotorama's purchase of Nordisk were so far advanced that former Minister of Trade, Jens Hassing-Jørgensen, now again the managing director of Revisionsbanken, participated on behalf

1213 NFS:I,25.DFI. Unpagn. Minutes of the Board of Directors Meeting (10 December 1921).

1214 NFS:I,25.DFI. Unpagn. Minutes of the Board of Directors Meeting (10 December 1921).

1215 NFS:I,25.DFI. Unpagn. Minutes of the Board of Directors Meeting (19 May 1922).

1216 NFS:I,25.DFI. Unpagn. Minutes of the Board of Directors Meeting (19 May 1922).

1217 NFS:I,25.DFI. Unpagn. Minutes of the Board of Directors Meeting (8 June 1922).

of Nordisk, and the managing director of Aarhus Privatbank, Christian D.A. Andersen, acted for Fotorama. Andersen stated that Fotorama had a loan of 2.6 million kroner in connection with the expansion and rebuilding of their Aarhus estate. Fotorama could only loan capital to purchase Nordisk if they could offer a repayment on their former loan, which Fotorama could not. Various solutions were discussed until July, one of these being that Olsen offered to pay Fotorama's 2.6 million debt in order to make the amalgamation go through.[1218] The negotiations petered out rather than being concluded. Eventually, Nordisk settled for extending its contract with Fotorama concerning film rental in Denmark and Norway.[1219]

Olsen must have seen the amalgamation with Fotorama as one of the few options left if Nordisk was to stay in business. He had personally been willing to supply the capital Fotorama needed if the deal could go through, and he had gone to Berlin to find out how an amalgamation with Fotorama could fit in with the contracts still existing between Nordisk and UFA.[1220] When the amalgamation failed, Olsen announced that he wished to resign as Director General as of 1 September 1922. He would, however, like to continue as a member of the board of directors. Fabricius voiced his suspicion that Olsen's true motive for resigning was to save Nordisk the expenses of his wages, and that Olsen wished to continue as hitherto with or without the title of managing director. The board thanked Olsen for this gesture, and he continued as Director General.[1221] One reason that Olsen announced his wish to retire might be that five years earlier, the transfer agreement he had signed with UFA stipulated that Olsen had to continue as Director General for another five years.[1222] Stæhr asked to be released from his contract as well, and continue after 1 July 1922 only as manager in Frihavnen until his contract with Nordisk expired.[1223]

Before the general meeting in 1921, when the company's deficit was made public, Olsen had suggested a 50 per cent reduction of the share capital,[1224] and after the negotiations with Fotorama broke down, he repeated this suggestion. Lamm opted for liquidation, but Olsen now advised against it.[1225] Instead it was decided in August 1922 to depreciate the share capital to either a third or 40 per cent, but not until the following year.[1226] While liquidation was contemplated, Frost and office manager Gøte reported that they had been to Berlin to negotiate with UFA. Nordisk would take over UFA's shares in Kinografen,

1218 NFS:I,25.DFI. Unpagn. Minutes of the Board of Directors Meeting (26 July 1922).

1219 NFS:I,25.DFI. Unpagn. Minutes of the Board of Directors Meeting (15 August 1922).

1220 NFS:I,25.DFI. Unpagn. Minutes of the Board of Directors Meeting (9 June 1922).

1221 NFS:I,25.DFI. Unpagn. Minutes of the Board of Directors Meeting (26 July 1922).

1222 Bundesarchiv-Filmarchiv R109-139. Deutscher Besitz, Nordisk Kopenhagen.

1223 NFS:I,25.DFI. Unpagn. Minutes of the Board of Directors Meeting (26 July 1922).

1224 NFS:I,25.DFI. Unpagn. Minutes of the Board of Directors Meeting (29 June 1921).

1225 NFS:I,25.DFI. Unpagn. Minutes of the Board of Directors Meeting (26 July 1921).

1226 NFS:I,25.DFI. Unpagn. Minutes of the Board of Directors Meeting (15 August 1922).

worth 491,700 kroner of the collected share capital of 600,000 kroner, all of the share capital in Skanlandia, worth 200,000 kroner, and 211,000 kroner worth of shares in Kinopalæet. UFA would then get Nordisk's shares in Fotorama, worth 725,000 kroner, 125,000 kroner in cash, and Nordisk would hand over its shares in the DAMRA syndicate.[1227] The former agreement between Nordisk and UFA to rent out each other's films would terminate.[1228] Two weeks later, Olsen could report to the board that Nordisk had indeed disentangled itself from UFA.[1229] Skanlandia was dismantled, and, to strengthen Nordisk's position in the cinema Kinopalæet, further shares worth 67,000 kroner were bought.[1230]

With the investment in Metropolteatret and the deal with UFA, Nordisk secured a good position in Copenhagen cinemas. Kinopalæet was the new huge Copenhagen cinema temple built by Constantin Philipsen in 1918, and Philipsen, who had the cinema license, became Nordisk's "silent partner".[1231] Philipsen relinquished his position as manager in return for a salary and a mortgage bond worth at least 80,000 kroner.[1232]

Nordisk had an opportunity to expand in Scandinavia as well. In late 1922, Fabricius negotiated with Lars Bjørck about taking over a rental business in Sweden; Bjørck owned five cinemas, managed thirty, and had the rights to distribute Famous Players' films in Scandinavia.[1233] Although the takeover entailed several other partners, it was still advantageous to Nordisk. However, credit with Revisionsbanken was needed to carry through the deal,[1234] and when this was denied, the deal fell through.[1235]

In February 1923, Felix Kallmann, UFA's representative on the board at Nordisk, pointed out that the large, unpaid debts which had grown to 5.2 million kroner constituted an unsustainable situation in the long run; the company's share capital had to be reduced as soon as possible. The board expected that such a reduction could wait until the general meeting, but on Kallmann's advice the board decided to reduce the share capital from nine million kroner to three, and write off 778,678.49 kroner, primarily in old negatives.[1236] On 8 March 1923, this was unanimously accepted with 4,272 votes at a general meeting, and in November 1923, UFA got rid of its last shares

1227 NFS:I,25.DFI. Unpagn. Minutes of the Board of Directors Meeting (15 August 1922).

1228 NFS:I,25.DFI. Unpagn. Minutes of the Board of Directors Meeting (7 March 1923).

1229 NFS:I,25.DFI. Unpagn. Minutes of the Board of Directors Meeting (30 August 1922).

1230 NFS:I,25.DFI. Unpagn. Minutes of the Board of Directors Meeting (26 September 1922).

1231 See Dinnesen and Kau, *Filmen i Danmark*, 34.

1232 NFS:I,25.DFI. Unpagn. Minutes of the Board of Directors Meeting (7 August 1923); Constantin Philipsen Collection. DFI. Letter from A/S Kinopalæet to Constantin Philipsen (28 June 1924).

1233 NFS:I,25.DFI. Unpagn. Minutes of the Board of Directors Meeting (10 October 1922).

1234 NFS:I,25.DFI. Unpagn. Minutes of the Board of Directors Meeting (27 October 1922).

1235 NFS:I,25.DFI. Unpagn. Minutes of the Board of Directors Meeting (6 February 1923).

1236 NFS:I,25.DFI. Unpagn. Minutes of the Board of Directors Meeting (6 February 1923).

in Nordisk. This was 308,000 kroner worth of shares which were sold for 181,720 kroner.[1237]

The reduction of the share capital changed the power structure at Nordisk. In the early summer of 1923, a group of shareholders led by stockbroker Christian Bencard had started a grand-scale purchase of Nordisk shares. The rate went up from 61 to 87, and rumour had it that the group owned 1.5 million kroner in shares. During World War I, Bencard, a young man in his mid-twenties, had made a fortune on the stock market through his company, Bencard & Pontoppidan, and he was a gambler by nature.[1238]

The group of shareholders appointed Paul G. Cohn to state their case, and in October 1923, Bencard and Cohn confronted the board at Nordisk. The group represented one million kroner in shares and made three demands: Nordisk should be compelled to save money, especially on the costly director's wages, Cohn was to be a member of the board, and the fiscal year should follow the calendar year. Moreover, it was suggested that half-term accounts should be made public in order to avoid mistrust concerning the transactions of the company. Nordisk's board had held a preliminary meeting and was prepared for these demands. Cohn became a member of the board, but the board did not think the director's wages were too high since qualified directors came at a price, and the matter of when the fiscal year was to start and end was postponed to a later time. Cohn scrutinized the accounts and suggested liquidation – a matter already proposed by the shareholders but vetoed by the board.[1239]

At the subsequent board meeting, Cohn reported that he had studied Nordisk's accounts and found them satisfactory, but he doubted whether it was at all possible to continue the company and make it profitable. Nordisk's film production only just managed to make ends meet, and Cohn pointed out that 40 per cent of the expenses were for administration. If these expenses could not be reduced, Cohn would find it difficult to appease those shareholders who wished to liquidate Nordisk. The board decided to form a committee that would investigate the future of Nordisk. Board member Fabricius felt that Nordisk was in a time of transition; things might still get better. Olsen agreed and argued that if this proved wrong, they could liquidate; he directly told Cohn that he was "[...] willing to resign from the board of directors if this was required of him. Cohn just had to nod, and he would resign."[1240]

Bencard pressed on, both to get further one of his people on the board of directors, and also for a payment of dividends, which had not happened since 1918. This would be possible if Colosseum in Flensburg was sold for 135,000

1237 Bundesarchiv-Filmarchiv R-109-673. A.S. Nordisk Films Komp.

1238 I am indebted to Henning and Mogens Bencard for sharing information about their uncle Christian Bencard.

1239 NFS:I,25.DFI. Unpagn. Minutes of the Board of Directors Meeting (23 October 1923).

1240 NFS:I,25.DFI. Unpagn. Minutes of the Board of Directors Meeting (6 December 1923).

kroner. However, Colosseum had not yet been sold, and in any event, when and if that happened the money was earmarked for film production, but Olsen was willing to lend Nordisk the capital necessary for production.[1241] The board answered Bencard that it was sympathetic to having a further member of the shareholders on the board, and also to paying dividends.[1242]

There was another board meeting in March 1924. The sale of Colosseum dragged on. The potential buyer, Otto Hammerstein, who had been Nordisk's representative in DAMRA, had to sell 15,000 bottles of wine before he had enough capital to take over the cinema, and for this reason, it would be difficult to pay dividends. Kinografen had not been as profitable as Nordisk hoped; it brought in only 53,818.81 kroner, and Olsen estimated that the six films planned for the season would break even, at best. He did not even know where to find the money for the company's administrative expenses. Bencard demanded ten per cent dividends for the shareholders. The money was to come from the sale of Colosseum, and from selling the company's shares in the Austrian film company Sascha. These transactions would not entirely cover the ten per cent, so the board contemplated offering Bencard shares in Paladsteatret at the rate of 125 kroner per share. Drescher pointed out that these shares were now at the rate of 180, and Olsen guessed that Bencard would still be willing to buy at the rate of 130. The board asked Cohn to tell Bencard that the matter of dividends could not be decided immediately.[1243]

The situation was once again at a deadlock, and liquidation was once more brought up. Olsen argued that if liquidation would result in the shareholders getting 100 per cent that would settle the matter. One possibility was that Fotorama took over Nordisk's shares in Kinopalæet and Kinografen for the sum of 800,000 kroner, and perhaps even the studios in Valby and the printing laboratory, but Drescher and Ramm both found this to be too big a mouthful for Fotorama. The result was that Olsen estimated that liquidation would bring in between 1.5 million and 1.8 million kroner for the company. The board had committed itself to giving Bencard assurance that the shareholders would get some kind of dividend. Drescher found that if dividends were to be paid, Nordisk was in the peculiar situation of having to pay from its cash and at the same time take a loan to continue the business. The choice was between continuing film production and paying dividends to the shareholders. Cohn once more sent word to Bencard's people to inform them that under the present circumstances, a ten per cent payment was impossible. The company assets would bring in much less than expected, for which reason the board was against a liquidation at the present time.[1244]

On 13 March 1924, the old board held its last meeting. Fabricius opened with

1241 NFS:I,25.DFI. Unpagn. Minutes of the Board of Directors Meeting (18 December 1923).

1242 NFS:I,25.DFI. Unpagn. Minutes of the Board of Directors Meeting (18 December 1923).

1243 NFS:I,25.DFI. Unpagn. Minutes of the Board of Directors Meeting (7 March 1924).

1244 NFS:I,25.DFI. Unpagn. Minutes of the Board of Directors Meeting (8 March 1924).

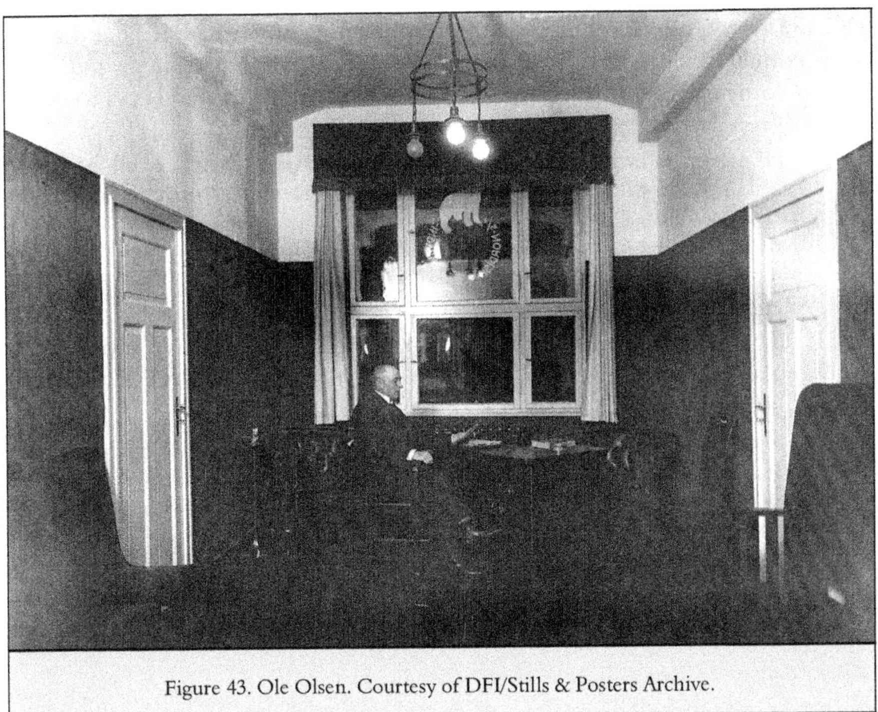

Figure 43. Ole Olsen. Courtesy of DFI/Stills & Posters Archive.

a report from his meeting with the shareholder group on the previous day. The group now represented 1.7 million kroner worth of shares and was deeply dissatisfied with the management at Nordisk. Fabricius had agreed that the old board would resign if this would calm things down. Bencard and a series of other representatives of the shareholder group met with the board and brought forth two complaints. When the shareholders had suggested liquidation they were told that the company was likely to survive and might yield a profit next year. However, the ten per cent dividends which the board had accepted had not been paid, so a new board of directors was needed. The shareholders had trusted the board and the management, but now they voiced severe scepticism against Olsen's credibility. Moreover, Olsen was said to have circulated false rumours about Nordisk on the stock market through his agent, "Jeweller Smith", and finally, the circumstances concerning the share expansion in 1916 should be investigated – as should, in fact, all Nordisk's transactions all the way back to 1914. Olsen did not feel responsible and dismissed the accusations as stock-market rumours. Drescher perceived the accusations as a call for the board to resign – and such was the outcome. The minutes of the old board's last meeting report an altercation in which Olsen denies having said that "[...] he would surely get the better of stockbroker Bencard".[1245]

The only point on the agenda at the general meeting of 29 March 1924 was the

1245 NFS:I,25.DFI. Unpagn. Minutes of the Board of Directors Meeting (13 March 1924).

election to the board of directors. Olsen did not show up at all, but a group with connections to the Copenhagen Stock Exchange appeared, and these would come to influence the development of Nordisk in the years to come. *Politiken* reported:

> It has been quite a while since the old guard has been seen together – all the known faces that made their mark on the stock exchange in the turbulent years. But yesterday at Nordisk Film's general meeting, they came out in force: *Carousel Charles, The Game Changer, Ole Loads-of-Money, the Luxury Inspector, the Bricklayer, Soothsayer Jensen*, and whatever their names might be.[1246]

Olsen had long wished to quit, and now he was phased out of Nordisk. In 1921, he became vice chairman of the board, in 1922, he retired more or less as Director General, and in 1924, Olsen left Nordisk for good. He told the newspaper *Berlingske Tidende*:

> I need some rest now. I am no spring chicken, and the last couple of years have not exactly been a walk in the park. I hope we are at the end of this, and the considerable write-offs made by my company will be the last. And then I think someone else should take over.[1247]

The words spoken at the last board meeting, however, suggest that Olsen might have hoped for a different demise. He was 61 years old.

1246 Merchand, "Nordisk Films sidste Sensationsstykke", *Politiken* (30 March 1924).

1247 "Ole Olsen fratræder som Direktør for Nordisk Film Co.", *Berlingske Tidende* (30 July 1924).

Recapitulation

At the outset of this book, there were the questions: How was Nordisk Films Kompagni able to range among the leading film companies in the world, and why did the company eventually fail to maintain this position? This book has described and analysed the company's development from 1906 to 1924. The perspective of this book is Nordisk as a business enterprise, and the overall assumption is that Nordisk was established first and foremost as a business. The aim was to make money, and the reasons for the company's success and later crisis in the silent era must be found in Nordisk's ability to organize and embrace change. The reorganizations and changes which Nordisk went through were founded on the company's sense of where to find the biggest profits. Olsen's talent for reading the development of the film industry correctly, and for planning and carrying through new strategies accordingly, was the reason that Nordisk gained a firm foothold on the international market and was able to maintain its position.

The stable management of the company and the safety net provided by the collaboration with the Copenhagen banks since 1912 were prerequisite for the changes and Nordisk's ability to meet the increasing demands of the market. Nordisk possessed, as Neergaard points out, the organizational capabilities required to carry through the strategic decisions decided on by the management. The present study has focused on four major phases through which Nordisk's reorganization or new combinations achieved and maintained its position as an international film company. Nordisk acted wisely in the first three cases, i.e. the establishing of the company, the reorganization related to the production of feature films, and partly in the expansion policy during the war. However, the company's plans to enter a grand-scale transatlantic alliance with UFA and Famous Players after the war failed.

The innovations or new combinations directing these changes were not invented by Olsen, but he had the entrepreneurial skills to commercialize them successfully. Olsen was no inventor in the domain of film, but was among the first to introduce the new commodity in Denmark. He then decided to go one step further by establishing his own production, and when long feature films were launched, Nordisk improved the quality, which entailed a new organization of production, distribution, and exhibition. Through its expansion policy, Nordisk created a new organization on the German, Central European and Russian markets. And after the war, Nordisk tried to enter into a new type of organization through film trade. If these plans had materialized, they would have led to a monopoly-like transatlantic alliance. Nordisk continued to innovate even after it was established and hence followed Schumpeter's idea that innovation does not only come from the entrepreneur but also from the company as such.

Although film cannot be said to be a mass-produced product as characterized by Chandler's definition of an MIE, Nordisk's organization resembles an MIE because the central issue was to produce many articles in a departmentalized production process at low cost, and to distribute the articles as widely as possible. By expanding, Nordisk followed the development of an MIE; it expanded horizontally, and later established itself as a vertically integrated company. The attempted diversification after the World War also resembles the development of an MIE.

Earlier Danish film historians, notably Ulrichsen, Neergaard and Engberg, tend to blame aesthetics for Nordisk's initial success and later decline. I concur with Christensen and Tybjerg in their view that Nordisk's success and demise cannot be explained solely by the artistic quality of the films. Nordisk's organizational dispositions played a part, and external forces weighed heavily as well. Olsen launched his film production at a time when film-making were undergoing colossal growth, and, although not among the first and already established companies, Nordisk could get a share of the international market. Nordisk spent resources on heightening the technical quality of its films, but it remains a question whether the contents of the films differed significantly from other products on the market. Olsen quickly built an organization that ensured a stable production as well as sales of the films. By making the transition to feature films, Nordisk gained a competitive advantage on the world market. The company's large-scale production of films that were distributed widely was the key to Nordisk's success. Its efficient mode of production was a prerequisite for the expansion strategy during World War I. Engberg's theory that Nordisk's crisis was caused by a stagnating quality and an overproduction of unsellable films after the war, a crisis which Engberg even believes had begun even before the war, is highly disputable. The films did not end up on a shelf, they were actually sold. What sent Nordisk into a crisis was a combination of various circumstances: the changing economic climate, the company's loss of both investments and the distribution network built up during the war, Nordisk's bad reputation among the Entente Powers after the war, the growing influence of American films on the world market, and the lost investments in American films as well as in foreign currency in the early 1920s.

The debts incurred by Nordisk after the war did not come from film production, but from failed investments, and after the share capital was written down, Nordisk lacked the means and the ability to regain a share of the international market. Moreover, Nordisk was not created as a company producing films exclusively for a Danish market. The last years of World War I and the post-war years revealed Nordisk's vulnerability as a company from a small country that had to adapt to international economic situations.

Selling the films was the key to Nordisk's Golden Age in the early 1910s and until 1917. When Nordisk lost its network of distribution, cinemas and its lucrative distribution deals at a time when the American film industry was gaining a foothold on the world market, the basis for Nordisk's "mass production of films" disappeared.

With help from the international film research in existence, I have been able to place Nordisk in a broader perspective, and in the development of film history at large, from the days when film was a fairground attraction until it established itself as a fully developed industry. For some years, Nordisk belonged among the biggest and most trend-setting companies in the world, and this even at a time when film was still finding its feet in an industrial, institutional sense. As far as form and style were concerned, Nordisk played a part in this development, especially in the introduction of feature films, which caused a revolution in the world of cinema. My book is a contribution to that mapping out of the early international film industry which Ron Mottram, among others, finds wanting.

This study offers a considerably more plausible and source-based explanation of Nordisk's development than earlier works. Of course, the quality of the films has indeed played a part, but as it happens, a source-based, systematic, comparative analysis between Nordisk's production and those of other companies has not yet been previously made. This book tries to offer a coherent description of Nordisk in the silent era, and it sheds light on a series of details and events. As mentioned, more can be done in this respect. The Nordisk Film Collection contains countless opportunities for further research on Danish and international silent films, and especially in the period when the polar bear stood tall among the kings of the international film industry.

Sources and Bibliography

Det Danske Filminstitut (The Danish Film Institute)

Nordisk Film Samlingen (The Nordisk Film Collection)

The major source material for this book is the Nordisk Film Collection which comprises great parts of Nordisk's office archives mainly from ca. 1906 to 1960. The greater part of the collection consists of material from the silent era, approximately half of the 30 metres of shelves in the collection.

The collection was formerly stored in the attic of Paladsteatret's and in Nordisk's Valby studios. In 1975, the collection was donated to the Danish Film Museum and is now at DFI, 55 Gothersgade, Copenhagen. The collection was investigated and catalogued in the years 1999–2001 by researcher Lisbeth Richter Larsen and is now open to the public. Through DFI's library database Bibliorama you can search the collection at Nordisk: https://ext.kb.dk/F/?func=file&file_name=find-b&local_base=NORDISK. An introduction to the collection is to be found in Richter Larsen's article "The Nordisk Film Collection – an Introduction".[1248] The parts of the collection which are of special interest to the present study are:

Minutes of Board Meetings

Since Nordisk became a limited company in 1911 and until the company went into receivership in 1928, the minutes of the board meetings were a decisive source documenting the decisions taken by the management.

Certain crucial questions have been decided in subcommittees from which there are no minutes or letters. Proposals and other issues referred to in the minutes are in many cases unaccounted for.

Copy Books

The copy books contain letters sent from the company from 1906 to 1915 – ca. 35,000 letters. After 1915, a new archiving system was introduced, which unfortunately has not been preserved. All copies have been investigated in connection with this book, but some of these are illegible, either because of the handwriting or because the text has been damaged by wear and tear.

1248 See Richter Larsen (2002), 196–206.

Appendixes referred to in the letters have been lost. Incoming letters have not been preserved, for which reason the contexts of many letters have been left to conjecture.

Scrapbooks

The earliest material in the Nordisk Film Collection, a short newspaper article about Olsen from 1899, is found in the scrapbooks. There are ten scrapbooks, of varying size, and most of them comprise 150 pages. Besides these scrapbooks, the collection also contains the later director of Nordisk Carl Bauder's private scrapbooks. The books hold clippings from Danish newspapers, but also from foreign magazines and periodicals. The clippings are not exclusively related to Nordisk Film; some are about other Danish or foreign companies, or pertain to people with relations to Nordisk. With a few exceptions, most of the newspaper articles quoted in this book are from the scrapbooks.

Distribution Protocols

Already since 1906, Nordisk kept detailed protocols of the number of copies sold of each film, of when the film was shipped and of which countries received it. Unfortunately, the protocols of 1908–1912 have not survived, and it is still uncertain whether the protocols were kept up to date. If copies of a film from 1915 were still sold in 1918, it is my impression that this was not entered in the protocols, but, on the whole, it is my guess that these cases were rare indeed. From certain periods we have two protocols for each film, but, apart from a few instances, the two protocols in such cases concur.

Besides the archives mentioned, the book refers to the following in the DFI Collections:

Personal and Case Files, DFI

Ever since the Danish Film Museum was established in 1941, the library has collected clippings from printed material about persons, films, companies or film-related matters.

Special Collections

DFI has a series of special collections which include private collections stored in uncatalogued crates. Materials from the following have been used:

Axel Graatkjær
Constantin Philipsen
Ebbe Neergaard
Olaf Fønss
Robert Dinesen

Interviews

Since the beginning of the1950s and until the early 1970s, the Danish Film Museum did interviews with people who had been active in the film industry during the silent era. The interviewers were for the most part Marguerite Engberg and/or Arne Krogh. The interviews take the shape of conversations rather than structured interviews, and as they were done many years after the fact, there is quite a gap between the events and the interviews. The interviews were done in a time of great respect for authorities, and we are left with the feeling, especially in the case of interviews with actresses, that the interviewers steer clear of controversies and anything untoward. The interviews with directors and technical staff are more informative than the interviews with actors; the latter category tends to be more anecdotal. Several of the interviews are undated. Thirty of the interviews have been researched for relevant material, and the following are referred to:

Edith Buemann, interviewed by Marguerite Engberg, undated.
Robert Dinesen, interviewed by Arne Krogh in Berlin (19 August 1960).
Ivan Eibye, interviewed by Marguerite Engberg (22 April 1958).
Mrs Elsas-Hansen and Joachim Nielsen (15 April 1970).
Axel Graatkjær, undated.
Louis Halberstadt, interviewed (17 December 1957).
Alma Hinding, undated.
Carlo Jacobsen, undated.
Viggo Larsen, interviewed (22 October1956).
Alfred Lind, interviewed by Arne Krogh and Marguerite Engberg (ca. 1954).
Joachim Nielsen, interviewed by Marguerite Engberg (4 February 1958).
Joachim Nielsen II, interviewed by Arne Krogh and unknown interviewer (7 October 1976).
Arnold Vilhelm Olsen, interviewed by Arne Krogh (24 May 1962).
Zanny Petersen, undated.
Helvig Ferdinand Rimmen, interviewed by Arne Krogh (9 November 1954).

Nordisk Films Kompagni Archives, Valby

Some of what is missing in the Nordisk Film Collection was found in an attic at Nordisk Films Kompagni in Valby, among other things some contracts and correspondence between Nordisk and directors, actors, scriptwriters and administrative staff. The majority of the archives has since been donated to DFI, but unfortunately not all. The whereabouts of the remaining part are unknown, but all of the material has been photographed, and the photos are in DFI's possession.

Ole Olsen's Private Archives

Olsen apparently burned most of his private files in 1933, and the sparse written material Olsen left behind now belongs to his family. This mostly concerns Olsen's official papers such as his document of citizenship, driver's license, passport etc. Most of this is known through Poul Malmkjær's biography on Olsen, and the majority of these papers are photographed and in the possession of DFI. The private archive is held at Bente Ole Olsen.

State Archives

The Danish National Archives

The collections at Danish National Archives are immense, and it has been difficult for me to find the papers relevant to Nordisk. In the light of the company's expansion policy during the war, it is actually surprisingly little I have been able to unearth from official files in Denmark.

However, my examination of the protocols of incoming and outgoing correspondence from the Ministry of Trade 1914–1918 and the Foreign Ministry 1914–1928 has yielded some results.

Erhvervsarkivet, part of the Danish National Archives

Minutes from General Assembly at Hotel Royal 1908–1923 (Fotorama).

District Archives for Sealand, Lolland-Falster and Bornholm, now a part of the Danish National Archives

Copenhagen Police, First Department:
Protocol of granted and refused applications for cinema licenses 1905–1929.

District and High Court:
Bailiff's Court verdicts 1910–1912.
Name Register 1892–1917.
Trade Register 1910–1912.

Museum of Slaughterhouses, Roskilde, now part of Danish Agricultural Museum, Gl. Estrup

Copenhagen City Archives

Trade Register:

A6662 (Nordisk Films Kompagni/Ole Olsen) app.: 626/07, 759/07, 1302/08, 209/1911.
B1489 (Nordisk Films Kompagni & Biograf Theater A/S).
B2763 (A/S Nordisk Films Kompagni) app.: 208/1911, 980/1911.
B3113 (A/S Nordisk Films Kompagni) app.: 468/1912, 1371/1912, 49/1916, 36/1917.
B4826 (A/S Nordisk Films Kompagni) app.: 877/1917.

Danish Actors Guild

Negotiation protocol
Danish Actors Guild's membership magazine

Periodicals

Filmen/Kinobladet (1912–1927)

Biografbladet and *Skandinavisk Films-Revue* (1913)

Der Kinematograph (1907–1916)

Deutsches Bundesarchiv-Filmarchiv Berlin-Lichterfelde

The Bundesarchiv's UFA collection contains a lot of material on Nordisk Film's transactions in Germany, Austria-Hungary, Switzerland and Holland during World War I. The overall collection number is R 109.

Literature

Anonymous, *Faran från Nordisk Films Co. Et varningsrop fran Tyskland* (Stockholm: Hedberg & Krook, 1916).

Abel, Richard, "Pathé's Stake in Early Russian Cinema", *Griffithiana*, no. 38/39 (October 1990): 242–252.

Abel, Richard, *The Cine Goes to Town. French Cinema 1896–1914* (Berkeley etc.: University of California Press, 1994).

Abel, Richard, *The Red Rooster Scare. Making Cinema American, 1900–1910* (Berkeley: University of California Press, 1999).

Abel, Richard (ed.), *Encyclopedia of Early Cinema* (London: Routledge, 2005).

Ackerman, Carl W., *George Eastman* (London: Cable and Company Ltd., 1930).

Allen, Robert C., *Vaudeville and Film, 1895–1915* (New York: Arno Press, 1980).

Allen, Robert C. and Douglas Gomery, *Film History. Theory and Practice* (New York: McGraw-Hill, 1985).

Altenloh, Emilie, *Zur Soziologie des Kino* (Frankfurt am Main: Stroemfeld/Roter Stern, 2012).

Andersen, Esben Sloth, *Joseph A. Schumpeter* (Copenhagen: Jurist og Økonomforbundets Forlag, 2004).

Andersen, H., *Filmen. I social og økonomisk belysning* (Copenhagen: C.E.C. Gad, 1924).

Anderson, Robert, "The Motion Picture Patents Company. A Reevaluation", in Tino Balio (ed.), *The American Film Industry* (Madison: The University of Wisconsin Press, 1985), 133–152.

Andersson, Lars-Gustaf, "Et filmbolags uppgang och fall", *Filmrutan*, no. 4 (Winter 1992): 15–24.

Arnedal, Poul, *Nordisk Film – en del af Danmark i 100 år* (Copenhagen: Aschehoug, 2006).

Bächlin, Peter, *Der Film als Ware*. PhD-thesis Basel: Universität Basel 1945, facsimile (Basel: Edition Kunst und Gesellschaft, 1972).

Bakker, Gerben, "Stars and stories. How films became branded products", in John Sedgwick and Michael Pokorny (ed.), *An Economic History of Film* (London: Routledge, 2004), 48–85.

Bakker, Gerben, "The Decline and Fall of the European Film Industry: Sunk Cost, Market Size, and Market Structure, 1890–1927", *Economic History Review*, vol. 58, no. 2 (2005): 310–351.

Bakker, Gerben, *Entertainment Industrialised* (Cambridge: Cambridge University Press, 2008).

Bardèche, Maurice and Robert Brasillach, *The History of Motion Pictures* (New York: Norton, 1938).

Behn, Manfred (ed.), *Schwarzer Traum und weiße Sklavin. Deutsch-dänische Filmbeziehungen 1910–1930* (München: edition text + kritik, 1994).

Behn, Manfred, "Krieg der Propagandisten", "Filmfreunde", "Der Ludendorff-Brief", "Großeinkauf", in Hans-Michael Bock and Michael Töteberg (ed.), *Das Ufa-Buch. Kunst und Krisen, Stars und Regisseure, Wirtschaft und Politik* (Frankfurt am Main: Zweitausendeins, 1994), 28–35.

Behn, Manfred, "Reaktionen auf die Nordisk in Deutschland zwischen 1914 und 1917". Unpublished lecture held at the seminar Danish-German Relations and Interactions in Film, Københavns Universitet/Goethe Institut Kopenhagen (3–4 November 1995), in my possession.

Bergsten, Bebe, *Ole Olsen. The Great Dane and the Great Northern Film Company* (Los Angeles: Locare Research Group, 1973).

Bernstein, Matthew, *Controlling Hollywood. Censorship and Regulation in the Studio Era* (New Brunswick, New Jersey: Rutgers University Press, 1999).

Bernardini, Aldo and Vittorio Martinelli, *Il cinema muto italiano 1911, prima parte* (Roma: Centro Sperimentale di Cinematografia, 1995).

Birett, Herbert, *Das Filmangebot in Deutschland 1895–1911* (München: Filmbuchverlag Winterberg, 1991).

Blom, Ivo, *Jean Desmet and the Early Dutch Film Trade* (Amsterdam: Amsterdam University Press, 2003).

Blom, Ivo, "Infrastructure, open system and the take-off phase. Jean Desmet as a case for early distribution in the Netherlands", in Frank Kessler and Nanna Verhoeff (ed.), *Networks of Entertainment* (Eastleigh: John Libbey Publishing, 2007), 137–144.

Bock, Hans-Michael and Michael Töteberg (ed.), *Das Ufa-Buch. Kunst und Krisen, Stars und Regisseure, Wirtschaft und Politik* (Frankfurt am Main: Zweitausendeins, 1994).

Boje, Per, *Ledere, ledelse og organisation 1870–1972. Dansk industri efter 1870*, vol. 5 (Odense: Odense Universitetsforlag, 1997).

Boje, Per, *Danmark og multinationale virksomheder før 1950* (Viborg: Odense Universitetsforlag, 2000).

Bordwell, David, Janet Staiger and Kristin Thompson, *The Classical Hollywood Cinema. Film Style and Mode of Production to 1960* (London: Routledge, 1985).

Bordwell, David, "Contemporary Film Studies and the Vicissitudes of Grand Theory", in David Bordwell and Noël Carroll (ed.), *Post Theory: Reconstructing Film Studies* (Madison: University of Wisconsin Press, 1996), 3–36.

Bordwell, David, *Figures Traced in Light* (Berkeley: University of California Press, 2005).

Bordwell, David, "Nordisk and the Tableau Aesthetic", in Dan Nissen and Lisbeth Richter Larsen (ed.), *100 Years of Nordisk Film* (Copenhagen: Det Danske Filminstitut, 2006), 80–95.

Bowser, Eileen, *The Transformation of Cinema, 1907–1915* (New York: Charles Schribner's Sons, 1994).

Brusendorff, Ove, *Filmen: dens navne og historie*, vol. I-III (Copenhagen: Universal Forlaget, 1939–1941).

Burch, Noël, "A Primitive Mode of Representation?", in Thomas Elsaesser (ed.), *Early Cinema. Space, Frame, Narrative* (London: BFI, 1990), 220–227.

Burrows, Jon, "When Britain Tried to Join Europe: The Significance of the 1909 Paris Congress for the British Film Industry", *Early Popular Visual Culture*, vol. 4, no. 1 (April 2006): 1–19.

Chandler Jr., Alfred D., *Scale and Scope. The Dynamics of Industrial Capitalism* (Cambridge, Massachusetts: The Bellknap Press of Harvard University Press, 1990).

Cherchi Usai, Paolo, "The Scandinavian Style", in Geoffrey Nowell-Smith (ed.), *The Oxford History of World Cinema* (Oxford: Oxford University Press, 1997), 151–159.

Christensen, Thomas C., "Isbjørnens fald. Nordisk Films Kompagni og første verdenskrig", in Helle Kannik Haastrup and Torben Kragh Grodal (ed.), *Sekvens 97. Filmæstetik og Billedhistorie. Filmvidenskabelig årbog 1997* (Copenhagen: Institut for Film og Medievidenskab, Københavns Universitet, 1997), 229–239.

Christensen, Thomas C., "Nordisk Films Kompagni and the First World War", in John Fullerton and Jan Olsson (ed.), *Nordic Explorations: Film Before 1930* (Sydney: John Libbey & Company Pty Ltd., 1999), 12–17.

Clemence, Richard V. (ed.), *Essays On Entrepreneurs, Innovations, Business Cycles, and the Evolution of Capitalism. Joseph A. Schumpeter* (New Brunswick: Transaction Publishers, 1988).

Dick, Bernard F., *Engulfed. The Death of Paramount Pictures and the Birth of Corporate Hollywood* (Lexington: The University Press of Kentucky, 2001).

Diederichs, Helmut H., "The Origins of the Autorenfilm", in Paolo Cherchi Usai and Lorenzo Codelli (ed.), *Prima di Caligari. Cinema tedesco, 1895–1920* (Pordenone: Biblioteca dell'Immagine, 1990), 380–400.

Dinnesen, Niels-Jørgen and Edvin Kau, *Filmen i Danmark* (Copenhagen: Akademisk Forlag, 1983).

Drum, Jean and Dale D. Drum, *My Only Great Passion. The Life and Films of Carl Th. Dreyer* (Lanham, Maryland: Scarecrow Press, 2000).

Elsaesser, Thomas, "The New Film History", *Sight & Sound*, vol. 55, no. 4 (Autumn 1986): 246–251.

Elsaesser, Thomas, "The Presence of Pathé in Germany", in Michel Marie, Laurent Le Forestier and Catherine Schapira (ed.), *La firme Pathé Frères 1896–1909* (Paris: Association française de recherche sur l'histoire du cinéma, 2004), 393–406.

Engberg, Harald, "Filmen", in Svend Dahl (ed.), *Danmarks Kultur ved Aar 1940*, vol. 8 (Copenhagen: Det Danske Forlag, 1943), 154–169.

Engberg, Marguerite, "Verdens første 'lange' film?", *Kosmorama*, no. 17–18 (Season 1956): 126–127.

Engberg, Marguerite, *Dansk stumfilm – de store år* (Copenhagen: Rhodos, 1977).

Engberg, Marguerite, *Registrant over danske film 1896–1930*, vol. I-V (Copenhagen: Institut for Filmvidenskab, 1977–1982).

Engberg, Marguerite, "Danske stumfilm i USA", in Kaare Schmidt (ed.), *Sekvens. Filmvidenskabelig Årbog 1980* (Copenhagen: C.A. Reitzels Boghandel A/S, 1980), 103–116.

Engberg, Marguerite, "Er det nat eller dag? Om rekonstruktion af danske film", *Kosmorama*, no. 198 (Winter 1991): 40–43.

Engberg, Marguerite, "Nordisk in Denmark", in Karel Dibbets and Bert Hogenkamp (ed.), *Film and the First World War* (Amsterdam: Amsterdam University Press, 1995), 43–49.

Engberg, Marguerite, "The Restoration of Silent Films Produced by Nordisk Films Kompagni", in Dan Nissen, Lisbeth Richter Larsen, Jesper Stub Johansen and Thomas C. Christensen (ed.), *Preserve Then Show* (Copenhagen: Det Danske Filminstitut, 2002), 152–157.

Engberg, Marguerite, "Plagiarism, and the Birth of the Danish Multi-Reel Film", in Dan Nissen and Lisbeth Richter Larsen (ed.), *100 Years of Nordisk Film* (Copenhagen: Det Danske Filminstitut, 2006), 72–79.

Finler, Joel W., *The Hollywood Story* (London: Wallflower Press, 2003).

Fønss, Olaf, *Films-erindringer gennem 20 Aar* (Copenhagen: Nutidens Forlag, 1930).

Gabler, Neal, *An Empire of Their Own. How Jews Invented Hollywood* (New York: Anchor, 1988).

Gall, Lothar, Gerald D. Feldman, Harold James, Carl-Ludvig Holtfrerich and Hans E. Büschgen, *Die Deutsche Bank 1870–1995* (München: Verlag C.H. Beck, 1995).

Gandrup, Richardt, *Redaktør Louis Schmidt – en levnedsbeskrivelse* (Copenhagen: C.E.C. Gad, 1957).

Gaudreault, André, "The Infringement of Copyright Laws and its Effects (1900–1906)", in Thomas Elsaesser (ed.), *Early Cinema: Space, Frame, Narrative* (London: BFI Publishing, 1990), 114–122.

Ginzburg, Seymon, *Kinematograf dorevoliutsionnoi Rossii* (Moscow: Agraf, 1963), 163–165.

Goergen, Jeanpaul, "'Neue Filme haben wir nicht erhalten'. Die deutsche Filmpropaganda 1917/18 in Dänemark", in Manfred Behn (ed.), *Schwarzer Traum und weiße Sklavin. Deutsch-dänische Filmbeziehungen 1910–1930* (München: edition text + kritik, 1994), 30–40.

Göktürk, Deniz, "Atlantis oder: vom Sinken der Kultur. Die Nobilitierung des frühen Kinos im Autorenfilm", in Manfred Behn (ed.), *Schwarzer Traum und weiße Sklavin. Deutsch-dänische Filmbeziehungen 1910–1930* (München: edition text + kritik, 1994), 73–86.

Göktürk, Deniz, "Market Globalization and Import Regulation in Imperial Germany", in Karel Dibbets and Bert Hogenkamp (ed.), *Film and the First World War* (Amsterdam: Amsterdam University Press, 1995), 188–197.

Grau, Robert, *The Theatre of Science. A Volume of Progress and Achievements in the Motion Picture Art* (New York, London: Broadway Publishing Company, 1914).

Green, Theodor, *Greens danske Fonds og Aktier*, vol. 1908, 1910, 1912, 1914, 1916, 1917, 1919, 1923, 1926, 1929 (Copenhagen: Børsen).

Greve, Ludwig, Margot Pehle and Heidi Westhoff (ed.), *Hätte ich das Kino! Die Schriftsteller und der Stummfilm* (Stuttgart: Ernst Klett, 1976).

Gunning, Tom, "The Cinema of Attractions. Early Film, Its Spectator and the Avant-Garde", in Thomas Elsaesser (ed.), *Early Cinema. Space, Frame, Narrative* (London: BFI, 1990), 56–62.

Hampicke, Evelyn, "Vom Aufbau eines vertikalen Konzerns. Zu David Olivers Geschäften in der deutschen Filmbranche", in Manfred Behn (ed.), *Schwarzer Traum und weiße Sklavin. Deutsch-dänische Filmbeziehungen 1910–1930* (München: edition text + kritik, 1994), 22–29.

Hampicke, Evelyn, "The Danish Influence: David Oliver and Nordisk in Germany", in Thomas Elsaesser (ed.), *A Second Life: German Cinema's First Decade* (Amsterdam: Amsterdam University Press, 1996), 72–85.

Hanisch, Michael, *Auf den Spuren der Filmgeschichte. Berliner Schauplätze* (Berlin: Henschel Verlag, 1991).

Hending, Arnold, *Stjerner i Glashuse* (Valby: Winkelmanns Forlag, 1936).

Hending, Arnold, *Da Isbjørnen var lille* (Copenhagen: Urania, 1945).

Hending, Arnold, "Det københavnske Hollywood", *Historiske meddelelser om København*, 4th series, vol. 4 (Copenhagen: C.E.C. Gad, 1954–1957), 641–688.

Hertogs, Daan and Nico De Klerk, *Disorderly order. Colours in silent film: The 1995 Amsterdam Workshop* (Amsterdam: Stichting Nederlands Filmmuseum, 1996).

Horak, Jan-Christopher, "Die Anti-UFA", in Hans-Michael Bock and Michael Töteberg (ed.), *Das Ufa-Buch. Kunst und Krisen, Stars und Regisseure, Wirtschaft und Politik* (Frankfurt am Main: Zweitausendeins, 1994), 78–79.

Horak, Laura, "The Global Distribution of Swedish Film", in Mette Hjort and Ursula Lindqvist (ed.), *A Companion to Nordic Cinema* (Chichester, West Sussex: Wiley-Blackwell, 2016), 457–483.

Horwitz, Alfred, *Minut-Millionærer, Økonomiske Tidsbilleder fra Krigs – og Efterkrigsaarene* (Copenhagen: Levin & Munksgaard, 1923).

Hyldtoft, Ole, "Den anden industrielle revolution – I forskningen og i Danmark", *Den jyskehistoriker*, no. 102–103 (December 2003): 18–46.

Idestam-Almquist, Bengt, "Nordisk Tonefilm och dess fäder", in *Ur en Isbjörns memoarer: Nordisk tonefilm 1929–1954* (Stockholm: Nordisk Tonefilm, 1954).

Idestam-Almquist, Bengt (Robin Hood), *Svensk film före Gösta Berling* (Stockholm: Bokförlaget Pan/Nordstedts, 1974).

Iversen, Gunnar, "Inventing the Nation: Diorama in Norway 1888–1894", *Early Popular Visual Culture*, vol. 9, no. 2 (May 2011): 123–129.

Jacobs, Lewis, *The Rise of the American Film. A Critical History* (New York: Hartcourt, Brace & Company, 1939).

Jahrbuch der Filmindustrie 1922/23 (Berlin: Verlag der Lichtbild-Bühne, 1923).

Jahrbuch der Filmindustrie 1926/27 (Berlin: Verlag der Lichtbild-Bühne, 1927).

Jones, Cadance, "Co-evolution of Entrepreneurial Careers, Institutional Rules and Competitive Dynamics in American film, 1895–1920", *Organization Studies*, vol. 22, no. 6 (2001): 911–944.

Jones, Geoffrey, *Multinationals and Global Capitalism* (Oxford: Oxford University Press, 2005).

Jonkman, Rixt, "Any ID? Building a database out of the Jean Desmet archive", in Frank Kessler and Nanna Verhoeff (ed.), *Networks of Entertainment* (Eastleigh: John Libbey Publishing, 2007), 312–319.

Kallmann, Alfred, *Die Konzernierung in der Filmindustrie, erläutert an den Filmindustrien Deutschlands und Amerikas* (PhD-thesis, Würzburg: Universität Würzburg, 1932).

Kepley Jr., Vance and Betty Kepley, "Foreign films on Soviet Screens, 1922–1931", *Quarterly Review of Cinema Studies*, vol. 4, no. 4 (Fall 1979): 428–442.

Kessler, Frank and Nanna Verhoeff (ed.), *Networks of Entertainment* (Eastleigh: John Libbey Publishing, 2007).

Kreimeier, Klaus, *The UFA Story. A History of Germany's Greatest Film Company 1918–1945* (New York: Hill and Wang, 1996).

Kragh-Jacobsen, Svend, "Manden med Ideerne", in Svend Kragh-Jacobsen, Erik Balling and Ove Sevel (ed.), *50 Aar i dansk film* (Copenhagen: A/S Nordisk Films Kompagni, 1956), 9–14.

Lähn, Peter, "Afgrunden und die deutsche Filmindustrie. Zur Entstehung des Monopolfilms", in Behn, Manfred (ed.), *Schwarzer Traum und weiße Sklavin. Deutsch-dänische Filmbeziehungen 1910–1930* (München: edition text + kritik, 1994), 15–21.

Lähn, Peter, "Paul Davidson, the Frankfurt Film Scene, and AFGRUNDEN in Germany", in Thomas Elsaesser (ed.), *A Second Life. German Cinema's First Decade* (Amsterdam: Amsterdam University Press, 1996), 79–85.

Lamm, Alfred, *Erindringer og Tanker* (Copenhagen: Gyldendalske Boghandel, Nordisk Forlag, 1928).

Lange, Ole, *Jorden er ikke større... H.N. Andersen, ØK og storpolitikken 1914–37* (Copenhagen: Gyldendal, 1988).

Larsen, Lisbeth Richter, "Isbjørnejagten", *Film*, no. 8 (April 2000): 12–13.

Larsen, Lisbeth Richter, "The Nordisk Film Collection – an Introduction", in Dan Nissen, Lisbeth Richter Larsen, Jesper Stub Johansen and Thomas C. Christensen (ed.), *Preserve Then Show* (Copenhagen: Det Danske Filminstitut, 2002), 196–206.

Leyda, Jay, *Kino. A History of the Russian and Sovjet Film* (New York: Collier Books, 1973).

Ligensa, Annemone, "'A Cinematograph of Feminine Thought': *The Dangerous Age*, Cinema and Modern Women", in Klaus Kreimeier and Annemone Ligensa (ed.), *Film 1900. Technology, Perception, Culture* (New Barnet: John Libbey, 2009), 225-236.

Lipschütz, Rahel, *Der Ufa-Konzern. Geschichte, Aufbau und Bedeutung im Rahmen des deutschen Filmgewerbes* (PhD-thesis, Berlin: Berliner Universität, 1932).

Locher, Jens, *Hvorledes skriver man en Film?* (Copenhagen: V. Pios Boghandel – Povl Branner, 1916).

Løkkegaard, Finn, "Nordisk Films Kompagnis industrifilm fra årene 1916–18", in *Fabrik og Bolig: Det industrielle miljø i Danmark*, no. 1 (1981): 17–25.

Low, Rachael, *The History of British Film 1906–1914* (London: George Allen & Unwin Ltd., 1949).

Ludendorff, Erich, *General Ludendorffs Krigserindringer 1914–1918* (Copenhagen: H. Aschehoug og Co., 1919).

Malmkjær, Poul, *Gøgler og Generaldirektør* (Copenhagen: Gyldendal, 1997).

Malmkjær, Poul, "I begyndelsen var billedet", *Film*, no. 40 (December 2004/January 2005): 26.

Messter, Oskar, *Mein Weg mit dem Film* (Berlin: Max Hesses Verlag, 1936).

Mørch, Søren, *Det store bankkrak* (Copenhagen: Gyldendal, 1986).

Mottram, Ron, *The Danish Cinema before Dreyer* (Metuchen, N.J.: Scarecrow Press, 1988).

Mottram, Ron, "The Great Northern Film Company. Nordisk Film in the American Motion Picture Market", *Film History,* vol. 2, no. 1 (1988): 71–86.

Mühl-Benninghaus, Wolfgang, "Newsreel Images of the Military and War, 1914–1918", in Thomas Elsaesser (ed.), *A Second Life. German Cinema's First Decade* (Amsterdam: Amsterdam University Press, 1996), 175–184.

Mühl-Benninghaus, Wolfgang, *Vom Augusterlebnis zur UFA-Gründung* (Berlin: Avinus-Verlag, 2004).

Müller, Corinna, "Emergence of the Feature Film in Germany Between 1910 and 1911", in Paolo Cherchi Usai and Lorenzo Codelli (ed.), *Prima di Caligari. Cinema tedesco 1895–1920* (Pordenone: Biblioteca dell'Immagine, 1990), 94–113.

Müller, Corinna, *Frühe deutsche Kinematographie. Formale, wirtschaftliche und kulturelle Entwicklungen 1907–1912* (Stuttgart: J.B. Metzler, 1994).

Musser, Charles, "Pre-classical American cinema: its changing modes of film production", in Richard Abel (ed.), *Silent Film* (New Brunswick, N.J.: Rutgers University Press, 1996), 85–108.

Neergaard, Ebbe, *Historien om dansk film* (Copenhagen: Gyldendal, 1960).

Nielsen, Jan, *A/S Filmfabriken Danmark: SRH/Filmfabriken Danmarks historie og produktion* (Copenhagen: Multivers, 2003).

Nørgaard, Erik, *Levende Billeder i Danmark* (Copenhagen: Lademann, 1971).

Nørrested, Carl, "Over de nordisks grænser", *Kosmorama*, vol. 37, no. 198 (Winter 1991): 50–66.

Olsen, Ole, *Filmens Eventyr og mit eget* (Copenhagen: Jespersen og Pios Forlag, 1940).

Quaresima, Leonardo, "Dichter, heraus! The Autorenfilm and the German Cinema of the 1910s", *Griffithiana*, no. 38/39 (October 1990): 101–120.

Refskou, Morten Mandel, "Kælkebakker, ambulancer og brandvagter. Sophus Falck og hans kamp for at kommercialisere redningstjenesten", *Historisk Tidsskrift,* no. 105 (2005): 381–417.

Ring, Peter S., Stefanie A. Lenway and Michelle Govekar, "Management of the political imperative in international business", *Strategic Management Journal*, vol. 11, no. 2 (1990): 141–151.

Sadoul, Georges, *Histoire générale du cinéma*, vol. II: *Les pionniers du cinéma 1897–1909* (Paris: Éditions Denoël, 1948).

Salmon, Stéphanie, *Pathé. A la conquête du cinéma 1896–1929* (Paris: Tallandier, 2014).

Sandberg, Mark, "Pocket Movies. Souvenir Cinema Programmes and the Danish Silent Cinema", *Film History*, vol. 13, no. 1 (2001): 6–22.

Sandfeld, Gunnar, *Den stumme scene* (Copenhagen: Nyt Nordisk Forlag, 1966).

Saunders, Thomas J., "Von Dafco zu Damra", in Hans-Michael Bock and Michael Töteberg (ed.), *Das Ufa-Buch. Kunst und Krisen, Stars und Regisseure, Wirtschaft und Politik* (Frankfurt am Main: Zweitausendeins, 1994), 70–71.

Schepelern, Peter (ed.), *100 års dansk film* (Copenhagen: Rosinante, 2001).

Schröder, Stephan Michael, *Weiße Wiedergängerkunst, schwarze Buchstaben. Zur Interaktion von dänischer Literatur und Kino bis 1918* (unpublished PhD-thesis, Berlin: Humboldt-Universität, 2003).

Schröder, Stephan Michael and Vreni Hockenjos (ed.), *Historisierung und Funktionalisierung. Intermedialität in den skandinavischen Literaturen um 1900* (Berlin: Nordeuropa-Institut der Humboldt-Universität, 2005).

Schröder, Stephan Michael, "Screenwriting for Nordisk 1906–1918", in Dan Nissen and Lisbeth Richter Larsen (ed.), *100 Years of Nordisk Film* (Copenhagen: Det Danske Filminstitut, 2006), 96–113.

Schröder, Stephan Michael, *Ideale Kommunikation, reale Filmproduktion. Zur Interaktion von Kino und dänischer Literatur 1909–1918*, series *Berliner Beiträge zur Skandinavistik*, vol.18/I & II (Berlin: Berliner Beiträge zur Skandinavistik, 2011).

Schröder, Stephan Michael, "Den danske isbjørns sejr på den 1. Internationale Kinematograf-Industri-Udstilling i Hamborg 1908", in Stephan Michael Schröder and Martin Zerlang (ed.), *1908: Et snapshot af de kulturelle relationer mellem Tyskland og Danmark* (Hellerup: Spring, 2011), 124–156.

Schumpeter, Joseph A., *Capitalism, socialism and democracy* (London: George Allen & Unwin Ltd., 1976).

Schumpeter, Joseph A., *The Theory of Economical Development* (New Brunswick: Transaction Publishers, 2006).

Sedgwick, John and Michael Pokorny (ed.), *An Economic History of Film* (London: Routledge, 2004).

Singer, Ben, "Fiction tie-ins and narrative intelligibility 1911–18", *Film History*, vol. 5, no. 4 (1993): 489–504.

Skands, Laurids, "Filmens Liv", *OLE*, no. 3 (1926): 1–32.

Skytte, Asbjørn, "Ole Olsen og Nordisk Films Kompagni", in Stig Brøgger, Claus Hesselberg and Asbjørn Skytte (ed.), *Dansk Film, Sophienholm* (Lyngby: Lyngby Taarbæk Kommune, 1981), 64–73.

Sørensen, Knud Rønn, *Den danske filmindustri (prod., distr., konsumtion) indtil tonefilmens gennembrud* (Copenhagen: Københavns Universitet / Institut for Filmvidenskab, 1976).

Stein, Hendrik, *Omkring Københavns Børs. Børsliv i Begyndelsen af det 20. Århundrede* (Copenhagen: Børsens Forlag, 1937).

Swedberg, Richard (ed.), *Entrepreneurship* (Oxford: Oxford University Press, 2000).

Thompson, Kristin, *Exporting Entertainment. America in the World Film Market 1907–1934* (London: British Film Institute, 1985).

Thompson, Kristin, "The Rise and Fall of Film Europe", in Andrew Higson and Richard Maltby (ed.), *"Film Europe" and "Film America". Cinema, Commerce and Cultural Exchange 1920–1939* (Exeter: University of Exeter Press, 1999), 56–81.

Thompson, Kristin, *Herr Lubitsch Goes to Hollywood* (Amsterdam: Amsterdam University Press, 2005).

Thompson, Kristin and David Bordwell, *Film History. An Introduction* (New York: McGraw-Hill, 2004).

Thorsen, Isak, "The Rise and Fall of the Polar Bear", in Dan Nissen and Lisbeth Richter Larsen (ed.), *100 Years of Nordisk Film* (Copenhagen: Det Danske Filminstitut, 2006), 53–71.

Thorsen, Isak, "We Had to Be Careful – the Selfimposed Regulations, Alterations and Censorship-strategies of Nordisk Films Kompagni", *Scandinavian-Canadian Studies,* no. 19 (2010): 112–128. Reprinted in John Tucker (ed.), *Evaluating the Achievement of One Hundred Years of Scandinavian Cinema: Dreyer, Bergman, Von Trier, and others* (Lewiston: Edwin Mellen Press, 2012) and published online in a slightly revised Danish version: Isak Thorsen, "'Vi maatte passe paa' – Selvcensur og selvregulering i Nordisk Films Kompagnis produktion", *Kosmorama,* no. 62 (2016) (www.kosmorama.org).

Thorsen, Isak, "Nordisk Films Kompagni Will Now Become the Biggest in the World", *Film History*, vol. 22, no. 4 (2010): 463–478.

Thorsen, Isak, "Ole Olsen's Sense of Film", *Journal of Scandinavian Cinema*, vol. 2, no. 1 (2012): 27–32.

Thorsen, Isak, "Nordisk Film and Asta Nielsen", in Martin Loiperdinger and Uli Jung (ed.), *Importing Asta Nielsen. The International Film Star in the Making 1910–1914* (New Barnet: John Libbey, 2014), 25–38.

Toeplitz, Jerzy, *Geschichte des Films*, vol. 1: *1895–1928* (Berlin: Henschel, 1992).

Traub, Hans, *Die Ufa. Ein Beitrag zur Entwicklungsgeschichte des deutschen Filmschaffens* (Berlin: UFA-Buchverlag, 1943).

Tsivian, Yuri, "Some Prepatory Remarks on Russian Cinema", in *Testimoni silenziosi: Film Russi 1908–1919*, research and co-ordination by Yuri Tsivian (Pordenone: Biblioteca dell'Immagine, London: British Film Institute, 1989), 24–42.

Tybjerg, Casper, *An Art of Silence and Light* (unpublished PhD-thesis, Copenhagen: Københavns Universitet, 1996).

Tybjerg, Casper, "Orientalisme i dansk stumfilm", in Helle Kannik Haastrup and Torben Kragh Grodal (ed.), *Sekvens 97. Filmæstetik og Billedhistorie. Filmvidenskabelig årbog 1997* (Copenhagen: Institut for Film og Medievidenskab, København Universitet, 1997), 213–228.

Tybjerg, Casper, "Teltholdernes verdensteater",13–28, "Spekulanter og Himmelstormere", 29–62, "Et lille lands vagabonder", 63–89, in Peter Schepelern (ed.), *100 års dansk film* (Copenhagen: Rosinante, 2001), 13–89.

Tybjerg, Casper, "Dreyer and the National Film in Denmark", *Film History*, vol. 13, no. 1 (2001): 23–36.

Tybjerg, Casper, "Searching for Art's Promised Land. Nordic Silent Cinema and the Swedish Example", in Mette Hjort and Ursula Lindqvist (ed.), *A Companion to Nordic Cinema* (Chichester, West Sussex: Wiley-Blackwell, 2016), 457–483.

Ulrichsen, Erik, "La belle époque", in Svend Kragh-Jacobsen, Erik Balling and Ove Sevel (ed.), *50 Aar i dansk film* (Copenhagen: A/S Nordisk Films Kompagni, 1956), 29–39.

Ulff-Møller, Jens, *Biografvæsenets udvikling, bevillingssytemet og biografloven af 1922* (unpublished Master-thesis, Copenhagen: Københavns Universitet, 1988).

Ulff-Møller, Jens, *Hollywood's 'film wars' with France: film-trade diplomacy and the emergence of the French film quota policy* (New York: University of Rochester Press, 2001).

Ulff-Møller, Jens, "Edouard Partsch: Pathé's Danish affiliation 1909–1924", in Michel Marie, Laurent Le Forestier and Catherine Schapira (ed.), *La firme Pathé Frères 1896–1909* (Paris: Association française de recherche sur l'histoire du cinéma, 2004), 413–421.

Uricchio, William, "German University Dissertations with Motion Picture Related Topics: 1910–1945", *Historical Journal of Film, Radio and Television*, vol. 7, no. 2 (1987): 175–190.

Yangirov, Rashit, "Pavel Gustavovich Thiemann", in *Testimoni silenziosi: Film Russi 1908–1919*, research and co-ordination by Yuri Tsivian (Pordenone: Biblioteca dell'Immagine, London: British Film Institute, 1989), 589–590.

Youngblood, Denise J., *Soviet Cinema in the Silent Era, 1918–1935* (Michigan: UMI Research University Press, 1985).

Youngblood, Denise J., *The Magic Mirror: Moviemaking in Russia* (Madison: University of Wisconsin Press, 1999).

Vasey, Ruth, "The World-Wide Spread of Cinema", in Geoffrey Nowell-Smith (ed.), *The Oxford History of World Cinema* (Oxford: Oxford University Press, 1997), 53–62.

Wasko, Janet Marie, *Relationships Between the American Motion Picture Industry and Banking Institutions* (unpublished PhD-thesis, Urbana, Illinois: University of Illinois at Urbana-Champaign, 1980).

Zimmerschied, Karl, *Die deutsche Filmindustrie, ihre Entwicklung, Organisation und Stellung im deutschem Staats- und Wirtschaftsleben* (PhD-thesis, Frankfurt am Main: Universität Frankfurt, 1922).

Websites

Adriaensens, Vito, "'Kunst og Kino'. The Art of Early Danish Drama", *Kosmorama*, no. 259 (2015), (accessed on 1 May 2017, http://www.kosmorama.org/Artikler/Kunst-og-Kino.aspx).

Piispa, Lauri, "Garrison, Star of the Russian Screen", *Kosmorama*, no. 267 (2017), (accessed on 1 May 2017, http://www.kosmorama.org/Artikler/Garrison-Star-of-the-Russian-Screen.aspx).

Audio-visual sources

Lorentz, Svend Aage, *Eventyret om dansk film I – Filmen kommer til Danmark (1896–1909)* (Copenhagen: Det Danske Filminstitut, 1996).

Salto, Ivan, *Nordisk Films 50 års jubilæum*, radio-montage aired 4 November 1956 (Copenhagen: Danmarks Radio, 1956). Held at Det Danske Filminstitut.

Appendices

Appendix 1. Danish Kroner to Euro

1 DKK Year	Equals in 2016	Euro 7,44 DKK, april 2017
1906	67,08	9,02
1907	65,18	8,90
1908	64,57	8,68
1909	63,97	8,60
1910	63,39	8,52
1911	63,39	8,52
1912	61,14	8,22
1913	59,56	8,01
1914	58,06	7,81
1915	49,35	6,62
1916	41,87	5,63
1917	36,17	4,86
1918	30,98	4,17
1919	26,17	3,52
1920	21,93	2,95
1921	25,78	3,47
1922	30,30	4,07
1923	29,15	3,92
1924	27,53	3,70

Consumer Price Index. Statistics Denmark: Denmark (accessed 1 May 2017, http://www.dst.dk/da/Statistik/emner/priser-og-forbrug/forbrugerpriser/forbrugerprisindeks).

Appendix 2. Alternative endings

Negative no.	Title	Notes and sources
801	BALLETDANSERINDEN (THE BALLET DANCER, August Blom, 1911)	Alternative ending indicated in the script. DFI.
803	TVILLINGEBRØDRE (THE TWINS, William Augustinus, 1912)	NFS:II,20.DFI, 620.
806	JERNBANENS DATTER (THE LITTLE RAILROAD QUEEN, August Blom, 1911)	NFS:II,18.DFI, 45.
853	DR. GAR EL HAMA I (DR. GAR EL HAMA, THE ORIENTAL POISONER I, Eduard Schnedler-Sørensen, 1911)	NFS:II,25.DFI,19 and 119.
890	SCENEN OG LIVET (ALL THE WORLD'S STAGE, Robert Dinesen, 1912)	NFS:II,20.DFI, 421.
913	TAVSHEDSEDEN aka DYREKØBT VENSKAB (DEADLY PURCHASED FRIENDSHIP, August Blom, 1912)	Alternative ending indicated in the script. DFI.
915	NAAR KÆRLIGHEDEN DØR (WHEN LOVE DIES, director unknown, 1912)	NFS:II,20.DFI, 971.
921	DEN SORTE KANSLER (THE BLACK CHANCELLOR, August Blom, 1912)	NFS:II,20.DFI, 917.
948	MØLLENS HEMMELIGHED (THE SECRET OF THE MILL, Eduard Schnedler-Sørensen, 1912)	NFS:II,21.DFI, 448.
958	ET DRAMA PAA HAVET (FIRE AT SEA, Eduard Schnedler-Sørensen, 1912)	Russian ending has survived.
972	HANS VANSKELIGSTE ROLLE (HIS MOST DIFFICULT PART, August Blom, 1912)	NFS:II,23.DFI, 127.
984	FØDSELSDAGSGAVEN (THE BIRTHDAY GIFT, August Blom, 1912)	NFS:II,24.DFI, 108.
1035	DRAMAET I DEN GAMLE MØLLE (THE DRAMA IN THE OLD MILL, Robert Dinesen, 1913)	Alternative ending indicated in the script. DFI.
1044	MELLEM BRØDRE (HIS UNKNOWN BROTHER, Robert Dinesen, 1913)	NFS:II,29.DFI, 39.
1047	ATLANTIS (August Blom, 1913)	Russian ending has survived.
1057	SKANDALEN PAA SØRUPGAARD (THE VICAR'S DAUGHTER, Hjalmer Davidsen, 1913)	NFS:II,27.DFI, 693–694 and NFS:II,29.DFI, 39.
1064	CHATOLLETS HEMMELIGHED (THE SECRET OF THE OLD CABINET, Hjalmar Davidsen, 1913)	NFS:II,29.DFI, 39.
1065	ELSKOVSLEG (LOVE'S DEVOTEE, Holger-Madsen, August Blom, 1913)	Alternative ending indicated in the script. DFI.
1072	PRINSESSE ELENA (THE PRINCESS' DILEMMA, Holger-Madsen, 1913)	NFS:II,29.DFI, 520.
1089	FYRSTINDE SPINAROSA DANSER (THE GAMBLER'S WIFE, Holger-Madsen, 1913)	NFS:II,29.DFI, 579.
1092	FANGENS SØN (THE CONVICT'S SON, Hjalmar Davidsen, 1913)	NFS:II,29.DFI, 520.
1095	MIDNATSSOLEN (THE MIDNIGHT SUN, Robert Dinesen, 1913)	NFS:II,30.DFI, 315 and 650.
1100	MILLIONÆRDRENGEN (THE ADVENTURES OF A MILLIONAIRE'S SON, Holger-Madsen, 1914)	NFS:II,30.DFI, 325.
1125	INDERPIGEN (THE ETERNAL BARRIER, Robert Dinesen, 1914)	Alternative ending indicated in the script. DFI.

Negative no.	Title	Notes and sources
1129	Et Kærlighedsoffer (I Will Repay, Robert Dinesen, 1914)	Alternative ending indicated in the script. DFI.
1145	Guldkalven (The Golden Calf, Hjalmar Davidsen, 1914)	Alternative ending indicated in the script. DFI.
1222	Sønnen (Her Son, August Blom, 1914)	Alternative ending indicated in the script. DFI.
1246	Evangeliemandens Liv (The Candle and the Moth, Holger-Madsen, 1914)	Alternative endings have survived.
1261	Krig og Kærlighed (Love and War, Holger-Madsen, 1914)	Alternative ending indicated in the script. DFI.
1266	I Farens Stund (The Fortunes of War, Robert Dinesen, 1914)	Alternative ending indicated in the script. DFI.
1287	En Skilsmisse (The First Quarrel, Lau Lauritzen Sr., 1914)	Alternative ending indicated in the script. DFI.
1288	Et Liv (The Little Street Singer, Alfred Cohn, 1914)	Alternative ending indicated in the script. DFI.
1289	Dr. Gar el Hama IV (Dr. Gar el Hama, the Oriental Poisoner IV, Robert Dinesen, 1914)	Alternative ending indicated in the script. DFI.
1301	Hjerter er Trumf (From Forge to Footlight, Hjalmar Davidsen, 1915)	Alternative ending indicated in the script. DFI.
1312	Børsens Offer (In the Shadow of Death, Alexander Christian, 1915)	Alternative ending indicated in the script. DFI.
1314	Den, der Sejrer (Nobody's Daughter, August Blom, 1915)	Alternative ending indicated in the script. DFI.
1318	Manden med de ni Fingre II (The Man with the Missing Finger II, Anders Wilhelm Sandberg, 1915)	Alternative ending indicated in the script. DFI.
1323	De mystiske Z-straaler (The Deathly Dance, George Schnéevoigt, 1915)	Alternative ending indicated in the script. DFI.
1324	Notitsen i Morgenbladet (The Buried Secret, Holger-Madsen, 1915)	Alternative ending indicated in the script. DFI.
1342	Den Dødsdømte (Condemned to Death, Holger-Madsen, 1915)	Alternative ending indicated in the script. DFI.
1343	En Fare for Samfundet (Love The Conqueror, Robert Dinesen, 1915)	Russian ending has survived.
1353	Danserindens Hævn (The Dancer's Revenge, Holger-Madsen, 1915)	Alternative ending indicated in the script. DFI.
1453	Alibisvindlerne (The Twin Counterfeiters, Alexander Christian, 1916)	Alternative ending indicated in the script. DFI.
1496	Manden uden Smil (Father Sorrow, Holger-Madsen, 1916)	Alternative ending indicated in the script. DFI.
1518	Børnenes Synd (The Sins of the Children, Holger-Madsen, 1916)	Alternative ending indicated in the script. DFI.
1556	Nattevandreren aka Edison Macs Dagbog (Out of the Under World, Holger-Madsen, 1916)	Alternative ending indicated in the script. DFI.
1634	Brændte Vinger (The Book of Tears, Emanuel Gregers, 1917)	Alternative ending indicated in the script. DFI.
1681	Tidens Barn (A Child of the Present Time, Martinius Nielsen, 1917)	Alternative ending indicated in the script. DFI.

Negative no.	Title	Notes and sources
1785	BLADE AF SATANS BOG (LEAVES FROM SATAN'S BOOK, Carl Theodor Dreyer, 1921)	English ending has survived.
1789	LAVINEN (ROCKS OF LIFE, Emanuel Gregers, 1919)	Alternative ending indicated in the script. DFI.
1791	DE EPIDEMISKE SYGDOMMES BEKÆMPELSE (The Fight Against Epidemic Diseases, director unknown, 1919)	Alternative ending indicated in the script. DFI.
1806	DEN FLYVENDE HOLLÆNDER (THE PHANTOM SHIP, Emanuel Gregers, 1919)	Alternative ending indicated in the script. DFI.
1844	PRÆSTEN I VEJLBY (THE HAND OF FATE, August Blom, 1922)	English ending has survived.
1848	MADSALUNE (LOVE IN EXILE, Emanuel Gregers, 1921)	Extra ending made for Denmark. Indicated in the script.
1880	JOKEREN (THE JOKER, Georg Jacoby, 1927)	Alternative ending indicated in the script. DFI.

Note: In his article "The Great Northern Film Company: Nordisk Film in the American Motion Picture Market" Ron Mottram quotes a letter from Nordisk to Nordisk Film in New York in which an alternative ending for BRISTET LYKKE is mentioned. See Mottram, "The Great Northern Film Company", 79. To the best of my knowledge the letter refers to PRINSESSE ELENA and not BRISTET LYKKE. NFS:II,27.DFI, 939. Letter from Harald Frost to Great Northern Film Co, New York (30 September 1913).

Index

CPSIA information can be obtained
at www.ICGtesting.com
Printed in the USA
BVOW06s0938081217
502314BV00010B/390/P